THE TRANSFORMATION OF LEARNING

The Transformation of Learning gives an overview of some significant advances of the cultural-historical activity theory, also known as CHAT in the educational domain. Developments are described with respect to both the theoretical framework and research. The book's main focus is on the evolution of the learning concept and school practices under the influence of cultural-historical activity theory. Activity theory has contributed to this transformation of the current views on learning, both conceptually and practically. It has provided us with a useful new approach to the understanding of learning in cultural contexts.

Bert van Oers is a professor of the cultural-historical theory of education at VU University in Amsterdam. He is an honorary doctor at the University of Jyvaskyla in Finland. He has published two books in English: *Narratives of Childhood* and *Symbolizing and Modeling in Mathematics Education*. His work has been published in many journals, including *Learning and Instruction*; *Journal of the Learning Sciences*; *European Early Childhood Education Research Journal*; and *Mind, Culture, and Activity*.

Wim Wardekker is an assistant professor in the Department of Theory and Research in Education at VU University in Amsterdam, and he is a professor of Quality of Education at Windesheim University of Professional Studies in Zwolle, The Netherlands. His work has been published in journals such as *Educational Review*; *Mind, Culture, and Activity*; and the *Journal of Moral Education*.

Ed Elbers is professor of communication, cognition, and culture at Utrecht University. His research is on communication processes in the context of learning and instruction, particularly in multiethnic classrooms. He was guest editor of *Learning and Instruction* and *European Journal of Psychology of Education*, and he is the author of many articles and book chapters.

René van der Veer is Casimir Professor of the History of Education at Leiden University. He has published widely on the history of developmental psychology and education. Among the books he has coauthored are *Main Currents of Critical Psychology*, *Understanding Vygotsky*, *The Vygotsky Reader*, *Reconstructing the Mind*, *The Social Mind*, and *Lev Vygotsky*.

The Transformation of Learning

Advances in Cultural-Historical Activity Theory

Edited by

BERT VAN OERS

VU University, Amsterdam

WIM WARDEKKER

VU University, Amsterdam
Windesheim University, Zwolle

ED ELBERS

Utrecht University

RENÉ VAN DER VEER

Leiden University

CAMBRIDGE UNIVERSITY PRESS
Cambridge, New York, Melbourne, Madrid, Cape Town, Singapore,
São Paulo, Delhi, Dubai, Tokyo

Cambridge University Press
32 Avenue of the Americas, New York, NY 10013-2473, USA

www.cambridge.org
Information on this title: www.cambridge.org/9780521156981

First published 2008
Reprinted 2009
First paperback edition 2010

A catalog record for this publication is available from the British Library.

Library of Congress Cataloging in Publication data

The transformation of learning : advances in cultural-historical activity theory /
Bert van Oers . . . [et al.].
    p.   cm.
Includes bibliographical references and index.
ISBN 978-0-521-86892-1 (hardback)
1. Learning – Philosophy.   2. Educational anthropology.   3. Cognition and culture.
I. Oers, B. van (Bert)
LB1060.T73   2008
370.15′23–dc22   2007019986

ISBN 978-0-521-86892-1 Hardback
ISBN 978-0-521-15698-1 Paperback

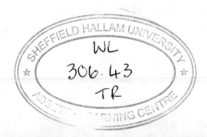

Contents

Contributors

Josué García Amián Universidad Pablo de Olavide, Sevilla, Spain

Ronald Arendt Institute of Psychology, State University of Rio de Janeiro, Brazil

Igor M. Arievitch College of Staten Island, City University of New York, United States

Chik Collins School of Social Sciences, University of Paisley, Scotland

Harry Daniels Department of Education, University of Bath, United Kingdom

Sonja de Groot Kim Kean University, Union, New Jersey, United States

Mariëtte de Haan Department of Pedagogical and Educational Sciences, Faculty of Social Sciences, Utrecht University, The Netherlands

Anne Edwards Department of Educational Studies, University of Oxford, United Kingdom; formerly at the Centre for Sociocultural and Activity Theory Research, School of Education, University of Birmingham, United Kingdom

Ed Elbers Department of Pedagogical and Educational Sciences, Faculty of Social Sciences, Utrecht University, The Netherlands

Hartmut Giest Institute of Primary School Education, University of Potsdam, Germany

Laura Gómez Faculty of Psychology, National Pedagogical University, Mexico

Beatriz Macías Gómez Estern   Universidad Pablo de Olavide, Sevilla, Spain

Fernando Luis González Rey   Pontificia Universidade Católica de Campinas, Brazil

Mariane Hedegaard   Department of Psychology, University of Copenhagen, Denmark

Ricardo Ottoni Vaz Japiassu   State University of Bahia (UNEB), Brazil

Peter E. Jones   Department of Communication and Media, Sheffield Hallam University, Sheffield, United Kingdom

Lin Mackenzie   Centre for Sociocultural and Activity Theory Research, School of Education, University of Birmingham, United Kingdom

John C. Moore   Colorado State University, Director of the Natural Resource Ecology Laboratory, Fort Collins, Colorado, United States

Wendy Naughton   Instructor of Chemistry, Minneapolis Community and Technical College, Minneapolis, Minnesota, United States

Jrène Rahm   Université de Montréal, Faculté des Sciences de l'Éducation, Montréal, Québec, Canada

Sylvia Rojas-Drummond   Faculty of Psychology, Universidad Nacional Autónoma de México, Mexico City, Mexico

José Antonio Sánchez Medina   Universidad Pablo de Olavide, Sevilla, Spain

Jocelyn Solis (deceased)   Developmental Psychology, CUNY Graduate Center, and School of Education, Brooklyn College, City University of New York, United States

René van der Veer   Child and Education Studies, Faculty of Social and Behavioral Sciences, Leiden University, The Netherlands

Bert van Oers   Department of Theory and Research in Education, Faculty of Psychology and Education, VU University, Amsterdam, The Netherlands

Maricela Vélez   National Pedagogical University, Mexico

Wim Wardekker   Department of Theory and Research in Education, Faculty of Psychology and Education, VU University, Amsterdam, The Netherlands; and Windesheim University of Professional Studies, Zwolle, The Netherlands

Rupert Wegerif   School of Education, University of Exeter, United Kingdom; formerly at the Centre for Language and Communications, Faculty of Education and Language Studies, Open University, United Kingdom

Preface

This book is an outcome of a congress of the International Society for Research in Activity Theory (ISCRAT – nowadays known as ISCAR) that was organized in 2002 in Amsterdam. The main theme of this congress was "dealing with diversity," and about 800 scholars from all over the world addressed this issue more or less directly from different perspectives. This book brings together a number of lectures that were delivered there and that illustrated some of the remarkable advances that were under way with regard to learning theory. Now, a couple of years later, the chapters in this book still contribute to the ongoing discussions within activity theory on learning, development, and teaching. We are grateful that Cambridge University Press is willing to publish this volume.

A few preliminary comments need to be made with regard to the spelling in this book. As scholars of many different countries and cultures were involved in the congress, we received many papers that were written with slightly different spellings of English words. The editors decided not to convert the differences into one universal spelling system. There is no reason why one system (American or British or whatever dialect of English) should dominate other acceptable ways of spelling. So the reader will find chapters with British English spelling and others with American English. This was our way of dealing with this diversity.

Another remark should be made with regard to the transcription of Russian names. Although there is a universal library transcription system for Russian names and words, different authors still use their own culture-bound ways of transcribing Russian names and words. Here we also decided not to impose one system of transcription throughout the volume but to respect each author's way of transcribing. So the readers will find different spellings of names – for example, Leont'ev, Leontev, Leontiev; Vygotsky,

Vigotski, Vygotskij; and Luria, Lurija. We believe that there is no confusion as to the identity of the author referred to.

Finally, we hope that this book will find its way to all those people interested in the development of Vygotskian thinking and activity theory.

Bert van Oers
Wim Wardekker
Ed Elbers
René van der Veer

INTRODUCTION

1

Learning and Learning Theory from a Cultural-Historical Point of View

Bert van Oers

CULTURAL EVOLUTION AND THE TRANSFORMATION OF LEARNING

Over the past century, social scientists have become increasingly sensitive to the cultural nature of human development. The human mind especially has been gradually acknowledged as a contextualised phenomenon, leading to the concept of the social mind. In their historical overview, van der Veer and Valsiner (2000) have demonstrated that this notion of "the social mind" has various roots that go back into the history of European thinking of (at least) the nineteenth century. The works of Vygotsky, Lurija, and Leont'ev on the cultural historical theory of human development, as well as Dewey's work on thinking and education, have played significant roles in the development of this point of view. Still, many scholars in psychology, education, anthropology, and sociology oriented to the cultural-historical (or sociocultural) tradition are putting much effort into elaborating this point of view and discovering its dynamics and mechanisms.

There is much consensus nowadays that culture influences the content and course of development and learning. Rogoff (2003, pp. 3–4) has specified the relationship between culture and development: "People develop as participants in cultural communities. Their development can be understood only in the light of the cultural practices and circumstances of their communities – which also change." Communities are defined as "groups of people who have some common and continuing organization, values, understanding, history and practices" (p. 80). From this point of view, Rogoff demonstrates that human behaviour and habits vary considerably among cultural communities and between historical periods. This regards table manners, child-rearing practices, and schooling, but also the ways of emotional expression, such as loving and grieving. In a similar way, Gauvain (2001) points out that sociocultural contexts (including their deliberately organised routines and practices, as well as their more or less fixed patterns embodied in playthings, tools, physical structures, power structures, and even social languages; see Bourdieu, 1991) play decisive roles in creating opportunities for development.

There is much empirical and theoretical evidence that, indeed, individual developmental courses may differ enormously depending on the system (or "developmental niche"; see Super & Harkness, 1986) in which they are positioned. These systems function like ecological environments, balancing patterns of mutually influencing factors. However, this is not a mechanistically functioning deterministic system. The ideas and theories that the participants in this system have about the system and its crucial elements are not the least influential determinants of the dynamics of the system (see also Bronfenbrenner, 1979). By the same token, educators' interactions with children are directly based upon their belief systems and theories about the nature of children, child development, knowledge, society, pedagogy, and so on. And different interactions tend to result in different developmental outcomes.

Hence, there is much empirical and theoretical support for the claim that development depends on culture, and varies with cultural-historical settings. Or is it just the forms of expression (of development) that change over time and place? Is all development not intrinsically related to learning and other fundamental structural changes that basically remain the same over the centuries? And what about learning? Is learning perhaps basically an invariant process? Or will it be transformed in accordance with changing cultural and historical settings? Is the learning process essentially different under different interactive conditions? In order to find answers to these questions let us turn to the history of learning itself.

THE HISTORY OF LEARNING THEORIES

Because learning has been central to the evolution of humanity, it is no surprise that so many scholars have reflected on the nature of learning. We can read treatments on learning in Plato and Aristotle, and they were probably not the first intellectuals who were interested in learning. Their views on the matter have significantly influenced many later theories of learning across Western cultural history. Plato's view on learning, as we can find in his *Politics*, is primarily didactical and focuses on learning processes that can be managed for cultural and political aims. Aristotle's ideas about learning more clearly describe a learning theory, as we can read in his *Nicomachean Ethics*, where he writes, for example, "For the things we have to learn before we can do, we learn by doing, e.g. men become builders by building and lyre players by playing the lyre; so too we become just by doing just acts, temperate by doing temperate acts, brave by doing brave acts" (book II, 1103a, 32–1103b, 2).

Aristotle obviously advocates a theory of learning that we would call today "learning by doing." This theory still echoes more than two millennia later in the works of John Dewey and remains a popular view on learning.

Many more lines of development could be depicted with regard to theories of learning over the centuries. Van der Veer and Valsiner (2000) already pointed out that the development of theoretical points of view is based on *interdependent processes*: theories react on other theories, borrow concepts from other theories, and emerge in a cultural context, employing the currently available imaginations and tools. Theories always form a *history of theories*. Similarly we can talk about the history of learning theories.

Most theories of learning agree with the definition that learning is "a relatively permanent change in behaviour which occurs as a function of practice" (see, e.g., Saltz, 1971, p. 5), but the mechanisms they postulate for the explanation and analytic description of learning differ between theories. The choice of the mechanisms and the nature of the explanations furthermore depend on fundamental epistemological and anthropological points of view. As an example, we can refer to the famous computer metaphor that dominated theories of learning in the middle of the twentieth century. The belief in the analogy of computer functioning and human thought and learning was strongly related to epistemological conceptions of "knowledge" as a collection of units that could be processed mechanically with the help of symbols and production mechanisms (like if–then rules). We can expect that future theories of learning will also try to cope with the demands of the knowledge society and view learning as a process of coding, retrieving, and exchanging information about conceptual artefacts and cultural ideas. A powerful version of such a theory was recently published by Carl Bereiter (2002), and he is also very explicit about his epistemological starting points (e.g., the Popperian World III interpretation of knowledge).

The history of learning theories is rich and populated with many more or less closely related theories. It is obvious that the description of the learning process changes over time. Another issue, however, should also be addressed with regard to the understanding of learning. In what sense can we talk about the *transformation of learning*? Is it really learning that is transformed or is it just the theories of learning? In addressing this issue here, I try to show in what way learning can be seen as a historically transforming phenomenon.

CAN LEARNING BE TRANSFORMED?

The idea that learning is essentially a universal process is strongly reinforced by developments in neurobiology. Neurobiologists have demonstrated that changes in behaviour can become permanent because they are stored in the organism's body at a molecular level in the neural system. As a result of acting, special parts of the brain and nervous system are activated and repeated actions enhance the efficacy of the synapses between the neurons involved in that action. This phenomenon is named long-term potentiation (LTP) and is widely discussed and often accepted as a mechanism that is involved in the explanation of memory and learning (see Shors & Matzel, 1997, for a critical overview). The effects of LTP can last from hours to days and can eventually be everlasting when the correlated actions are practiced regularly. Recent neurobiological research discovered that often antagonistic processes (like long-term depression) can also be involved in remembering and learning. Although neurobiologists still do not completely understand the mechanisms of long-term potentiation and long-term depression (LTD), it is generally believed that mechanisms like these are involved in remembering and learning.

As a result of these chemical changes at the microlevel of neurons (especially in the hippocampus, cortex, cerebellum, and amygdala), the organism will remember and execute these actions easily when evoked by appropriate stimuli. There is reason to believe that these mechanisms are universal, occurring in both animal and human beings, and stable over the evolution of organisms. In this view, further understanding of the mechanisms of LTP and correlated biochemical mechanisms should provide final insights into the molecular basis of learning and memory in vertebrates. In that sense, there seems to be no transformation of learning: learning is always basically the same process of LTP or LTD.

Research has shown that LTP can be aroused or blocked by different causes. Drugs or genetic manipulations can block hippocampal LTP and impair performances on particular tasks (see again Shors & Matzel, 1997). So they lead to more or less permanent changes in behaviour but not as a result of (repeated) practice. It is important to see that such changes in long-term potentiation cannot be called a result of learning (in the ordinary psychological sense of that word). Learning is always related to actions (material, perceptual, verbal, or mental) performed by the learning person. As was demonstrated by several psychologists (e.g., Reber, 1993; van Parreren, 1951), the actions do not need to be intentional in order to evoke learning processes: unintentional, subconscious, or object-driven actions (like those, e.g., in perceptual processes) can also result in permanent changes of behaviour, that is, in learning. Their learning effect will also result from the impact that they have at the molecular level. It is evident that all actions may result in changes at the cell-molecular level (called LTP or LTD). *Actions are essential in the learning process.* If we exclude causes like drugs and genetic manipulation, we can conclude that, without actions, the neurological system will not be specifically affected and will not lead to sustained performance of those actions.

The conclusion that actions of some kind must always be involved in learning processes has important theoretical consequences. Notwithstanding the essential relevance of molecular processes in learning, it is obvious now that learning cannot be identified with its neurobiological processes at the molecular level. Conceiving of learning as identical with LTP is committing a *pars-pro-toto* mistake, comparable to defining a car by its engine (or steering wheel) or a human being by its brain. Learning is indissolubly connected to both acting and bioneurological processes.

THE CULTURAL DIMENSION OF LEARNING

The assumption that acting plays an essential role in learning processes has far-reaching consequences for the theory of learning. Different actions will affect different parts of the brain and will result in different locations of LTP or LTD and even (slightly) different neuronal networks. The idea of the plasticity of the brain and its dependence on human action is an important tenet of modern developmental neuropsychology (see, e.g., Johnson, 2005; see also Luria, 1973). This insight, however, also essentially leads to the basic conclusion of the cultural nature of learning. Different cultures and generations will get their children and pupils involved in different types of actions, depending on the educators' worldview, epistemological beliefs, and image of the child and of a future society. In this sense we can maintain that learning is indeed transformed during cultural history in accordance with the prevailing psychological, epistemological, and scientific points of view, in accordance with pedagogical, sociological, and cultural views on the child and its position in the world. So it is not only the descriptions that change but also the process of learning itself.

TRANSFORMATION OF LEARNING

Over the past fifty years educators' and teachers' views have radically changed regarding how children should be involved in learning. In the early twentieth century, learning was almost exclusively based on pupils' copying actions of the teacher and repeating these actions until they could be performed auto-matically and independently. These drill-and-practice methods of teaching have gradually evolved into forms of meaningful learning based on inten-tional and guided problem solving by the pupils. Both types of learning start out from different types of actions, triggering different regions of the brain. In many domains of cultural learning, the learning processes have been radically transformed from drill-and-practice learning into negotiation of meanings (see, e.g., Bruner, 1990, 1997). Although the final molecular processes may be similar in some abstract sense, the nature of learning as a human activity has radically changed. We only have to look at the classrooms of the 1950s and today's classrooms, for example, in the domain of mathematics learning. The rote learning of arithmetical sums based on endlessly digesting rows of sums has changed into a classroom where pupils are involved in solving meaningful problems on the basis of analysis of problem situations, planning of activities, discussion of different solutions, reflection on outcomes, and the like. The types of learning actions are radically different, although both approaches may end up with classrooms of pupils mastering the ordinary calculations.

Many examples could be given from other subject areas. It should be clear, however, that the transformation of the learning processes is a cultural process that is not taking place everywhere at the same time. Some areas of learning are still based on the same processes as centuries ago. The way people transmit cultural narratives in families or in some communities of practice is still more or less the same as a hundred years ago (see, e.g., Rogoff, 2003; Wertsch, 2002). The way people learn depends on the culture they live in.

TRANSFORMATION BY LEARNING

The view on learning that emerged from Vygotsky's thinking was always strongly based on the belief of the cultural nature of learning. Vygotsky called his approach the cultural-historical theory of human development, and he tried to show that development and learning both depend on the ways pupils and educators interact and learn to share cultural tools. The structure and the meaning of the tool in a community, in particular, strongly influence the actions that people accomplish, and as such the cultural tool is a strong semiotic determinant of the learning process (see, e.g., Wertsch, 1998, for further explanation). On the other hand, Vygotsky (1984, p. 258) also emphasised the changing nature of the contexts of development in his notion of the social situation of development. When the social situation of development changes, the course of development and learning will change as well.

In his elaboration of the cultural-historical activity theory, Leont'ev (1975) has demonstrated that different levels of analysis should be distinguished. He demonstrated that most actions (*dejstvie*) are basically a moment in the realisation of a certain activity (*dejatel'nost'*), at a certain time and in a certain place. Activities can be accomplished only in specific actions. Extending these distinctions to the level of learning, we can see that learning to participate in activities requires particular actions and can even produce new actions through collaborative reflection on the meaning of different actions within the activity. This calls for a type of learning that is based on negotiations of meaning, exchange and construction of new meanings, and similar actions. Although the discursive actions involved may be common practice in the context of scientific communities, they can be seen as a revolutionary transformation of learning in school practices over the past decades. It is based on the cultural belief in the developmental potentials of pupils and on the belief in the educational value of interaction and participation.

It is still a matter of dispute how precisely the activities should be organised, and how the participation should be regulated, in order to promote understanding and deep learning. Most chapters of the present book are focused on questions related to this particular issue. The diversity of relevant aspects and possible solutions is immense, but the authors in all the chapters are basically dealing with this underlying problem of the transformation of learning through meaningful cultural activities.

But with regard to *actions*, we can also distinguish specific types of learning processes. In these cases, the regulation of the performance of pupils' actions is often focussed on mastery of these actions, or the building of automatic operations. At first sight, it may seem that the learning is not transformed in these cases, as learning is still based on execution and repetition of actions. However, in order to make the automatisation process meaningful, it is important to build on meaningful actions and to transform the actions stepwise, as was demonstrated in the works of Gal'perin (see also Arievitch in this volume). Research by Gal'perin and his students has demonstrated that this can be achieved only when the learning actions are performed reflectively and in combination with anticipatory actions that predict the outcomes of the actions performed (see, e.g., Šabel'nikov, 1982). This approach results in completely different action patterns leading eventually to automatisation. As a result of psychological research (e.g., that of Šabel'nikov), the actions that underlie this type of learning have been transformed from practicing prefixed actions to anticipatory actions. The strong reflective and anticipatory basis of automatisation processes will probably result in molecular processes in different locations of the brain from what would be the case in the drill-and-practice approach to automatisation. The final result may be the same, but the learning as a human performance is definitely transformed.

THE DIVERSITY OF LEARNING GOALS

All chapters in this book contribute to the argument of transformed learning.[1] In particular, the authors of the chapters try to show the starting points and the various solutions to the process of meaningful learning in cultural contexts. Some chapters focus on the assumptions and basic tenets of this approach to learning (Section I), others focus on specific problems and how they can be addressed from this activity point of view (Sections II and III).

The different chapters dwell on different domains of culture or adopt different educational goals. The goals of learning especially can have decisive influence on how the actions are organised and regulated and what strategies are selected for the accomplishment of one's goals. As such, the learning goals may also have an impact on the process of transformation of learning.

Different general goals can be distinguished in the different chapters of this book:

Learning to perform: These learning processes aim at appropriation of specific meaningful actions within a particular cultural context. Most of the time educators carefully guide these learning processes. Reflection, anticipation, and feedback are important elements in the organisation of these action patterns. Motor and perceptual learning are examples of this type of learning processes.

Learning to make meaning: These learning processes aim at the distribution and improvement of the contents (subject matter) of learning. This learning is basically discursive: meanings are explained, discussed, transformed, and shared through collective codes (like inscriptions). Important examples of this type of learning can be found in the areas of conceptual and subject matter learning.

Learning to participate: This form of learning focuses on the genres of acting in social contexts; the learner is assisted to appropriate the rules and tools of the community in order to participate independently, critically, and creatively within the borders of the community's practices.

---

[1] For summaries of all the chapters, see the introductions to the different sections of the book.

Learning to be: This type of learning addresses the learner's identity by focussing on the learner's motives, ambitions, and moral and aesthetical values. The actions to be performed here start out from the learner's personal sense and are constantly evaluated with the help of personal values and norms.

The book discusses the transformation of learning that has occurred as a result of cultural-historical studies of human behaviour and development. The different chapters present diverse solutions to problems that emerge when applying this paradigm. The different aims of learning presented here can be used as a speculative classification system for the reading of the chapters and summarising the conclusions in the pursuit of a new structured paradigm of learning.

References

Bereiter, C. (2002). *Education and mind in the knowledge age.* Mahwah, NJ: Lawrence Erlbaum.

Bourdieu, P. (1991). *Language and symbolic power.* Cambridge: Polity Press.

Bronfenbrenner, U. (1979). *The ecology of human development.* Cambridge, MA: Harvard University Press.

Bruner, J. S. (1990). *Acts of meaning.* Cambridge, MA: Harvard University Press.

Bruner, J. S. (1997). *The culture of education.* Cambridge, MA: Harvard University Press.

Gauvain, M. (2001). *The social context of cognitive development.* New York: Guilford Press.

Johnson, M. (2005). *Developmental Cognitive Neuroscience.* London: Blackwell.

Leont'ev, A. N. (1975). *Dejatel'nost', soznanie, licnost'* [Activity, consciousness, personality]. Moscow: Politizdat.

Luria, A. R. (1973). *The working brain: An introduction to neuropsychology.* Harmondsworth: Penguin.

Reber, A. S. (1993). *Implicit learning and tacit knowledge: An essay on the cognitive unconscious.* New York: Oxford University Press.

Rogoff, B. (2003). *The cultural nature of human development.* New York: Oxford University Press.

Šabel'nikov, V. K. (1982). *Formirovanie bystroj mysli* [The formation of fast thinking]. Alma Ata: Mektep.

Saltz, E. (1971). *The cognitive bases of human learning.* Homewood: Dorsey Press.

Shors, T. J., & Matzel, L. D. (1997). Long-term potentiation: What's learning got to do with it? *Behavioral and Brain Sciences, 20,* 597–655.

Super, C. M., & Harkness, S. (1986). The developmental niche: A conceptualization of the interface of child and culture. *International Journal of Behavioral Development, 9,* 545–569.

van der Veer, R., & Valsiner, J. (2000). *The social mind: Construction of the idea.* Cambridge: Cambridge University Press.

van Parreren, C. F. (1951). *Intentie en autonomie in het leerproces* [Intention and autonomy in the learning process]. Amsterdam: Noord-Hollandsche Uitgeversmaatschappij.

Vygotsky, L. S. (1984). Problema razvitija [The problem of age]. In L. S.Vygotsky, *Sobranie sočinenij* (Vol. 4, pp. 244–268). Moscow: Pedagogika.

Wertsch, J. (1998). *Mind as action.* Oxford: Oxford University Press.

Wertsch, J. (2002). *Voices of collective remembering.* Cambridge: Cambridge University Press.

SECTION ONE

TENETS OF ACTIVITY THEORY

Introduction to Section One

Exploring Vygotsky's Legacy: The Meaning of Mediation

René van der Veer

When Vygotsky died in 1934, he left us with a set of general guidelines (e.g., true insight into a phenomenon can be gained only by studying its genesis, individual mind can be explained only by looking outside individual mind), methods of investigation (e.g., the method of double stimulation), and specific ideas (e.g., the systemic structure of mind and brain, the notion of scientific concepts, the zone of proximal development), but not with a fully coherent and systematically elaborated theory. With hindsight we can see that many of these guidelines, methods, and ideas were clearly historically or logically connected, but at the time Vygotsky did not always spell out their connection.

Take, for example, what Vygotsky called the genetic law of mental development and his concept of the zone of proximal development. The genetic law of mental development stated that "every function in the cultural development of the child appears on the stage twice, in two planes, first, the social, then the psychological, first between people as an interpsychological category, then within the child as an intrapsychological category" (Vygotsky, 1931/1983, p. 145; cf. Vygotsky, 1997, p. 106). The law clearly stated that private mental processes originate in the social interaction with other people and was present in Vygotsky's writings from at least 1931.

The concept of the zone of proximal development (the difference between joint and independent performance) was developed several years later. That concept was formulated by Vygotsky from 1933 onward (cf. Chaiklin, 2003; van der Veer & Valsiner, 1991) and arose in the context of the assessment of intelligence. As is well known, Vygotsky claimed that what the child is able to do with the help of a more able person (joint or aided performance) is predictive of his future independent performance. In other words, joint or interpsychological performance precedes or creates and hence predicts independent or intrapsychological performance.

15

Formulated in this way, one can see at once that Vygotsky's concept of the zone of proximal development can be seen as a simple transposition of the general genetic law of mental development to the domain of prognosis. It is as if Vygotsky realized that if the one precedes the other, the one may be used to predict the other (cf. Valsiner & van der Veer, 2000, p. 379). At the time, however, Vygotsky did not make the link between these concepts explicit, and the fact is that we do not even know whether he considered them to be clearly linked.

This is just one example of many more that could be given. It demonstrates that much still needs to be done to clarify Vygotsky's concepts, to argue their inner coherence, to elaborate specific applications of his ideas, and so on. The present section presents part of this important theoretical endeavor. On the basis of Vygotsky's ideas concerning mediation, the authors provide provisional answers, suggest specific interpretations, raise certain questions, and demonstrate how these ideas have been elaborated by later theorists.

In Chapter 2, van der Veer discusses the method of double stimulation. He distinguishes between two interpretations of this method. According to the first interpretation, the method can be used to lay bare the process of internalization. According to the second and more radical interpretation, the method of double stimulation actually creates the process of internalization and hence mental development. This latter interpretation is defended and elaborated by Arievitch (Chapter 3) and Giest (Chapter 6). In his discussion of the forbidden-color task, van der Veer further raises the issue of the necessity of a stage of material mediation as a prerequisite for semiotic mediation for each and every task (as defended by Gal'perin; see Chapter 3). His discussion also illustrates that the original investigations carried out by Vygotsky, Luria, Leontiev, and their students were often no more than mere arguments for a certain plausible point of view and not the rigorous proof thereof. Finally, in his discussion of Rodriguez and Moro (1999), van der Veer pays attention to the preverbal semiotic means that escaped Vygotsky's attention and yet seem very important in the process of negotiation about meaning that takes place in any culture.

In Chapter 3, Arievitch argues that Gal'perin's theory avoids the extremes of overestimating linguistic mediational means (said by some to be characteristic of Vygotsky) and their underestimation (said by Arievitch to be characteristic of Leontiev). Gal'perin's so-called procedure of the stepwise formation of mental actions involves the deliberate and guided transformation from material actions, via overt and covert speech to thinking. This procedure formed a great improvement on the original experiments with the method of double stimulation during which it was often not clear to the subjects how the material aids provided could improve their performance or how the transition from material to verbal mediation could take place (see Chapter 2). The procedure of the stepwise formation of mental actions has proved its value in carefully designed experiments and in school curricula. As Arievitch explains, however, Gal'perin went much further by positing that the procedure is not just another educational device but also a means to reveal the true object-bound and social nature of our innermost feelings and actions.

In Chapter 4, Daniels takes up the issue of nonverbal mediation through artifacts. Whereas Gal'perin shows that with children one can devise a careful procedure using both material and verbal mediation to create theoretical thinking, and Giest argues that in the case of adults computer programs can stimulate the development of thinking, Daniels suggests yet another potential form of mediation involving children, that of wall displays in schools. Unstated rules of proper drawing may be relayed through these displays rather successfully as witnessed by the surprising similarity of children's drawings within one school. Daniels's findings raise the important issue of the regulation of children's behavior by other semiotic means than speech. Whereas Gal'perin's stepwise procedure and Giest's programs show a strong emphasis on language, the findings of Rodriguez and Moro and of Daniels demonstrate the important role of the preverbal and nonverbal or paraverbal regulation of development.

In Chapter 5, Jones brings us back to the issue of language, which was of such paramount importance for Vygotsky and many of his Russian students. He argues that, developmentally speaking, language is not just an expression of inner mental states but a material cultural tool that is transmitted in social interaction and helps to create these inner mental states. Through the child's engagement with others who already act, think, and communicate in this way; verbal acts help to form psychological processes, including unconscious ones (cf. Chapter 3). This argument seems in perfect agreement with Vygotsky's Humboldtian position (van der Veer, 1996a; 1996b). Jones further suggests that the verbal instruction is the perfect candidate for a linguistic unit of analysis. This interesting suggestion reminds us of the suggestion originally made by the French psychologist Pierre Janet (1929) – and often quoted by Vygotsky – that language is originally a command to perform some action (Valsiner & van der Veer, 2000). Jones's emphasis on the social and action-based nature of language has much in common with that of Janet and deserves to be explored further.

In Chapter 6, Giest contrasts the method of double stimulation, now called the causal-genetic method, with the classical experiment. Whereas the classical experiment presupposes a passive subject who reacts to the stimuli that are presented, the causal-genetic method presupposes creative subjects who interpret and change their environment and thereby themselves (cf. Chapter 2). Unlike Arendt (Chapter 7), Giest posits that such a position is incompatible with the tenets advanced by the Geneva School founded by Piaget. Giest connects the causal-genetic method with the concept of the zone of proximal development arguing that using tools or being helped by others allows one to reach new developmental zones. The question then arises whether computer programs can provide the necessary tools or help. On the basis of empirical findings, Giest argues that sophisticated programs (constructed after ideas advanced by Davydov and others) can indeed lure the adult students into more advanced, theoretical thinking. Cooperation with adequate programs creates a zone of proximal development for adults just like cooperation with a more able adult creates a zone of proximate development for the child. In a way, then, Giest's chapter forms a belated answer to the criticism voiced against the concept of proximal development in the mid 1930s – namely, that the concept would exclude the possibility of adult learning (cf. van der Veer, 2002).

Arendt, in Chapter 7, reflects upon the nature of the person-culture relationship. The person generates knowledge on the basis of a socially constituted world. Unlike Giest (cf. Chapter 6), Arendt believes that such a view allows us to combine the cultural-historical approach with the work of Piaget's school. Children do not "receive" cultural models but are confronted with conditions that stimulate reflection, lead to reconceptualization of these conditions, and so on. Arendt argues that meaning is constructed in this dialectical process. His final conclusion, with Glasersfeld, that the meanings attached to words by different speakers of a language community are "at best compatible" brings us to the issue of the construction of personal sense addressed by González in the next chapter.

What happens when individual children acquire language in the process of social interaction? This question is addressed by González in Chapter 8. González takes up the issue of sense versus meaning raised by Vygotsky in the 1930s. Roughly speaking, the meaning of words coincides with their description in the dictionary and is shared by all members of a language community. However, each individual person may also attach a personal sense to words based on his or her specific experience (e.g., the word "ship" may get a negative connotation after a shipwreck). The personal sense of words is thus always subjective and emotional. González argues that each person develops a private and ever changing fabric of subjective senses that are constrained but not determined by the social situations in which the person participates.

Taken together, these chapters present us with an interesting overview of the work that has been done and is still being done concerning Vygotsky's concept of mediation. Like many other concepts discussed by Vygotsky, the concept of mediation was relatively underdetermined (cf. Daniels, 2001), and modern interpretations are necessary and indeed inevitable. It is only by exploring the possible meanings of Vygotsky's concepts that we can make sense of his scientific legacy.

References

Chaiklin, S. (2003). The zone of proximal development in Vygotsky's analysis of learning and instruction. In A. Kozulin, B. Gindis, V. S. Ageyev, & S. M. Miller (Eds.), *Vygotsky's educational theory in cultural context* (pp. 39–64). Cambridge: Cambridge University Press.

Daniels, H. (2001). *Vygotsky and pedagogy*. New York: Routledge Falmer.

Janet, P. (1929). *L'évolution psychologique de la personnalité*. Paris: Chahine.

Rodriguez, R., &. Moro, Ch. (1999). *El mágico número tres: Cuando los niños aún no hablan*. Barcelona: Paidós.

Valsiner, J., & van der Veer, R. (2000). *The social mind: Construction of the idea*. Cambridge: Cambridge University Press.

van der Veer, R. (1996a). The concept of culture in Vygotsky's thinking. *Culture & Psychology, 2*, 247–263.

van der Veer, R. (1996b). On some historical roots and present-day doubts: A reply to Nicolopoulou and Weintraub. *Culture & Psychology, 2*, 457–463.

van der Veer, R. (2002). Vygotsky criticized. *Journal of Russian and Eastern European Psychology, 38*, 3–9. (dated November–December 2000, vol. 6)

van der Veer, R., & Valsiner, J. (1991). *Understanding Vygotsky: A quest for synthesis*. Oxford: Blackwell.

Vygotsky, L. S. (1931/1983). Istoriya razvitiya vysshikh psikhicheskikh funktsii. In A. M. Matyushkin (Ed.), *Sobranie sochinenii. Tom tretii. Problemy razvitiya psikhiki* (pp. 6–328). Moscow: Pedagogika.

Vygotsky, L. S. (1997). The history of the development of higher mental functions. In R. W. Rieber (Ed.), *The collected works of L. S. Vygotsky: Vol. 4. The history of the development of higher mental functions* (pp. 1–125). New York: Plenum Press.

2

Multiple Readings of Vygotsky

René van der Veer

Vygotsky's work has prompted several interpretations. Older theories naturally spark a range of interpretations, especially if the work of an investigator is sufficiently rich. After all, the reading of historic works is inevitably done on the basis of present-day and personal knowledge and possibly with an eye to the future. As our knowledge is constantly changing, so will our interpretations of the writings of the classic scholar whose work we are studying. In this sense, the need to restudy historic works may perhaps be compared to the need to regularly retranslate classic novels to adjust them to the newest standards. The older translations are no longer acceptable in light of the current knowledge and language. Another way to look at this phenomenon is to consider the process of creating new interpretations and new translations of classic works in terms of Piaget's concepts of assimilation and accommodation, where both the reader and the text will always be transformed in the reading process (van der Veer, 1999a).

Among the older interpretations of Vygotsky's work, I would like to mention the analyses by Wertsch (1985), Cole and colleagues (1978), the younger Leontiev (1990), Tulviste (1991), Yaroshevsky (1989, 1993), Kozulin (1990), and Puzyrej (1986). Interesting newer interpretations have been advanced by, again, Cole (1996), Veresov (1999), and Toomela (2000). Each of these scholars emphasizes different aspects of Vygotsky's work and creates, as it were, his own Vygotsky. But these were only the interpretations of Vygotsky's work published in English or Russian. If we take a broader look and include publications in other languages, then the picture gets even richer. Interesting versions of Vygotsky's thinking have been advanced by such authors as Blanck (1984), Brossard (2004), Keiler (1997, 2002), Kohl de Oliveira (1993), Rissom (1985), Rivière (1984), and Schneuwly and Bronckart (1985) and no doubt in other works in still other languages that I am not able to read.

Given that Vygotsky kept revising his ideas and that he left us a conceptual framework that was far from finished when he died, one may discern many topics in his writings that lend themselves to different interpretations – for example, the notion of natural functions, the idea of scientific concepts, the analysis of consciousness, the notion of internalization, and the concept of the zone of proximal development, to mention but a few. The concept of the zone of proximal development has been taken by some as a concept that deals with the influence of education on development. Some have analyzed, for example, how classroom discussions can promote the zone of proximal development in students, or what kind of teaching is needed to promote children's use of language for self-regulation (Moll, 1990). Others have seen the concept as a means to assess learning potential. These researchers have used the zone of proximal development as an individual difference metric designed to provide information about individual students. In other words, they have investigated whether measurement of aided and unaided performance on IQ tests yields important prognostic information, as was suggested by Vygotsky in the early 1930s (Brown & Ferrara, 1985; Brown & French, 1979).

In my view, many of these different interpretations are important, and I myself attach special importance to those interpretations which confront Vygotsky's notions with findings of modern research that come from quite different paradigms, whether from cognitive science, sociobiology, or any other area. To give an exotic example, I would find it extremely interesting to see Vygotsky's notion of consciousness compared to those of modern thinkers such as Dennett, Damasio, and Searle. Rather than condemning other paradigms or schools in psychology for their limited views, I think we should encourage open debates on these topics.

MULTIPLE READINGS

In the present chapter I focus on two interpretations: the suggestion that Vygotsky was first and foremost an innovator of experimental method, and the claim that Vygotsky was above all a semiotic thinker. Both ideas are far from new and have been advanced repeatedly, but I would like to explore them somewhat further to see whether they still hold and to see what new empirical or theoretical research has been done to either prove or disprove these claims.

Let me begin with the notion that Vygotsky was an innovator of experimental method. Here reference is often made (by people such as Valsiner and Puzyrey) to Vygotsky's experimental *method of double stimulation*. The basic idea of this method can be described as follows (Valsiner & van der Veer, 2000; van der Veer & Valsiner, 1991).

The experimenter specifies a certain task for the research subject or participant, but rather than observing how the subject deals with this task on his own, so to speak, he supplies the subject with tools or means that, if used, may help the subject to solve the task. Thus, the subject is presented with two different sources of stimulation: the task or problem to be solved, and the means or instruments through which it can be solved.

For example, the subject is told to learn a series of pictures by heart (after repeated presentation) and is given a pencil and paper to help him perform that task. Subjects might then write down simple codes or make schematic drawings that enable them to reproduce the series of pictures.

The rationale for this approach was that it would "externalize" the problem-solving process, as it were, because the subject presumably will make use of the visual, material objects to guide his problem-solving efforts. In other words, we can literally see by what means the subject solves the problem. It also emphasized that the subject is an active agent who selects for his own use whatever objects or tools are available. Different subjects will presumably use different tools or the same tools in different ways. Finally, the method of double stimulation highlighted the process-oriented view that Vygotsky held – namely, we can understand mental processes only to the extent that we can lay bare their process of becoming, their genesis. Presuming that all mental processes at first rest upon material aids, the method of double stimulation was supposed to lay bare the initial stage of the internalization process of higher mental functions.

There is, however, a more radical interpretation of this method of double stimulation. I am referring to the view advanced by Puzyrey (1986), which says that in psychology we cannot study what is but only what becomes. And that, moreover, by introducing external means (say, mnemotechnical means), the experimenters themselves are changing the behavior (say, memory) they wish to study. In a sense, then, the processes of mind are always changed by the means we introduce to study them, whether material or nonmaterial, and in that sense we are always studying artifacts. Our study of the subject changes the subject, and this is as it should be, says Puzyrey. Borrowing a term from a Russian philosopher, he calls this situation "non-classical" (cf. Asmolov, 1998).

In Puzyrey's analysis of the method of double stimulation then, Vygotsky becomes related to researchers such as Kurt Lewin and his collaborators (e.g., Dembo, Zeigarnik). After all, Lewin likewise argued that the subject's behavior is always and inevitably a function of the investigative situation that includes the experimenter and that behavior can be understood through the developmental analysis of the dynamic interaction of various forces operating in the field, which in Vygotsky's case would include the tools supplied (van der Veer, 2000; van der Veer & Lück, 2002).

Puzyrej's view has been criticized but I find it sufficiently interesting to mention it here, because it is one of the few genuine analyses of the value of the method of double stimulation. However, I now shift to a more matter-of-fact analysis of the method of double stimulation. I wish to analyze how the method worked out in Vygotsky's investigative practice in order to explore its real strengths and weaknesses. To this goal, I now turn to the most famous piece of research done with the method of double stimulation, namely Leontiev's (1931, 1932) memory studies, conducted as a doctoral dissertation under the supervision of Vygotsky. In these studies Leontiev made use of the so-called forbidden-colors task.

The Forbidden-Colors Task

This task was based on a well-known game in which children are asked to answer eighteen questions and to avoid certain answers. The answers to be avoided are specified in advance. In Leontiev's case, participants were asked to avoid two color names and to avoid repeating one and the same color name. For example, if the forbidden colors were yellow and blue, the experimenter might ask the subject "What color is the sun?" and the subject would have to avoid the obvious answer "yellow." Also, he might first ask for the color of leaves and several questions later for the color of grass, and the subject would have to avoid the answer "green" in both cases. Of the eighteen questions asked, only seven required a color answer. The other questions were simple questions about the subject's life and preferences (e.g., "Do you like dogs?" or "Do you ever listen to music?").

The forbidden-colors game is a task that requires concentration and memory and that proves surprisingly hard for younger children. The new element Leontiev introduced – in accordance with the idea of double stimulation – was to supply the children with colored cards to aid their performance. With a number of children from different age groups and a group of adult students, Leontiev played the forbidden-color game once without color cards and another time with color cards. The results are shown in Table 2.1.

The first thing we note is that the number of errors goes down with increasing age in both conditions. Also, the number of errors is less for the "card use" condition for all age groups. For younger children, however, the number of errors does not seem to differ very much between conditions.

Table 2.1. Number of errors in
Leontiev's forbidden-color task

Age	No cards	Cards
5–6	3.9	3.6
8–9	3.3	1.5
10–13	3.1	0.3
22–27	1.4	0.6

For adults the difference between the two conditions is also less noticeable. From informal observations, Leontiev inferred that children of all ages use the cards frequently but that the youngest ones did so in an unsystematic way and in a manner that betrayed that they simply did not grasp how the cards might help them to obtain a better performance. The older children used the cards in a much more systematic fashion and obtained good results with them. The adults, however, no longer seemed to use the cards but nevertheless obtained an excellent performance in both conditions. As was usual for that time, Leontiev did no statistical analyses. Also, his number of subjects was quite low (n = 30). Nevertheless, to him and Vygotsky these general trends seemed sufficiently clear and easy to interpret.

Leontiev's interpretation was that the five- to six-year-old children did not know how to handle the color cards. Although they manipulated the cards, they did not include them in the problem-solving process, and therefore we may conclude that their problem-solving behavior was unmediated – that is, it did not involve the use of auxiliary means. It seemed, then, that their performance reflected their "natural" abilities unaided by cultural instru-ments. The children who were, respectively, eight to nine and ten to thirteen years old were able to make intelligent use of the color cards (e.g., by turning upside down a color card corresponding to a color name just mentioned and selecting future color answers from the color cards not yet turned upside down so as to avoid repeating a specific color) and apparently profited from this strategy by making less errors in the cards condition than in the no-cards condition. Hence, their performance seemed mediated by the color cards. Children of this age are not dependent on some "natural" ability but can make intelligent use of cultural means. Finally, the adults did not make use of the colored cards but nevertheless obtained an excellent performance. Also, for adults the difference between the no-cards and cards conditions was rather small. To Leontiev, this could only mean that the adults relied upon *internal* mediation, that is, their performance was not based on the use of the colored cards but on the use of language (e.g., the subjects probably said to themselves things like "I must not say 'yellow' or 'blue,'" or "I already used 'green'"). This meant that adults do not rely upon their "natural" abilities and do not make use of external cultural instruments. Rather, they rely upon the powerful cultural means of internal, private language.

Leontiev and Vygotsky interpreted these findings from their cross-sectional experiment as if they reflected a general trend in cognitive development. That is, they speculated that at a certain age cognitive processes shift from being externally mediated to being internally mediated. This would form a perfect illustration of Vygotsky's general claim that all higher mental processes shift from external mediation to internal mediation as they are being mastered. In this interpretation, what the colored-cards experiment lays bare is an internalization process. By watching how children of different ages make use of external supports, we can lay bare or externalize the roots of adult cognitive functioning, which always originally rests upon the use of external means. Using the method of double stimulation, we have come closer to an understanding of an otherwise inaccessible and therefore incomprehensible adult cognitive process.

Complications: The Use of Different Strategies

Leontiev's and Vygotsky's interpretation of the experimental results made perfect sense and was entirely in line with the central tenets of cultural-historical theory. However, if we take a more detailed look at the experimental procedure and at the nature of the task, then the interpretation of the experimental results turns out to be more complicated and less straightforward.

First, it was unclear to what extent Leontiev explained the different possible uses of the colored cards to the subjects. There are various ways the subjects might use them. When asked a color question, the subject might simply *turn upside down* a colored card after each color question. This strategy works because the children received nine colored cards: two of them were forbidden, but the remaining seven could be used in the way I indicated because only seven out of eighteen questions were about a color. In fact, in quite a few cases the children used the cards in exactly this way. Another strategy would be to put colored cards out of sight or to move them in some way to clearly distinguish used or forbidden cards from cards that can still be used. Leontiev claimed that some strategies were more advanced than others, but that need not bother us here. What is more important at this stage is that Leontiev seems to have been very inconsistent in his instruction: some children were simply given the cards with no instruction at all, whereas others were explicitly told how to use them. This makes it rather difficult to say what his results reflected.

Second, some questions that required a color answer were clearly more difficult than others. For instance, a question like "What color is the sea?" is undoubtedly easier to answer than a question such as "What color is your shirt?" The question about the sea can be answered truthfully with different colors as the color of seawater tends to vary. This gives the child the possibility to avoid a forbidden answer. The question about the particular shirt one is wearing allows for much fewer degrees of freedom *unless* the subject is prepared to give an untruthful answer or has a rich color vocabulary. For example, if the forbidden color is red and the subject is wearing a red shirt, and he is confronted with the question, "What color is your shirt?" he can avoid making an error only by either giving a patently false answer ("My shirt is blue") or giving a very sophisticated answer, like saying that the shirt is "scarlet." This was apparently not against the rules of the game, and Leontiev hinted that older subjects made more use of the possibility to give false or sophisticated (i.e., arbitrary) answers. Younger children probably did not understand that they were allowed to give such answers to the color questions. Again, this fact makes it difficult to say what Leontiev was actually measuring. Was it the readiness to provide untruthful answers? Was it the ability to produce sophisticated color names? Or still something else?

A Replication Study

To clarify these issues and to separate different possible effects, I have done a replication study (with considerably more subjects, a counterbalanced design, and so on) in which I introduced the possibilities of card use and the possibility of using verbal strategies in a more systematic manner (van der Veer, 1994). For each child or adult, the whole experiment consisted of six series (see Table 2.2).

During the first series the subject was asked eighteen questions, but no rules about forbidden answers were specified. This was done to familiarize the subjects with the nature of the situation. After series 1, the subjects were told that the task would become harder and that they would have to avoid giving certain answers in the next series. The words to be avoided were then specified, and series 2 of the game was played. After series 2, the colored cards were introduced with the remark that "these might help in winning the game." The subject then went through series 3 and 4. Finally, before the fifth series the subjects were explicitly told how to use the colored cards, and

Table 2.2. Different conditions in the replication of
the forbidden-color experiment

Series 1
Introduction of rules of the game
Series 2
Introduction of cards
Series 3
Series 4
Explicit instruction
Series 5
Series 6

Source: Van der Veer, 1994.

Table 2.3. Number of errors in van der Veer's (1994)
replication of the forbidden-color experiment

Age	No cards	Cards	Instruction
5–6	3.4	3.3	1.8
8–9	2.6	2.2	0.6
10–13	2.2	1.5	0.6
21–30	1.6	1.0	0.6

Note: The results of the series 2–3 and 4–5 have been averaged
for the sake of simplicity.

two ways of using them (putting forbidden or used cards aside or turning
them over) were shown by the experimenter. In addition, the subjects were
told that it was allowed to give "funny" answers, like saying that the sea was
red or pink. In this way, the instruction both demonstrated ways of using the
colored cards and hinted at the use of a verbal strategy. The results in terms
of the number of errors are shown in Table2.3.

As can be seen from Table 2.3, the results of our replication study partially
confirmed Leontiev's findings. The number of errors decreased with age,
and after explicit instruction the number of errors decreased significantly.
However, the introduction of colored cards as such, without instruction,
seemed to have little effect. In fact, it was not statistically significant (van der
Veer, 1994).

It was observed that explicit instruction before series 5 and 6 was effective
in enhancing card use. Also, the number of errors went down significantly for
series 5 and 6. It would seem then that the use of the colored cards effectively
diminishes the number of errors. However, the instruction before series 5 and

6 concerned both the possible ways to use the colored cards and the possibility of using verbal strategies. What caused the lower number of errors? Was it indeed the card use or the use of verbal strategies? Rather surprisingly, when I computed the correlation between card use and number of errors, it turned out that there was virtually no relation – that is, more card use does not correspond with higher performance. That leaves the use of verbal strategies as a possible explanatory factor for the enhanced performance. Indeed, it was found that after the instruction before series 5 and 6 the number of "funny," arbitrary answers given by the subjects rose significantly. Also, it was found that the frequency of arbitrary answers was negatively correlated with the number of errors made – that is, giving more arbitrary answers is associated with making fewer errors (van der Veer, 1994).

What do these results mean? In my view, the results indicate that card use is probably not very effective in diminishing the number of errors made. At any rate, when both the possible ways of card use and the idea of giving arbitrary answers are explained to the subjects, they pick up both elements, but the strategy of giving arbitrary answers proves far more effective in diminishing the number of errors. And subjects of all age groups proved able to make use of this strategy. That means, in my view, that the forbidden-colors game formed too crude a test for the internalization hypothesis. It is probably not a very fruitful idea to think that all mediating devices necessarily go through an external material phase. That is, one may posit that all internal means originate in the external world, but this does not necessarily imply that they originate as material objects, such as colored cards.

The forbidden-colors experiment was also unfortunate insofar as it suggested that for each specific task one can discern periods of, respectively, no mediation, external mediation, and internal mediation. In reality, it would seem that children confront each new task armed with a whole repertoire of internal mediating devices that proved effective in other tasks. At any rate, it seems a little naive to expect that children up to thirteen years old had to rely exclusively on external mediating devices such as the colored cards. Rather than positing a necessary object stage in the internalization process, then, we should think in terms of semiotic guidance by the adult and the acquisition of different semiotic means by the child. That brings me to the second topic of my chapter.

Vygotsky as Semiotician

It is, of course, quite commonplace to think of Vygotsky as a semiotic thinker. Vygotsky was profoundly influenced by the linguists of his time (van der Veer

& Valsiner, 1991) and repeatedly emphasized the role of signs in what he termed the higher mental or psychological processes. This emphasis on signs and language became increasingly prominent in his writings, and toward the end of his career the role of word meanings became particularly dominant (van der Veer, 1997).

Different researchers have attempted to expand Vygotsky's schematic ideas about the semiotic regulation of behavior. In their study of mother-child dyads, for example, Wertsch (1985) and others have shown how the process of self-regulation emerges from other-regulation by means of language. The mother scaffolds or guides the child's activity with words and gradually gives her child more responsibility to perform the task successfully on his or her own. This model seemed very plausible, although Wertsch has rightly remarked that we need to specify in more detail what semiotic means are being used in social interaction. One problem is that the semiotic means studied by Wertsch and others rely heavily on language use – the children in these studies are being introduced to a cultural task (e.g., making a jigsaw puzzle) by verbal means. In a joint problem-solving process, the children's behavior is primarily guided and developed by the mother's words. In recent studies, however, it has been pointed out that very young children need not be introduced into cultural tasks by means of language but can be introduced to cultural meanings through other semiotic methods such as gestures. This view, incidentally, is from my perspective entirely compatible with Vygotsky's framework and with Wertsch's investigations. One of the studies about preverbal semiotic guidance was done by Rodriguez and Moro (1999). A concise discussion of this study seems important both for its intriguing results and for the fact that it does not seem to have reached the English-reading audience (van der Veer, 1999b).

What Rodriguez and Moro did was to try and find out how babies are introduced by their mothers to the proper use of simple cultural objects. These cultural objects were two simple toys: a toy truck and a toy telephone (see Figures 2.1 and 2.2).

As can be seen in Figure 2.1, the truck was somewhat unusual, as it contained holes of an irregular shape through which the child could put objects of a similar shape so they would drop into the truck. The truck was of the type beloved by modern parents who wish to promote the sensomotoric and cognitive development of their child, and its design was clearly inspired by the materials once developed by Montessori. The telephone, likewise, was somewhat special and unlike modern genuine telephones; one had to dial the number in the old-fashioned way and for some reason, perhaps to introduce the child to the notion of a mobile telephone, it had wheels. In addition,

Figure 2.1. Toy truck (after Rodriguez & Moro, 1999, p. 134).

Figure 2.2. Toy telephone (after Rodriguez & Moro, 1999, p. 135).

and for reasons that are beyond my understanding, both truck and telephone
had smiling faces painted on their front side.

Now, one might think that the proper use of such objects is obvious and
follows from their design. This is mistaken, however; in reality the proper
use of these objects is entirely conventional and children need to learn them

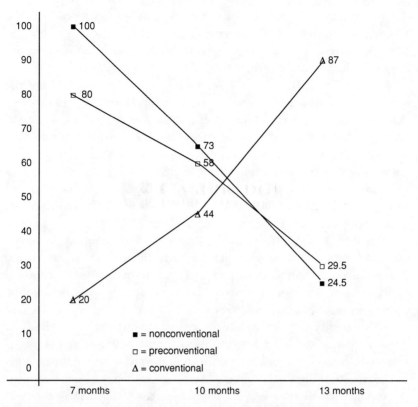

Figure 2.3. Percentages of nonconventional, preconventional, and conventional use of a toy truck at different ages during mother-child episodes (after Rodriguez & Moro, 1999, p. 224).

from adults. That is, a truck can be stuck into one's mouth, it can be used to physically abuse a good friend, it can be handed over as a present, and one can put certain objects in it. It is only the latter use that can be called the proper or conventional use of toy trucks, and mothers desperately seek to promote it and to eliminate the other uses. That they are quite successful at it can be seen from Figure 2.3.

Here we see the nonconventional, preconventional, and conventional use of the truck at the age of, respectively, seven, ten, and thirteen months. The conventional use was to put an object in the truck through one of the holes. Preconventional use was any behavior that remotely resembled that action, such as touching one of the holes with the hand or sticking a finger in it. As we can see, seven-month-old babies rarely use the object in a proper way and thirteen-month-old babies often do. But how do the babies learn it? All by themselves? No, Rodriguez and Moro made a quite convincing case that the children are introduced to the meanings of these objects through a variety of semiotic means employed by the mother in dyadic (or rather triadic, because the object they concentrate on makes a difference) interaction.

What are the semiotic means the mothers have at their disposal? First, the mothers can *model* the required act by repeatedly performing it in a slow and deliberate way. For example, the mother takes an object and slowly puts it into the proper hole of the truck. The movement can be and is often accompanied by language (like all other gestures), but it need not be. This semiotic means is the most effective one to attract the attention of the youngest children of seven months. Modeling or "remote demonstration," as Rodriguez and Moro call it, is easy to understand because the action involves the concrete (and socially desired) manipulation of the object.

More difficult to grasp for children are what Rodriguez and Moro call "immediate demonstrations" when the mother makes the child perform the conventional act or initiates that act and tries to make the child continue it. For example, the mother may try to elicit proper telephone behavior by putting the receiver to the child's ear.

Still more difficult for the children is *signaling* or *pointing*. Adults often point to a part of the object or to the object as a whole. However, pointing is difficult to understand for young children as the proper use of the object is not demonstrated but only suggested. Indeed, like dogs and other animals, the youngest children look at the pointing finger rather than in the right direction. Pointing thus proves far less effective in attracting the attention of the child to the object. Signaling or pointing can be made more effective by introducing redundancies, such as repeating the gesture, making the pointing gesture iconic (e.g., putting a finger in one of the truck's holes), or touching the object. But it remains an ineffective semiotic means to guide the behavior of the youngest babies.

That pointing is quite ineffective with young children can be shown by looking at the different behaviors that immediately follow such a semiotic means (see Figure 2.4). For instance, when the children are seven months old, pointing to the toy by the mother elicits the conventional use of the toy in only 8 percent of the mother-child interaction episodes, whereas 35 percent of the children simply watch the mother's action (Rodriguez & Moro, 1999, p. 237). This is true even when the pointing is made redundant by, for instance, repeating it. This means that, for the youngest children, pointing hardly ever leads to the conventional use of the toys and only in a minority of cases is effective in drawing the child's attention to the object.

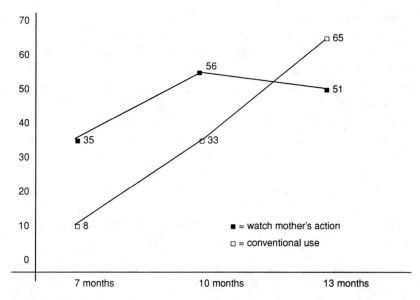

Figure 2.4. The effect of pointing for children of different ages in percentages per mother-child episode (after Rodriguez & Moro, 1999, p. 237).

Incidentally, mothers seem to realize the relative effectiveness of the more "difficult" semiotic means, and with the little ones they primarily make use of modeling or immediate demonstrations. This seems a perfectly adequate strategy because, as Rodriguez and Moro convincingly argue, it is on the basis of these simple semiotic means, which involve the actual use of the object, that the more abstract semiotic means become understandable for the child later on. Thus, we can see that the effectiveness of pointing increases when the child grows older, and in thirteen-month-old children pointing elicits proper behavior in already 65 percent of the children (see Figure 2.4). Rodriguez and Moro (1999) argue that the effectiveness of the more abstract semiotic means (including language) increases because they are being repeatedly presented in conjunction with the more simple ones such as modeling.

I cannot do full justice here to Rodriguez and Moro's (1999) detailed and meticulous analysis of the semiotic means employed and their results, but I do think the authors made a quite convincing case for the claim that we must analyze preverbal semiotic means in much more detail. Children are introduced to various social practices with the help of various signs of ascending complexity when they do not yet understand language. They do not simply discover or copy the conventional uses of objects, because this is beyond their abilities, but are gradually introduced to them by their caregivers through the use of subtle and increasingly abstract semiotic means. This conclusion is entirely in line with Vygotsky's theory but extends it in a significant way. In some of his writings Vygotsky was prone to consider the preverbal stage in children's cognitive development as a period during which children do not make use of cultural instruments – indeed, as a period that is not yet influenced by cultural factors at all (van der Veer & Valsiner, 1991). Later research, such as that by Rodriguez and Moro discussed previously, demonstrated that much subtle adult-child interaction and communication precede the acquisition of language proper by the child. These adult-child interactions prepare the ground for much of the child's later cognitive development and continue for a substantial part of childhood in Western society. Preverbal development, then, is a thoroughly cultural process that takes place in the social matrix that Vygotsky so perfectly described.

CONCLUSIONS

Vygotsky's claim that human mental processes are regulated by semiotic means and that they originate in social practices is still valid. The method of double stimulation is one way to study that process; the analysis of social interactions (whether dyadic or triadic) is another one. However, the replication of Leontiev's memory study showed that we must take care in interpreting its results. It was rightly established by Leontiev that five- and six-year-old children do not by themselves understand how to make use of the colored cards as cultural instruments (or rather: that they do not see how to turn the cards into instruments). However, this finding did not prove that the youngest children were unable to use cultural instruments in general. Further, Leontiev rightly established that adults make more use of internal cultural means or instruments than children do. However, this did not prove that children made no use of internal cultural instruments, let alone that they are still incapable of using them. In our replication study, we found that younger children are capable of making use of internal cultural devices (e.g., giving "funny" answers, or producing sophisticated color names) and that such semiotic devices are more effective in enhancing performance than the use of external cultural means. That finding suggests that semiotic devices can be effective at a much earlier age than Leontiev expected and that one need not posit that all internal means originated as or rested upon material objects.

Our discussion of the study conducted by Rodriguez and Moro (1999) yielded a similar reinterpretation of Vygotsky's cultural-historical theory.

We cannot regard the preverbal stage in child development as a stage that is quasi-natural as Vygotsky and Leontiev sometimes implied in their writings (van der Veer & Valsiner, 1991). It is true that the acquisition of oral speech has a tremendously important influence on the child's cognitive processes and problem-solving behavior, as Vygotsky argued. But that finding should not blind us to the fact that, before the acquisition of oral speech has been accomplished, enormously important developments take place that are based upon the use of semiotic means by the caregivers of the child. Entirely in line with Vygotsky's more general tenets, we can claim that the child's cognitive development rests upon the growing understanding of and guidance by signs such as pointing. As Rodriguez and Moro (1999) demonstrate, the preverbal stage is characterized by a subtle joint meaning, creating a process that paves the way for language development proper.

It is by amending and extending Vygotsky's and Leontiev's theories in the ways I have sketched that we can argue the fruitfulness of the cultural-historical paradigm. In that complex task we must not avoid an open debate with other schools of thought.

References

Asmolov, A. (1998). *Vygotsky today: On the verge of non-classical psychology.* Commack, NY: Nova Science Publishers.

Blanck, G. (1984). *Vigotski: Memoria y vigencia* [Vygotsky: Legacy and validity]. Buenos Aires: C & C Ediciones.

Brossard, M. (2004). *Vygotski: Lectures et perspectives de recherches en éducation* [Vygotsky: Readings and research perspectives in education]. Villeneuve d'Ascq: Presses Universitaires du Septentrion.

Brown, A. L., & Ferrara, R. A. (1985). Diagnosing zones of proximal development. In J. V. Wertsch (Ed.), *Culture, communication, and cognition: Vygotskian perspectives* (pp. 273–305). Cambridge: Cambridge University Press.

Brown, A. L., & French, L. A. (1979). The zone of potential development: Implications for intelligence testing in the year 2000. *Intelligence, 3,* 255–273.

Cole, M. (1996). *Cultural psychology: A once and future discipline.* Cambridge, MA: Belknap Press of Harvard University Press.

Cole, M., John-Steiner, V., Scribner, S., & Souberman, E. (Eds.). (1978). *Mind in society: The development of higher psychological processes.* Cambridge, MA: Harvard University Press.

Keiler, P. (1997). *Feuerbach, Wygotski & Co.* Berlin: Argument.

Keiler, P. (2002). *Lev Vygotskij: Ein Leben für die Psychologie* [Lev Vygotsky: A life for psychology]. Weinheim: Beltz Verlag.

Kohl de Oliveira, M. (1993). *Vygotsky: Aprendizado e desenvolvimento um processo sócio-histórico* [Vygotsky: Learning and development in the sociohistorical process]. São Paulo: Editora Scipione.

Kozulin, A. (1990). *Vygotsky's psychology: A biography of ideas.* New York: Harvester Wheatsheaf.

Leontiev, A. A. (1990). *L. S. Vygotskiy.* Moscow: Prosveshchenie.

Leontiev, A. N. (1931). *Razvitie pamyati: Eksperimental'noe issledovanie vysshikh psikhologicheskikh funktsiy* [The development of memory: An experimental investigation of the higher psychological functions]. Moscow and Leningrad: Uchpedgiz.

Leontiev, A. N. (1932). The development of voluntary attention in the child. *Journal of Genetic Psychology, 40,* 52–81.

Moll, L. C. (1990). *Vygotsky and education: Instructional implications of sociohistorical psychology.* Cambridge: Cambridge University Press.

Puzyrey, A. A. (1986). *Kul'turno-istoricheskaya teoriya L. S. Vygotskogo i sovremennaya psikhologiya* [L. S. Vygotsky's cultural-historical theory and contemporary psychology]. Moscow: Izdatel'stvo Moskovskogo Universiteta.

Rissom, I. (1985). *Der Begriff des Zeichens in den Arbeiten Lev Semenovic Vygotskijs* [The concept of sign in Lev Semenovich Vygotsky's writings]. Göppingen: Kümmerle Verlag.

Rivière, A. (1985). *La psicología de Vygotski* [Vygotsky's psychology]. Madrid: Visor.

Rodriguez, R., &. Moro, Ch. (1999). *El mágico número tres: Cuando los niños aún no hablan* [The magical number three: When children do not yet speak]. Barcelona: Paidós.

Schneuwly, B., & Bronckart, J. P. (Eds.). (1985). *Vygotsky aujourd'hui* [Vygotsky today]. Neuchatel: Delachaux & Niestlé.

Toomela, A. (2000). *Cultural-historical psychology: Three levels of analysis.* Tartu: Tartu University Press.

Tulviste, P. (1991). *The cultural-historical development of verbal thinking.* Commack, NY: Nova Science Publishers.

Valsiner, J., & van der Veer, R. (2000). *The social mind: Construction of the idea.* Cambridge: Cambridge University Press.

van der Veer, R. (1994). Leont'ev's forbidden colors game: An argument in favor of internalisation? In R. van der Veer, M. H. van IJzendoorn, & J. Valsiner (Eds.), *Reconstructing the mind: Replicability in research on human development* (pp. 233–254). Norwood, NJ: Ablex Publishing.

van der Veer, R. (1997). Some major themes in Vygotsky's theoretical work: An introduction. In R. W. Rieber & J. Wollock (Eds.), *The collected works of L. S. Vygotsky: Vol. 3. Problems of the theory and history of psychology* (pp. 1–7). New York: Plenum Press.

van der Veer, R. (1999a). Piaget in the plural: The story of his reception in Latin America. *Culture & Psychology, 5,* 217–222.

van der Veer, R. (1999b). El desarrollo semiótico. *Anuario de Psicologia, 30,* 130–133.

van der Veer, R. (2000). Tamara Dembo's early years: Working with Lewin and Buytendijk. *Journal of the History of the Behavioral Sciences, 36,* 109–126.

van der Veer, R., & Lück, H. (2002). Berliner Gestaltpsychologie in Aktion: Zur Diskussion der Experimente von Tamara Dembo [The Berlin Gestalt psychology in action: On the discussion of Tamara Dembo's experiments]. *Geschichte der Psychologie, 10,* 40–55.

van der Veer, R., & Valsiner, J. (1991). *Understanding Vygotsky: A quest for synthesis.* Oxford: Blackwell.

Veresov, N. (1999). *Undiscovered Vygotsky*. Frankfurt am Main: Peter Lang.

Wertsch, J. V. (1985). *Vygotsky and the social formation of mind*. Cambridge, MA: Harvard University Press.

Yaroshevsky, M. G. (1989). *Lev Vygotsky*. Moscow: Progress.

Yaroshevsky, M. G. (1993). *L. S. Vygotskiy: V poiskakh novoy psikhologii* [L. S. Vygotsky: In search of a new psychology]. St. Peterburg: Izdatel'stvo Mezhdunarodnogo Fonda Istorii Nauki.

3

Exploring the Links between External and Internal Activity from a Cultural-Historical Perspective

Igor M. Arievitch

After decades of being dominated by individualist (behaviorist, cognitivist, or physiology-driven) and reductionist notions, psychology has recently turned to contextual and cultural facets of human development. New attention to culture greatly contributes to, and necessitates, a substantial reconceptualization of the very nature of cognitive and other psychological processes as well as the ways to study them. Although the impact of culture, in one form or another, is acknowledged in almost all research branches that exist in psychology today, there is arguably one family of approaches that places this issue at the very center of its theory and methodology. This family of approaches encompasses studies in distributed cognition (e.g., Hutchins, 1996), situated learning (e.g., Lave & Wenger, 1991), cognitive evolution (e.g., Donald, 2001), sociocultural research (e.g., Cole, 1996; Wertsch, 1998), science and technology studies (e.g., Latour, 1999), and even history of psychology (e.g., Morawski, 2001). The principal assumption of this approach is that human cognition is a social collaborative activity that cannot be reduced either to physiological processes in the brain or to any individual information processing occurring "in the head." Instead, cognition is viewed as stretching beyond the individual isolated mind – into the cultural systems of artifacts and activities that allow for the cognitive processes to be accomplished and into the social communities of which these processes are only a part.

A substantial, and arguably pivotal, contribution to this paradigmatic shift has been made by scholars of the cultural-historical school of thought, beginning with its founders – Vygotsky, Luria, and Leontiev – and also by the proponents of this approach who helped to introduce, disseminate, and further develop it in Western psychology (Cole, 1996; Rogoff, 2003; Scribner, 1985; Wertsch, 1998; and others). In addition, in the most recent wave of international scholarship this approach is now being further expanded, specified, and applied to new research areas, such as education, organization studies, computer-human interaction, and others (e.g., Chaiklin, 2002; Engeström 1987; Glassman, 2001; Packer & Goicoechea, 2000; Wells, 1999).

One part in the Vygotsky school legacy, however, has yet to be fully assimilated into contemporary culture- and activity-centered studies, although it has important implications for the ways these studies can shape the overall landscape in psychology. This part of the legacy is associated with the works of Piotr Galperin, who was a contemporary of Vygotsky, Luria, and Leontiev and shared with them many basic assumptions of the cultural-historical psychology. Importantly, besides these shared assumptions, his works contain highly original insights into many fundamental problems of psychology and can be viewed as a pivotal elaboration of the cultural-historical framework. This elaboration, I argue, is critically important for the future of the whole project initiated by Vygotsky and continued today on an international scale – not only for its internal coherence but also for its ability to have a broad impact on psychology and education.

What constitutes the unique and important contribution by Galperin with a direct relevance for today's research on cultural dimensions of human development is the central question of the present chapter. I believe that addressing this question is one of the pathways that can help to fill the major gap existing in today's culture- and activity-oriented research, a gap that is impeding its growth and transformation into a truly influential approach, potentially capable of revolutionizing the very foundations of psychology in the new century. Exploring Galperin's works is promising because this scholar, continuing important insights by Vygotsky and Leontiev, turned out to be the only psychologist in this school who most consistently explored in his theoretical and empirical studies one of the central issues in the cultural-historical agenda – how external material actions get transformed into mental actions. Galperin came to realize that, without providing a consistent account of how new mental actions emerge out of meaningful human activity, the whole cultural-historical project is in constant danger of falling into the familiar traps of either old mentalist psychology or physiological reductionism. He devoted his career to conceptualizing the formation of the individual mind – as a unique capacity of humans to perform actions on the internal plane – within a profoundly sociocultural account of human development.

A unique core component of Galperin's approach – a conceptualization of psychological aspects of human activity, distinct from its physiological, logical, or sociological aspects – allowed him to understand in a new, promising way many traditional research and educational topics, such as knowledge representation, problem solving, comprehension, transfer, and learning and development, as well as many controversies that have been dividing the science of the mind since its inception. Such a research orientation also helped Galperin to avoid yet another, relatively new form of reductionism – the tendency to dissolve the individual mental activity in a broader reality of cultural practices, social organizations, and linguistic discourse (for the analysis of the latter form of reductionism, see Stetsenko & Arievitch, 1997). The fundamental cultural-historical framework put forth by Vygotsky and Leontiev, combined with the advanced understanding of mental processes themselves as forms of object-related activity, made it possible for Galperin to conceptualize the mind in a nonmentalist way.

In this chapter, I first discuss Galperin's place in the cultural-historical line of research and chart the common metatheoretical background of this school of thought. Then I describe how Vygotsky and then Leontiev made important steps in answering the central question of how the mental is formed out of the material and point to some gaps in their accounts. After that, I present Galperin's account and argue that Galperin's understanding of internalization and related concepts of mental action formation and internalization can serve as unifying bases for developing a sociocultural research agenda.

COMMON GROUNDS OF THE CULTURAL-HISTORICAL ACTIVITY THEORY

To understand Galperin's views, one has to consider his relation to the broader context of the cultural-historical activity theory. This relation is quite complex because, on the one hand, at the level of foundational premises and assumptions, Galperin firmly belongs to this school of thought. On the other hand, Galperin was an original thinker who proposed his own unique system of ideas that were often developed in arguments and sometimes even in a direct opposition to ideas of other cultural-historical theorists.

Galperin became acquainted with Vygotsky and his theory in the 1930s after joining the group of scholars headed by Leontiev in Kharkov, and the beginning of his career as a psychologist has been profoundly influenced by this acquaintance. All of his subsequent research was carried out within a collaborative project shaped (at least in its foundation) by Vygotsky, especially through his close lifelong ties with Leontiev (for details, see Arievitch & van der Veer, 2004).

In particular, Galperin shared the important concern of the cultural-historical approach with constructing psychology not on the basis of the phenomena of consciousness as they appear in introspection (i.e., not from the content of mental representations), and not on the basis of the phenomena of behavior as they appear in observation. Neither could the internal workings of the brain, as a process separate from the conditions of life, be taken as a starting point for explaining psychological processes. Instead, the major pathway to explore these processes was to trace their origin in the relations that link individual organisms and their environment, focusing on how these relations develop in evolution and history. This research orientation very clearly underlies Leontiev's central notion that psychological processes emerge in activities that connect living organisms with their environment and that human development is driven by the logic and dynamics of practical activities (Leontiev, 1978, 1981). The same orientation is particularly evident in Vygotsky's last work, *Thinking and Speech* (1987). He regarded psychological processes as developing in connection with the changes in social practice in which these processes are embedded, for example, linking the development of scientific concepts to school practices and the development of word meaning as a means of activity of communication (cf. Minick, 1987).

The question about the function of mind in the broader context of life (i.e., in regulating activities of organisms in the environment), rather than in the workings of physiological processes or narrowly defined behavior, put forward by Vygotsky and his associates, defied the traditional "entities-bound" worldview. Instead, this question was grounded in an alternative worldview and an alternative version of causality – the worldview in which the complex dynamics of self-evolving activities of organisms in their real life environment, and the notions of "organism-environment" as a unified system of interactions, emerged in opposition to the view of the universe as composed of separate discrete entities. The emergence of this worldview has been a complex and lengthy development that included the merger of Darwinian evolutionary thinking with the growing knowledge about the physiology of higher nervous processes (e.g., by Helmholtz, Sherrington, Sechenov, Pavlov), and the new notion of acting in meaningful situations as the unit of analysis for psychology based on the study of social conduct and its maladies.

The centrality of this general orientation is transparent in the threefold interrelated emphasis of the cultural-historical approach on (1) studying psychological processes in their development (i.e., in ontogeny, phylogeny, and the history of human civilization); (2) viewing human mental functioning as emerging out of specifically human forms of life and social practice, including the processes of transmitting the collective cultural experience of previous generations; and (3) exploring the mediating role of cultural tools and the processes of their internalization as pivotal elements in such transmission and in the genesis of the human mind.

This research orientation common to cultural-historical psychology guided Galperin's work from his early study on tool use in the mid-1930s to his late investigations on the stepwise formation of mental actions (e.g., Galperin, 1998b). Like Vygotsky and Leontiev, he also strove to understand psychological processes as an integral part of the relations between living organisms and their environments (which are inherently social for humans). He also pursued the analysis of internalization of cultural tools as the pathway for the development of human psychological processes.

An additional unifying theme that distinguishes Galperin's approach (even in comparison to other representatives of the cultural-historical framework) was his persistent quest to understand the specific functions of psychological processes and the precise conditions that make their emergence within broader material activities necessary. With this quest guiding his work, Galperin developed an original research agenda, ultimately arriving at a coherent system of ideas and a distinct research program, implemented by himself and several generations of his co-workers and followers (e.g., Obukhova, 1972; Podolskij, 1987; Talyzina, 1975) in areas as diverse as the history and theory of psychology, the methodology of psychological research, and the psychological foundations of education.

Galperin's focus on these questions can be seen as a result of his affiliation with the cultural-historical framework with its interest in how psychological processes originate from and within real-life contexts. At the same time, it appears that among cultural-historical scholars Galperin was the first who realized the centrality of these questions (already very early on in his career; see Galperin, 1997), provided elaborate answers to them, and placed these answers at the very foundation of his further research.

Given the highly original character of his views, can Galperin be considered part of the cultural-historical activity framework at all? In my view, this is certainly the case; moreover, without Galperin's elaboration of the core questions of the cultural-historical framework – mediation by cultural tools, internalization, the relation between external material processes and mental functions – this framework would lack internal consistency and conceptual tools to deal with many vexing problems that keep resurfacing in contemporary theoretical and empirical studies. A potential to approach all these problems in a revolutionary new way was present in Vygotsky's project in the form of many nascent ideas and insights. However, further elaboration and conceptualization was needed to transform this potential into a fully fledged theory of mind and development.

As this is an actively debated issue (see, e.g., Kozulin, 1986; van der Veer & Valsiner, 1991), I would like to reiterate that in my view this was generally the same Vygotskian research line, despite several shifts in emphasis, sometimes quite substantial, and the same explicit criticism that existed within the cultural-historical school (for the analysis of this criticism viewed as an extension of the same research line, see Haenen, 1996b). It was not a different line, as is sometimes portrayed in order to contrast Vygotsky and Leontiev's perspectives. Galperin's own firm view was that there was a fundamental continuity between Vygotsky's, Leontiev's, and his own theory – although, no doubt, he developed all the core concepts in his own way (Galperin, 1992b). Suffice it to say that – following Vygotsky – both Leontiev and Galperin used as their starting point the unique character of human development, based on appropriation of human culture and cultural tools, both material and symbolic. The concept that became pivotal for both Leontiev and Galperin – "the object-related meaningful activity" – is itself very indicative. Each and every component of it implies specifically human objects, human meanings, and human forms of activity; therefore, all are necessarily social, cultural, and historical forms, that is, mediated by tools and signs.

In my view, contrasting Vygotsky to Leontiev, as well as Galperin with these scholars in some recent discussions (e.g., Kozulin, 1986), comes, at least partly, from a narrow interpretation of their views and concepts in a rather "technological" or "technical" way. In relation to Vygotsky, this narrowness manifests itself in understanding his concept of social interaction only as a direct interpersonal communication ("information exchange") mediated by various sign systems. In relation to Leontiev, the same narrowness manifests itself in understanding his concept of human actions and activity merely and strictly as being material transformations of a given situation. In both cases, the cultural-historical nature of social interaction, of symbolic systems, and of human activity is being overlooked. If one considers the underlying cultural-historical core of all those concepts, central to both Vygotsky and Leontiev, as well as to Galperin, the kinship between their theories becomes evident.

THE DEVELOPMENT OF A NEW PSYCHOLOGICAL PARADIGM

Vygotsky made an important step toward resolving one of the key problems of psychology – how to overcome the centuries-old dichotomies of "external versus internal" and "individual versus social." For him, the specific structure of human interaction was a "material" one that was appropriated from the social into the individual domain. Social interaction mediated by cultural tools and symbols, for Vygotsky, was the source of psychological development. The ontological significance of this step is difficult to overestimate.

The impassable barrier between the external world and internal mental phenomena was broken. Human mind was conceived of as originating not from the functioning of the brain and not as something entirely different from productive activities, cultural practices, and social interactions, but as a direct product of these external forms of human life. To be sure, the sociogenetic view did exist in psychology before Vygotsky (not to mention a long philosophical tradition), most prominently in the works of Baldwin, Mead, Janet, and some others, and Vygotsky was certainly influenced by these works (cf. Valsiner & van der Veer, 2000). Nevertheless, it was Vygotsky who brought different sociocultural ideas together, gave them a new powerful interpretation, and structured them as a new alternative paradigm in psychology.

At the same time, many potentially promising lines of thought and research were left uncompleted by Vygotsky, quite understandably given his untimely death. The idea of social interaction as the driving force of individual mental development could serve as an attractive starting point; yet it remained unclear what exactly in this interaction could be viewed as the core component making the individual mind develop. The "general sociogenetic law" of human development (a transition from interpersonal communication to intrapersonal forms of dialogue and thinking; see Vygotsky, 1987) presented a refreshing outline of human development, but the particular stages and detailed regularities of such transition were not specified. The idea of mediation of all human mental processes by cultural tools provided a fascinating insight into the unique character of human mental functioning; yet it was difficult to explain how external tools are employed by internal (mental) processes to their benefit and then become integrated into these processes. Finally, the concept of the zone of proximal development was a potentially powerful instrument for reshaping the views on the role of instruction in development; yet it remained unspecified what kind of processes took place within this zone that led to a cognitive change.

In addition, Vygotsky's position regarding the initial sources of internal psychological processes contained a twofold, and not an unambiguous, explanation. On the one hand, as just mentioned, Vygotsky believed that all higher, specifically human, psychological processes take root from social interaction and that their development entails complex processes of mediation by cultural tools. However, he also seemed to assume that some lower (or natural) psychological processes (such as elementary perception, attention, and memory) are present in the child from birth and that their genesis has little to do with cultural influences. Vygotsky's whole system of ideas aimed at addressing the issue of how the lower, natural psychological functions become gradually transformed into cultural, higher processes. Signs and symbols, according to Vygotsky, play a major role in this transformation by "growing into" the natural psychological process and changing its character from the immediate, elementary function to a culturally mediated and voluntary function, for example, of attention, memory, and so on – hence, Vygotsky's strong stance on the decisive role of the mastery of language and speech, as the major sign system, in the child's mental development.

Interestingly, one consequence of such a focus of Vygotsky on the centrality of speech was that in his writings the interpersonal communication (primarily in verbal dialogues) emerged as the most characteristic, prototypical form of social interaction and the main driving force of individual mental development. Vygotsky's further thinking along these lines resulted in his assumption that word meanings and their mastery could serve as a unit of analysis and the main subject matter of psychological study. Because word meanings exist only in individual or social consciousness, choosing the word meaning as the unit of analysis could potentially lead to the interpretation of mental development as being the result of a "communication of minds." This is exactly what happened in many interpretations of Vygotsky, in which interpsychological functioning became viewed as "socially distributed consciousness" (see, e.g., Bruner, 1985), rather than the broader reality of human social practice. It went almost unnoticed that the emphasis on verbal meanings and social consciousness as the origins of human development to some extent undermined Vygotsky's own initial claim about the external origins of the individual mind (Vygotsky, 1997).

In brief, by using the notion of lower psychological processes that were presumably biologically driven, Vygotsky in fact admitted that some "internal" plane existed before the acquisition of social and cultural experiences takes place. In addition, the strong emphasis on verbal forms of interaction left room for the mentalist interpretations of the development of mind. This led to a certain tension between the main message of Vygotsky's overall program – that of the cultural-historical origin and development ("construction") of human mind as a foundation for a new psychological paradigm – and some of his specific explanations, concepts, and terminology that allowed for a tacit but restraining presence of the traditional mentalist assumptions within the new paradigm.

To address these unanswered questions and inconsistencies in the studies of Leontiev and his colleagues (Galperin among them), the concept of activity has been introduced to the cultural-historical framework as a basic explanatory principle. Leontiev took as a starting point the assumption that all psychological processes, not only the cultural ones, originate from "outside" the organism – from meaningful object-related (external) activity. Therefore, although within the same Vygotskian research agenda, the focus was shifted from internalization of symbols and signs within the processes of social interaction to the emergence of mental activity within external object-related meaningful activity.

The genetic link between external (or material) and internal (or mental) activity became the focal point in Leontiev's studies. He maintained that "the process of internalization is not the transferal of an external activity to a preexisting, internal 'plane of consciousness': It is the process in which this internal plane is formed" (Leontiev, 1981, p. 163). Therefore, more explicitly than in Vygotsky's account of internalization, the very existence of something "internal" before the acquisition of social and cultural experience was questioned by Leontiev. However, Leontiev did not further elaborate on this conceptualization either theoretically or empirically. After Vygotsky's death, the efforts of Leontiev and his associates were directed toward the demonstration of the close relationship between an individual's mental and external object-related activity. These studies resulted in rich experimental evidence that the cognitive performance intrinsically depends on an individual's external activity. For example, it has been demonstrated that unintentional (nondeliberate) memorization of the items presented in the experiment was dependent on the specific place of these items in the structure of the individual's external activity, namely, on whether those items represented the goal of the activity or were part of some technical conditions of the activity (P. I. Zinchenko, 1983). In other experiments, through vocalizing a standard tone and attuning the sound to a prescribed amplitude, the participants learned to distinguish this amplitude in the follow-up tasks with an accuracy that was very close to that of people with a "perfect pitch"; however, if this tone was not vocalized at the previous stage, the participants remained almost at the same level of performance as they were before learning (Leontiev, 1981).

In these and other studies by Leontiev and his partners, it has been shown that the way in which external activity was organized had a remarkable influence on an individual's mental activity. Along with Vygotsky's and Leontiev's earlier studies on memory and attention, this important evidence revealed an intrinsic link between external object-related activity and mental processes. The cultural-historical idea that there was no absolute barrier between external behavior and mental activity and that they are genetically and structurally interrelated was given further empirical grounding. However, after this relationship had been established in a number of spectacular experiments, its specific character was not further analyzed by Leontiev and his colleagues. The exact ways in which external activity exerted such a powerful effect on mental functioning remained unclear.

Most importantly, the question of how the transformations of external activity lead to the emergence of new forms of mental activity – that is, how "the internal plane is formed" – has been neither explicitly formulated nor investigated in Leontiev's works. Instead, he concentrated on the analysis of just one aspect of object-related activity – its motives and goals as the most obviously psychological aspects of activity (cf. V. P. Zinchenko, 1985). In his later research, Leontiev (1978, 1981) was primarily concerned with conceptualizing the general structure of activity and the links between its levels; thus, for example, he defined various components of activity through their differential relations to the activity's motives and goals. He also devoted great attention to how conscious actions turn into automatic operations. The main distinctive feature of operations is that they are automatic processes related to and determined (in their content) by concrete conditions in which activity is performed, whereas actions are regulated by conscious control and directly related to the goals of activity. Another key concept of Leontiev's (1981) theory – the concept of leading activity – was also defined through the emergence of new motives and goals within activity and the changing relations between them.

One can also notice one quite paradoxical feature of Leontiev's theory: his otherwise profoundly cultural-historical analysis of object-related activity tells us very little about the role of speech as the specifically human form in which the content of activity is represented. In contrast to Vygotsky, who scrutinized in detail the function of speech in internalization, Leontiev acknowledged the critical role of speech in human mental functioning only at a very general metatheoretical level. In Leontiev's concrete studies, the function of speech was not examined. It was Galperin who combined Vygotsky's emphasis on the role of speech with Leontiev's focus on the role of external object-related activity in his empirical study of mental development.

Galperin continued Leontiev's line of research in his analysis of how external processes of activity generate mental processes. At the same time, Galperin argued that there was a great need to clarify how the transformation of the initially external activity into its "internal" form takes place. He believed that neither the communicative aspects of joint activity (addressed by Vygotsky) nor the powerful impact of material activity on the individual's mental performance (established by Leontiev) was completely sufficient:

It was impossible to clarify what substantive connection existed between mental activity and "object-related activity" and, consequently, the content of mental activity itself. The difficulty was that the objective content of external activity was conceived as something indisputably non-psychological, whereas the "true content" of mental activity was considered something nonobjective. This created an insuperable barrier to resolution of the most important question . . . namely, understanding mental activity itself as being fully substantive, i.e., as being also "object-related" activity. Mental activity itself continued to remain inaccessible for objective analysis. As a result, the role of external activity in the effectiveness of mental activity and its development was objectively reduced to the position of a system of conditions. . . . Previously it had not been taken into account, but now it was demonstrated that it was necessary to take this system into account. Nevertheless, the external remained external, and the internal remained internal. Even the use of signs as instruments of mental activity and their "growing from the outside inwards" (i.e., the use of "for oneself" and "in one's mind"), without an explanation of what exactly took place in this case or how external activity and its external instruments changed, were unable to alter the former views of mind. (Galperin, 1992b, p. 54)

In line with this critique, Galperin has built his whole theory around these intractable questions – how the mental, psychological emerges out of the material, nonpsychological. Having accepted the general premises about the cultural-historical origins of mental processes, he undertook further steps in developing this approach.

FROM MATERIAL ACTIVITY TO MENTAL PROCESSES

Galperin's conceptualization of how external activity becomes internal, or how the mental plane of functioning is formed, was one of several important cornerstones of his whole approach to human development. His own original answer to this question can be regarded as a pivotal component in the general edifice of the cultural-historical theory. While answering the question as to how the internal plane is formed, Galperin proposed a number of novel ideas about the very nature of psychological functioning, including the nature of mind, with these ideas forming a comprehensive foundation for a consistently nonreductionist theory of human development.

First, one needs to note Galperin's general focus on the functions of psychological processes as the foundation for conceptualizing their nature. His analysis here was based on clarifying the role of psychological regulation as an important mechanism in the adaptation of living organisms to the ever-changing environment. Following the general premises of the cultural-historical school, Galperin insisted on viewing psychological processes not as an isolated reality sui generis, but as processes that are included in the natural chain of events that take place in the life of organisms in their environments. Galperin understood psychological processes as specific forms of activity allowing for new kinds of adaptation that became necessary due to the growing complexity of environments in which automatic forms of behavior did not suffice for the survival of the organisms. Because of this emphasis, much of Galperin's work was devoted to the analysis of evolutionary conditions for the emergence of new, psychological forms of activity that represent a "response" to increasingly complex environments. On the one hand, this allowed Galperin to show the continuity in the development of mental functioning in evolution and, on the other hand, to reveal certain features of psychological processes that characterize the specifically human mental development.

In accordance with his general logic, Galperin viewed the emergence of mental regulation as resulting from the growing contradiction between the increasing inconstancy of the environment for organisms that became increasingly mobile and the need to immediately perform relevant and precise actions without preliminary physical trials. Such trials, if unsuccessful, could cost the organism its life, Galperin maintained. What was needed was an entirely new mechanism of adaptation where actions would not be carried out physically but first investigated on the basis of an image presented "ideally" (mentally). Galperin argued that the mental image makes it possible to thoroughly examine an emerging new situation and to anticipate the consequences of any action prior to its physical execution.

Further, the specifics of human mental functioning were conceived of by Galperin as a result of a radical change in the way of life of our human ancestors that took place at the dawn of human civilization. Humans developed collaborative, social forms of life in which they acted together and employed increasingly complex tools to meet the challenges presented by their environment. It is within such collaborative and tool-mediated practices that the specifically human mental processes emerged in human evolution. Clearly this reasoning was in line with Vygotskian thought, although it represented Galperin's (1976) own interpretation. Human ability to employ tools in accordance with their collectively developed purpose became an important part of conceptualizing the human mind by Galperin; his early works already focused on the experimental demonstration of how children gradually master the specifically human way of tool use and thus also develop specifically human ways of thinking (Galperin, 1998a).

Throughout Galperin's research, the critical question to address was how human mental activity is formed out of the transformation of external activity. It is here that Galperin's contribution is particularly substantial in light of today's controversies and gaps in sociocultural theories and research. He created a new methodology, the "stepwise formation of mental actions," aimed at the exploration of how a new psychological process (mental action) emerges out of a nonpsychological, material process (material action). With this method, Galperin was able not just to passively observe the emergence of a new psychological process but to actively construct it in carefully designed experimental procedures. He was able to expose and actively guide the internalization of a new activity by the individual. The procedure of the stepwise formation of mental actions has been described many times by Galperin himself and by other authors (e.g., Galperin, 1992a; Haenen, 1996a). For the purposes of this chapter, it is important to point to several key features of this procedure.

The formation of any mental activity according to Galperin's stepwise procedure was framed as a teaching-learning experiment. It started with carrying out the activity (i.e., solving a given problem) at the material level, that is, as an activity based on the material supports necessary for the learner to solve the problem successfully. Such material supports included models of objects, graphic representations of the problem situation, and, most importantly, the "orientation card" with the succinct description of goals, tools, and the steps necessary to carry out the activity. In this way, all the substantial conditions and components of the activity were made easily comprehensible for the learners.

Once the activity was mastered by the learners at the material level, the material supports were removed and the learner was required to perform the activity in overt speech, that is, to describe out loud every step of the activity while performing it. Carrying out the activity verbally was a critical step in internalization of the activity. In Galperin's view, speech was the only way to transform the external activity into mental activity. Only speech made the activity abstract and generalized enough to gradually enable the learner to carry out the activity mentally, "in the mind."

The next important transformation was carrying out the activity in covert speech, while silently talking to oneself. At this stage, the activity got increasingly abbreviated and automated. The vocal aspect of speech began to recede to the background, gradually fading and giving way to "pure" (nonverbalized) meanings as the major content of action. The result was a generalized image of action in which the "internal representation" of its content, in the form of meanings, became the only focus of an individual's activity. At the final stage of formation, this activity appeared as "pure" thought, in which individuals operated with meanings per se, rather than with words – that is, rather than with external, verbalized representations of meanings.

By taking material object-related activity as the starting point of mental activity formation, Galperin continued Leontiev's activity approach in its major thrust of conceptualizing psychological processes as originating in the external practical activity. Moreover, he further developed this approach by including the specific content of activity (its particular conditions, goals and tools, sequence of necessary steps, and the like) in psychological analysis of the activity formation. This constituted a substantial step in comparison to Leontiev, who focused only on the motivational aspects of the activity. Further, by emphasizing the crucial function of speech in internalization, Galperin clearly continued Vygotsky's tradition that focused on the central role of culturally evolved semiotic systems, especially language, in mental development. Finally, by integrating the speech as the major mechanism of forming "internal actions," described as acting based on meanings, and revealing the crucial import of abbreviated internal speech as the foundation of thought, Galperin in fact was able to reveal the sequence of events leading to the formation of internal actions as such. Thus, he showed how external action becomes transformed into thought, in a sequence of rather comprehensible, not mysterious, events involving gradual metamorphoses of action from external into internal modes of existence. It should also be noted that the function of internal speech in this overall process described by Galperin was compatible with Vygotsky's well-known analysis in *Thinking and Speech* and, moreover, represented an important extension and specification of this analysis.

In his later research, Galperin (1998b) implemented his method for studying various types of processes, such as conceptual thinking, perception, and language development. For example, Galperin has experimentally demonstrated how the material form of monitoring and checking one's own performance in children gradually becomes transformed into a new psychological process, the process of attention. In this experiment, children who were in the beginning highly inattentive to spelling errors learned to check the spelling of a text presented by the experimenter. Galperin assumed that the material activity of monitoring and checking one's performance is a genetic prototype (a material analog) of the psychological process of attention because they both have the same essential function: to improve the quality of some activity (such as an activity of writing) in which it serves as a counterpart.

On the basis of this assumption, children were first taught to perform monitoring and checking of spelling in a material form – by breaking down the words in the text into syllables with pencil and checking the spelling syllable by syllable, following the order written down on the "orientation card" provided by the experimenter. After the activity of spelling-checking had been mastered on the material level, children progressed to performing that same activity verbally, that is, describing their actions in detail out loud, without using a pencil and the orientation card anymore. After that, under the guidance of the experimenter, they gradually transitioned to talking to themselves, without overt speech, while carrying out the same activity. As children achieved this stage, their verbal descriptions of their own actions became increasingly abbreviated and the performance got increasingly accelerated. In the end, children were able to carry out monitoring and checking of spelling entirely "in the mind," smoothly and without mistakes. In other words, children who used to be extremely inattentive to spelling errors acquired the ability of a high-quality attention to spelling as the result of a specially organized learning process (Galperin & Kabylnitskaia, 1974).

Therefore, attention has been shown in its genesis – as an abbreviated, "mental" form of monitoring that stemmed from the material activity of monitoring and checking one's own performance. These genetic roots are substantially obscured in nongenetic views of attention, such as most cognitive theories of attention. In other words, Galperin's study of attention has empirically shown how certain (material) forms of the individual's external activity are gradually transformed into other (mental) forms of that same external activity. It was, perhaps, the first empirical demonstration of how the dualistic dichotomies of "external" and "internal" could be eliminated (for details, see Galperin, 1989).

The significance of Galperin's study of the stages in which mental actions are formed can be fully appreciated when it is viewed as a novel attempt to conceptualize mental processes in a nonmentalist way. This study provides theoretical tools for understanding human development as essentially embedded in sociocultural contexts and intimately connected with the specifics of these contexts, while at the same time leaving room for conceptualizing what traditionally has been described as individual cognition and mind. Although Galperin used many traditional notions and metaphors, such as "internal" action, internalization, cognitive processes, and acting "in the mind," his account was in fact aimed at overcoming the traditional concept of mind as an individual internal container in which thoughts are born and function on their own grounds.

The paradox worth emphasizing is that Galperin's "internal" or mental actions (and other seemingly internal processes), in his theorizing, were actually not internal in the traditional meaning of the term. This can be explained through Galperin's analysis of different kinds of actions, which was part of his conceptual system underlying the procedure of stepwise formation of mental actions.

Galperin distinguished between the ideal ("nonmaterial") actions that can be performed only in the physical presence of the problem situation and ideal actions that can be carried out in abstraction from the physical situation. The former type of action is common to animals and humans. The latter type of action, which Galperin termed mental actions per se, is specific only to humans. It is exactly this type of action that underlies a wide variety of seemingly different phenomena related to acting "in the mind," such as manipulating with mental models studied in cognitive psychology, or the inner speech studied by Vygotsky (for details, see Arievitch & van der Veer, 1995).

These types of action, performed in abstraction from the physical situation, although termed "mental actions," are, in Galperin's interpretation, not internal, mental faculties, nor are they a reflection of brain processes. They are object-related actions, as all other human actions are, the only difference being that mental actions are carried out in a special form, that is, without their physical execution. Conceptualizing mental activity itself as an object-related activity implies that it occurs in the objective, outer world. Perhaps most importantly, mental activity is carried out not according to any internal, mysterious "mental" laws of mind but according to the laws and to "the stubborn facts" of the external world. It is performed in compliance with particular characteristics of external objects and processes. Therefore, mental actions have the same objective content as the relevant material actions in a particular field.

In brief, any human action, both mental and material, is characterized by its object-relatedness. To be successful, such an action has to follow the logic and relationships of the external objects and processes. And it cannot be explained by referring to some inherently "internal" components, whatever is usually meant by that – for example, purely physiological processes. Understanding human action in any of its guises, including "mental" or "internal," as following the objective rules of the outer world and demonstrating how mental actions emerge from external actions constituted Galperin's way of eliminating the dualism of mental and material, external and internal processes.

The concrete character and content of emerging actions may be, of course, quite different. For example, when a chess player analyzes the actual standing on a chessboard or when a child classifies objects – these two activities differ from one another in their operational makeup. Nevertheless, they all are the result of basically the same process of internalization – the specifically human type of mastering new actions that starts from the fully fledged material form and culminates in the abbreviated, mental form of action. Therefore, Galperin's analysis of mental action formation detailed in his "stepwise procedure" opened up the possibility to understand the transition from external to internal planes of action as a fundamental mechanism of human learning and development.

To summarize, Galperin's account of how mental actions are formed demonstrated the genetic link between external and mental activity and the particular mechanism of how "external" becomes "internal" – without implying the dualistic dichotomy between these two planes, the dichotomy that to some extent was still tacitly present in Vygotsky's and Leontiev's accounts. Such a dichotomy was eliminated by viewing mental processes themselves as a specific form of object-related activity, and by conceptualizing internalization both as a transformation of certain (material) forms of an individual's external activity into other (mental) forms of that same external activity and as a specifically human form of appropriation of new knowledge and skills. In this sense, it appears that we can overcome the dualistic dichotomies without discarding individual cognition and the "internal" plane of action. Instead, they can be reconceptualized in a nonmentalist way, based on a clearer understanding of the transitions from external to internal planes of activity, as elucidated by Galperin.

It should be noted that such a reconceptualization would further entail expanding on the notion that even seemingly solitary mental activities of individuals remain not only always external (i.e., object-related, as previously explained) but also profoundly social – the aspect that Galperin had in mind in principle but never directly addressed in his research. That is, his notion that studying the human mind does not have to entail any traditional mentalist constructs should be complemented with the notion that individual development is based on acquiring social ways of dealing with reality and on learning how to carry out activities in a shared social world and in constant dialogue with this world. In this sense, the future task is to merge Galperin's line of research with the ideas that focus more directly on the interactional dimensions of development, initially proposed by Vygotsky and today continued in research, for example, on participatory learning in cultural communities (see Rogoff, 1990, 2003), collaborative cognition (Bearison & Dorval, 2002), and dialogic inquiry (Wells, 1999). It is along these lines that a broader picture of human development in its diverse dimensions is likely to emerge, highlighting all of these dimensions as being the collective processes of shared social endeavors that continue to be such endeavors even when carried out by individuals.

CONCLUDING REMARKS

Contemporary sociocultural theory is still struggling with the problem of how to analyze the culturally constructed nature of the mind without losing the aspect of individual mental functioning (cf. Hatano & Wertsch, 2001; Minnis & John-Steiner, 2001). Overcoming the dominant metaphor of mind as information processing strictly "in the head," not linked to the contexts of social and cultural practices, has led many researchers of the sociocultural orientation away from considering mental processes, leaving these processes under the purview of traditional cognitive psychology. This situation results in substantial gaps and a limited explanatory power of sociocultural accounts of human development, impeding their progress toward a truly influential approach that could reshape the very foundations of psychology.

One possible way to close these gaps is to advance our understanding of human development as an inherently sociocultural process, yet entailing a uniquely human ability to act "mentally" that emerges as a transformation of external object-related activity and does not exist apart from it. Galperin's contribution can be viewed as an elaboration of a nonmentalist view of mental processes, grounded in the general premises of the cultural-historical psychology but adding a crucial piece to it in his explanation of how exactly the external turns into internal in human activity without losing its object-oriented character. In this account Galperin opened up the ways to study the mind beyond the metaphor of a "mental container" (cf. Bereiter, 2002), or of any other mentalist construct. Thus the foundations have been laid to address in a novel way the traditional issues of knowledge representation, problem solving, comprehension, and the like, without falling into the traps of a dichotomous mentalist thinking that viewed these processes as a separate mental reality "in the head." This line of research can serve as a valuable source of ideas for bringing individual cognition and cultural context together.

References

Arievitch, I. M., & van der Veer, R. (1995). Furthering the internalization debate: Galperin's contribution. *Human Development, 38* (2), 113–126.

Arievitch, I. M., & van der Veer, R. (2004). The role of non-automatic regulation of activity: From Lipps to Galperin. *History of Psychology, 7* (2), 154–182.

Bearison, D. J., & Dorval, B. (2002). *Collaborative cognition: Children negotiating ways of knowing.* Westport, CT: Ablex Publishing.

Bereiter, C. (2002). *Education and mind in the knowledge age.* Mahwah, NJ: Lawrence Erlbaum.

Bruner, J. (1985). Vygotsky: A historical and conceptual perspective. In J. V. Wertsch (Ed.), *Culture, communication, and cognition: Vygotskian perspectives* (pp. 21–34). Cambridge: Cambridge University Press.

Chaiklin, S. (2002). A developmental teaching approach to schooling. In G. Wells and G. Claxton (Eds.), *Learning for life in the 21st century: Sociocultural perspectives on the future of education.* London: Blackwell.

Cole, M. (1996). *Cultural psychology: A once and future discipline.* Cambridge, MA: Harvard University Press.

Donald, M. (2001). *A mind so rare.* New York: W. W. Norton.

Engeström, Y. (1987). *Learning by expanding: An activity approach to developmental research*. Helsinki: Orienta-Konsultit.

Galperin, P. Ia. (1976). *Vvedenie v psikhologiju* [Introduction to psychology]. Moscow: Izd-vo Moskovskogo Universiteta.

Galperin, P. Ia. (1989). The problem of attention. *Soviet Psychology, 27* (3), 83–92. (Original work published 1976)

Galperin, P. Ia. (1992a). Stage-by-stage formation as a method of psychological investigation. *Journal of Russian and East European Psychology, 30* (4), 60–80. (Original work published 1978)

Galperin, P. Ia. (1992b). The problem of activity in Soviet psychology. *Journal of Russian and East European Psychology, 30* (4), 37–59. (Original work published 1977)

Galperin, P. Ia. (1997). Pismo k A. N. Leontievu, 1940 [Letter to A. N. Leontiev, 1940]. *Vestnik Moskovskogo Universiteta, 14* (3), 3–7.

Galperin, P. Ia. (1998a). Razlichie v ispol'zovanii orudii u cheloveka i vspomogatel'nykh sredstv u zhivotnykh i ego psikhologicheskoe znachenie [The difference between human tool use and the use of auxiliary means in animals and its psychological significance]. In P. Ia. Galperin, *Psikhologiia kak obyektivnaya nauka* [Psychology as a rigorous science] (pp. 37–93). Moscow: Academy of Pedagogical and Social Sciences. (Original manuscript written 1935)

Galperin, P. Ia. (1998b). Metod, fakty i teorii v psikhologii formirovaniia umstvennykh deistvii i poniatii [The method, facts, and theories in the mental actions and concepts formation]. In P. Ia. Galperin, *Psikhologiia kak obyektivnaya nauka* [Psychology as a rigorous science] (pp. 389–398). Moscow: Academy of Pedagogical and Social Sciences. (Original manuscript written 1966)

Galperin, P. Ia., & Kabylnitskaia, S. L. (1974). *Eksperimentalnoe formirovanie vnimaniia* [Experimental formation of attention]. Moscow: Izdatelstvo MGU.

Glassmann, M. (2001). Dewey and Vygotsky: Society, experience, and inquiry in educational practice. *Educational Researcher, 30* (4), 3–14.

Haenen, J. (1996a). *Piotr Galperin: Psychologist in Vygotsky's footsteps*. New York: Nova Science Publishers.

Haenen, J. (1996b). Piotr Galperin's criticism and extension of Lev Vygotsky's work. *Journal of Russian and East European Psychology, 34* (2), 54–60.

Hatano, G., & Wertsch, J. V. (2001). Sociocultural approaches to cognitive development: The constitutions of culture in mind. *Human Development, 44* (2), 77–83.

Hutchins, E. (1996). *Cognition in the wild*. Cambridge: Cambridge University Press.

Kozulin, A. (1986). The concept of activity in Soviet psychology. *American Psychologist, 41* (3), 264–274.

Lave, J., &. Wenger, E. (1991). *Situated learning: Legitimate peripheral participation*. Cambridge: Cambridge University Press.

Latour, B. (1999). *Pandora's hope: Essays on the reality of science studies*. Cambridge, MA: Harvard University Press.

Leontiev, A. N. (1978). *Activity, consciousness and personality*. Englewood Cliffs, NJ: Prentice-Hall.

Leontiev, A. N. (1981). *Problems of the development of the mind*. Moscow: Progress. (Original work published 1959)

Minick, N. (1987). The development of Vygotsky's thought: An Introduction. In R. Rieber & A. S. Carton (Eds.), *The collected works of L. S. Vygotsky: Vol. 1. Problems of general psychology* (pp. 17–36). New York: Plenum Press.

Minnis, M., & John-Steiner, V. P. (2001). Are we ready for a single, integrated theory? *Human Development, 44* (5), 296–310.

Morawski, J. (2001). Gifts bestowed, gifts withheld: Assessing psychological theory with a Kochian attitude. *American Psychologist, 56*, 433–440.

Obukhova, L. F. (1972). *Etapy razvitiia detskogo myshleniia* [Stages in the development of the child's thinking]. Moscow: MGU.

Packer, M. J., & Goicoechea, J. (2000). Sociocultural and constructivist theories of learning: Ontology, not just epistemology. *Educational Psychologist, 35* (4), 227–241.

Podolskij, A. I. (1987). *Stanovlenie poznavatelnogo deistviia: Nauchnaia abstraktsiia i realnost* [The genesis of cognitive action: Scientific abstraction and reality]. Moscow: Izdatelstvo MGU.

Rogoff, B. (1990). *Apprenticeship in thinking: Cognitive development in social context.* New York: Oxford University Press.

Rogoff, B. (2003). *The cultural nature of human development.* New York: Oxford University Press.

Scribner, S. (1985). Vygotsky's use of history. In J. V. Wertsch (Ed.), *Culture, communication, and cognition: Vygotskian perspectives* (pp. 119–145). Cambridge: Cambridge University Press.

Stetsenko, A., & Arievitch, I. M. (1997). Constructing and deconstructing the self: Comparing post-Vygotskian and discourse-based versions of social constructivism. *Mind, Culture, and Activity, 4* (3), 160–173.

Talyzina, N. F. (1975). *Upravlenie protsessom usvoeniia znanii* [Guiding the process of knowledge acquisition]. Moscow: Izdatelstvo MGU.

Valsiner, J., & van der Veer, R. (2000). *The social mind.* Cambridge: Cambridge University Press.

van der Veer, R., & Valsiner, J. (1991). *Understanding Vygotsky: A quest for synthesis.* Oxford: Blackwell.

Vygotsky, L. S. (1987). *Thinking and speech.* In R. Rieber & A. S. Carton (Eds.), *The collected works of L. S. Vygotsky: Vol. 1. Problems of general psychology* (pp. 39–285). New York: Plenum Press.

Vygotsky, L. S. (1997). The history of the development of higher mental functions. In R. Rieber (Ed.), *The collected works of L. S. Vygotsky: Vol. 4. The history of the development of higher mental functions* (pp. 1–125). New York: Plenum Press.

Wells, G. (1999). *Dialogic inquiry: Towards a sociocultural practice and theory of education.* Cambridge: Cambridge University Press.

Wertsch, J. V. (1998). *Mind as action.* New York: Oxford University Press.

Zinchenko, P. I. (1983). The problem of involuntary memory. *Soviet Psychology, 4*, 9–33.

Zinchenko, V. P. (1985). Vygotsky's ideas about units for the analysis of mind. In J. V. Wertsch (Ed.), *Culture, communication, and cognition: Vygotskian perspectives.* Cambridge: Cambridge University Press.

4

Reflections on Points of Departure in the Development of Sociocultural and Activity Theory

Harry Daniels

In this chapter I attempt to clarify, elaborate, compare, and contrast sociocultural approaches to learning. After addressing the tension between accounts of mediated action and activity (or semiotic and activity-based accounts), I reflect on the notion of tool or artefact as mediator between individual and social and suggest that this requires further clarification. My next step is to address the issue of the production of tools or artefacts in contexts, asking how we understand the production of tools or artefacts in terms of the social relations that obtain in the circumstances in which they were produced. Lastly, I discuss the need to extend the analysis beyond words and ask how we can develop methodologies that enable us to explore effects of activity that is mediated by and through nonverbal means. I illustrate this section through reference to empirical work.

THE TENSION BETWEEN ACCOUNTS OF SEMIOTIC AND ACTIVITY-BASED MEDIATION

The concept of "mediation" opens the way for the development of a non-deterministic account in which mediators serve as the means by which the individual acts upon and is acted upon by social, cultural, and historical factors. There is considerable tension and debate as to the nature of such factors. Some approaches have tended to focus on semiotic means of mediation (Wertsch, 1991), whereas others have tended to focus more on activity itself (Engeström, 1993). Engeström argues that the positioning of Leontiev, one of the progenitors of activity theory, as someone who took no account of semiotic mediation was and is erroneous.

A careful reading of Leontiev's work reveals that both mediation by signs and subject-subject relations do play an important role in his theory. Proponents of the cultural-historical school repeatedly point out that

communication is an inherent aspect of all object-related activitie
tiev's account of the emergence of speech and language emphasises the orig
inal unity of labour actions and social intercourse. So, there is a curious
discrepancy between the ways Leontiev is read by critics and by those sympathetic to his ideas (Engeström, 1990, p. 7).

Here it is suggested that the supposed origins of differences are not responsible for the tensions that have developed. Lave (1993, p. 20) has discussed
some of these tensions between the research traditions:

The major difficulties of phenomenological and activity theory in the eyes of
the other will be plain: Those who start with the view that social activity is its
own context dispute claims that objective social structures exist other than in
their social interactional construction in-situ. Activity theorists argue, on the
other hand, that the concrete connectiveness and meaning of activity cannot be
accounted for by analysis of the immediate situation.

The terms that are used to describe these positions are not without their
problems. The field abounds with descriptors such as "sociocultural psychology" and "cultural historical activity theory," each of which has been defined
with great care. Confusion can still persist as a result of genuine differences
in emphasis. Some think, for example, that the emphasis on the historical
plane has been diminished as theories have been transferred from Russian to
Western academic cultures.

We would agree that "cultural-historical" and "sociohistorical" are more
appropriate terms when referring to the heritage we recognize from Vygotsky, Leontiev, Luria, and many other Soviet psychologists. We believe that
"sociocultural" is a better term when it comes to dealing with how this heritage has been appropriated in contemporary debates in the human sciences,
at least in the West (Wertsch, Del Rio, & Alvarez, 1995, p. 6). Yet Wertsch
et al. continue to assert that "the goal of a sociocultural approach is to expli-
cate the relationships between human action, on the one hand, and the
cultural, institutional, and historical situations in which this action occurs
on the other" (p. 11).

This position has led Wertsch (1998) to advance the case for the use of
mediated action as a unit of analysis in social-cultural research because,
in his view, it provides a kind of natural link between action, including
mental action, and the cultural, institutional, and historical context in which
such action occurs. This is so because the mediational means, or cultural
tools, are inherently situated, culturally, institutionally, and historically. As
Cole (1996, p. 333) remarks, "So the level of activity is present in Wertsch's
formulation; it is simply backgrounded when he focuses on the processes

of mediated action." Engeström (1993, p. 66) points out the danger of the relative undertheorising of context: "individual experience is described and analysed as if consisting of relatively discrete and situated actions while the system or objectively given context of which those actions are a part is either treated as an immutable given or barely described at all."

Cole (1996, p. 334) tries to develop a middle line between the two traditions:

[M]ediated action and its activity contexts are two moments of a single process, and whatever we want to specify as psychological processes is but a moment of their combined properties. It is possible to argue how best to parse their contribution in individual cases, in practice, but attempting such a parse "in general" results in empty abstractions, unconstrained by the circumstances.

The development of this line of argument represents a significant challenge to our field.

THE NOTION OF TOOL OR ARTEFACT AS MEDIATOR BETWEEN INDIVIDUAL AND SOCIAL

Vygotsky describes psychological tools as devices for mastering mental processes. They were seen as artificial and of social rather than organic or individual origin. This emphasis on the self-construction through and with those tools which are available brings two crucial issues to the foreground. Firstly, it speaks of the individual as an active agent in development. Secondly, it affirms the importance of contextual effects in that development takes place through the use of those tools which are available at a particular time in a particular place. He distinguishes between psychological and other tools and suggests that psychological tools can be used to direct the mind and behaviour. In contrast, technical tools are used to bring about changes in other objects. Rather than changing objects in the environment, psychological tools are devices for influencing the mind and behaviour of oneself or another. Vygotsky argues that the ways in which tools and signs are used varies as a function of context and the child's own development. He refers to the "natural history of the sign" as a way of emphasising that, in the course of development, the psychological function that may be fulfilled by signs may also develop and change. Thus, speech may have several functions (e.g., labelling and planning). In the early stages of development, Vygotsky suggests that speech may assume an important labelling function in that it enables the child to identify a particular object, to single it out and distinguish it from others. He argues that increasing sophistication in the use of language allows the child to become progressively more independent of the sensory field (Vygotsky, 1978, p. 32).

In the discussion of memory and thinking that constitutes chapter 3 of *Mind in Society*, Vygotsky stipulates that radical transformations take place in the relationships between psychological functions as a result of such mediated psychological activity. He suggests that "for the young child, to think means to recall; but for the adolescent, to recall means to think" (1978, p. 51). Human memory is seen as a function that is actively supported and transformed through the use of signs.

Just as a mold gives shape to a substance, words can shape an activity into a structure. However, that structure may be changed or reshaped when children learn to use language in ways that allow them to go beyond previous experiences when planning future action ... once children learn how to use the planning function of their language effectively, their psychological field changes radically. A view of the future is now an integral part of their approaches to their surroundings. (Vygotsky, 1978, p. 28)

Thus from Vygotsky's (1981, pp. 139–140) perspective the use of psychological tools introduces several new functions connected with the use of the given tool and with its control; abolishes and makes unnecessary several natural processes, whose work is accomplished by the tool; and alters the course and individual features (the intensity, duration, sequence, etc.) of all the mental processes that enter into the composition of the instrumental act, replacing some functions with others (i.e., it re-creates and reorganises the whole structure of behaviour just as a technical tool re-creates the whole structure of labour operations).

Psychological tools, just as material tools, are the products of human cultural historical activity. Pea describes what can be thought of as the sedimentation of cultural historical legacies in tools. He also draws attention to the way in which this legacy may appear "natural" or indeed be rendered invisible. This process may leave the observer with the impression that a person acting with tools is behaving intelligently in a way that reveals his own individual or asocial capability.

[Invented tools] turned from history into nature, they are invisible, unremarkable aspects of our experiential world.... these tools literally carry intelligence in them, in that they represent some individual's or some community's decision that the means thus offered should be reified, made stable, as a quasi permanent form, for the use by others.... as such tools become invisible, it becomes harder to see them as bearing intelligence; instead we see intelligence as residing in the individual mind using the tools. (Pea, 1993, p. 53).

This process may happen as much with persons as with objects. Cole's (1996) proposal is that the concept of tool should be treated as a subcategory of the superordinate notion of artefact. Just as objects do, people may act as mediating artefacts.

The notion of artefact raises a central concern in the philosophy under-pinning many sociocultural psychologies – the relation between the ideal and the material. Bakhurst (1995) has done much to clarify the contribution of the Russian philosopher Ilyenkov to our understanding of the framework within which so much of the Russian perspective on mediation may be read. A starting point from which to untangle some of the ramifications of this philosophical position is with reference to the concept of "objectification." It is with this concept that connection can be made to the cultural historical production of the artefacts that humans use to order and construct their lives. The idea of meaning embodied – or, as I have suggested, sedimented – in objects as they are put into use in social worlds is central to the conceptual apparatus of theories of culturally mediated, historically developing practical activity.

This notion of "objectification" (*opredmechivanie)* is easiest to understand in the case of artefacts. What distinguishes an artefact from a brutally physical object? (e.g. what distinguishes a table from the raw material from which it is fashioned?). The answer lies in the fact that the artefact bears a certain significance which it possesses, not by virtue of its physical nature, but because it has been produced for a certain use and incorporated into a system of human ends and purposes. The object thus confronts us as an embodiment of meaning, placed and sustained in it by "aimed-oriented" human activity. (Bakhurst, 1995, p. 160)

This process is part of the conceptual apparatus that is associated with Ilyenkov's philosophy of ideality. This provides an account of the way in which humans inscribe significance and value into the very physical objects of their environment. This "ideality" results from "the transforming, form creating, activity of social beings, their aim mediated, sensuously objective activity." As Bakhurst (1995, p. 173) notes "Ilyenkov's transcendental account of the origin of subject and object in activity portrays nature as a kind of shapeless raw material given form by human agency. Nature is the clay on which humanity inscribes its mark."

Cole (1994, p. 94) joins with Bakhurst in theorising artefacts as being both ideal (conceptual) and material: "Artifacts exhibit a dual nature in that they are simultaneously ideal and material. Their creators and users exhibit a corresponding duality of thought, at once grounded in the material here and now, yet simultaneously capable of entertaining the far away, the long ago, and the never has-been."

A theory of mediation through artefacts infers that in the course of human activity meaning is sedimented, accumulated, or deposited in things. These meanings are remembered both collectively and individually. The artefact is thus both material and ideal. How is the relationship, this intertwining, to be conceptualised?

Holland and Cole (1995) use discourse and schema theory to elaborate the concept of cultural artefact. Discourse theory is used to initiate a discussion of representations or artefacts that operate in the social world, may be regarded as cultural products, and exhibit historical legacies. Speech genres and stories both reveal these qualities. Schema theory is used to explore the possibilities for mental representations that are socially formed and are modifiable.

The approach is based on the belief that by studying individuals' developing ability to acquire knowledge from or produce discourse, one is investigating fundamental characteristics of how individuals acquire, represent, and construct extended knowledge structures. Although these theories may well be sufficient for treating internal and external structures as independent entities, a theory is required that posits their dynamic mutual influence.

Wertsch (1998) and Bruner (1990) both analyse narrative and historical texts as cultural tools. Wertsch (1998) emphasises that tools or artefacts such as "conventional" stories or popular histories may not always "fit" well with a particular personal narrative. As ever with a Vygotskian account, there is no necessary recourse to determinism. Wertsch (1998, p. 108) suggests that individuals may resist the way in which such texts "shape their actions, but they are often highly constrained in the forms that such resistance can take." This emphasis on the individual who is active in shaping a response to being shaped by his engagement with cultural artefacts is central to the Vygotskian argument. The relative emphasis on agency (whether individual or collective; Wertsch, 1998) and the affordances (Gibson, 1979) that social, cultural, and historical factors offer form the stage on which the development of new and improved forms of thought are enacted.

Clearly, the concept of cultural artefact has developed considerably since the concept of a psychological tool was discussed by Vygotsky. In my mind there are at least two further areas of development that should be considered. Firstly, there is the search for a unit of analysis, which, as Tudge notes, integrates the various aspects of the activity system.

Meanings, tools and goals all necessarily relate the individual and the social world of which the individual is part, for they are all formed in socio-cultural context. Understanding how the use of tools (psychological or physical) is jointly constructed by the developing child and by the culture in which the child is developing, with the assistance of those who are already more competent in the use of those tools and in culturally appropriate goals. These units of analysis therefore integrate the micro-social contexts of interaction with the broader social, cultural and historical contexts that encompass them. (Tudge & Winterhoff, 1993, p. 67)

Much has been done to develop the analysis of activity systems, yet this analysis proceeds without a conceptual language that allows the macro–micro relation to be explored within a coherent language of description. This language would allow researchers to describe macrostructures and their associated cultural artefacts to be described with reference to a common analytical framework. As Bernstein (1993) notes, "Once attention is given to the regulation of the structure of pedagogic discourse, the social relations of its production and the various modes of its recontextualising as a practice, then perhaps we may be a little nearer to understanding the Vygotskian tool as a social and historical construction." How do we understand the production of tools or artefacts in terms of the social relations that obtain in the circumstances in which they were produced?

Vygotsky's emphasis on humans mastering themselves through the use of symbolic, cultural systems carries with it implications concerning the origins and availability of such artefacts. My interest here is in the creation of new cultural forms through human activity. This form of externalisation is a form of production, whose results are used, as Vygotsky reminds us, as tools of development. This theme has recently been extended by the Russian philosopher Lektorsky (1999, pp. 66–67) in his insistence that "Humans not only internalize ready-made standards and rules of activity but externalise themselves as well, creating new standards and rules. Human beings determine themselves through objects that they create. They are essentially creative beings."

It has been suggested that whilst Vygotsky discussed the general importance of language and schooling for psychological functioning, he failed to examine the social systems in which these activities occur. Ratner (1997, p. 103) argued that the resulting analysis is one that overlooks the real world of social praxis in which forms of speech are produced and used:

The failure of activity theorists to identify the concrete social organization of activity can be traced all the way back to Vygotsky and Luria. For all their stated emphasis on the sociohistorical nature of psychology, Vygotsky and Luria did not consider the ways in which concrete social systems bear on psychological functions. They discussed the general importance of language and schooling for psychological functioning, however they failed to examine the real social systems in which these activities occur and reflect. This omission is evident in Vygotsky's *Experimental Study of Concept Formation*. Here, Vygotsky stated that social life is important for the development of conceptual thinking in adolescence.

However, instead of analyzing the social demands and activities that occur during adolescence, he postulated that a new abstract use of words during adolescence generates concept formation. Vygotsky never indicated the social basis for this new use of words. His social analysis thus reduced to a semiotic analysis which overlooked the real world of social praxis.

Researchers such as Christie (1999) and Tul'viste (1987) have shown various forms of relation between specific cultural contexts and specific cultural products. My interest is in developing a language of description and analysis that can be used in research concerned with this relation. It is at this point that I turn to the work of the late Basil Bernstein.

Bernstein's work is concerned with interrelations between changes in organisational form, changes in modes of control, and changes in principles of communication. His language of description is generated from an analysis of power (which creates and maintains boundaries in organisational form) and control (which regulates communication within specific forms of interaction). Initially, he focuses on two levels: a structural level and an interactional level. The structural level is analysed in terms of the social division of labour it creates (classification) and the interactional level with the form of social relation it creates (framing). He defines modalities of pedagogic practice in terms of principles for distinguishing between contexts (recognition rules) *and* for the creation and production of specialised communication within contexts (realisation rules). Modalities of pedagogic practice and their discourses may then be described in terms directly referenced to the theory. Features of cultural artefacts may be described in terms of the cultural context of their production. Bernstein (1993) argues that much of the work that has followed in the wake of Vygotsky "does not include in its description how the discourse itself is constituted and recontextualised."

Bernstein's approach to analysis can be applied to different levels of school organisation and various units within a level. This allows the analysis of power and control and the rules regulating what counts as legitimate pedagogic competence to proceed at a level of delicacy appropriate to a particular research question. The development and application of language of description that meets the specification developed by Bernstein will facilitate the enhancement of activity theory.

HOW DO WE DEVELOP METHODOLOGIES THAT ENABLE US TO EXPLORE THE EFFECTS OF NONVERBAL ARTEFACTS?

Vygotsky attached the greatest importance to the content of educational curricula but placed the emphasis on the structural and instrumental aspects of that content, the significance of which was mentioned in our analysis of the implications of McLuhan's phrase "the medium is the message." In this approach it is quite possible to regard the school itself as a "message," that is, a fundamental factor of education, because, as an institution and quite apart from the content of its teaching, it implies a certain structuring of time and space and is based on a system of social relations between pupils and teacher, between the pupils themselves, between the school and it surroundings, and so on (Ivic, 1989).

In different schools (or cultures), actions and objects signify different meanings. Indeed, at a very general level it is possible to conceive of cultures or schools as worlds of signs and signs about signs (Hawkes, 1977). In a sense, adapting to cultural change is a process of adapting to changing systems of signification. For a child, particularly a child who finds learning difficult, moving from home to school is itself an act of cultural change and, for some, entails culture shock. That which is taken to signify competence in one culture may signify incompetence in another or irrelevance in a third. How then does a school transmit to children the criteria that are taken to signify appropriate learning? What are the cues offered to children in their attempts to read the signs of schooling? It is argued here that art displays are part of the system of signs that constitute the culture of schools, that through these acts of publicity the principles that regulate the curriculum are realised.

To have a "nice bright classroom with lots of good display work" is one of the commonly held indicators of good teaching practice. Display work is important not only to parents but also to children. Children like having their work displayed on the wall. This very public way in which a teacher shows approval of a child's activity is highly valued. By putting works of art on the wall the teacher is telling the child that he or she approves of it and at the same time is offering a model of good practice to the rest of the class. This, of course, is one of the reasons why children feel so proud when their work is displayed: their friends are being offered their work as a model. The way in which work is selected for display and the way in which the display is arranged is effectively an act of publicity of the teacher's desired model of good practice. Such publishing activities have focussed the attention of theorists in the fields of art and education. "Publicity is the culture of the consumer society. It propagates through images that society's belief in itself" (Berger, 1972, p. 139).

These two schools were structured in very different ways: one in which there is a variety of highly structured subjects where the children have little choice over what they will learn, the other where a broad, integrated thematic approach is taken within which children and teachers are relatively autonomous in their actions. These two approaches approximate to the "collection" and "integrated" types identified by Bernstein (1977): one in which things must be put together and the other where things are kept apart.

When illustrating the differing nature of the criteria the child is supposed to acquire in different teaching situations, reference is made to the teaching of art. In what is termed the visible pedagogy, which is associated with the collection type of curriculum with its strong classification and framing, the following example is given:

What are the children doing? They are making facsimiles of the outside. They are learning a reproductive aesthetic code. They may be drawing or painting figures, houses, etc. The teacher looks at the product of one child and says, "That's a very good house, but where is the chimney?" or "There are no windows in your house," or "That man has got only three fingers," etc. Here the child is made aware of what is missing in the production and what is missing is made explicit and specific, and subject to finely graded assessment. (Bernstein, 1977, p. 119)

In the invisible pedagogy in the integrated-type curriculum realised through weak classification and framing,

The children have a large sheet of paper, and not a small box of paints but an assembly of media whereby their unique visual imagination may be momentarily revealed. This is allegedly not a reproductive aesthetic code, but a productive aesthetic code. The teacher here is less likely to say, "What's that?", is less likely explicitly to create in the child a consciousness of what is missing in the product: the teacher is more likely to do this indirectly, in a context of general, diffuse support. Where the transmission realises implicit criteria, it is as if the acquirer is the source of the criteria. (Bernstein, 1977, p. 119)

These statements come very close to describing the practices of the two schools used in this study. Clearly these schools should not be taken as examples of pure types but rather as complex systems that embody significant differences. These differences are revealed in the notes taken in art lessons in two schools to be referred to here as CH and TC.

ART LESSON OBSERVED IN CH SCHOOL

The teacher read Maurice Sendak's story called *Where the Wild Things Are*. She then told the children that they were going to "make pictures of the wild things." The teacher had prepared a number of different pieces of paper and proceeded to distribute these pieces of paper to the children. Each piece of paper had an outline of a "wild thing" on it, and most of them had sections or areas of the paper marked off. Each section contained a code number and thus could be translated by a key at the bottom of the piece of paper. The children followed the key, which dictated the material to be used to "fill in" the sections or areas marked on the paper. The "wild things" were thus constructed.

The department head said of art lessons, "We are interested in the results of art, of good productions rather than 'experiencing' the materials."

ART LESSON OBSERVED IN TC SCHOOL

The children were given different grades of paper, powder paint, and a piece of foam rubber or sponge. The teacher then told the children to wet the paper and flick paint at it with the sponge. The children were encouraged to use different kinds of paper with different degrees of dampness. They were told to experiment with ways of applying the powder paint. Similar differences in pedagogic practice were noted on every observation day.

Gearhart and Newman (1980, p. 183) argued that, for the nursery school children they studied, learning the social organization of a classroom and learning its curriculum could not be distinguished: "What children know about drawing is intimately tied to what they understand of drawing activities undertaken in a particular social context." They discussed the importance of the way the teacher spoke to the children about their drawings and also drew attention to the particular form of pedagogy in the classroom: "drawing was also being learned from the teacher's efforts to teach the organizational independence of individual production tasks. Reflexively, this individual task organization was being learned from the teacher's efforts to teach independently planful drawing."

Whilst Gearhart and Newman's study is of interest, it failed to undertake the comparative work needed to show the ways that learning to draw differs under different forms of classroom social organisation. Also, following as it does an explicitly Vygotskian experimental approach, it lacks the potential for describing and analysing the social organisation of the classroom in structural terms (Wertsch, 1985). In its failure to do this it confines interpretation to a very local domain. Equipped with the detail of the principles regulating classroom practice available in Bernstein's model, a comparative study aimed at producing data of more general interpretive value is anticipated. Through focussing on wall display rather than pupil-teacher and teacher-pupil verbal communications, a wider perspective on semiotic mediation is being drawn.

It is important to note that the photographs that are to be discussed here are representative of each school's display work. All the work displayed at one time in both schools was recorded, and selected examples are presented.

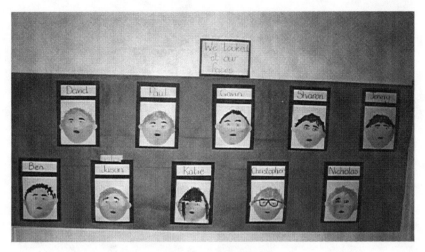

Figure 4.1. Picture A.

The selection was made by the teachers of the classes of nine- to twelve-year-old children in each school. That is, the (two) teachers in each school were shown the entire sample of photographs for their school and asked to select the three that best represented the school's display work. Emphasis was laid on the display rather than the individual pictures. Equally important is the fact that all the teachers responsible for this display work viewed their efforts as the result of a "commonsense" approach to the task. They did not regard themselves as having been instructed or coerced to work in this way nor did they regard their work as potentially different in form from display work in any other school. These photographs are displayed in Figures 4.1 through 4.6.

INTERPRETATION OF DISPLAYS

What then is revealed by an inspection of a sample of the display work in these schools? The control over what is expected is clearly high in displays A, B, and C. In A, the faces all have the same structure – they are all the same shape! In B the faces of the flowers are structurally similar. The faces were all yellow, all on the same plates, all with red lips and all had eyebrows. The levels of similarity in C are so marked that they require no comment.

On the other hand, the control over what is taught or expected is of a very different nature in D, E, and F. In D, there is an integrating theme of transport, and yet children have produced different illustrations relating to

Figure 4.2. Picture B.

Figure 4.3. Picture C.

the central theme. These are drawn, crayoned, or painted using a variety of techniques. In E and F there are no underlying themes and the work is very varied in terms of the techniques used and the content portrayed. It seems there are at least two principles at this level of control, which distinguish the schools. In one school there is a high degree of control over what is to be

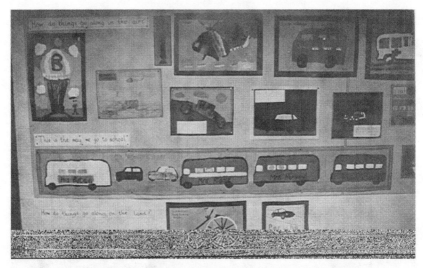

Figure 4.4. Picture D.

Figure 4.5. Picture E.

portrayed and also over the techniques and materials to be used. In the other school, the level of control over these factors is much lower.

Each school appears to some extent to have a characteristic style of structuring the displays. Whereas in A and B the pictures are arranged in straight

Figure 4.6. Picture F.

lines with regular spacings between pictures, in D, E and F the pictures are closely grouped in irregular patterns. It is perhaps not entirely coincidental that in picture D the work displayed was produced by children in the age range five through fourteen, whereas each display in the other school was produced by one age group only. These two factors perhaps reveal underlying levels of classification. On the one hand, ages and individuals are grouped and, on the other, separated by clearly marked boundaries. It is in this way possible to argue that the principles on which the curriculum is organised are realised in the way work is displayed. Yet this analysis is from the point of view of a detached adult; the question remains as to what the children perceive in these situations.

The work of Vygotsky rests on the assumption that in order to understand the individual one must first understand the social relations in which the individual exists. The evidence presented here accords with the Vygotskian view of the social origin of higher mental functions. The school environments were specified in terms of what is ultimately their social nature. It has been demonstrated that the principles that regulate these environments are relayed through the wall displays in these schools. The different aesthetic principles of the schools in question are contained within very different institutions. It is not the purpose of this study to say whether one set of aesthetic principles is better than another, but rather to demonstrate the transmission of these and other social constructs.

The arrangements through the production, selection, and combination of children's painting were shown to act as a relay of the deep structure of the pedagogic practice of particular schools, although as far as the teachers were concerned, they were simply mounting wall displays rather than using wall displays explicitly as relays of the focus of their practice. Whilst they were keen to create a good impression through their wall display work, they were not aware of their expression of the underlying principles of school practice.

If we follow the directions given by Vygotskian psychology, it would seem profitable to investigate the meaning of cultural artefacts beyond speech for children as a step in the process of understanding what counts as important in a particular school (Wertsch, 1985). In the investigation of wall display it is important to remember that the children also produced the pictures and thus were socialised by that activity. The products of these socialising activities are then selected, combined, and organised by the teacher in a way that celebrates and announces the expected competences required of a particular school and/or classroom. Rather than reading backwards from statistics describing the outputs of schooling, it would seem worthwhile for us to consider what is relayed to children by particular activities. From this perspective, schools may be considered as generators of a specialised semiotic. The meaning of these signs for the participants in the practice of schooling then becomes the object of study. The study of wall displays indicated that children from different schools "saw" different meanings in the same displays. They were oriented towards different sets of recognition and realisation rules. Here lies the possibility for the development of an interesting theoretical development – the bringing together of work within semiotics, new Vygotskian psychology, and symbolic interactionist and structuralist sociology for the sake of the development of an overall theoretical perspective.

References

Bakhurst D. (1995). Lessons from Ilyenkov. *Communication Review* 1 (2), 155–178.

Berger, J. (1972). *Ways of seeing.* London: BBC Publications/Penguin.

Bernstein, B. (1977). *Class codes and control: Vol. 3. Towards a theory of educational transmissions* (2nd rev. ed.). London: Routledge & Kegan Paul.

Bernstein, B. (1993). Foreword. In H. Daniels (Ed.), *Charting the agenda: Educational activity after Vygotsky* (pp. xiii–xxiv). London: Routledge.

Bruner J. S. (1990). *Acts of meaning.* Cambridge, MA: Harvard University Press.

Cole, M. (1994). A conception of culture for a communication theory of mind. In D. Vocate (Ed.), *Intrapersonal communication: Different voices, different minds.* Mahwah, NJ: Lawrence Erlbaum.

Cole, M. (1996). *Cultural Psychology: A once and future discipline.* Cambridge, MA: Belknap Press of Harvard University.

Christie, F. (Ed). (1999). *Pedagogy and the shaping of consciousness.* London: Continuum.

Engeström, Y. (1990). *Activity theory and individual and social transformation.* Open address at the Second International Congress for Research on Activity Theory, Lahti, Finland, May 21–25.

Engeström, Y. (1993). Developmental studies of work as a testbench of activity theory: The case of primary care medical practice. In S. Chaiklin & J. Lave (Eds.), *Understanding practice: Perspectives on activity and practice* (pp. 64–103). Cambridge: Cambridge University Press.

Gearhart, M., & Newman, D. (1980). Learning to draw a picture: The social context of an individual activity. *Discourse Processes, 3,* 169–184.

Gibson, J. J. (1979). *The ecological approach to visual perception.* Boston: Houghton Mifflin.

Hawkes, T. (1977). *Structuralism and semiotics.* London: Methuen.

Holland, D., & Cole, M. (1995). Between discourse and schema: Reformulating a cultural-historical approach to culture and mind. *Anthropology and Education Quarterly, 26* (4), 475–490.

Ivic, I. (1989). Profiles of educators: Lev S. Vygotsky (1896–1934). *Prospects, 9* (3), 427–436.

Lave, J. (1993). The practice of learning. In S. Chaiklin & J. Lave (Eds.), *Understanding practice: Perspectives on activity and contest* (pp. 3–34). Cambridge: Cambridge University Press.

Lektorsky, V. A. (1999). Activity theory in a new era. In Y. Engeström, R. Miettinen, & R.-L. Punamäki (Eds.), *Perspectives on activity theory* (pp. 65–69). Cambridge: Cambridge University Press.

Pea, R. D. (1993). Practices of distributed intelligence and designs for education. In G. Salomon (Ed.), *Distributed cognitions: Psychological and educational considerations* (pp. 47–87). Cambridge: Cambridge University Press.

Ratner, C. (1997). *Cultural psychology and qualitative methodology: Theoretical and empirical considerations.* London: Plenum Press.

Tudge, J. R. H., & Winterhoff, P. A. (1993). Vygotsky, Piaget, and Bandura: Perspectives on the relations between the social world and cognitive development. *Human Development, 36,* 61–81.

Tul'viste, P. (1989). Education and the development of concepts: Interpreting results of experiments with adults with and without schooling. *S-4, 27* (1), 5–21.

van der Veer, R., & Valsiner, J. (1991). *Understanding Vygotsky: A quest for synthesis.* Oxford: Blackwell.

Vygotsky, L. S. (1978). *Mind in society: The development of higher psychological processes.* Cambridge, MA: Harvard University Press.

Vygotsky, L. S. (1981). The development of higher forms of attention. In J. V. Wertsch (Ed.), *The concept of activity in Soviet psychology* (pp. 189–140). New York: Sharpe.

Vygotsky, L. S. (1987). *The collected works of L. S. Vygotsky: Vol. 1. Problems of general psychology.* New York: Plenum Press.

Wertsch, J. V. (1985). *Vygotsky and the social formation of mind.* Cambridge, MA: Harvard University Press.

Wertsch, J. V. (1991). *Voices of the mind: A sociocultural approach to mediated action.* Cambridge, MA: Harvard University Press.

Wertsch, J. V. (1998). *Mind as action.* Oxford: Oxford University Press.

Wertsch, J. V., Del Rio, P., & Alvarez, A. (Eds.). (1995). *Sociocultural studies of mind.* Cambridge: Cambridge University Press.

5

Language in Cultural-Historical Perspective

Peter E. Jones

From the point of view of the tasks of a science of language, the cultural-historical approach to the human mind is not a metatheory or philosophy standing above the sciences in the sense of a set of general ideas to be applied to or confirmed in specifically linguistic material. It is, rather, a particular science whose findings and implications, by the nature of its subject matter, cannot but interconnect in intimate fashion with those of a linguistic science. From this perspective, the task before a science of language is, therefore, to "prove this systematic connection" with the achievements of the cultural-historical tradition "both in general and in particular" (Engels, 1975). Indeed, this is the way Vygotsky and his colleagues approached their own scientific work. For them, the cultural-historical approach to the mind was itself developed as an attempt to "prove the systematic connection" between human psychological processes and the processes of sociohistorical emergence and evolution identified and studied by Marx and Engels and expressed theoretically in their "materialist conception of history." It is this concrete knowledge of the dynamic of human social life as well as of the nature and development of thinking with which students of language must reckon and in relation to which they must make their own distinctive contribution.

The materialist conception of history, and the cultural-historical theory with it, understands that humanity – all human faculties, practices,

My thanks to Anna Stetsenko, who invited me to deliver a conference presentation based on this paper at ISCRAT 2002 in Amsterdam. The paper was written in the hope of starting a debate in CHAT circles on the need to critically distance ourselves from orthodox approaches to language. But it is not intended as a comprehensive, still less definitive, statement of what a "cultural-historical linguistics" might look like. In particular, the considerable contribution of the late A. A. Leont'ev to the identification and discussion of foundational problems of language and the "sign" is not addressed.

knowledge, and relations – is a work in progress. Humanity is an unfinished project and the fate of that project is in our own hands: it is the job of us all to struggle to find and mobilise the intellectual, practical, and physical resources to put an end to material want and the exploitation of human beings by other human beings. The theoretical task that such a struggle poses, in linguistics or psychology or anywhere else, is therefore part of a struggle to free human minds from the intellectual shackles constantly generated and reproduced through the inhuman conditions in which we live. From this perspective the linguistic theories of, for example, Chomsky and others of similar persuasion, predicated on immutable properties of language and mind, on the fragmentation ("modularisation") of mind and consciousness, on the ultimate unfathomability of human imagination and will – such theories speak to this unfreedom by speaking this unfreedom: we are ruled, they tell us, by our own faculties, which confront us as fixed, isolated, and mutually unintelligible shards of human being and potential. These theories mirror our alienated state, expressing in their methodologies, in their assumptions, and in their analytical and theoretical categories the distortion that these inhuman life conditions effect.

At the same time, the positive discoveries of different schools of linguistics must not be lost or overlooked because of the ideological gloss that is put over them. A cultural-historical linguistics must, therefore, relate in a positive and critical manner to these approaches. The subject matter of a science of language is linguistic communication as a social activity, as a creative bodily art, enacted and produced between people in the meaningful matter of sound or gesture. Its task is to uncover and reconstruct the specific and distinctive dynamic and emergence of concrete instances of human communicative intercourse. If there is no doubt that the communicative phenomena we generally refer to as "language" constitute a proper object of special scientific study, our preliminary discussion forces us to think critically about where and how to begin our investigation of them and about the way in which we go about our theoretical endeavour. If we take it that language, whatever its peculiarities, is a "form of culture" (Sapir, 1963) we must take care, when working out our theoretical concepts and categories, not to distort or mystify our linguistic object by making its cultural essence unrecognisable and unrecoverable; the distinctive forms and patterns of linguistic communication are an affirmation not of their autonomy or independence from practical and mental activity but of their role as an instrument of symbolic mediation of such activity. Human social activity, then, not only lies behind these forms and patterns but moves in them and through them as the very *substance* of linguistic communication.

LANGUAGE AND HUMAN ACTIVITY

According to Vygotsky (1999, p. 68), "if at the beginning of development stands the deed, independent of the word, then at the end stands the word becoming a deed; the word, making human action free." This passage summarises Vygotsky's most complete and rounded exploration of the role of language in the child's thinking and action and affirms the central significance of language for the cultural-historical view of the mind. Indeed, his claim that the word makes "human action free" places language at the core of the pivotal problem of cultural-historical psychology, that of "free action," the conscious, voluntary, and purposeful action that human individuals engage in (see Jones, 2002, for further discussion). Vygotsky argues that the ability to communicate in language plays a determining role in the emergence of the capacity for free action and, consequently, is intrinsically bound into the whole system of practical and mental activities that constitute our human way of life. Let us begin, then, by exploring some aspects of the picture of human social life that Vygotsky presupposes in his research on language, action, and thought.

Human communities, creating and reproducing themselves historically through activities of social production ("labour" in Marx's sense; see Marx, 1976) constitute complex, dynamic systems characterised by an intricate division of labour. Vital tasks and functions are distributed amongst individuals in specific ways conditioned in large measure by the level of development of technique, technology, and knowledge that the community inherits and builds upon. This intricate and evolving social coordination presupposes the conscious participation of community members, which includes their ability to develop specialised skills and to engage in actions that are subordinated to the tasks and needs of the community as a whole.

Human social existence rests on an intimate dependency between the objects that are produced to satisfy human needs, the means of producing them, and the social relations between people engaged in production. Consequently, the objects of people's needs, because they are produced in this socially organised fashion, always serve as a form of intercourse between people, ultimately connecting up each individual with every other. Because our needs are satisfied by such humanly produced objects, our needs are always directly needs for other people and therefore an affirmation of our connectedness to others. This means that it is the community of producers themselves who in fact create and develop their own human needs, as well as the ability to develop new ways of satisfying them and, as a result, new needs to be satisfied. Thus, human needs are always as much a historical product as is productive activity along with the forms of social organisation through which production takes place. Ultimately, then, any individual human action has as its presupposition the mental and physical practices of an entire historically developed community and is, in that sense, an action of the whole of society.

In producing and reproducing its means of life, the community reproduces itself as a community of human individuals in these historically specific relations to one another, individuals who feel these humanly produced objects as needs and who are capable of appreciating them – of enjoying or fearing them – as the source of pleasure and pain, as objects of attention and desire, as models and ideals to be emulated and attained, as instruments to master – in short, of making them into the very substance of their practical and mental interactions with other people. This way of life makes us thinkers as well as producers or, more accurately, makes us producers of thoughts and intentions as well as of objects. As a consequence, our own mental powers are part of the productive resources of the community and become themselves the object of attention and manipulation from the earliest times. Human social life, then, is conscious life. But the fact that human beings live a conscious life does not mean that they are immediately conscious of the origins of their consciousness and of their humanity. Because they act as conscious individuals, conscious of the role and position that the community allots to them, this does not mean that the historically developing logic of social organisation and development is transparent to them. Consciousness, because it is always the property of people living in a particular way, cannot magically transcend the historical conditions of its existence. The ability to penetrate the mysteries of our own origins and development is itself a long (and unfinished) work of history, with specific preconditions and presuppositions of its own.

A closer look at any human community will confirm that it is a unity of a great many diverse and simultaneously occurring practical and mental activities, but a unity that consists in the mutual interconnections and exchanges constantly taking place between the different individuals engaged in these different activities. Here, a modern example of useful labour, such as building a house, will serve to illustrate the point.[1] If we follow the process through, we will find that the house begins to take shape on the architect's drawing board, with the drawing passing to a team of builders, who convert it into a real structure in brick, which is then inhabited and becomes a family home.

---

[1] For the purposes of this discussion, I take the activity of house building as an example of the "labour process" only, rather than as a unity of the "labour process" and the "valorization process" as is the case in capitalist production (Marx, 1976).

The path from need to goal to idea to reality already presupposes a world of objects and people in specific relations and is in itself a process of production of various objects – words, drawings, plans, foundations, walls – that leads us along a chain of people with specialised mental and physical skills and roles. The object is the final outcome of a complex metamorphosis in which the need of one person becomes an object constructed by a second person on the basis of an idea developed by a third. In turn, each stage of this process is itself the intersection of many other processes – industrial, technical, and scientific, for example. All these different processes work to their own logic and at their own peculiar pace, but they are all bound up with one another, conditioning and influencing one another, and passing into one another. In fact, we find the same unity or integration of diverse practical and mental actions in the individual person. Our builder, for example, integrates in his or her person the conscious mental states of intention and goal orientation, the inner verbal thinking process involved in understanding and interpreting instructions, the directly symbolic and communicative acts of discursive interchange, and the physical actions of digging, lifting, and placing.

The social organization that human communities display is also a natural formation; it is part of nature and exerts a particular influence on the natural world from which it springs and which is the source of its life and power. The human community develops and exercises its own distinctive socially organised powers by using and changing nature, by exploiting its powers and affordances in the production of the means of life, and, in the process, learning to fathom nature's innermost secrets, to anticipate and consciously direct its elemental forces.[2]

Consequently, all the different activities and attributes of individuals within the evolving human community together with the objects they fashion collectively from nature's materials form an integral whole developing under its own impetus, driven by its internal possibilities and contradictions.

This perspective on human social life affords no grounds for the various dualisms that continue to bedevil the human sciences: the dualisms of thinking and being, of mind and world, of body and mind, of thought and action. These dualistic positions express an alienated human condition in which the essential unity of human practical and mental powers is expressed, contradictorily, in their separation, fragmentation, and dispersal amidst antagonistic social divisions and relations. The overcoming of such dualistic chimeras is, therefore, not a theoretical issue alone but entails a struggle to overcome

---

[2] "When man engages in production, he can only proceed as nature does herself, i.e. he can only change the form of the materials" (Marx, 1976, p. 133).

in practice, in real life, the alienation from which they draw their strength. A concrete understanding of human practice dispels these dualisms and, thereby, removes the theoretical and empirical foundations for the compartmentalisation of linguistic and cognitive processes into independent, innately determined "modules" and, more generally, for the biological determinist view of human nature (see Jones, 2003b).

A closer look at our simplified house-building example allows us to appreciate the properties of "labour in a form in which it is an exclusively human characteristic" (Marx, 1976, pp. 283–284), in which "a result emerges which had already been conceived by the worker at the beginning, hence already existed ideally" (p. 284). Before the house exists as a physical object in real space, it exists *ideally*, or as the *idea* of a house, in a number of different forms: on paper in the architect's office, in the minds and public discourse of the planners, in the plans and verbal instructions given to the builders, in the minds and discourse of the builders as they dig the foundations and lay the first bricks. The "ideal house," embodied in the symbolic object of the design, creatively interpreted and modified in the actual real-life conditions in the imagination of the builders, motivates and guides at all times the actions of those who effect its transformation into the real thing.

Our example suggests that some instances of linguistic communication may function as "ideal" activity. First of all, our communicative actions may have a "planning function" (Levina, 1981) in which the desired outcome of joint activity, along with the means and course of activity, can be consciously anticipated, worked out, and presented to all concerned as a common goal. This planning of the result in an "ideal form" allows the technical and social problems that have arisen or will arise in the course of activity to be identified, addressed, and resolved. At the same time, linguistic communication may have an "organizing function" (Vygotsky, 1999) that allows the different partial tasks and skills involved in joint activity to be distributed and coordinated in situ amongst individuals and groups of individuals who are working in relative isolation. The symbolic "tool," like the real tool, then, is an instrument of human activity. Moreover, planning and organising, as special activities or phases within activity, presuppose specific kinds and forms of social relation between the producers so that the cognitive and the social-interactional are ultimately inseparable.

The coordination of collective activity through language presupposes individuals who are capable of using language as a means of organising and controlling their own actions and behaviour within the communal task. Indeed, in order to go about their allotted task, individuals must approach and undertake what they are doing *as a task*, that is, as an action carried out *for and with others* in pursuit of the "ideal" aim, fixed in advance in symbolic acts.[3]

Language, then, serves not only as a directly social means of intercourse but as "a means of psychological action on behaviour, one's own or another's, a means of internal activity directed toward mastering man himself" (Vygotsky, 1997a, p. 62). That is, it is this ability to use language to actively formulate "ideal" aims as motivation for oneself and others and to subordinate one's own and others' actions and behaviour to the achievement of these aims, which is the very essence of Vygotsky's "free action" and, indeed, the very foundation of individual self-consciousness.[4] Individuals must be aware of how their own actions relate to the actions of others on the spot, to others not present, and to the common goal, and, therefore, be able to relate critically to their own practice as if from the outside, that is, through the eyes of these others. Language is necessarily interwoven in the entire history of the development of the individual human personality so that, for example, the transition from the so-called holophrase of the very young child to the complex and sophisticated utterance of the four-year-old is an aspect of the cultural-historical "mastery of one's own behaviour"; of the development of the will, an aspect of the development of this child as a human personality, as a cultural being; and, therefore, of the development of the community itself and of culture as a whole.[5]

But if language makes human action free, then who or what makes language? In the cultural-historical perspective, there is nowhere to look for an answer to the question of the ultimate origins of language but within the dynamic of "free action" itself. If language makes such a powerful contribution to human activity, then this is only because language belongs to that activity, arising from within that activity to play a special role within it. In our house-building example, we made a distinction between the "ideal"

---

[3] Cf. Vygotsky's (1999) discussion of this task-related consciousness in child development: "The situation in which people begin to act, just like things, as a whole acquires for him a social significance. The situation presents itself to him as a task posed by the experimenter and the child feels that behind this the whole time stands a person, whether this person is directly present or not. The child's own activity acquires its own significance within the system of social behaviour and, being directed towards a definite goal, is diffracted through the prism of social forms of his thinking."

[4] "With the help of speech the child first acquires the ability to master his own behaviour, to relate to himself as if from the side, to consider himself as an object. Speech helps him to master this object via the previous organization and planning of his own actions and behaviour" (Vygotsky, 1999).

[5] "Cultural devices of behavior do not appear simply as external habit; they comprise an inalienable part of the personality itself, rooted in its new relations and creating their completely new system" (Vygotsky, 1997a, p. 91).

activity of talking and drawing and the physical activity of building. However, this distinction is only between different sides of *one* activity, because the symbolic activity is merely a phase of the building activity itself. In the discourse of architect and planners, it is a *house* that is being constructed and not just *words*; the drawing and talking are *part of* the "doing."[6] The purpose of linguistic communication here, the meaning of the language symbols used and the source of that meaning, must be sought in the role language plays within the social activity of house building that it helps to realise. The purpose and end point of this process of activity, of course, lies in the real object that is its result. Thus, language serves this process or, in Vygotskian terms, *mediates* it, forming an intermediate link within the chain of practical actions resulting in the finished product. At certain points within that process, in planning, discussing, and so on, the entire process is concentrated and contained in discourse and other symbolic means: at these points the symbols *are* the activity.

Thus, if language plays an organising role within activity, it is because the activity being performed creates a need for organisation of precisely this kind. Activity spontaneously gives rise to linguistic communication, which, as a form of symbolic mediation of that activity, can never lose its connections with, and its influence on, activity, however much those connections are obscured by the process of social differentiation and stratification. Language is the solution to the problem of coordinating and subordinating the developing practical and mental actions of individuals engaged in productive activity of the distinctively human kind. More specifically, the utterance as a form of connection of one individual to another is the active resolution of the contradictions that arise within free action. Consequently, the power that language has within activity is ultimately due to the kind of activity being performed. Language is made by human communities as a necessary instrument for living together in a human way, as an instrument of their collective activity, and its power ultimately remains the reflected power of their collective work and of the possibilities inherent in it; it is the power of the community condensed into a symbolic form.

If language develops *from* activity, then it is as a development *of* activity: in language human activity acquires a new form, expressed not only in physical actions, in the production of useful objects, but also in the production of meaningful symbols. The architect is engaged in building a house, but building it in "ideal" or symbolic form. This symbol is the very activity of

---

[6] As Vygotsky (1997b, p. 248) says, the engineer studying a blueprint "is studying a machine and not a blueprint."

house building "transformed . . . into a special object with which [a person] can operate specially without touching and without changing the real object up to a certain point" (Ilyenkov, 1977, p. 278). Thus, with the help of language and other symbolic systems, "man builds new forms of action first mentally and on paper, stages battles on maps, works on mental models" (Vygotsky, 1997a, p. 90). Language is such an instrument for human action, an instrument that is a specialised and differentiated form of human action itself.

Language, then, is one of the essential attributes of freely acting people, of "socialised humanity" (Marx), of historically definite men and women collectively working out the possibilities for interaction with the natural world that the social form of life offers them. To understand the origins and functioning of language means to try to come to grips with the process by which the community of individuals, through their own activity, produce and reproduce for themselves all the necessary material, intellectual, aesthetic, and spiritual organs of their collective life activity. Indeed, a clear perspective for the unity of the human sciences is offered in this attempt to understand the developing community as the active subject of its own historical process (as is argued by Mikhailov, 1990).

LINGUISTICS AND PSYCHOLOGY

Linguists and psychologists today tend to see linguistics as part of cognitive psychology or "cognitive science" (Lakoff and Johnson, 1999)[7] because it seems self-evident to them that, firstly, there are such "things" as semantic structures, grammatical categories, and, secondly, that these things are, like thoughts and intentions, mental states of the individual person and, therefore, psychological phenomena. Furthermore, if psychological processes are equated with brain processes, then psychology in turn, and linguistics with it, collapses into biology.[8]

The view of language as a mental phenomenon has important consequences for the methodology of linguistics. The most important is that the utterance, "the concrete act of verbal interchange" (Voloshinov, 1973), is relegated to the status of a more or less imperfect "realisation" of the primary

---

[7] I exclude from consideration here the socially oriented linguistics of Malinowski and the Firthian tradition. For a critical evaluation of "cognitive linguistics" see Jones (1999, 2001).

[8] Cf. Chomsky (1975) for the clearest statement of this position: "The theory of language is simply that part of human psychology that is concerned with one particular 'mental organ,' human language" (p. 36); "Linguistic theory . . . is an innate property of the human mind. In principle, we should be able to account for it in terms of human biology" (p. 34).

mental constructs, giving us the basic position referred to by Roy Harris (1981) as the "telementation fallacy." Indeed, for some theorists the derivative status of actual utterances places them outside the scope of linguistic science altogether. Chomsky (1986), for example, sees the subject matter of linguistics as a system of mental computation, which he refers to as "I-Language" (where "I" means individual and internal), whereas the utterance belongs to "E-Language" ("E" for external). In E-Language the properties of language proper (i.e., I-Language) are inextricably mixed and contaminated with all kinds of unrelated and extraneous properties to do with real-time social interaction that are irrelevant to the linguist. On this view, as Sperber and Wilson (1986, p. 173) put it, "the fact that humans have developed languages which can be used to communicate is interesting, but it tells us nothing about the essential nature of language," because the "activities which necessarily involve the use of a language ... are not communicative but cognitive."

Some other approaches in linguistics, while perhaps recoiling from the extreme biological reductionism of the Chomskyan programme, nevertheless share a view of linguistic phenomena as the product and expression of inner mental constructs or rules (even, e.g., Tomasello, 2003).

Vygotsky would have considered the "mentalist" position on language to be not the result of scientific discovery in relevant fields (as has been claimed recently by Lakoff and Johnson, 1999) but to be the enduring legacy in the human sciences of an old-fashioned "metaphysical" or "idealist" conception of human behaviour according to which "Not only the maturing youth's growing into separate spheres of culture – law, ethics, art, religion, professional life – but these very cultural spheres arise due exclusively and purely to a mind process, an internal, self-powered mind" (Vygotsky, 1997a, p. 12).

For Vygotsky, the mentalist position sees everything upside down when it looks at human behaviour. It takes what is primary in human behaviour and thought, namely the historically developed cultural practices of the community, to be derivative of what is actually "a genetically secondary stratum in the development of behavior" (1997a, p. 106), that is, the individual mind. Now, Vygotsky (1981), too, calls the word a "psychological tool." However, his conception of psychological tools, indeed of human psychological processes generally, puts him at odds with the mentalist conception because he does not mean that language has its origins in psychological processes, but that it comes to assume a psychological function, and thereby to take on a psychological character, in the course of the development of the individual person. For Vygotsky (1981), language is completely social in nature, an instance of what he refers to as "higher cultural activity" and, as such, an "interpsychological" function that is produced by and between people, and therefore by more than one mind, as a form of their active mutual interconnection.

If we pursue this line of thought, then it becomes clear that language consists not of mental phenomena, although mental phenomena are involved in its production, but in the activity of producing visible, audible, tangible, and palpable *objects* in the material of the physical stuff of sound, gesture, or marks on paper or on the computer screen. It is these very *un*psychological objects, existing as bodily movements or indeed quite outside of our bodies and minds as the products of these movements, that have meaning, just like the painting, the sculpture, or the musical composition; it is these special, sensuous objects that are true or false, beautiful or ugly, noble or vulgar, sophisticated or clumsy, vibrant or bland, inspirational or dulling. Communicating is, indeed, sculpting in sound or some other physical material, the fashioning, in real time and space, of an object whose meaning is its being a form and means of intercourse between us. The sensuous *and* meaningful objects that we call utterances, or texts, or diagrams are human subjectivity itself in objectified form and are therefore as much a part of human nature as hands and eyes.[9]

Linguistic communication can take place only through this investing of natural material with the "artificial" property that we call "meaning." But this process of investment is not a mental act per se or the expression of an already existing psychological state: the meaning of the communicative act is the function of the actual sounds or gestures within social activity (Mikhailov, 1990). Linguistic *meaning* starts life in the meaning*ful material* of social intercourse. For a child, the process that has come to be known as "language acquisition" is the process of creating with others this meaningful substance in daily interactions. This is no Chomskyan process of "exposure" to language in which the child's mind correlates words directly with already existing meanings in some a priori "language of thought," but is the very formation of meaning in the material of the physical signals that pass between the child and others.[10] What is referred to as "grammar," similarly, must be seen not as a mental phenomenon but as a property or function of this real material outside of our heads. It may well be objected that grammar and meaning, like beauty, are in the eye of the beholder or hearer. But, first of all, it is what the eye *sees*, and not the eye or visual image itself, that is beautiful;

9 Or more so, because hands and eyes, if lost or damaged, can be replaced by "artificial," culturally created (and therefore linguistically mediated) instrumental functions or social relations. Human subjectivity necessarily takes the form of objects because all distinctively human activity is the production of objects; cf. Marx (1959): "man is at bottom objects."

10 This is the process that Lock (1980) aptly refers to as "the guided reinvention of language."

and, secondly, an eye for beauty, like a musical ear or any other human faculty, is formed in the course of our human dealings with one another and with the humanly created objects that are the measure and model of beauty. The immediate consequence of this view for linguistics is that the utterance – the "concrete act of verbal interchange" – in the form of the act of creation of this real sensuous object in sound, gesture, and the like must be restored to its rightful place as the essential and primary object of scientific investigation.

Of course, there is no doubt that an ability to produce, apprehend, and appreciate this meaningful linguistic material has its *presuppositions* in the natural, biological functions and processes in the newborn child as well as in the prior development of specific psychological functions. But in the Vygotskian view, these presuppositions remain presuppositions or preconditions and cannot determine either the nature or the course of human mental and linguistic development. The specifically human ways of acting, thinking, and communicating can be formed only through the child's engagement with others who already act, think, and communicate in this way.[11] The consequence for the child of inclusion in the whole system of "intermental" activities, those which are specifically communicative and those mediated by language, is that these natural and already developed psychological functions are altered and transformed into elements of the "higher" cultural activity of free action. Thus, to create a meaningful utterance, for example, to say the name of an object to gain attention or recognition, is to exercise such psychological functions as perceiving, remembering, recognising, and categorising (Ilyenkov, 1997, p. 57). But the ability to name things, to categorise and classify them in accordance with a linguistic designation, is neither an innate capability nor the direct expression of a psychological process that has developed independently of language (e.g., Piagetian "sensorimotor intelligence"). It is, rather, a result of the process of engaging in human activity mediated by linguistic communication in which psychological processes are "verbalised." In other words, such verbal acts help to form such distinctively human psychological processes.

In this respect, language is no different from other cultural activities, all of which depend on psychological processes, which, in turn, depend on specialised brain activity. But this does not make cultural actions into psychological phenomena or states of the brain. House building depends on specific psychological processes but is no more a psychological phenomenon than

---

[11] Cf. Mikhailov (1990, p. 72): "Only joint action with adults and peers which has become an organic mode of his/her life, only the understanding of him/her by other people renders intelligible his/her own actions and the words and objects participating in these actions."

the actual house that is built, or the tools used to build it. Indeed, the ability to undertake any kind of skilful goal-oriented practice can arise only through a lengthy process of actually engaging in the social activity of a goal-oriented application of materials and tools, and the handling and consumption of the finished product. Just as the psychological processes necessary for the successful use of a tool can only be formed in and through the actual purposeful use of the tool in its relevant function, so too the mental processes involved in the use and understanding of language are actually formed through and as a result of the process of engaging in communication as a form of direct social connection. Psychological processes, including all the "unconscious cognitive mechanisms" accorded such importance in cognitive linguistics (Lakoff and Johnson, 1999), constitute a dimension of cultural action and are only formed in and through active participation in action.

At the same time, thinking, speaking, writing, and so on, of course, depend on brain activity of a specific kind. But in order for the brain to help us think in this human way, we must give it the tools of human thought to practice with, to struggle with, to make sense of, to adapt to, and to master. The brain's ability to help us think and communicate is created in each individual's practical struggle to create utterances as instruments of communication and verbal thinking.

Language use, however, not only presupposes specialised psychological processes but is a conscious, and therefore mind-dependent, activity. Are we not forced to conclude, then, that language is, after all, the expression of mental states, this time, conscious ones? It is certainly true that there could be no language without the conscious mind. But from a cultural-historical perspective, the conscious mind itself – indeed, the whole inner world of the personality – is formed through a process at the centre of which is the "internalization" or involution of the "ideal" or symbolic forms of mediation of action, including language. Language as a historically developed cultural tool is a factor in the very formation of human consciousness, which itself develops, therefore, as a distinctive, differentiated component of human activity, of social being. Furthermore, language as direct interpersonal communication and language when it has metamorphosed into the processes of conscious inner direction and thought – language as an immediately social event and language as the events of inner speech and thought – are two different poles of the social act of linguistic communication and are dialectically interconnected.

This now puts a quite different spin on the connection between the linguistic and the psychological: the psychological dimension of language understanding is formed from the activity of linguistic communication itself; the linguistic *becomes* the psychological. All higher mental activity has this same beginning in people relating to one another in their practical and intellectual

activity by means of artificially created objects. These forms of active intercourse mould the natural psychological endowment of the child into new
shapes and functions, thereby creating their own inner supports as these
directly social forms of behaviour and objective means of intercourse are
transformed into individual mental activity. This is the general process
referred to by Vygotsky as the "law of cultural development of behaviour"
which he states in the following way:

Every function in the child's cultural development appears twice: first, on the
social level, and later, on the individual level; first, between people (interpsychological) and then inside the child (intrapsychological). This applies equally
to voluntary attention, to logical memory, and to the formation of concepts.
All the higher functions originate as actual relationships between individuals.
(Vygotsky, 1978, p. 57)

The specific implications for language and its involution are also presented:

The most important and fundamental of the genetic laws which our research
into higher mental functions has led us is that any symbolic activity of the child
was always at some point a social form of cooperation and preserves throughout
its development up to its highest point a social mode of functioning. (Vygotsky,
1999, p. 56)

This position immediately rules out the possibility of innate linguistic
or conceptual categories and is incompatible with the idea of biologically
fixed psychological or linguistic abilities or processing mechanisms. On the
contrary, for Vygotsky (1997a, p. 39) "the process of mental development in
man is part of the total process of the historical development of humanity."
To talk, as we are doing here, of "language" or "psychological processes" is not
to assume, therefore, the existence of fixed, universal, mental capacities that
underlie and define these phenomena. Linguistic and psychological processes
are not transhistorical or ahistorical phenomena. Any language – indeed, any
act of linguistic communication – is a historically and culturally specific form
of social intercourse that will differ from all others in its forms and meanings
and, therefore, in its psychological dimensions, too. Just as the linguistic forms
and functions created in an instance of communication between a young
child and his or her mother are very different from those involved in writing
a chapter like this, or a text message between friends over mobile phones, so
too are the psychological processes involved in these communicative acts.

For this reason, it is quite wrong to conceive of the origins of language or
of human mental abilities in terms of a single event that took place in the
distant past or as a process whose course has run (cf. Taylor, 1997). On the
contrary, language is *still originating*, along with the psychological processes

involved in communicating. In the processes of linguistic differentiation and development going on all around us (now text messages, email, etc.), we see essentially the same process of originating that was at work in the historical emergence of human culture and human language as part of culture. For that reason, empirical investigation of linguistic differentiation, provided that it is able to place this process concretely within the dynamic of linguistically mediated social activity, can allow powerful insights into the emergence and development of communicative skills in the species.

WHERE SHOULD A SCIENCE OF LANGUAGE BEGIN?

Human social activity is the very *substance* of linguistic communication. So when we look at language we are actually looking at the social process in its entirety as that process is reflected and refracted through the form of symbolic mediation of that process.[12] But this situation clearly poses difficult problems for a science of language: given this concrete unity of all practical and mental faculties in the human community, how is it possible to legitimately isolate and meaningfully study a distinctively linguistic object? The problem is made more complicated by the fact that language itself has many different properties, aspects, and functions and has innumerable direct and mediated links with social action. It would be easy to unwittingly include within our conception of language all kinds of phenomena that have no essential relation to linguistic communication as such. Conversely, when extracting language from its social matrix, we might leave something essential behind and end up with an incomplete or impoverished object that makes no sense in and of itself. So where do we begin? What do we take as the starting point for our analysis? How do we distinguish between those phenomena that are central and those that are accidental and peripheral, between the essential and the historically transient? As an illustration of the problem, let us briefly examine a number of proposed starting points for linguistic analysis.

The Design Features Approach

The "design features" approach of Hockett and Altman (1968) was developed as a framework for the comparison of human language with animal communication systems. The method involved identifying the essential and

---

[12] Sapir (1949, p. 69): "The understanding of a simple poem...involves not merely an understanding of the single words in their average significance, but a full comprehension of the whole life of the community as it is mirrored in the words, or as it is suggested by their overtones."

distinctive ingredients of language and then using these as a point of reference for analysis and evaluation of animal systems. Although they identified sixteen features in all, the feature at the top of their list is "vocal-auditory channel," by which is meant: "The sender of the signal employs a vocal tract to produce a message, and the receiver employs an auditory system to process the signal."

The assumption is that human language is designed as *spoken* language with the implication that sign language or writing is derivative from speech. This was a commonly accepted view in linguistic circles until relatively recently. It lies behind the work of such scholars as Lieberman, who have investigated the origins of human language by reconstructing hominid vocal tracts from fossil evidence in order to see whether the individuals concerned would have been able to produce the range of speech sounds that humans produce today. The assumption that speech is *biologically* primary rests on the near universality of spoken language in the world's communities but also draws support from evidence that infants are predisposed to pay particular attention to the human voice and are particularly sensitive to sounds within the frequency range of human speech.

From a cultural-historical perspective, however, the assumption of the primacy of speech is unfounded. The linguistic properties that speech sounds have, whether phonological or grammatical properties, indeed their very function as speech sounds, are due entirely to the social functions of such sounds. Whatever pleasure and interest the sound of the human voice may have for the infant, the transformation of this sound into a *linguistic* instrument is a work of social activity. There is no natural predisposition or predilection for *spoken* language because there is none for *language*; human beings communicate only because they lead a social existence, and to this end they will exploit whatever physical means (including the resources of their own bodies and brains) are necessary or most effective in the circumstances. This is the lesson of the historical process of the development of varied communicative means and technologies, continuing today through the development of digital communication. Moreover, comparative studies of spoken language and sign language acquisition have disconfirmed the hypothesis of a bias in favour of speech in the newborn child.

Language as a Set of Sentences

Let us take quite a different starting point, say, the idea of language as a "set of sentences," following Chomsky (1957). The sentence certainly looks more like a specifically linguistic phenomenon than a vocal tract. Even a superficial study of sentences reveals special kinds of patterning that cannot be straightforwardly accounted for in terms of nonlinguistic behaviour.[13] The description and analysis of linguistic *form* in the shape of syntactic patterns, however, cannot be the starting point for a science of language because form is always the *form of something*. Any such "formal" patterns constitute at best merely a contextually conditioned aspect of the integral whole of the meaningful utterance. Taken in themselves, they are abstract and inert, because they have their cause and also their functional effects only within the meaningful communicative act. The sentence as a formal construct is the outcome of a procedure that overlooks or ignores the culturally situated and culturally determined process of communicative interchange. In this way, the Chomskyan approach effects a reduction of communicative activity to an arbitrary, formal pattern that has no intrinsic relation to the social activity it mediates. Accordingly, what constitutes a product and means of social intercourse is misconstrued as the manifestation of an a priori state of the brain (cf. Jones, 2003a, 2003b).

The problem with both the approaches we have examined has to do with the nature of the initial theoretical abstraction. The first approach equates language with one of its accidental historical manifestations and thereby mistakenly attributes linguistic properties to the raw material stuff of language; the Chomskyan approach, focussing on one aspect of the living utterance independently of its source within and connections to the whole, sees such patterns as the direct expression of an intrinsically syntactic component of the human mind and mistakenly attributes linguistic properties directly to the natural state of the brain. From very different starting points, we end up with distinctively linguistic properties being attributed to natural material independently of the social function of the material. Both approaches, then, involve abstract and one-sided views of the phenomenon, focussing on and reifying in ahistorical fashion either accidental and historically transient aspects of linguistic activity or the results of this seen independently of the activity itself. Neither approach, therefore, makes it possible to develop a concrete scientific conception of language as an attribute of social humanity.

Beginning from Origins

Another approach might be to try to trace language back to its very earliest manifestations in child development or in the history of the species on the

---

[13] "Linguistics would seem to have a very peculiar value for configurative studies because the patterning of language is to a very appreciable extent self-contained and not significantly at the mercy of inter-crossing patterns of a non-linguistic type" (Sapir, 1949, p. 74).

assumption that the particular circumstances of the origins of a phenomenon give the best clue as to its genuinely distinctive nature. The difficulty here, however, is knowing when to stop rewinding, because every stage of language development that we look at has its own history in earlier behaviour: behind the sentence lies the utterance, behind the utterance lies the wordless communicative interchanges between mother and infant, behind them the babbling and crying of the infant, etcetera. But crying is not language: this regression does not yield up the true origins and history of the object of study but merely takes us beyond that object and into the history of quite unrelated processes.[14] Looking at the historical sequence of events, therefore, is no shortcut to an understanding of the distinctive logic of our particular object of study but merely forces us into a potentially infinite regress. This approach substitutes an often arbitrary account of the temporal succession of empirical events for an understanding of the causal determinations and inner interconnections between elements within the relevant system of phenomena. It confuses the historically accidental circumstances of the birth of the phenomenon with the logic of the process of its generation, a logic that, far from being lost in the distant past, is, in the case of language, still at work today.

The problem of the origins of language is approached quite differently in the cultural-historical perspective. If language arises within social life as a necessary link in the chain of activity, that role cannot have disappeared with the passage of time. On the contrary, if the emergence of language presupposes social activity, then its impact on such activity is to make it, in turn, dependent on language. In this way, what is an essential condition of the development of language – namely, organised social action – becomes the result or consequence of language itself. Consequently, the truly necessary *conditions* of the emergence of language are present and are constantly being recreated as an *effect* or *consequence* of language itself. As Ilyenkov (1982, p. 210) explains, "a logical consideration of the higher stage of development of an object, of an already developed system of interaction, reveals a picture in which all the really necessary conditions of its emergence and evolution are *retained* and all the more or less accidental, purely historical conditions of its emergence are absent."

From this point of view, the historical problem of the origins of language is to be solved, at least in outline, by an investigation of the "logic" of language-mediated activity today or, more accurately, of the role of language in such activity: understanding the historical preconditions and conditions for the

---

[14] Ilyenkov (1982) refers to this method as "abstract historicism."

emergence of language means understanding the effects and consequences of language on the social process as a whole.

The Word Becoming a Deed

Whatever the difficulties facing a linguistic science, we may take some comfort from the fact that they are no different from those facing any natural or social science: "Each science obviously reflects in its categories only specific forms and laws of a concrete system of interacting phenomena constituting its special subject-matter, making abstraction from everything else, despite the fact that without this 'everything else' its subject-matter is impossible and inconceivable" (Ilyenkov, 1982, p. 120).

Furthermore, the cultural-historical tradition is not working in a theoretical vacuum but against the backdrop of a rich body of knowledge about language already accumulated throughout the history of linguistics. And, in fact, the historical development of schools of linguistics presents different ways of tackling the methodological problems we have outlined. It is, therefore, necessary for a cultural-historical linguistics to develop through a critique of linguistics and, thereby, a critical overcoming of the one-sided, abstract, and reductionist tendencies of linguistics as well as a critical reappropriation of the genuine achievements and advances in linguistic thought which that history offers, as indeed was the practice of Vygotsky himself (see Lee, 1985).

With this discussion in mind, let us pursue the methodological implications of our cultural-historical perspective. Language, it was argued, is a product of "free action." But free action is itself a consequence of the development of language. We appear to have created a vicious circularity at the very outset of our investigation. But instead of shying away from this paradox let us consider it instead to be a reflection of how the relationship between language and action looks on the surface. Let us assume that it records quite accurately, if also abstractly, the dialectical interaction between them.

Human communities, as we have seen, are complex systems in constant motion. All sides and elements of the system – including language – have grown up and developed in interaction with all others. But this essential unity between all aspects of social existence does not present itself as a homogenised mush where all ingredients seamlessly blend into one another. Rather, it is, like the human body, a "unity in diversity" (Ilyenkov, 1982, following Marx), a system of differentiated organs each with its own specialised function and distinctive position in the vital process. Indeed, differentiation *means* difference: system element A is different from system element B; A does what element B does not, and vice versa; A does what it does *because* B (and C, D, E, etc.) does not do this but does something else. It is this pattern of presences and absences, of positives and negatives, distributed amongst the elements of the system that binds them together into the system and constitutes both the basis of their interaction and the continuously recreated consequence of it. Now we begin to see the answer to one element of our methodological conundrum. While each element depends on all the others, this dependency is expressed not by an *identity* of function, form, or position with all the others but, on the contrary, in its very *difference* from them, in its differentiated, specialised position amongst them. Each element, then, has its own distinctive *causal action* upon all the other elements, and so the task of science is to identify and account for this distinctive causal force, which is, at the same time, a form of the action of the system as a whole.

In the case of language, we have argued that its place is within the chain of social activity and that it works as the symbolic mediation of activity. It remains, then, to look for the initial and most basic case of the exercise of this symbolic or "ideal" force. In Vygotsky's terms we are looking for a "unit of analysis": "By *unit* we mean a product of analysis which, unlike elements, retains all the basic properties of the whole and which cannot be further divided without losing them" (Vygotsky, 1962, p. 4).

The method of analysis into units leads to what Ilyenkov (1982, p. 226) calls the "concrete fullness of abstraction," that is, an abstraction that "expresses the concrete characteristics of the objectively simplest further indivisible element of a system of interaction, a "cell" of the analysed whole."

To pursue this idea, what phenomenon exemplifies the simplest instance of the differentiated and qualitatively distinctive causal action of language? Vygotsky (1962) took "word meaning" as his unit of analysis and therefore as the starting point of his investigation. But his subject was "verbal thinking," whereas ours is language. A clue is given in Luria's application of the same methodological principle in his analysis of human action (of "free action" in Vygotsky's terms). Luria (1961, p. 26) identifies his own "unit of analysis" in the following passage: "It would not be wrong to state that *the accomplishment of a simple action on verbal instruction* can be regarded as the core of voluntary behaviour regulated by speech" (emphasis in original).

While this is a definition of "voluntary behaviour regulated by speech" rather than of language, it suggests a way to resolve our own specifically linguistic problem. Is the "verbal instruction" on which a "simple action" is "accomplished" not in fact an instance of the kind of unit we are looking for? Does the verbal instruction not offer us the simplest case of "the word *becoming a deed*"? Although only the attempt to construct a linguistic theory on this basis will allow us to tell for sure, the verbal instruction looks like a promising example of such a "unit." The instruction is a distinctively linguistic phenomenon that has a special role within an ongoing social interaction. Although everything essentially linguistic about it is due to its being a form and means of human activity, a typical instruction marks the point at which the communicative act has differentiated itself from its matrix of practical action to become itself an identifiable and distinctive act that is an independent, causal factor within that action. An instruction is a symbolic link in the chain of action, redirecting an ongoing action towards a new goal. Produced by one person, it is transformed by another person directly into an action. In actual fact, this is an oversimplification of the situation: there is no such thing as "an instruction" or "the instruction" in general. Rather, what we tend to refer to as "instructions" are simply uniquely created instances of interindividual communicative regulation or guidance of activity.

These situated acts of communicative exchange carried out by conscious participants in practical action ("sympractic speech"; Luria 1998) in which immediate transitions between word and deed are effected are the primary reality of linguistic form and meaning and the only possible foundation for the emergence and development of communicative skills in the child, because it is only when words come to have dependable consequences within practical intercourse that the child can make them, take them, and trust them, as a special means of relating to others in a human way. The distinctive dialogic relations between utterances, which have become the subject of so much theoretical attention in recent years, also have their source here. Utterances are initially rooted in particular action-related relations between participants. Some utterances, like the instruction, initiate and shape action in relation to a goal, whereas others register and confirm or reject the results of action initiated or prompted verbally. This is the necessary beginning of a process in which the communicative and directly practical dimensions of activity differentiate out as distinct but interdependent moments of skilled and purposeful activity and in which the skilled ability to plan action – implicit in the instruction and other forms of verbal regulation of behaviour – begins to develop.

In short, then, the instruction has all the requisite ingredients of a distinctive and irreducible linguistic "unit":

1. It is an objective, sensuous object fashioned from sound, gesture, or some other material.
2. It is a form of intercourse between people who are already in certain social relations and engaged in certain joint activities.

3. It is a form of joint action in which the word of one person is transformed into the action of another.
4. It is a conscious action and therefore an act of will and an expression of emotion.
5. It integrates and transforms the "lower" psychological processes into the "higher" form of human cultural action.
6. It is a cognitive as well as directly communicative action.
7. It is a special phase of action, forming a moment of transition between past and future actions.
8. It does not simply trigger or initiate a practical action but causes its specific formation in accordance with the ideal, verbally expressed goal.
9. It is the very act of creation of linguistic form and meaning.

CONCLUSIONS

In summary then, I have argued that a cultural-historical approach to language involves the following assumptions and claims:

• The reality of what we call "language" is communicative activity, a purely cultural form of activity, a product and means of the self-creation of human beings through the productive activity known as "labour."
• Language arises as a differentiated form of human activity whose role is the symbolic mediation of activity.
• Language is the "ideal form" of human activity, allowing the conscious formation and coordination of goal-directed action.
• A typical, simple, or basic case of distinctively linguistic communication is an instruction or other verbal prompt to practical action.
• The instruction is our unit of analysis for language and will be the starting point for our investigation of the distinctive properties of communicative behaviour within joint practical activity.

References

Chomsky, N. (1957). *Syntactic structures.* The Hague: Mouton.
Chomsky, N. (1975). *Reflections on language.* New York: Pantheon.
Chomsky, N. (1986). *Knowledge of language: Its nature, origin, and use.* New York: Praeger.
Engels, F. (1975). *Anti-Dühring.* Moscow: Progress.
Harris, R (1981). *The language myth.* London: Duckworth.
Hockett, C. F., & Altman, S. A. (1968). A note on design features. In T. A. Sebeok (Ed.), *Animal communication* (pp. 61–72). Bloomington: Indiana University Press.

Ilyenkov, E. V. (1977). *Dialectical logic.* Moscow: Progress.

Ilyenkov, E. V. (1982). *The dialectics of the abstract and the concrete in Marx's "Capital."* Moscow: Progress.

Ilyenkov, E. V. (1997). *The dialectics of the abstract and the concrete in theoretical- scientific thinking* (in Russian). Moscow: Rosspen.

Jones, P. E. (1999). The embodied mind: Contrasting visions. *Mind, Culture and Activity, 6* (4), 274–28.

Jones, P. E. (2001). Cognitive linguistics and the Marxist approach to ideology. In R. Dirven, B. Hawkins, & E Sandikcioglu (Eds.), *Language and ideology: Vol. 1. Theoretical cognitive approaches* (pp. 227–251). Amsterdam: Benjamins.

Jones, P. E. (2002). "The word becoming a deed": The dialectic of "free action" in Vygotsky's "Tool and sign in the development of the child." In D. Robbins & A. Stetsenko (Eds.), *Voices within Vygotsky's non-classical psychology: Past, present, future* (pp. 143–159). New York: Nova Science.

Jones, P. E. (2003a). Critical realism and scientific method in Chomsky's linguistics. In J. Cruickshank (Ed.), *Critical realism: The difference it makes* (pp. 90–107). London: Routledge.

Jones, P. E. (2003b). New clothes for an old emperor: "Evolutionary psychology" and the cognitive counter-revolution. *Mind, Culture, and Activity, 10* (2), 173–180.

Lakoff, G., & Johnson, M. (1999). *Philosophy in the flesh: The embodied mind and its challenge to Western thought.* New York: Basic Books.

Lee, B. (1985). Intellectual origins of Vygotsky's semiotic analysis. In J. V. Wertsch (Ed.), *Communication and cognition: Vygotskian perspectives* (pp. 66–93). Cambridge: Cambridge University Press.

Levina, R. E. (1981). L. S. Vygotsky's ideas about the planning function of speech in children. In J. V. Wertsch (Ed.), *Communication and cognition: Vygotskian perspectives* (pp. 279–299). Cambridge: Cambridge University Press.

Lock, A. (1980). *The guided reinvention of language.* London: Academic Press.

Luria, A. R. (1961). *The role of speech in the regulation of normal and abnormal behaviour.* Oxford: Pergamon Press.

Luria, A. R. (1998). *Language and consciousness* (in Russian). Rostov on Don: Fenix.

Marx, K. (1959). *Economic and philosophical manuscripts of 1844.* Moscow: Progress.

Marx, K. (1976). *Capital.* Harmondsworth: Penguin.

Mikhailov, F. T. (1990). *Social consciousness and the self-consciousness of the individual* (in Russian). Moscow: Nauka.

Sapir, E. (1949). *Selected writings of Edward Sapir in language, culture and personality* (D. G. Mandelbaum, Ed.). Berkeley: University of California Press.

Sapir, E. (1963). *Language: An introduction to the study of speech.* London: Rupert Hart-Davis. (Originally published 1921)

Sperber, D., & Wilson, D. (1986). *Relevance: Communication and cognition.* Oxford: Blackwell.

Taylor, T. J. (1997). *Theorizing language: Analysis, normativity, rhetoric, history.* Oxford: Pergamon.

Tomasello, M. (2003). *Constructing a language.* Cambridge, MA: Harvard University Press.

Voloshinov, V. N. (1973). *Marxism and the philosophy of language.* New York: Seminar Press.

Vygotsky, L. S. (1962). *Thought and language.* Cambridge, MA: MIT Press.

Vygotsky, L. S. (1978). *Mind in society: The development of the higher psychological processes.* Cambridge, MA: Harvard University Press.

Vygotsky, L. S. (1981). The instrumental method in psychology. In J. V. Wertsch (Ed. & Trans.), *The concept of activity in Soviet psychology* (pp. 134–143). Armonk, NY: M. E. Sharpe.

Vygotsky, L. S. (1997a). The history of the development of the higher mental functions. In R. W. Rieber (Ed.), *Collected works of L. S. Vygotsky: Vol. 4. The history of the development of higher mental functions* (pp. 1–125). New York: Plenum.

Vygotsky, L. S. (1997b). Problems of the theory and history of psychology. In R. W. Rieber & J. Wollock (Eds.), *Collected works of L. S. Vygotsky: Vol. 3. Problems of the theory and history of psychology* (pp. 63–79). New York: Plenum.

Vygotsky, L. S. (1999). Tool and sign in the development of the child. In R. W. Rieber (Ed.) *The collected works of L. S. Vygotsky: Vol. 6. Scientific legacy* (pp. 1–68). New York: Kluwer Academic/Plenum.

6

The Formation Experiment in the Age of Hypermedia and Distance Learning

Hartmut Giest

It is well known that learning tasks and demands in science education present substantial difficulties for the majority of students (Aikenhead, 1994; Solomon & Aikenhead, 1994; Yager, 1996; see also Mikkilä-Erdmann 2001; Vosniadou et al. 2001; Wiser & Amin 2001). International comparisons (e.g., TIMSS – Third International Mathematics and Science Study, Martin & Kelly 1996; Baumert, Lehman, et al. 1997; and PISA – Programme for International Student Assessment, http://www.pisa.oecd.org, Baumert et al., 2001) reveal considerable problems concerning application tasks, problem solving, scientific argumentation, and the like, whereas reproductive tasks and skills are better mastered. In my view these results indicate that most of the students have tremendous problems in theoretical thinking. Science education suffers – among other shortcomings – from a predominant orientation toward isolated, nonsituated facts that are seldom applied to real-life situations, and this orientation leads to difficulties in understanding and a loss of sense and motivation in many students. One reason for this situation is the preference in today's classroom for an often unrelated, single-discipline approach as a means to interpretation and understanding. This approach is no longer viable, however, because mankind's problems are becoming more and more complex and their understanding and solution require the application of a transdisciplinary approach to address this complexity.

Mankind's problems are a consequence of developmental conflicts of complex systems (ecology, economy, climate, democracy). These systems are characterized by opposing tendencies. The systems will develop only if these tendencies are in an interplay (forming a unit); if not, a conflict may appear that hinders the system's development. So, in order to solve complex problems, disciplinary thinking has to be complemented by transdisciplinary thinking, which also has to include skills in dialectical thinking.

Thinking dialectically means thinking in units of contradictions (oppositions)[1] and in mental systems. And thinking dialectically requires a high degree of theoretical thinking.

The limitations of disciplinary science instruction require a transdisciplinary approach that includes not only different sciences but also arts, which might make available different kinds of acquisition (Huber, 2001; Reinhold & Bünder, 2001). This step might help overcome the crisis of science education (Black & Atkin, 1996; Reinhold & Bünder, 2001), which is mainly a sense crisis in the view of students. Transdisciplinary instruction has to put mankind's problems and their solution in the center and has to ask whether and how disciplinary science can contribute to the solution of such complex problems.

Modern society is characterized by the need for lifelong learning in order to enable citizens to cope with a steadily (exponentially) growing knowledge base. Therefore, another main task of today's schools consists in preparing students for lifelong learning. That means, first of all, to enable students to learn and think independently and efficiently. *Self-directed learning* in connection with *modern media* might be a solution for those problems of modern society. Therefore, we focused our research on the formation of *theoretical (systemic) thinking* and *distance learning* with means of *modern media*.

Because the student's ability to think theoretically is, in my eyes, strongly connected with successful learning science (Giest & Lompscher, 2003), we looked for ways that promise an efficient formation of theoretical thinking in classrooms. But this can be done only if the research focuses on the essential psychological[2] aspects of theoretical thinking. The investigation of the nature of theoretical thinking is identical with the investigation of its development. To investigate theoretical thinking means to focus the research on the conditions of its development. The most adequate method of psychological research of the development of higher (culturally determined) psychic functions that we know is the causal-genetic method elaborated by Vygotsky and his collaborators. Within the framework of the causal-genetic method,

---

[1] One of the main concepts of dialectics (Hegel and others) is the concept of contradiction. That means that all phenomena and processes of the world consist of opposing features or aspects, for example, attraction and repulsion, continuity and discontinuity, dualism of wave and particle, assimilation and dissimilation, and so on. Such oppositions are the driving force of development.

[2] The term "psychological" has two meanings – corresponding to psychology as a science and to phenomena and processes studied by this science. In several languages, including German, for the second meaning the term "psychic" is used.

investigation and formation are two sides of the same coin. In some respect, formation is the culturally determined counterpart of maturity, which is naturally determined, but we must not forget that there is an interaction between both. Vygotsky pointed to the social, cultural character of learning, to the joint activity between adult and child in which the child is reaching his or her zone of proximal development. Development is strongly connected with social learning and interaction between competent and less competent partners. But what happens in the context of modern media and distance learning? Is it possible to apply the causal-genetic method here in order to investigate the formation and development of theoretical thinking in learners in instructional settings using distance learning and hypermedia?

In this chapter I draw the attention to some of the main theoretical aspects of the causal-genetic method. Next, after reviewing problems related to self-directed learning, I consider principles of applying the causal-genetic method, using multimedia and distance learning in instructional settings. Then I report on an empirical investigation in order to show how to apply those principles and also to draw some conclusions from our research.

THE CAUSAL-GENETIC METHOD AS A RESEARCH METHOD OF ACTIVITY THEORY: THEORETICAL PREREQUISITES

Although Vygotsky's work has received much attention in recent psychological research, the full methodological basis of his approach is not well known. This might be a result of the philosophical tendency of pragmatism in connection with modern constructivist approaches (Miettinen, 2002), or it might be that Vygotsky and his approach are not seen in the framework of a consistent theoretical approach (cf. activity theory) but more as a heuristic means (which is not wrong at all) – that is, as a broader cultural-historical approach useful in investigating human development and psychic functions. However, activity theory is strongly connected with Vygotsky and his approach (see Engeström, 1978, 1990; Engeström, Miettinen, & Pumäki, 1999; Lektorskij, 1990; Leontiev, 1978, 1981; Lompscher, 2002; and many others). In order to benefit from this approach, one has to know its methodological and theoretical roots.

In the relevant literature, often less attention is paid to the theoretical roots of a given concept or problem (Chaiklin, 2003; Fichtner, 1999). The basic ideas of elaborated theories are used in isolation in order to answer a research question and to realize an investigational program. The causal-genetic method (Merkys, 1996) and the zone of proximal development (Chaiklin, 2003; Fichtner, 1999) are examples of such basic concepts. The concept "zone of proximal development" is often found in recent psychological and pedagogical work but that of the causal-genetic method, which is inseparably connected with the former concept, is rarely found in the literature. Sometimes one can read the demand to overcome the causal-genetic method and to switch to the empiric-analytical paradigm (Saldern, 1998), ignoring that with the latter paradigm it is possible only to describe development but not to explain it (Giest, 1997) and that, without the causal-genetic method (which is the original research method of the cultural-historical school), this theoretical approach would not have been able to reach its original results (Merkys, 1996).

The causal-genetic method is a method of experimental "production" of the development of certain psychological phenomena like concepts, ideas, and actions in order to study real developmental processes and their conditions under specified experimental conditions. If you can reach a certain level or quality of psychic phenomena determined beforehand by creating and implementing special conditions and controlling the process experimentally, you will be able to explain – not only describe – the developmental process to a certain degree and make proposals for changing the corresponding practice for reaching certain aims.[3]

Might it be that the concept of the zone of proximal development fits better in modern constructivist theory than that of the causal-genetic method? Going back to the theoretical roots of "modern" concepts and paying more attention to activity theory might be very important because of the recent discussions concerning neurobiological research and genetic engineering. For example, the new neurobiological theory (see Kurzweil, 2000; Maturana & Pörksen, 2002; Roth, 2002) could overcome reductionism and face new perspectives by paying more attention to the concept and theory of activity and its perspective for the investigation and understanding of human nature.

Why is the causal-genetic method not well known in the scientific community? Why does this aspect of Vygotsky's work not seem to be up-to-date and useful, not of fruitful use in the eyes of today's psychologists? Looking at the history of science, we find two different roots and basic ideas in scientific thinking: the idea and concept of *evolution* sensu Darwin, and the idea and concept of *activity* sensu Marx. The basic difference between the two

---

[3] The causal-genetic method is characterized by a transformation or adaptation of a scientific experiment to research on the human mind and thinking. Therefore Vygotsky used the term "experimental-genetic method." The cornerstone of this method is to investigate especially higher (that means culturally-historically determined) human psychological functions in the process of their development by creating the conditions that mainly cause the development (therefore the term "causal-genetic method").

ideas concerns the relation between human being and environment: Darwin pointed to "adaptation *to* the environment" as a basic idea, whereas Marx referred to "the adaptation *of* the environment." Basic to and pioneering for modern thinking was Darwin's idea that the existing living world was not created according to some plan or organized by an idea existing beforehand but evolved as an effect of the interdependence between environment and living beings. The feature that can explain it all is the ability of living beings to bring themselves more or less actively in line with the environment. The fitting into the environment explains the developmental potential of a living being – the survival of the fittest. This idea was fascinating and explained the evolution from the variety of life up to the development of the human being by self-organization. No ideas or principles or order-organizing rules were needed that come from outside. So humans became similar to all other living beings. This had tremendous consequences for the investigation of the human being because it was now possible to investigate humans using the methods of science.

Adaptation was a powerful idea that could answer a variety of questions about the existing appearances and forms of life on Earth. It was a relatively simple principle with an enormous explanatory power. It is relevant today if we look at modern evolutionary biology. So it is not surprising that this idea has significantly influenced mankind's thinking. This is also true for psychologists. The idea of active adaptation to the environment also influences mental development: theories are rejected if they are no longer applicable or if they cannot explain the phenomena. Thus mental structures are changed in order to enable individuals to orientate and interact with the environment more adequately (to cope with the demands of life). The two basic processes are assimilation (the structure adapts to the environmental stimulus by quantitative change) and accommodation (as soon as qualitative changes or new structuring is required). This is equilibrium – the active production of a balance between inside and outside, between mental structure and environment. And this is the basic principle of constructivist theories in psychology (Glasersfeld, 1995).

Activity theory (Engeström 1978, 1990; Engeström et al. 1999; Lektorskij 1990; Leontiev 1978, 1981; Lompscher 2002; and others) arrives at analogous statements. But there is, however, a serious difference: the basic idea is not "evolution," that is, the idea of adaptation to the environment, but "revolution," that is, change of the environment. The dialectical analysis of human history, as it was done, for example, by Hegel and particularly by Marx, showed not only that humans adapt to the environment but also that they change it in accordance with their demands (from agriculture, the use of fire, the construction of houses, to the manipulation of genes). Activity is not an active adaptation to the environment but the transformation of the environment and – in interrelation with it – of humans themselves. Although this idea is not new, it has only begun to prove its explanatory potential. Among the first who applied this idea to psychology were Vygotsky and one of his closest students, Leontiev. This was, and still is, Vygotsky's contribution to modern psychology and to human science in general.

In short, the main difference between constructivism (in all its varieties) and activity theory consists in that the activity from which both start will be interpreted differently in accordance with the background of various basic concepts and paradigms: activity in the view of constructivism means the humans' active adaptation to the environment. Simply put: things are such that we cannot change them; therefore we must come to terms with them and adapt to the conditions of nature and society. Activity in the context of activity theory means active adaptation (change due to activity) of the environment to the humans' needs. Or, in simple terms: the environmental conditions are not suitable, so let us change them in order to be able to lead a better life and to cope better with the demands of life.

Bearing in mind these different basic approaches, it will be clear that a researcher who bases his investigations on the idea of evolution must adopt another research program and use methods of investigation different from those adopted by the researcher who bases his work on the idea of activity. In some respects, the comparison between the classical scientific experiment and the causal-genetic method shows just this difference.

COMPARISON OF CLASSICAL EXPERIMENT AND CAUSAL-GENETIC METHOD IN HUMAN RESEARCH

If we take adaptation as the basic idea, we can use classical science methods in order to investigate humans. The basic idea in the classical scientific experiment as applied to psychology is that independent variables cause changes in dependent variables by activating internal psychological conditions, processes, and structures (which are in principle not accessible from outside, not directly observable by the researcher). This idea allows the application of the experimental method as a scientific method.

The classical scientific experiment includes the following characteristics:

- It is directed toward the investigation of *objects* changing under experimentally controlled conditions.
- Even in human science, the research object will not be treated as a subject, but as an object (see Figure 6.1). Because the subject's activity "disturbs" the investigation in the investigational design, interactions between

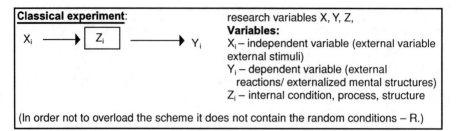

Figure 6.1. Classical experiment in human research.

researcher, method (material), and the object – here the person to be investigated – have to be minimized. For example, when using a psychological test, the participant should not think about the test because the object to be measured (the participant) should not interact with the measuring instrument – this is a well-known problem of investigation in the field of quantum physics (see Heisenberg, 1977). A variety of human psychological processes may be investigated with this method but not typically human activity, that is, not the higher cultural psychological functions.

In general, the classical scientific experiment is not an adequate method to investigate the human as a subject of his (specifically human – i.e., intentional, conscious, motive-driven) activity and its development. Even "modern" empirical-analytical methods cannot solve the research problem of subjects (the researcher) investigating other subjects (human beings as subject of their activity) because they register correlational links between different variables and try to reconstruct the research object based on the measured data. Only the psychological functions developed so far can be reconstructed, but not those in development. And the reconstruction can only take into account what kind of variable was measured in the investigation. In the best case, this method allows one to describe development but not to explain it.[4]

THEORETICAL BASIS AND KEY FEATURES OF THE CAUSAL-GENETIC METHOD

In the search for an adequate method to investigate human development (especially the development of culturally determined psychological functions

---

[4] The other method that is rooted in humanities is the hermeneutic method. This is not the place to discuss it, but we should note that even this method is not very objective, although it also may be useful in many ways. Nevertheless, it is not the scientific method, which allows the investigation of subjects.

and structures), Vygotsky and his collaborators developed the causal-genetic method. I discuss here seven basic theoretical concepts for understanding the causal-genetic method.

Human Subjects

Unlike an object, which can be more or less simply influenced or changed by the experimenter, human subjects create their own development (changes) via their own activity. This activity is determined in particular by culture and embedded in a social and cultural context. Higher psychological functions determined by culture cannot be investigated by analysis of conditions outside of a subject, because the main condition is the subject's activity. Thus, the classical scientific experiment directed to the investigation of objects changing under controlled conditions is not applicable to human subjects.

Activity

Activity is not adaptation to the environment but acting on the environment in order to change it corresponding to inner needs (Leontiev, 1978). This is a basic idea Vygotsky found in Marx's works and, in my eyes, is the basic difference with Piaget and modern constructivist approaches. The latter focus on psychological development as an adaptation to the environment and explain development in terms of that adaptation (e.g., in equilibration theory).

Shared Activity

Activity is essentially shared activity: as Vygotsky (1987) pointed out, psychological functions and structures exist first between humans and then inside a human; they are first interpsychological functions before they become intrapsychological functions. Activity in particular has to be characterized as shared or common activity. Social communication and cooperation, real activity beginning with its external (i.e., social and object-related) forms and their internalization, are seen as principal conditions for promoting but also investigating human development.

Developmental Zones

What the subject is actually able to perform lies in the zone of actual performance. This zone characterizes the actual developmental state of an individual (leading activity, motives, psychological prerequisites, prior knowledge, skills, and abilities). This zone as well as the zone of proximal development is oriented toward development and not toward tasks. That is, the developmental zones are not characterized by the available or missing ability to cope with single requests or to solve this or that task, but – as Chaiklin (2003) points out – are oriented toward the whole personality (and not only of children). Its internal structure and development as a change in the structural relationship are brought about by the learner's activity in the social situation of development. The developmental zones are strongly related to a leading activity that characterizes a developmental period (and not an age period, as Chaiklin emphasizes).[5]

I agree with Davydov (1998) that the zone of proximal development is created in interaction between more and less competent partners (e.g., child and adult)[6] in the frame of shared (culturally determined) activity, but it is rarely related to matured psychological functions. Culturally determined development starts on the basis of interactions but on the other side of natural development. That is the inner reason why we need a school with cultural tasks, not to forget that school is a cultural invention. Vygotsky had no time to elaborate the theory of these zones (Allal & Ducrey, 2000; Carugati, 1999; see also Chaiklin, 2003), but because of its relatedness to the whole personality and the culture and common activity in the social context, the major point to be made is that these zones are maximally characterized by the sense or meaning of the activity and how the individual experienced the activity. In its turn, this experience is linked with the special needs of an individual and whether activity is able to satisfy these needs. But it also has much to do with the position of an individual in the society, with his or her leading activity. So the zone of proximal development is much more dependent on individuals' meaningfully experiencing a new activity than on the particularities of single performances, which may be available in the zone of proximal development.

[5] This corresponds to findings of modern cognitive and developmental psychology that point to strong similarities between cognition in adults and children. The main differences exist concerning cognitive capacity and metacognitive awareness and not in reasoning and basically different cognitive structures, as one can read in Piaget's work (Mähler, 1999; Meer, 1996; Metz, 1995; Sodian, 1998).

[6] Because for a long time developmental psychology was only oriented to development up to the age of adulthood, the aspect of joint activity appears in the literature in the form of adults and children sharing their activity. But the essence is the joint activity in which different subjects with different abilities are involved. Jointly solving problems, both subjects influence each other and each other's development. And this does not end at the age of twenty-one or twenty-five.

Investigation by Formation

Human's phylogenesis and ontogenesis is characterized by the fact that in situations of social cooperation and communication cultural tools (means) are generated and used in order to change environment according to shared and meaningful aims. Psychological functions developed in that activity are internalized cultural tools. In order to acquire those tools, the corresponding activity has to be acquired. Because this activity is essentially shared activity, social cooperation and communication are necessary conditions for its acquisition. By means of the shared activity, a common subject will be constituted, and common aims and a meaningful integration of the cultural tools, functions, and means will be jointly used. In that shared activity, the transformation of culture, of those cultural tools between jointly active humans, takes place. Instruction is only a very special kind of this activity, which is characteristic of humans' activity in general. So, in order to investigate the development of higher, cultural psychological functions, the respective activity has to be investigated, which means the investigation of higher, culturally determined psychological functions has to be done by means of their formation. This makes clear why formation is tied to instruction and instruction to development.

Instruction

Vygotsky claimed that instruction influences development only if it runs ahead of development. This does not mean that the zone of proximal development depends only on instruction, as suggested by Bruner (1970). Instruction is effective in promoting development when it offers learners a new activity that is meaningful for them. Thus, intrinsic motivation for self-directed learning emerges only when the student develops a personal sense and meaning of this new activity.

Lifelong Development and Learning

Finally, we have to add that development does not end with leaving school or university but is a process that will continue throughout life. So it might be a good idea to ask whether the concept of the zone of proximal development is also valid in adult development. Although Piaget (1970) argued that in illiterate cultures no stage of formal operations will be observable, and the investigations by Adey and Shayer (1994) showed that a lot of older students and adults could not cope with formal operations, it is becoming clear that the development of those cognitive functions does not depend on age. TIMSS and PISA also point to the lack of development and missed chances, which implies that students must develop their learning, activity, and personality in the age of adulthood after school.[7]

To summarize, it can be said that the causal-genetic method is a method to investigate especially higher human psychological functions within the process of their development by creating the conditions that primarily cause that development. Higher psychological functions have developed within the historical process of cultural development and have been caused by it. Culture is a result of humans' shared, socially determined activity. Therefore, activity is the main condition of the development of humans' higher psychological functions. Theoretical thinking (theoretical reasoning) is one of the most developed human psychological functions. Prerequisite to and a result of the development of theoretical thinking is a very special, highly developed human activity directed at cognition. In order to apply the causal-genetic method to the investigation of theoretical thinking, one has to make sure that the learner can acquire that special activity. Therefore, it is of highest importance that the learner will be introduced to the use of specific cultural tools essential for that activity. Hypermedia and distance learning represent such specific tools.

HYPERMEDIA AND DISTANCE LEARNING

Why do we focus our research on the causal-genetic method of the formation of theoretical thinking by means of distance learning and new media? We see two good reasons for hypermedia and distance learning. The first reason is strongly connected with the computer as a means, as a knowledge generator. Today's knowledge often is generated by computer use and Internet search. In the cases of genetic engineering, fractal geometry, modern medicine, physics, chemistry, economy, and ecology, the computer is part of the generation of

---

[7] This last point has much in common with learning and development by means of distance learning and new media. Learning in school can create only the basis for education. Education no longer characterizes a special period in life but is a lifelong requirement. It does not end with the age of twenty-five, and there might be important zones of proximal development that we do not know yet but which are waiting to be discovered and which should be made fruitful for lifelong development. This kind of development must be promoted with special means. Distance learning using computers and hypermedia might be such a means that could be used to foster cognitive development and learning, and not only in children.

scientific knowledge. Without computer use, nothing will happen. The second reason is the need for lifelong learning. Modern society is characterized by the need for lifelong learning in order to enable citizens to cope with a steadily (and exponentially) growing knowledge base. Self-directed learning in connection with modern media might be a solution for those problems of modern society. Distance learning using hypermedia offers possibilities for lifelong learning. Modern media, computer, the Internet, and hypermedia offer many more chances to individualized learning (concerning time, modes, etc.), allowing flexible access to different and unlimited sources of information and multicoding of information, as compared with traditional learning means.

The computer and other electronic devices offer new opportunities for learning and thinking (Fichtner, 1999). Indeed, these tools can make it easier to open up the world of knowledge. For instance, the computer can be used to gain information, to train thinking, to present results of one's own thinking, to communicate worldwide, and to simulate and produce and publish ideas. Using interactive programs in connection with simulation or the possibilities of digitalization and visualization of digitalized material allows, for instance, to experiment with complex systems in a new way that is possible only with the help of the computer. In this way, the computer becomes a psychological tool, a tool that allows us to principally enlarge the possibilities of thinking.

Thus, modern education needs to develop learning environments using modern media and distance learning. But presently there is still a lack of good educational programs, and many questions remain unanswered concerning self-directed learning using hypermedia and distance learning, and many problems are still unsolved (Mayer & Moreno, 2002; Mugler & Landbeck, 2000; Tenenbaum et al., 2001). One such problem is the evaluation of electronic educational programs with respect to learning and psychological development. Another one is the need for programs ensuring a high quality of learning effects (Fricke, 1995a, 1995b). In my view, this quality of learning depends on the formation of theoretical and dialectical thinking with respect to system education (see also Giest & Walgenbach, 2002; Walgenbach, 2000). Although special research has been done, until now it is not very clear under which conditions theoretical thinking develops and conceptual change takes place and also how theoretical thinking develops in relation to everyday thinking. This applies to the traditional classroom as well as to distance learning with new media. We assume that applying the causal-genetic method to learning with new media is a way to solve those problems and to find answers to some of the questions.

The special aim of our research is to help students to reach their zone of proximal development concerning theoretical, especially dialectical, thinking by means of distance learning. This research also serves as a theoretical and empirical basis for the development of in-service programs, in particular for teachers, and has special applications for adult education.

Three questions arise concerning the application of the causal-genetic method in instructional settings using distance learning with new media:

1. Is a teacher or tutor needed for a learner in order to reach the zone of proximal development?
2. Is direct interaction between learners needed, implying that distance learning without such interaction will be not very productive?
3. What role is played by modern media in order to achieve a good, modern education?

As pointed out previously, activity is in its essence shared activity. The social character of activity can be very concrete and direct – in the form of teachers, parents, or peers interacting with the learner, or it can be more abstract and indirect (in the form of cultural means, results of the activity of other people being presented in an instructional environment and standing for the corresponding activity, representing it). The amount of direct inter-action depends on the developmental state of the activity (zone of actual per-formance and sense, role of intrinsic motivation; cf. Mandl, 1997) acquired so far. This means that if the learner is able to make sense of a special activity, to integrate the means of that activity offered or presented by an instruc-tional environment into his own activity, self-directed learning is possible. If not, special help in the form of direct pedagogical interaction is needed.[8] The teacher always represents the cooperating part in shared activity, but this part can be represented by the instructional design without the teacher as well (e.g., the problem of learning and comprehension of texts).

Direct interaction is not always necessary. But we have to assume (and all our experiences with distance learning have shown it) that students like direct contact, specifically face-to-face interaction in classroom settings. In

---

[8] Self-directed learning is not identical with self-learning (without any instruction or cooperation with more competent partners). The pedagogical problem entails carefully adapting instruction to meet or better create the zone of proximal development beginning from an existing zone of actual performance. Often direct instruction fails in showing developmental effects in students because it does not meet their zone of proximal development. The same is true for self-learning (i.e., the situation of a single learner who does not share his activity with others) because it often remains within the zone of actual performance.

any case cooperation and communication among students and between tutor and students has to be made possible.

At this point we should emphasize that an emphatic and competent teacher is a strong factor in the instructional process. That fact complicates the formative experiments, that is, the application of the causal-genetic method in classroom experiments. Even if the investigational design pays some respect to the variable "teacher" (i.e., one takes two or more experimental and control classes, and in each case the same teacher works in different instructional designs), a good teacher makes his or her own method and will be successful under all conditions, whereas a poor teacher can use each method and will have less success in each case. Distance learning or learning with new media offers a way to control for the teacher variable in formative experiments applying the causal-genetic method. Other than in the programmed classroom (which was the former way to organize a teacher-independent instruction), modern media, the computer, the Internet, and hypermedia offer many more chances for individual learning (time, modes, proceeding, etc.), as well as flexible access to different and unlimited information and multicoding of information. Thus, with the computer and modern media, an instructional environment may be created that facilitates learning. Computers and modern media allow many facilities for activity (pictures, sound, text, interaction, simulation) with the help of which it is possible to simulate the activity virtually. That makes it much easier for the learners to integrate the means of activity presented by computer programs into their own activity and to learn efficiently.

In contrast to the programmed classroom, authentic experiences of activity are possible here, and the program greatly facilitates the generation of meaning and motives.

FORMATIVE EXPERIMENT AND DISTANCE LEARNING

What special conditions have to be taken into account to develop a formative experiment using modern media and distance learning? One may think of the following four considerations when developing an educational program based on activity theory.

First, the program must be aimed at the formation of learning activity (respectively, the activity to be learned). The structural components of activity have to be elaborated explicitly in the program – these are aims, learning tasks, and learning means (first of all, learning actions). In particular, the program must present and introduce the use of such cultural tools, which allow one to practice and acquire the activity to be formed. In addition, all the other instructional moments with respect to instructional psychology have to be taken into account: summaries as moments of instruction, control of learning, choice of the learning units by the learner, learners' control of learning speed, didactical elements, and use of cognitive strategies (see Glaser & Bassock, 1989; Merrill, 1991; Reigeluth, 1983, 1987; Wulfeck, Dickieson, Apple, & Vogt 1993).

Second, in order to allow the learners to construct their own knowledge on a theoretical level and to initialize knowledge construction as a continuing process of self-organization, the learning material has to be structured and constructed according to the epistemology of "ascending from the abstract to the concrete" (for details, see Giest & Lompscher, 2003; Lompscher, 1999). Using initial abstractions that contain the essence of the object to be learned or acquired, the learner will ascend by concretizing these initial abstractions and apply the relevant knowledge in practice. Although initial abstractions are similar to advanced organizers in some respects, they differ from them because of their clear orientation toward theoretical thinking. They are necessary means for theoretical thinking and concept formation. Vygotsky (1964, 1987, 1998) showed the difference between pseudoconcepts and real (scientific) concepts theoretically. Davydov (1990) and his collaborators elaborated this distinction in great empirical detail.

Third, the introduction to the object and the learning activity itself must be meaningful. Other than in instructional design (sensu instructional psychology; see Reigeluth, 1983, 1987), we must not only pay attention to present advance organizers (Ausubel, 1963) but must also ensure that the learners can experience learning as a meaningful authentic activity. They have to experience the valence and the evidence of the learning object, aims, and means.

Fourth, social interaction, cooperation, and communication must be emphasized. As pointed out previously, activity in its essence is shared activity. The social character of activity can be very concrete and direct, in the form of teachers, parents, or peers interacting with the learner; or it can be more abstract and indirect, in the form of cultural means or tools representing the activity of other people in materialized forms. Instructional design must integrate many interactive moments into the programs because it must represent an abstract cooperation partner to interact with the learner. In this way, the learner can be involved in shared activity by using the cultural tools presented by the program. Nevertheless, the program must also support direct forms of communication and cooperation in many ways: inside (Internet use) and outside the interaction with the computer (face-to-face communication).

EMPIRICAL RESEARCH: AN EXAMPLE FOR
A FORMATION EXPERIMENT

As a general question we have asked, Does an educational program using hypermedia and distance learning that is developed in line with the previously mentioned principles produce learning results in the direction of dialectical thinking?

We also asked, in particular, Does students' cognitive orientation change what concerns the demands of systemic thinking and the relation between antinomical versus dialectical thinking (thinking in dialectical units as a special form of theoretical thinking)?

To give an example, ecological problems are mainly caused by the contradiction between nature and highly developed, industrialized human culture.[9] They are often discussed out of incompatible, antinomical positions – one stands for nature and the other one for culture (in terms of formal logic – either A or B). But sustainable development is only possible if both sides form a unit that enables the development of both sides – nature and culture. The solution for ecological problems is not to abolish the contradiction but to ensure its development. But to understand this, one has to think in units of contradictions – dialectically.

Applying the causal-genetic method in an instructional setting of distance learning with new media, we developed a hypermedia module (a complex educational program).[10] This program (Web on CD with the given possibility to present it on the Internet) was developed from a special perspective on learning and instruction, namely the approach of learning activity and its formation (Davydov 1999; Giest & Walgenbach 2000; Lompscher 1999). The learner should be given the opportunity for self-directed study under special conditions that are derived from the theory of learning activity.

This program was especially aimed at transdisciplinary scientific thinking dialectical thinking, and self-directed learning as a reflection of the need for life-long learning. In order to make these aims reachable, the program must offer various possibilities for self-directed learning.

It must offer an *introduction into the program*, which is aimed at the creation of meaningful learning. It should ensure the motivational basis for

---

[9] But there are also natural disasters that give rise to ecological problems.

[10] The program's content involves a complex as well as motivating ecological problem: one of the complex problems of our world consists in the necessity to change the present relationship between humans and nature. So far, both sides form a contradiction: Nature rules over humans or vice versa. The environmental problems of our world may be solved only if an alliance between humans and nature is created.

self-directed learning and offer advance organizers so that the learner knows exactly what he can learn within the program. The example of water will introduce the learner to the main problem of the relationship between mankind and nature in terms of contradictions: chaos versus order; determining versus being determined. These contradictions serve as learning means and initial abstractions. They represent a special kind of transdisciplinary knowledge that allows the learner to integrate disciplinary knowledge. In this process these transdisciplinary initial abstractions become concretized. They help to organize the disciplinary knowledge in order to fit in a transdisciplinary frame. This frame is a prerequisite for creating new knowledge that can overcome antinomical thinking and create a unity between mankind and nature.

On the basis of this orientation, the program must offer *learning goals, learning tasks, learning actions*, and different interactive learning tools, but the learner himself has to decide whether he wants to use and integrate them into his own activity.

It must offer a *structure of successive learning fields* that constitute learning steps, but the learner himself decides how he follows the learning steps offered (each of them is constructed in a way that allows a successful and meaningful learning inside the single learning step). This way the program offers possibilities to adapt it to the learner's need. The learner does not have to adapt; rather, the program must be constructed in such a way that the learner himself always decides what he wants to study, not the other way round. It is very important that the learner never loses the control over his learning, his learning activity. Depending on his interests, the learner decides what he studies more intensively and where he stays on the surface of the program. Nevertheless, the learning steps are not arbitrary; only the intensity and the depth of study depend on the learner's choice. In these learning steps, the learner ascends from the abstract (antinomical contradictions between mankind and nature in terms of order vs. chaos, and determining vs. being determined) to the concrete (creating units of those contradictions thinking dialectically) and practices this thinking by creating utopias and participating in ecological practice (for details, see Giest & Walgenbach, 2002).

Finally, the program must offer *learning aids* in many ways (information, direct help, interactive programs to study a special theme or problem, and integrated links to relevant Web sites). The program purposefully encourages the learner to turn the computer off and to learn together with peers in cooperative work and also to work directly in nature.

In this way, it represents an offer for the learner to involve himself in a special activity. Much more than a traditional instructional program where the interaction with the program represents the classroom situation, the program offers diverse possibilities to create the classroom with and without a teacher while working with the program or stimulated by the program without using the computer. The program serves as a stimulation or encouragement for learning and as a prototype of a transdisciplinary project-classroom in secondary education. It was also created to make a special contribution to teacher training. In our estimation, it was very stimulating for our teacher-students to work with it.

Our random sample consisted of fifty students. We designed our empirical investigation in the form of a pretest, treatment, and post-test design. The procedure of the instructional experiment can be characterized by three steps: we gave a short introduction to the research program followed by the pretest; the students worked independently on the basis and with the help of our educational program (five sessions, one and a half hours each); and we conducted the post-test, and the students evaluated the program through a questionnaire.

SELECTED RESULTS

In order to investigate changes in student's cognitive orientation effected by our educational program, we asked them to rate the poles of antinomical concept pairs concerning different complex subjects. The complex subjects (systems) were society, democracy, ecology, climate, and education. For instance, the students were asked to describe in which relationship environmental systems should stand in regard to "order and chaos," and to "to be determined and to determine." They should describe the relationship of the features just mentioned by numbers between 1 and 6 (6 indicating of highest relevance, 1 of least relevance). The features were, on the one side: order, to be determined, regulation, human intervention, use; and on the other side: chaos, to determine, self-organization, no use, no intervention. We expected that thinking dialectically would bring both antinomical poles closer to each other and that they would be rated as similarly important.

As results we found differences on the rated scales across all systems and for each individual one and an increasing correlation between the pole pairs in the post-test. As can be seen in Figure 6.2, over all systems the difference between the poles decreases. Here we found a significant difference $p = .002$ (Wilcoxon nonparametric test for two related random samples). Looking at the five different complex systems (Figure 6.3), we found significant differences between pre- and post-test for society ($p < .001$), ecology ($p < .024$), and climate ($p = .046$). The pole differences became smaller. So we can

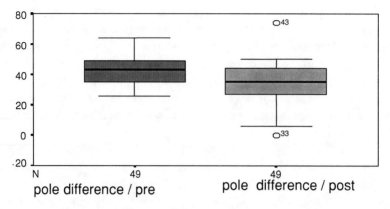

Figure 6.2. Difference of the rated poles across all systems.

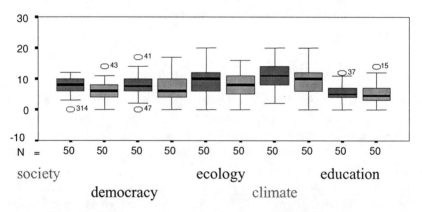

Figure 6.3. Difference of the rated poles across each individual system.

conclude that thinking in antinomies decreases. This interpretation is confirmed in the next results as well.

The analyses of the ratings showed increasing similarities concerning the five different systems. In the pretest, we found significant correlations ($r = .477, p < .01$) for society and democracy, climate and ecology. This is not very surprising, because one has to expect a correlation between systems that are connected. In the post-test, we found a significant correlation between climate and ecology; society, democracy, ecology, and education ($.498 \leq r \geq .398; p < .01$). Further, we found (as a trend) less negative correlation of the poles (e.g., order becomes generally less and chaos higher rated – the poles came closer). We may conclude that, concerning the various systems or the concepts that represent these systems, as the thinking in antinomies decreases, the differences between the systems become smaller. We can interpret this

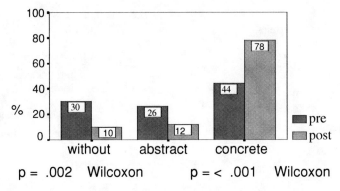

Figure 6.4. Concrete examples of concept pairs from everyday life: Concrete versus abstract.

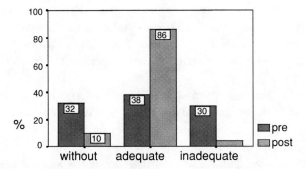

Figure 6.5. Concrete examples of concept pairs from everyday life: Adequate versus inadequate answers.

finding as an indication for transdisciplinary thinking and for crossing the boundaries of domain specific knowledge.

Subsequently, in order to get information about the explicitness, preciseness, and adequacy of the knowledge, we asked the students to give a concrete example for the concept pairs (order vs. chaos, determining vs. being determined, responsibility vs. freedom, reality vs. possibility) from everyday life.

We found that in the post-test the examples given by the students became more concrete (we registered fewer abstract concepts). In this respect the examples differ significantly in pre- and post-test (p = .002 Wilcoxon). In the post-test the examples became also more adequate (we registered fewer antinomies in the students' answers – p < .001 Wilcoxon). The number of the given answers (examples) in the post-test increased as well (fewer students without an answer – see Figures 6.4 and 6.5).

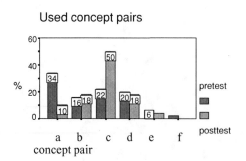

Legend of abscissa:

a)   without a solution

b)   order vs. chaos

c)   determining vs. being determined

d)   freedom vs. responsibility

e)   possibility vs. reality

f)   other answers

Figure 6.6. Concept pairs used in the students' examples.

When we compare the concept pairs used in the students' examples in pre- and post-test, it is conspicuous that order versus chaos and especially determining versus being determined were often used. The comparison between pre- and post-test showed overall an almost significant difference ($p = .065$), but the comparison between the categories "without a solution" and "determining versus being determined" showed a significant difference ($p = .02$) (see Figure 6.6).

It seems that this concept pair used as an initial abstraction has an excellent influence on students' dialectical thinking about everyday life situations. This motivated us to use the antinomian concept pair "determining versus being determined" in a program especially developed for primary school students.

Analyzing the students' texts, we noticed that in the post-test the students' descriptions were much more detailed than in the pretest. In the pretest we found more antinomies, whereas in the post-test the interaction was predominant. Some typical answers of the students that show this trend of development may illustrate this part of the investigation.

> Student 1 pretest: "Outside-determination of children by teachers will produce citizens who are not able to decide independently. The self-determination of the individual leads the human to learn to recognize the effects of his own actions."
>
> Student 1 post-test: "It is important to notice reality and to live with it, but it is also important to see the given possibilities (utopia) and to create possible reality."
>
> Student 2 pretest: "Freedom is a marriage without children; you can do what you like to do. Responsibility is a marriage with children. You must carry the responsibility and can't do what you want to do."
>
> Student 2 post-test: "Freedom isn't possible without responsibility; both form a unit."

The empirical investigation thus showed that the main hypothesis could be verified. The basic theoretical approach and its practical realization in the form of a hypermedia educational program that is based on the theory of learning activity shows a way to systemic education, to the formation of complex and dialectical thinking. What we could not show in this chapter is that aesthetic perception also developed in the direction of more sensitivity for situations close to nature and for the beauty of nature. So learning with the educational program produces changes not only in the cognitive but also in the aesthetical dimension of learning activity.

Under the condition of self-directed learning guided by the program, self-directed learning was registered. We found that students acquired knowledge and developed the ability to think more dialectically. In our eyes, this is also a prerequisite for a main component of systemic thinking. To be able to deal with complexity, the student must overcome linear and monocausal thinking and thinking in antinomies. The results of our empirical investigation showed that such a cognitive shift took place in our students.

CONCLUSIONS

The investigation showed that modern instructional design developed with respect to the needs of the formation of learning activity can encourage students' cognitive development in the direction of theoretical thinking, especially dialectical thinking. Using hypermedia and distance learning, university students reached a new level of thinking. This level does not mark as yet a new developmental state, but it points to the fact that it is an important step to reach a new zone of proximal development characterized by the student's growing ability to make practical use of theoretical thinking. We think it is important to notice that the zone of proximal development is a concept to be used with reference not only to child development but also to the development of adult learners. And it is important also for instruction in the frame of adult education.

From our viewpoint, hypermedia and distance learning will be an important means in adult education. We were able to show a way to promote dialectical thinking of students using hypermedia and distance learning. This was done in self-directed learning and we were able to describe some necessary conditions that must be taken into account when developing a program oriented toward self-directed distance learning: the program must be developed on the basis of a theoretical approach that is able to explain development – in our case the theory of the formation of learning activity. The structure of the course of study must be organized according to a well-defined epistemology – in our case, ascending from the abstract to the concrete. The program must offer possibilities for social interaction, cooperation, and communication, which also means that the learner must have the chance to adapt the course of study presented by the program to his or her needs by concretizing the (still abstract) means of learning offered by the program according to his or her concrete interests, prerequisites, and skills. And the program must offer the chance for a hiatus from the computer and encourage the student to study without the computer in real nature or together with peers, whether in face-to-face situations or by communicating and cooperating with the means of new media (chat, e-mail, video-conferencing, etc.).

We were able to show that the causal-genetic method is applicable to the use of modern media. The real social partner may not be present, but it is also possible to become involved in shared activity by interacting with an educational program that represents a new kind or new facets of a complex, not-yet-acquired activity. Working with the program must allow the learner to be involved in that special activity, which at the same time means that the program has to be oriented toward that sense-making activity as a whole and not toward single tasks. The formation of new psychological functions and structures is related to a special point of view concerning the concept of the zone of proximal development: New developmental stages and new levels of thinking are much more connected with an introduction to new cultural tools, to new levels of activity than with matured psychological functions. And as a result, they are much more dependent on instruction because the zone of proximal development (as well as the zone of actual development) is created by instruction. But more research is surely needed. In this investigation we were able to investigate only one way of constructing an educational program and of forming components of theoretical thinking. In further investigations we intend to focus on the construction of alternative programs derived from other learning theories that may lead to other conclusions for learning and instruction.

References

Adey, P. S., & Shayer, M. (1994). *Really raising standards: Cognitive intervention and academic achievement.* London: Routledge.

Aikenhead, G. (1994). A review of research into the outcomes of STS teaching. In K. Boersma, K. Kortland, & J. van Trommel (Eds.), *Science and technology education in a demanding society* (7th IOSTE Symposium) (pp. 13–24). Enschede: National Institute for Curriculum Development (SLO).

Allal, L., & Ducrey, P. (2000). Assessment of or in the zone of proximal development. *Learning and Instruction, 10* (2), 137–152.

Ausubel, D. P. (1963). *The psychology of meaningful verbal learning.* New York: Grune & Stratton.

Baumert, J., Klieme, E., Neubrand, M., Prenzel, M., Schiefele, U., Schneider, W., Stanat, P., Tillmann, K.-J., & Weiß, M. (Eds.). (2001). *PISA 2000: Basiskompetenzen von Schülerinnen und Schülern im internationalen Vergleich.* Opladen: Leske + Budrich.

Baumert, J., Lehmann, R., et al. (1997). *TIMSS – Mathematisch-naturwissenschaftlicher Unterricht im internationalen Vergleich.* Opladen: Leske + Budrich.

Black, P., & Atkin, J. M. (Eds.). (1996). *Changing the subject: Innovation in science, mathematics and technology education.* London: Routledge in association with OECD.

Bruner, J. (1970). *Der Prozeß der Erziehung.* Düsseldorf: Schwann.

Carugati, F. (1999). From Piaget and Vygotsky to learning activity. In M. Hedegaard & J. Lompscher (Eds.), *Learning activity and development* (pp. 211–234). Aarhus: Aarhus University Press.

Chaiklin, S. (2003). The zone of proximal development in Vygotsky's analysis of learning and instruction. In A. Kozulin, B. Gindis, V. Ageyev, & S. Miller (Eds.), *Vygotsky's educational theory and practice in cultural context* (pp. 39–64). Cambridge: Cambridge University Press.

Davydov, V. V. (1990). *Types of generalization in instruction: Logical and psychological problems in the structuring of school curricula* (J. Teller, Trans.). Reston, VA: National Council of Teachers of Mathematics.

Davydov, V. V. (1998). The concept of developmental teaching. *Journal of Russian and East European Psychology, 36* (4), 11–36.

Davydov, V. V. (1999). What is real learning activity? In M. Hedegaard & J. Lompscher (Eds.), *Learning activity and development* (pp. 123–138). Aarhus: Aarhus University Press.

Engeström, Y. (1978). *Learning by expanding.* Helsinki: Orienta Konsultit Oy.

Engeström, Y. (1990). *Learning, working and imaging: Twelve studies in activity theory.* Helsinki: Orienta Konsultit Oy.

Engeström, Y., Miettinen, R., & Punamäki, R.-L. (Eds.). (1999). *Perspectives on activity theory.* Cambridge: Cambridge University Press.

Fichtner, B. (1999). Activity theory as methodology: The epistemological revolution of the computer and the problem of its appropriation. In M. Hedegaard & J. Lompscher (Eds.), *Learning activity and development* (pp. 71–92). Aarhus: Aarhus University Press.

Fricke, R. (1995a). Evaluation von Multimedia. In L. J. Issing & P. Klimsa (Eds.), *Information und Lernen mit Multimedia – ein Lehrbuch zur Multimedia-Didaktik* (pp. 401–413). Heidelberg: Springer.

Fricke, R. (1995b). Über den richtigen Umgang mit Qualitätskriterien für Lernsoftware. Arbeiten aus dem Institut für Empirische Pädagogik und Instruktionspsychologie der TU Braunschweig, Bericht Nr. 14 (3/95).

Giest, H. (1997). Zur kausalgenetischen Methode in der Unterrichtsforschung. In E. Glumpler & S. Luchtenberg (Eds.), *Handbuch Grundschulforschung* (Vol. 1, pp. 167–179). Weinheim: Beltz, Deutscher Studienverlag.

Giest, H., & Lompscher, J. (2003). Formation of learning activity and theoretical thinking in science teaching. In A. Kozulin, B. Gindis, V. Ageyev, & S. Miller (Eds.), *Vygotsky's educational theory and practice in cultural context* (pp. 267–288). Cambridge: Cambridge University Press.

Giest, H., & Walgenbach, W. (2000). Entwicklung von Multimedia- Bausteinen zur Ökologischen Grundbildung. In R. Jänkel & W. Loschelder (Eds.), *Umweltforschung an der Universität Potsdam* (pp. 23–31). (Brandenburgische Umwelt Berichte -BUB-, vol. 8)

Giest, H., & Walgenbach, W. (2002). System-learning – a new challenge to education – bridging special field to transdisciplinary learning. In B. Zeltserman (Ed.), *Obrazovanije 21 veka: dostizhenija i perspektivij. Mezhdunarodnij sbornik teoreticheskikh, metodicheskikh i prakticheskikh rabot po problemam obrazovanija* (Education in the 21st century: Results and perspectives. International anthology of theoretical, didactical and practical work on problems of education) (pp. 21–37). Riga: Pedagogiskais centrs "Eksperiments."

Glaser, R., & Bassock, M. (1989). Learning theory and the study of instruction. *Annual Review of Psychology, 40,* 631–666.

Glasersfeld, E. v. (1995). *Radical constructivism: A way of knowing and learning.* London: Falmer Press.

Heisenberg, W. (1977). *Tradition der Wissenschaft.* Munich: Hanser. http://www.pisa.oecd.org.

Huber, L. (2001). Stichwort: Fachliches Lernen (Headword: Domain-specific learning). *Zeitschrift für Erziehungswissenschaft, 3* (1), 307–331.

Kurzweil, R. (2000). *The age of spiritual machines. Homo sapiens: Leben im 21. Jahrhundert – was bleibt vom Menschen?* Munich: Econ.

Lektorskij, V. A. (1990). *Activity: Theory, methodology, and problems.* Orlando, FL: Paul M. Deutsch Press.

Leontiev, A. N. (1978). *Activity, consciousness, personality.* Englewood Cliffs, NJ: Prentice-Hall.

Leontiev, A. N. (1981). *Problems of the development of mind.* Moscow: Progress.

Lompscher, J. (1999). Learning activity and its formation: Ascending from the abstract to the concrete. In M. Hedegaard & J. Lompscher (Eds.), *Learning activity and development* (pp. 139–166). Aarhus: Aarhus University Press.

Lompscher, J. (2002). The category of activity as a principal constituent of cultural-historical psychology. In D. Robbins & A. Stetsenko (Eds.), *Voices within Vygotsky's non-classical psychology: Past, present, future* (pp. 79–99). New York: Nova Science.

Mähler, C. (1999). Naive Theorien im kindlichen Denken. *Zeitschrift für Entwicklungspsychologie und Pädagogische Psychologie, 31* (2), 55–65.

Mandl, H. (1997). How should we learn to really learn? (Interview). *Learnline, 4,* 195–199.

Martin, M. O., & Kelly, D. L. (Eds.). (1996). *Third international mathematics and science study.* Chestnut Hill, MA: Boston College.

Maturana, H. R., & Pörksen, B. (2002). Der Schüler lernt den Lehrer. *Pädagogik, 7–8,* 75–77.

Mayer, R. E., & Moreno, R. (2002). Aids to computer-based multimedia learning. *Learning and Instruction, 12* (1), 107–120.

Meer, E. v.d. (1996). Gesetzmäßigkeiten und Steuerungsmöglichkeiten des Wissenserwerbs. In F. E. Weinert (Eds.), *Psychologie des Lernens und der Instruktion* (pp. 209–248). Göttingen: Hogrefe. (Enzyklopädie der Psychologie, Serie Pädagogische Psychologie, vol. 2)

Merkys, G. (1996). Kultur-historische Schule und Methodologie der pädagogisch-psychologischen Forschung. In J. Lompscher (Eds.), *Entwicklung und Lernen aus kulturhistorischer Sicht* (pp. 143–162). Marburg: BdWi-Verlag. (Internationale Studien zur Tätigkeitstheorie, vol. 4/1)

Merrill, M. D. (1991). Constructivism and instructional design. *Educational Technology, 31*, 45–53.

Metz, K. E. (1995). Reassessment of developmental constraints on children's science instruction. *Review of Educational Research, 65* (2), 93–127.

Miettinen, R. (2002). Varieties of constructivism in education: Where do we stand? *Lifelong Learning in Europe, 1*, 41–48.

Mikkilä-Erdmann, M. (2001). Improving conceptual change concerning photosynthesis through text design. *Learning and Instruction, 11* (3), 241–257.

Mugler, F., & Landbeck, R. (2000). Learning, memorization and understanding among distance learners in the South Pacific. *Learning and Instruction 10* (2), 179–202.

Piaget, J. (1970). L'évolution intellectuelle entre l'adolescence et lâge adulte (Intellectual evolution from adolescence to adulthood). *Human Development (1972) 15*, 1–15.

Reigeluth, C. M. (Ed.). (1983). *Instructional-design theories and models: An overview of their current status.* Hillsdale, NJ: Lawrence Erlbaum.

Reigeluth, C. M. (Ed.). (1987). *Instructional theories in action.* Hillsdale, NJ: Lawrence Erlbaum.

Reinhold, P., & Bünder, W. (2001). Stichwort: Fächerübergreifender Unterricht (Headword: Transdisciplinary classroom). *Zeitschrift für Erziehungswissenschaft, 3* (1), 334–357.

Roth, G. (2002). *Fühlen, Denken, Handeln: Wie das Gehirn unser Verhalten steuert.* Frankfurt am Main: Suhrkamp.

Saldern, M. v. (1998). Die Aufgabenfülle der Grundschule und ihrer Pädagogik. *Zeitschrift für Pädagogik, 44* (6), 907–924.

Sodian, B. (1998). Wissenschaftliches Denken. In D. H. Rost, *Handwörterbuch der Pädagogischen Psychologie* (pp. 566–570). Weinheim: Beltz, Psychologie Verlags Union.

Solomon, J., & Aikenhead, G. (Eds.). (1994). *STS Education: International perspectives on reform.* New York: Teachers College Press.

Tenenbaum, G., Naidu, S., Jegede, O., & Austin, J. (2001). Constructivist pedagogy in conventional on-campus and distance learning practice: An exploratory investigation. *Learning and Instruction, 11* (2), 87–112.

Vosniadou, S., Ioannides, A., Dimitrakopoulou, A., & Papademetriou, E. (2001). Designing learning environments to promote conceptual change in science. *Learning and Instruction, 11* (4–5), 381–420.

Walgenbach, W. (2000). *Interdisziplinäre Systembildung – Eine Aktualisierung bildungstheoretischer Ansätze.* Frankfurt am Main: Peter Lang.

Wiser, M., & Amin, T. (2001). "Is heat hot?" Inducing conceptual change by integrating everyday and scientific perspectives on thermal phenomena. *Learning and Instruction, 11* (4–5), 331–356.

Wulfeck, W. H., Dickieson, J. L., Apple J., & Vogt, L. (1993). The automation of curriculum development. Using the Authoring Instructional Materials (AIM) System. *Instructional Science, 21*, 255–267.

Vygotsky, L. S. (1964). *Denken und Sprechen.* Berlin: Akademie Verlag.

Vygotsky, L. S. (1987). *Ausgewählte Schriften* (Vol. 2). Berlin: Volk und Wissen.

Vygotsky, L. S. (1992). *Geschichte der höheren psychischen Funktionen.* Münster and Hamburg: Lit. (Fortschritte der Psychologie, vol. 5)

Vygotsky, L. S. (1998). *Thinking and speech.* In R. W. Reiber & A. S. Carton (Eds.), *The collected works of L. S. Vygotsky: Vol. 1. Problems of general psychology* (pp. 39–285). New York: Plenum Press.

Yager, R. E. (Ed.). (1996). *Science, technology, society: As reform in science education.* Albany: State University of New York Press.

7

Constructivism and Meaning Construction

Ronald Arendt

A *Tai-chi-chuan* apprentice follows the steps of the master in the beginning of his training. As he reaches a stage of proficiency, he creates his own interpretation of the movements proposed by his master. Being able to control the technique, he will reinvent the learned movements, adapting them to his own manner of interpretation. Without the initial context, he would not reach this stage of expertise. Experience made it possible to surpass the sociocultural determinism.

This chapter intends to analyze in some detail the example of the first paragraph. In its apparent simplicity, a series of complex questions is posed to the psychologist. How should we think about learning? What are the cognitive developmental processes? How should we define the influence of the context and the individual participation? Are we obliged to choose between an approach centered in the individual or the environment? My aim is to propose a solution to some of those questions, starting from the sociocultural theory. However, I think that it is important to establish my own theoretical position, although I cannot do it in a systematic form in this chapter. While I consider the conceptual ideas posed by Lev Vygotsky to be fundamental, as well as those advanced in contemporary developmental psychology by authors such as Scribner, Cole, Fogel, and Valsiner, I do not think that those positions are in conflict with the psychogenetic model proposed by Jean Piaget.

In this context, the analyses of the symposium "Piaget and Vygotsky Again: Anything New under the Sun?" presented at the Third Conference of the ISCRAT are of significance, as they indicated the sensibility of Piaget to the social questions and showed the viability of thinking about the relationship between psychogenetic and sociohistorical approaches. I think that an individual can reach a proficiency phase, in a constructionist sense, and *at the same time* reach a more elaborated stage in cognitive development from the viewpoint of Piaget's theory. Such assumptions are part of the conclusions

I reached in a study about the object of psychology (Arendt, 1999). The main problem is the *balance*, the *symmetry* of the relation of the individual with the environment. According to my conclusions, in contemporary psychological theories this relation is generally unbalanced. Either one attaches immense weight to the individual, to his or her subjective concerns, and allows for only a minimal role for the environment, or the individual is conceived of as a result of political, social, cultural, and historical forces antecedent to him and, in this case, his or her opportunity for development is viewed as being minimal. I think that it is necessary to reach a balance or symmetry in the theorizations of this relation, and that will be the leading argument in the course of this chapter.

CULTURAL DETERMINISM AND ITS SURPASSING

An author who nicely expresses the viewpoint I have just defended is Bronckart (2000). Emphasizing the importance of socialization as a fundamental developmental mechanism, he observes that such an assumption implies positing ourselves in the logic of the social interaction movement, which follows the stream of ideas in human sciences that analyze thinking as a phenomenon parallel to the construction of a sociocultural world. Influenced by Marxism, contemporary social interactionism will emphasize specific ingredients of human contexts (like collective activities, social formations, language) in semiotic mediation processes and in the construction of higher psychological functions. Defining culture as a semantic of the social, Bronckart stressed the importance of the effects of cultural dimensions on the development of the person. The conclusion of his chapter is of particular interest to the argument of this essay.

The contemporary person, Bronckart says, is formed in contact with a body of universalized knowledge, the content of which is marked by the formal character of this order of knowledge. In such a manner, even considering that the constitution of human thinking is marked by the cultural, development manifests itself in the progressive positioning of capacities of generalization and abstraction. "Thinking purifies itself, becomes out of context, taking the form of logical-mathematical implications" (Bronckart, 2000, p. 15). This tendency strengthens itself with the development of exchanges and confrontations between cultures of different origins. The multiplicity leads to comparison and to the possibility of taking distance with relation to particular cultural models. We note the proximity of this reasoning with the analysis of Rorty (1991) about ethnocentrism. Following him, we are at the start ethnocentric, and only in contact with other spaces of argumentation do we drop our particular viewpoint. This move out of the context and semantics of thinking, affirms Bronckart, seems to constitute the necessary condition for persons to permit their intervention in the developmental process of their group, not simply reproducing the cultural acquisitions but participating entirely in the collective process of alimentation and transformation of the whole collective constructions. In synthesis, "if the cultural affects or determines the initial phases of the development, the participation in the evolution and transformation of this dimension requires a deflection in the order of the cognitive, or better, of the psychological universal" (Bronckart, 2000, p. 15).

Bronckart's important conclusions, however, particularly those which concern the surpassing of the social by the individual, refer to adult individuals and their socialization process and formation of the superior stages of psychogenetic development. How do we think about the social when we are dealing with a child in development? Here, the constructivism of Ernst von Glasersfeld provides the answer.

THE RADICAL CONSTRUCTIVISM OF ERNST VON GLASERSFELD

Traditionally, constructivism is linked to the work of Piaget. My aim in this chapter is to introduce the constructivism proposed by Glasersfeld. In a debate following a speech in which Evelyn Fox Keller talked about the paradoxes of scientific subjectivity (in Schnitman 1994), she received a surprising critique by Glasersfeld: "it is impossible for me to agree with some of your positions," he said, "because they presume a society that is out there, in which everybody in a certain manner incorporates himself almost automatically and I don't know how this can be done." Fox Keller proposed to substitute "to observe" for "to produce," "to participate." Glasersfeld argued that those actions, obviously social, are concepts that must be constructed beforehand by the subject of experience and that *which* is not sociological. The society is not "out there." The social, in the viewpoint of the subject is a subjective experience. "How does society contribute to the construction of individuals?" asked Fox Keller. "The family is the mechanism by which societies produce individuals. The society defines what constitutes kinship. And it is through this activity that little children absorb, acquire their values, their social identities." Glasersfeld answered that he could agree with this, but noted that it is a description made from the *outside*. What is to "know" what the baby knows, he asked. If we presuppose that he reacts affectively to his mother, are we not supposing a reaction of a child to an adult world when we talk about interaction? The affect "in the viewpoint of the child is something that affects it, but he or she doesn't know what it is...he or she doesn't know in the beginning that this is an interaction with another or another thing. He or she experiences it. The child has to learn to distinguish, by itself in its experience, what the other is." At another moment, now in a debate following a speech by W. Barnett Pearce, Glasersfeld (in Schnitman, 1994, p. 284) argued, "nobody convinces someone with argumentations. He doesn't convince them with good or bad argumentations. People modify their viewpoints only by themselves, when they realize that something does not work." If we adopt the model of the metaphor proposed by Donald Davidson, to be developed later in this chapter, one could say that arguments do not carry meanings, but they provoke the individual, induce him to think them over, and attribute a meaning to them, based upon his own experience.

Giambattista Vico points with his "verum ipsum factum" in the direction of the construction of knowledge by the subject, opening the way to the "esse est percipi" by Georges Berkeley, to the biology of Jacob von Uexküll in the beginning of the twentieth century, and up to contemporary authors like George Kelly, Humberto Maturana, Francisco Varela, Heinz von Foerster, and Ernst von Glasersfeld. The basic principle of radical constructivism is that *every* kind of knowledge depends on the structure of the knower. The radical form comes from the refusal of any type of objective knowledge, a strategy that becomes clear in the treatment given to perception. Contrary to classical, empiricist formulae that argue that action is guided by perception, authors like Maturana and Varela invert the formulae and affirm that, in enacting (of the Spanish *en accion*), perception will be guided by the action of the individual in the environment. Constructivists like Glasersfeld simply refrain from statements about what might be in "outside reality." In this sense, second-order cybernetics, proposed by the physicist and cyberneticist Heinz von Foerster, will help us to take another, more complex look at the world. First-order cybernetics separates the subject of the object and assumes a world "down there," independent of the individual. It is circular.

We learn to see ourselves as parts of a world to understand, that we want to observe. The whole situation of description penetrates in a new field in which we must, suddenly assume the responsibility for our observations...; the references to a world independent of our observations are replaced by indications realized by the person himself. . . . The reflection about the meaning and purpose of the observations also gain another dimension; it begins to become clear for us why we ultimately want to know or experience. (von Foerster 1998, p. 16)

Instead of the correspondence to an external reality, Glasersfeld considers more adequate the concept of "fitness." Glasersfeld (1998) gives us several examples: a boat that navigates at night between reefs, a "blind flight" of a pilot operating by instruments, a pedestrian walking in a town that he does not know well. It would be viable to construct a "map of possible ways" for the individual, depending on his experience. Better, more adapted, existing solutions are not always available. The individual will have to elaborate those possible ways through his own reflected action. In connection with reflection about action, Glasersfeld (1997) gives a significant example. A little girl is playing with a ball that she goes on kicking, when suddenly she reaches a hill and, to her surprise, the ball rolls to her feet. Then she asks: "How did the ball roll toward me?" (p. 18). This example permits us to infer that in some sense the girl is attentive to her experience and can reflect about it. This is the kind of question that after several trials would lead an imaginative thinker to formulate an explanatory principle, says Glasersfeld. He wants to understand this act of creation, of individual invention.

In an essay in honor of Piaget, he criticizes approaches exclusively founded in social or cultural determinism. It is clear that Piaget did not ignore the role of social interaction. But he saw that there was a great quantity of knowledge acquired by the individual for himself. Glasersfeld (1997) gives two examples. Some of you, he observes, may have witnessed this striking phenomenon: some infants invent a quite spectacular method of moving around the room while sitting on their potties. They have certainly not been prompted, nor have they ever seen it performed by an adult. It is wholly their own accomplishment, constructed, one might say, in splendid isolation. In another example, Glasersfeld imagines Pythagoras observing the pattern of the tiled floor of congruent isosceles triangles set in squares. Suddenly Pythagoras saw that the squares formed over the long side of a triangle contained four of the triangles, and the square formed over the short side contained two. It was the first conception of the theorem that was to make him famous for thousands of years, says Glasersfeld. In both cases, significant new knowledge is constructed by an independent individual mind. The argument that potties or tiles are artifacts is not enough to question the novelty of such constructions, considering that they were not designed to work for locomotion or geometry, concludes Glasersfeld (1997, p. 22). In sum, the aim of constructivist investigations is to understand how the individual generates knowledge. If one presupposes a social nature through which children grow and are introduced to intellectual life, one cannot explain how those born in a linguistic community generate a new language.

It becomes, therefore, clear that Glasersfeld is not against the social dimension, his theoretical and methodological emphasis being the construction of this dimension by the individual. It is in this sense that I discuss the chapter of van Oers (2000) about knowledge transference.

CONTINUOUS RECONTEXTUALIZATION AND THE GENERALIZATION OF KNOWLEDGE AND SKILLS

The subject investigated by van Oers is the generality of learning outcomes. He argues that human beings do not have to reconstruct new repertories of actions all the time they encounter new situations. It would be better to conceptualize a recontextualization of those actions. The functionality of the learning outcomes, through a variety of situations, would be at the same time a personal re-creation of the meaning effected in each situation by the individual and a process of cultural influence that, involving other people, could be understood as *a co-reconstruction of cultural meanings*. Transference would be always *context-bound* and dependent on the meaning that the person attributes to the situation. To van Oers, the generalization of knowledge would be processed in the following way: the person facing a new situation would interpret it while requiring a specific type of activity and would actualize it as a function of what he or she knows about the resources that this activity requires, accomplishing the actions based on those resources or reinterpreting the situation as requiring another type of activity, or restructuring some element inherent to the activity. Searching for empirical evidence for this theoretical formulation, the author gives an account of a dialogue between a thirteen-year-old student and his teacher concerning the solution of a complex problem in physics. The conclusion of van Oers is that effectively a reconstruction occurred in the solution reached by the student, rather than a simple employment of common elements.

Although, in general, the analysis by the author in the discussion of his theoretical approach and its empirical example converge with the argument of this chapter, I would like to stress some disagreements. In his critique, van Oers concedes that the Swiss psychologist had already demonstrated that generalization is a constructive process. However, Piaget's contribution had two conceptual problems: his lack of attention for discursive processes and his proposal for a developmental model of stages. In opposition to Piaget, van

Oers (2000, p. 22) argues that "all types of generalization can be present at any moment, distributed over different participants in the process. When the student is still attempting to find an empirical generalization, the teacher can interact with the student on the basis of a more generalized theory, and in fact introduce this type of generalization in the discourse with the student." Van Oers does not see any reasons for the stages to follow one another, because they are often simultaneously present in the discourse, distributed over the participants. In Piaget's approach, the emphasis is primarily on the transition from one stage to another, whereas, in van Oers's viewpoint, transference or generalization focuses on transformation and continuity.

If the first critique of van Oers is consistent – after all, Piaget really did not deepen the study of discourse processes (whereas the thesis that he did not pay attention to the social dimension is no longer supported today) – I do not think that the second critique refutes the stage model proposed by Piaget. We should not forget that in van Oers's example the stages, "distributed over the participants," are distributed over an adult and a thirteen-year-old student. From a Piagetian point of view, the participants have already reached the superior stages of development, allowing their interchange. I do not think that "all types of generalization" could be present at any moment. Suppose, for example, that the teacher would submit the problem of physics to a child of an early stage, say, of six years old. She would not be able to solve the problem. Although I agree with the Vygotskian conception of the generalization of knowledge and skill as part of a reconstructive process in a contextualized task charged with meaning, I do not see why this should lead to the abandonment of a stage account based on Piaget.

Van Oers's analyses are obviously compatible with those of Richard Rorty. It suffices to see the title of an essay by Rorty, published in 1991: "Inquiry as Recontextualization: An Anti-dualist Account of Interpretation." In this chapter, however, I wish to finalize my argument in favor of individual agency in context with the discussion of an excellent text by Rorty about metaphor and meaning construction, based on Donald Davidson's thinking.

DAVIDSON AND RORTY ON METAPHOR

In an essay about metaphor, Rorty (1991) exposed ideas very close to the argument of this chapter. Rorty starts with a statement of philosopher Mary Hesse that metaphors are instruments indispensable to intellectual and moral progress. Rorty, on the one hand, agrees with Hesse about the importance of metaphor but, on the other, questions Hesse's position that metaphors carry meanings – more generally, that a metaphor has cognitive content. Rorty proposes that we follow Donald Davidson's account of metaphor, putting it outside the pale of semantics: A metaphorical sentence has no meaning other than its literal sense. Metaphors are now seen as unfamiliar events in the natural world – causes of changing belief and desires – rather than as representations of unfamiliar worlds that are symbolic rather than natural. For Davidson, metaphors allow for a greater knowledge of the world and are the causes of our ability to do a lot of things "e.g. be more sophisticated and interesting people, emancipate ourselves from tradition, transvalue our values, gain or lose religious faith – without having to interpret these latter abilities as functions of increased cognitive abilities" (Rorty, 1991, p. 163).

Rorty reminds us of an image of Willard Quine: the realm of meaning is a relatively small cleared area within the jungle of use, whose boundaries are constantly being both extended and encroached upon. To say "metaphor belongs exclusively to the domain of use" is to say that it falls outside the cleared area (Rorty, 1991, p. 164). Metaphors are related to unpredictable and irregular uses of language. If "understanding" or "interpreting" means "bringing under an antecedent scheme," then metaphors, says Rorty, cannot be understood or interpreted. But if we extend these two notions to mean something like "making use of" or "coping with," he continues, then we can say that we come to understand metaphors in the same way that we come to understand anomalous natural phenomena. We do so by revising our theories so as to fit them around the new material. We interpret metaphors in the same way we interpret such anomalies – by casting around possible revisions in our theories that may help to handle the surprises (p. 167). Rorty quotes Davidson saying that, if we "give up the idea that the metaphor carries a message," we can see that the various theories about "how metaphors work" do not "provide a method for deciphering an encoded content . . . but tell us (or try to tell us) something about the *effects* metaphors have on us." The acquisition of knowledge would be, after all, a psychological matter, argues Rorty (p. 168).

How does this process work? When live metaphors become literal, commonplace, and familiar, they die and transcend the line between being "mere" causes of belief and reasons for belief. In this manner, they can be described and expressed in an intentional language. In fine, when they are being "received" in the familiarization process, metaphors enter Quine's cleared area, but we cannot know beforehand how they will work.

CONCLUSIONS

In all the conceptual examples I presented – the positions of Bronckart, Glasersfeld, van Oers, Davidson, and Rorty – I tried to answer the questions posed in the introduction to this chapter, seeking to indicate the balance between the action of the individual and his interaction and involvement in an environment that constitutes him and is constituted by him, in the constant alternation of the experience lived by the subject and the challenges imposed on him while living in a specific context. I tried to indicate how this balance in the individual-society relation is confirmed by several postmodern contemporary approaches. In defending this balance, I argued for the coexistence of Piaget's and Vygotsky's conceptual models. In this conclusion, I want to stress the compatibility of my analyses with those of sociocultural theory, especially with the studies of communication and metacommunication (Branco, 2000; Fogel & Branco, 1997). Such studies of children appear to be particularly interesting for the argument of this chapter. If, as these works indicate, subjective configurations emerge through the influence of sociogenetic factors, these will have an effective impact only in relation to the individual action system, as I tried to discuss. If metacommunication systems are of fundamental significance in the construction of interaction patterns, the examples by Branco and his research group describe situations in which the children's agency points to a pause for reflection and meaning construction. The children, in those examples, are at the same time, through their experience, constructing the social dimension and reflecting about their environment and producing a recontextualization of their actions, giving new lived situations. Generally speaking, the various examples utilized in this chapter permit one to conclude that children or adults are called upon to reflect about and psychologically elaborate the solicitations of the environment.

In one of his more recent texts, dedicated to the constructivist approach of meaning construction, Glasersfeld (1999) argues that, if language games are an occasion for such meaning construction, they do not explain why children play them. Kenneth Gergen, following Glasersfeld, is aware of this and notes that "the constructionist is centrally concerned with such matters as negotiation, cooperation, conflict, rhetoric, ritual, roles, social scenarios, and the like, but avoids psychological explanations of micro social process" (Gergen quoted by Glasersfeld, 1999, p. 3). Glasersfeld does not see why those instances have to be antagonistic. The psychogenetic model that he defends "could help the socially oriented researchers to ground their findings far more solidly than by assuming that the knowledge and the language of a social group could be instilled into its members through the simple occurrence of language games and other forms of social interactions" (Glasersfeld, 1999, p. 3). Comparing English and French, Glasersfeld stresses the countless differences of conceptualization existing between the two languages. "Although individuals necessarily adapt the meaning they associate with words to what they perceive to be the usage of the community ... the meanings of the words they use is at best *compatible* in the linguistic interactions with other speakers; but such compatibility remains forever relative to the limited number of actual interactions the individual has had in his or her past. What speakers have learned to mean remains their own construction" (Glasersfeld, 1999, p. 10). This involvement of the individual in his environment, the one constituting the other, is the theoretical kernel of the social anthropological approach of Tim Ingold (2000), a precious example of the balanced proposal between the cultural and the psychological that I defend. But this I will discuss in another publication.

Let me finish this chapter with a phrase from a story by the Brazilian writer Guimarães Rosa: "One saw that he went on to repose on the saddle – surely he relaxed his body to dedicate himself to the enormous task of thinking."

References

Arendt, R. J. J. (1999). *Para onde vai a Psicologia? Por uma abordagem contemporânea da autonomia.* Tese de Professor Titular em Psicologia Social. Departamento de Psicologia Social e Institucional, UERJ, Rio de Janeiro.

Branco, A. (2000). *The Role of metacommunication as providing a basis for the development of the self.* Trabalho apresentado na III Conferência de Pesquisa Sócio-Cultural.Campinas, Unicamp.

Bronckart, J. P. (2000). *Les Processus de Socialisation. Le Déterminisme Culturel et son Dépassement.* Palestra proferida na III Conferência de Pesquisa Sócio-Cultural.Campinas, Unicamp.

Fogel, A., & Branco, A. (1997). Metacommunication as a source of indeterminism in relationship development. In A. Fogel, M. C. Lyra, & J. Valsiner (Eds.), *Dynamics and indeterminism in developmental and social processes* (pp. 65–92). Mahwah, NJ: Lawrence Erlbaum.

Glasersfeld, E. v. (1997). *Hommage à Jean Piaget.* www.oikos.org/Piagethom.htm.

Glasersfeld, E. v. (1998). *Welten konstruiren, die für alle gangbar sind.* Telepolis. Interview with Rudolf Maresch. www.heise.de/tp/deutsch/inhalt/co/2572/1.html.

Glasersfeld, E. v. (1999). *How do we mean? A constructivist sketch of semantics.* www.umass.edu/srri/vonGlasersfeld/onlinePapers/html/238.html.

Ingold, T. (2000). *The perception of the environment: Essays in livelihood, dwelling and skill.* London: Routledge.

Rorty, R. (1991). *Objectivity, relativism and truth.* In *Philosophical Papers* (Vol. 1). Cambridge: Cambridge University Press.

Schnitman, D. F. (1994). *Nuevos Paradigmas, Cultura y Subjetividad.* Buenos Aires: Paidos.

van Oers, B. (2000). *Continuous recontextualization and the generalization of knowledge and skills.* Trabalho apresentado na III Conferência de Pesquisa Sócio-Cultural. Campinas, Unicamp.

von Foerster, H. (1998). *Wir sehen nicht, dass wir nicht sehen.* Telopolis. Entrevista a Bernard Pörksen. www.heise.de/tp/deutsch/special/robo/6240/1/html.

8

Subject, Subjectivity, and Development
in Cultural-Historical Psychology

Fernando Luis González Rey

INTRODUCTION

One of the main goals of this chapter is to put Vygotsky in a perspective that differs from currently dominant interpretations of his work in Western psychology. Before I offer a rather different interpretation, however, I would like to comment on certain trends in the sociocultural approach to the interpretation of Vygotsky's works.

First, it is characteristic to separate Vygotsky from his historical and theoretical context – the Russian Revolution, Soviet psychology, and the influence of Marxism on Vygotsky's theoretical representations. When I refer to the influence of Marxism on his view about psychology, I am not suggesting any kind of linear relation between more philosophical Marxist categories and principles and Vygotsky's work. On the contrary, I would like to emphasize Vygotsky's creativity in the way he adopted Marxism in his psychological work. Marxism was present in Vygotsky's thinking – above all, in his general representation of psychological phenomena.

Second, at this moment some prevailing interpretations of Vygotsky appear as "correct" and updated, for example, those given by Bruner, Kozulin, Wertsch, and van der Veer. This trend has led some psychologists to consider Vygotsky's original works as old-fashioned and to reinterpret his views in the light of the currently fashionable narrative, semiotic, or discursive approaches. Because Vygotsky's work was unfinished, contradictory, and irregular, it allows a variety of interpretations, of which we have not seen the last.

Third, these trends are responsible for the current tension in the demarcation of the general integrative theoretical and methodological principles of the sociocultural approach. This tension is evident in the multiplicity of labels that are currently used by different authors, including the recent

"CHAT," which try to integrate activity theory and cultural-historical psychology. What is clear is that there are many lacunae in the legacy of Vygotsky and Soviet psychology in general.

In view of these trends, I elaborate here one aspect of Vygotsky's work to which authors have not paid much attention: the concept of "sense" and its implications for the development of the topic of subjectivity. When we refer to Vygotsky, we necessarily have to refer to Soviet psychology and the work of Rubinstein, because in spite of the differences between them, there were certain general principles that both shared. Using different categories and sets of problems, both Vygotsky and Rubinstein began to produce a new view of psychological phenomena. That view of the human psyche, developed in the 1930s in Soviet psychology, could be characterized by the following points:

- The dissolution of the representation of the human psyche as an internal, individual entity
- The representation of the human psyche as a complex system whose forms of organization do not exclude a permanent processual and dynamic character of the system
- The first general theory of the human psyche that was presented as a developmental theory
- The transcendence of several dichotomies that have historically characterized the development of psychology, such as conscious-unconscious, affective-cognitive, and social-individual
- The linking of action and human psyche, understood as the principle of the unity between activity and consciousness (Rubinstein) and through the concept of sense (Vygotsky).

The principles mentioned are not a sum of fragmented requirements; rather, they were foundational in relation to a new comprehension of the human psyche, behind which lay a new ontological definition of psychological phenomena, something that remains irreducible to its semiotic character. In fact, sense in Vygotsky's view or personality in Rubinstein's view represents a complex organization of the individual psyche that is permanently interwoven with the social subject's involvement, in which complex representations are the first step in a new representation of the human psyche, deserving further theoretical specification.

Subjectivity is used as a theoretical definition pointing to a new order of psychological phenomena, which represents another ontological domain: the order of subjective sense. Understanding psyche as a subjective phenomenon is beyond any attempt to explain it as a direct consequence of an objective or rational order. Contrary to prevailing trends in psychology, in which subjective processes have always been replaced by something different, like social discourse, biological drives, or narratives, Vygotsky focuses on psyche as a new order of phenomena, putting in the center of this order the concept of sense.

Criticism has been raised by some authors identified with postmodern theories, who consider subjectivity a remnant of modernity. Apart from the "new status" adopted in some interpretations of American pragmatism, and the now fashionable interpretations related to Heidegger, Nietzsche, and Wittgenstein, all such criticism has led to a rejection of any ontological status for the human psyche, which is defined only as a discursive order (see, e.g., the work of Harré, Shotter, and Brockmeier). This orientation has produced certain approaches, such as narrative psychology and social construction-ism, that are gaining more influence within sociocultural psychology. For the proponents of these theories, the word subjectivity seems to be a very old-fashioned expression. But even starting with the previously mentioned philosophers, it would be possible to support subjectivity as we have defined it within a cultural-historical perspective. However, that is not my point.

In my opinion, modernity primarily entered psychology via empiricism, in a specifically hard empiricist and atheoretical version, whose historical roots reflect a complex combination of philosophical trends, practices, and historical contexts. Particularly relevant here is the cultural and socioeco-nomic context that appeared at the end of the nineteenth and beginning of the twenty centuries in the United States, where the dominant positivistic approach in natural sciences strongly influenced the cult of methodology in psychology. This period has been critically analyzed by different authors (Danziger, 1990; Koch, 1981). The level of empiricism in psychology was stronger than in Comte's positivistic view.

The concept of subjectivity entails an attempt to understand ontology, not in its essentialist or causalistic version of being, but rather as a different domain of psychological phenomena, with its own organization of active, complex, irregular, recursive, and processual ways of organization, an attempt strongly influenced by Vygotsky's theoretical construction. It does not mean that the epistemological ghost of knowledge as a representation of reality should be revived: to recognize the active participation in the process of theoretical construction does not necessarily imply the direct reproduction of the studied phenomenon in theoretical representation. One of the best examples of this complex dialectic of the knowledge process is quantum mechanics.

Finally, in this introduction, I would like to comment on another ele-ment that should be present in our interpretation of Vygotsky as well as in the interpretation of Soviet psychology in general: the marks of Stalinism on Soviet psychology. In my opinion, two important marks of Stalinism on

Soviet psychology were its trend to objectify the psychological phenomenon and its focus on microanalysis of social events, which ignored the way in which macrosocial and economical facts become psychological configurations. These marks influenced Soviet psychology and also Western interpretations of it. In both Soviet and Western psychology, it is possible to observe some of the following characteristics:

- The objectification of Vygotsky's thinking, which among other effects led to a fragmentation in the use of more specific categories of Vygotsky's theory, considering them in a direct relation to practice and not as a moment of a system of thinking
- The emphasis on cognition and semiotic mediation, without consideration of other important psychological facts, such as emotion and personality, which were very much present in Vygotsky's works
- The preservation of certain dichotomies that were already overcome by Vygotsky and Rubinstein, like the dichotomy between external and internal and between subjective and objective, which leads one to consider the external as an objective phenomenon and the internal as a subjective one. (These divisions contribute to the preservation of the distinction between individual and social because the individual is considered subjective and social facts as objective, which leads one to consider social facts as objective determinants of individual subjective phenomena. This is one of the reasons for which I introduced the distinction between social and individual subjectivity; see González Rey, 1991.)
- The absence of macrosocial facts in the analysis of psychological production, separating, for example, the school context from the general social context within which school functions

Vygotsky invested much energy in understanding the principles of the organization of the human psyche, which – in Vygotsky's thinking – referred to some type of particular phenomenon. So, for example, the concept of the unity of consciousness was an attempt to formulate consciousness as a complex system. Through the concept of unity, Vygotsky tried to make visible a new organizational level of human psyche. In fact, Vygotsky preferred to use the term "consciousness" because it could better respond to the ideological demands of the prevailing Marxist interpretation in the political circles of the Soviet Union at that time. He always favored "consciousness" over "subjectivity." But the system that Vygotsky tried to define – through the term consciousness – was in fact much more complex than the possible boundaries of the concept of consciousness, something that was completely clear in numerous references throughout Vygotsky's work.

The term "cultural" is quickly expanding now with the integration of the role of culture in relation to the human psyche and development. In this chapter, I focus on the importance of rethinking the categories of subjectivity and subject within the development of cultural-historical psychology, a term introduced by Vygotsky and Rubinstein as they established the theoretical foundation of Soviet psychology. Subjectivity, from this perspective, has nothing to do with an essential, rational, and static entity, as it has been understood by some philosophical trends in modernity.

VYGOTSKY'S CONCEPT OF SENSE: ITS MEANING IN THE CONSTRUCTION OF THE TOPIC OF SUBJECTIVITY IN THE CULTURAL-HISTORICAL APPROACH

The concept of sense – introduced by Vygotsky as a complex organization of psyche – represents a kind of unity of subjectivity that gains an important heuristic value in the reconstruction of psychological theory from a completely new perspective. Vygotsky used the word "sense" from different points of view at different moments in his work. Thus, at first he emphasized the presence of sense in words, starting from Paulhan's theoretical position. Even in this approach to the term, Vygotsky underscored the psychological character of sense from the very beginning of its use. Later he emphasized sense as a psychological organization, as a system of senses, thus adopting the use of sense in its deeper psychological relevance. Because these discussions occurred only in Vygotsky's late works, this use of the term is not as well known in the West, although the topic was adopted and developed by some Soviet followers of activity theory, including A. A. Leontiev and B. Bratus in the 1980s.

In *Thinking and Speech*, in his reflection about Paulhan's contribution to the psychological analysis of speech, and on the basis of Paulhan's distinction between meaning and sense, Vygotsky, while keeping Paulhan's perspective of locating sense in the word, pointed out:

The word's sense is the aggregate of all psychological facts that appear in our consciousness as result of the word. Sense is a dynamic, fluid, and complex formation which has several zones that vary in their stability. Meaning is only one of these zones of the sense that the word acquires in the context of speech.... Ultimately, the sense of a word depends on one's understanding of the word as a whole and on the internal structure of personality. (Vygotsky, 1987a, pp. 275–276)

In Vygotsky's phrase, one may observe the distinction he made between sense and meaning. He began to consider sense within the complex psychological organization of the subject. In this quote, sense itself is expressed in

a word, but it is different from the word, and it embodies other psychological elements. Apart from Vygotsky's emphasis on sense and word in the
preceding quotation, he simultaneously understood sense as a system organized through different zones. Sense becomes a new type of formation that
characterizes itself as being in constant movement.

Vygotsky clearly viewed sense as an aggregate, an integration in the word
of different psychological elements. This indicates the heterogeneity of sense.
Later, he emphasized the complexity of sense as organization and the presence
of emotions in sense. Through the term sense, Vygotsky defined the subjective character of emotion, and he could definitively integrate emotion and
symbolic process, which was a permanent aspiration of his work. The inseparable relation of emotions and other psychical phenomena was defined by
him in different works, and it was particularly emphasized in "Emotions and
Their Development in Childhood," which was part of lectures that he delivered between March and April 1932, a little before *Thinking and Speech* was
published, in which he attributed particular importance to the term sense.

In relation to emotions, Vygotsky (1987b, p. 336) pointed out in this work:

Lewin demonstrated how one emotional state is transformed into another, how
one emotional experience is substituted for another, and how an unresolved
and uncompleted emotion may continue to exist in covert form. He also demonstrated how an affect enters into any structure with which it is connected. Lewin's
basic concept was that affective or emotional reactions cannot be found in isolation as a special element of mental life, an element of mental life that is subsequently united with others. The emotional reaction is the unique result of a
particular structure of mental processes.

Through the term sense, Vygotsky integrated emotions as a permanent
process of certain psychological functions: the functions of sense. The importance of sense in Vygotsky's representation of psyche has largely been ignored
for some time, although among Soviet psychologists the topic has always mer-
ited attention. A. A. Leontiev's (1992) comprehension of sense in Vygotsky's
works is particularly interesting. A. A. Leontiev tried to rescue the last period
in Vygotsky's creativity (from late 1933 until his death in 1934), emphasizing the transcendence of sense in Vygotsky's more advanced representation
of higher human psychological organization. Leontiev brought to his work
several interesting quotations from the later part of Vygotsky's writings: "In
the process of societal life...the emotions come into a new relationship
with the other elements of psychical life, new systems appear, new blending
of psychical functions; units of a higher order emerge, governed by special
laws, mutual dependencies, and special forms of connection and motion."

Immediately after this quotation, Leontiev (1992, p. 42) affirmed: "Just such a blending is the unity of 'intellect and affect.' It forms a dynamic system of senses."

This interpretation represents the more advanced moment of Vygotsky's ideas in relation to sense. Here, sense appears as a system, but the interesting thing is Vygotsky's emphasis on the complexity of the blending of psychological functions within which emotions enter into new relations with other elements of mental life. The emphasis on emotions was characteristic of Vygotsky's later works. His introduction of the category of sense led to a new step in the representation of the relationship between affect and cognition within the complex organization of human psyche. In relation to the process of development of sense Vygotsky (1982a, p. 22) wrote: "Generally speaking, the problem is not the unity of affect and intellect as such, but the realization of this unity in the form of a 'dynamic system of senses,' which embraces the 'dynamic of thought' (intellect) as well as the 'dynamic of behavior and concrete activity of personality.'"

In this quotation, the concept of sense is broadened. It integrates new psychological domains, becoming a complex whole in the light of which different psychological categories receive a new meaning, which progressively begins to appear within the system of sense. This is the case with categories such as personality, thinking, motive, and action. Sense is responsible for the wholeness of mental life.

The idea of this system, used as the cornerstone of a new view of subjectivity, was changed by A. N. Leontiev when he introduced the concept of personal sense. In my opinion, Leontiev did not use the term sense in order to develop a complex theory of the human psyche, which always was Vygotsky's intention. On the contrary, Leontiev reoriented Vygotsky's efforts centered on complexity by emphasizing activity. He represented the internal activity as being identical to external activity by its structure, which leads to a reification of activity to the detriment of its subjective character. This was clear throughout Leontiev's work. Thus, in one of his later publications, *Activity, Consciousness, and Personality*, Leontiev (1978, p. 60) stated:

We must say at once that the mutual transitions about which we are speaking form a most important movement of objective human activity in its historical and ontogenetic development. These transitions are possible because external and internal activity have a similar general structure. The disclosure of the common features of their structure seems to me to be one of the more important discoveries of contemporary psychological science. Thus activity that is internal in its form, originating from external practical activity, is not separated from it and does not stand above it but continues to preserve an essential, twofold connection with it.

A. N. Leontiev defined "personal sense" as a moment of activity organization. In spite of this fact, it is necessary to recognize that the category of personal sense introduced the topic of emotions in a new psychological dimension, contributing in this way to the recognition of the singular, personal character of sense.

But the use of the term personal sense did not lead to another level of theoretical construction within the frame of activity, because of the separation of personal sense from the topic of personality and, in general, from the topic of the whole organization of psyche as a different ontological domain of objective operations of activity. The way in which Vygotsky treated the topic of sense – continued by some of Leontiev's followers, including his son – emphasized sense as an organization, a system, and a formation. In a paper I wrote with Bratus (1982, p. 31), we pointed out:

> The formation of sense … is a dynamic and integral system that reflects the interaction of several motives within a motivational subsystem which expresses itself in a certain relation to the world, carrying out personal sense for the subject. This definition allows one to remove sense from an activity, emphasizing the systemic character of this psychical formation.

Unfortunately, this work, intended to rescue the category of sense, began in the 1970s in Soviet psychology, and it could not continue in all its richness due to profound changes in the country and in the field of psychology as well. The internal difficulties that developed in Russian psychology as a result of theoretical and methodological dispersion led to a deep crisis in the field at the time.

The idea of sense as a system has led different authors (e.g., Asmolov, Bratus, and González Rey) working within this framework to reformulate categories like personality, which appear to be more a system of sense than an internal structure. The concept of sense was used for the reconstruction of a general view of the human psyche, rescuing the complex and social character of individual subjective configuration (González Rey, 1991, 1995). On the other hand, use of this term allows one to present emotions in their subjective nature. The reconsideration of these psychological topics, such as personality and emotions, led to a complex representation of mental functions, which is not engulfed by narratives and discursive phenomena, something common in some Vygotskian interpretations. The category of sense opened a new perspective on the intelligibility of the complex configuration of the human psyche; however, in the current Western versions of sociocultural and activity theory, this perspective has not always been considered.

In his extension of the concept of sense to different domains of psychical life, Vygotsky (1987b, p. 333) pointed out: "The emotions are not 'a state within a state.' They cannot be understood outside the dynamic of human life. It is within this context that the emotional processes acquire their meaning and sense."

On the basis of this comment it is possible to draw conclusions about Vygotsky's emphasis on continuing the differentiation between meaning and sense. It also allows us to see the articulation of emotions and context in human life, within which emotions become elements of sense acquiring a subjective expression.

As was said before, the difference between meaning and sense has not been considered by most sociocultural authors, who have not understood the main principles on which Vygotsky developed his more general view of psyche. These principles were replaced by microlevel definitions focused on concrete problems and categories. So, for example, the zone of proximal development was separated from the higher psychological functions, while meaning was separated from sense, action was separated from personality, and so on. Nowadays, this trend is growing in the sociocultural approach and in narrative psychology, whose philosophical and epistemological orientations are quite different.

The sociocultural approach has emphasized activity and action in its comprehension of human processes, and sense does not appear in its conceptual repertoire. For example, as Rogoff et al. (1995, p. 129) wrote in relation to learning, "Within sociocultural approaches, the aim is to understand the developmental processes involved in activities, at the level of individual, interpersonal, and community (or cultural) processes."

This comprehension of such processes within an activity frame may hide socially produced elements of sense, which are separated by time and space from current activity. These elements represent an invisible moment produced by the subject in activity, without which it would be very difficult to understand the real social and historical character of any activity.

SUBJECTIVE SENSE AND SUBJECTIVE CONFIGURATIONS: THE CONSTRUCTION OF THE TOPIC OF SUBJECTIVITY IN THE CULTURAL-HISTORICAL APPROACH

In an attempt to differentiate sense in its subjective configuration from personal sense, I propose the term "subjective sense," trying to rethink the significance of sense for the development of a cultural-historical definition of subjectivity. I define subjective sense as a type of emotional and self-organized unity of subjectivity that characterizes itself in relation to dominant meanings and emotions, in an order in which one of these elements is not a direct expression of the other. So, these elements stand together in a new qualitative unity, defining a phenomenon that is simultaneously an emotional and symbolic one that also takes many paths in its organization and expression. Within the nature of sense, symbolic elements and emotions mutually evoke one another, without any linear relation between them.

Human psychological production is almost always involved with a production of sense, and in every human activity many different elements of subjective sense enter into new clusters during the subject's actions; however, subjective senses do not have only a chaotic and endless character; they also become integrated in different dynamic organizations that I label "subjective configurations" (González Rey, 1995).

The production of senses involved in human activity is inseparable from the subjective senses resulting from subjective configurations; therefore, personality – as a configured system of senses – is part of any subject action, not as a determinant of action, but as a moment of sense production that characterizes action. Of course, those senses involving personality represent a higher order in relation to those chaotic and unexpected senses that appear within the course of action, which is one of the reasons that explain why new senses are frequently defined in terms of current dominant subjective configurations. Sense resulting from personality regulation and senses produced in ongoing action become integrated with each other within the process of subjectivation of action. As Chaiklin and I have written, "there is always a personal sense that is present before, during, and after the action – and it is a psychological aspect of that action" (González Rey & Chaiklin, 2002). This means that in the process of sense production, we cannot separate the moment of the organized configuration from the new senses that appear in the course of an ongoing action or after the action. All these subjective senses represent the subjective moment of activity, structuring the endless movement of subjective configuration within development. Of course, there are not immediate changes in these configurations as a result of activity, but this continuous flow of senses – which characterizes different domains of human action – represents strong points of tension in the current organized configuration, tension that could lead to qualitative changes in dominant configurations. Relations between these types of senses would be responsible for the tension that characterizes human development, a tension that could be located by the interdependence between subjective configuration and local production of senses within human development. In other words, Vygotsky's concept of the "social situation of development" allows us to explain this type of contradiction as being characteristic of human development.

Subjective configurations represent a way to represent in theoretical terms the organization of senses as a system, a system that is always in tension in the course of human action and that simultaneously is involved as a moment of sense in any activity. These configurations do not represent static entities characterized by well-defined attributes: they are truly systems of subjective senses that integrate senses produced in different temporal moments and areas of human experiences that are part of the ongoing human action. This concept, as any new concept, is in a continuous process of change. Some time ago, I understood sense to be a complex of elements that enter in relation to each other, defining the subjective sense of any human experience. At this moment, I believe that subjective configurations are configurations of senses, which means that any element that becomes part of a configuration is in itself a subjective sense. To give an example, aggression, as an element of any human configuration, is not simply a contextual emotion or a trait but may be a complex sense based on historical events and relations of one subject in different areas of his or her life. All these areas subjectively appear organized in aggression as an element of sense. Sense is not the sum of data coming directly from social experiences. It is a complex network of hidden emotions and symbolic processes that are integrated with each other without following the logic of external living events, producing the new "logic" of a system of senses.

Elements of subjective configurations are not isolated elements that make sense only once they become part of the wholeness of one configuration. Each element is in itself configured as sense; this means that they have a particular history along which they became subjective sense, integrating many different emotions and symbolic expressions that finally became a sense production. So, for example, aggression as behavior in the face of a certain situation is not sense, but when aggression results from a complex qualitative integration of emotions and symbolic processes that has a history as a system integrating different zones of human experiences, such an aggression turns into a subjective sense. However, senses are not something static and unchangeable; they are always involved in certain kinds of configuration, within which each concrete subjective sense may change its subjective charge, becoming a new sense. Each concrete sense may simultaneously be part of different configurations, appearing differently in each of them, because sense production is not organized by addition as a sum. They represent a new qualitative order in each new configuration, within which they take part as a moment of different human experiences.

Aggression may be part of many different configurations, but emotions and symbolic expression associated with it in each of these configurations would be different, so aggression is not mere aggression as such: it becomes a moment in a production of subjective sense in different configurations of personality, in relation to which aggression may appear in many different ways. But aggression in itself is a configuration that may become dominant in certain contexts of the subject's action; in this case, aggression results from different scenarios of the subject's life, which are interconnected with each other in a particular way within subjective configurations. So, once aggression has become a subjective sense, it integrates emotions and symbolic expressions from different activities, events, and relations produced in very different times and social scenarios.

The feeling of hopelessness in a child that results from racial discrimination is felt in many different ways throughout his young life, and this may lead to emotions and symbolic production that could become integrated in aggression as a subjective configuration.

An infinite number of psychological elements could become integrated in aggression as subjective sense. Other possible elements that merge with an aggression configuration could be, for example, the anger experienced by a person during his childhood in witnessing his father's abuse of his mother. Both emotions, hopelessness and anger, become elements of a subjective sense of aggression coming into a new relationship with the other elements of psychical life. They do not merge in aggression as sense immediately after having the experience; it is a complex subjective process that cannot be followed by external behavioral evidence, because, as production of sense, it does not follow the logic of external evidence. Also, becoming part of an aggression-like configuration is not a result of personal repression in a concrete moment of lived experience. Psychological processes become subjective sense only as a result of historical processes within which they organize themselves in a new blending of psychological functions.

Subjective configurations represent a real system of senses configured in diverse human activities and experienced throughout human life. Configurations are historical, but within their organization there is not one moment in a linear dependency on the past. Elements of sense are not static; as part of one configuration they may express a different subjective sense compared to their presence in other configurations. Also it could happen that a specific subjective sense becomes dominant in one subject as part of different configurations involved in the same kind of subjective production. Take, for example, a person in prison. The subject, in the strength of his arguments, in his overcoming of his frustrations, and in his reaction in the face of difficulties, may configure a subjective sense associated with creating his own space in prison. Once this experience is in the past, and depending on the way family relations are evolving, this subjective sense configured in prison may lead in a family situation to aggression, uncertainty, and anxiety when the subject is confronted with the impossibility of getting his own space under new social conditions. Behind these different emotional expressions, the subjective sense in itself is the same.

Subjective configurations are different from person to person, and even the same kind of activity or experience is differently configured in each person. Subjective senses are a very complex and sensitive registration, configured not only as a result of explicit emotions and symbolic expressions directly produced in the relation of one person to another. Each relation or human experience is mediated by many different senses configured before this experience, which take part in the new production of sense that, in its appearance, has little to do with a lived concrete situation in which new senses are being organized. For this reason, subjective sense is a unity for understanding an irrational definition of subjectivity.

Parents, as an element of sense, may appear in many different ways in human configurations; therefore, these configurations are not directly defined within the social delimitation of the parent-child zone of experiences. These zones of experiences are articulated in a sense production, not as objective experienced spaces. One of the reasons that pathologies are not always evident in the social history of people is that the production of senses does not follow any evident or objective standardized logic. The heuristic value of a subjective configuration has to do with the possibility of identifying senses associated with life events and relations between persons that are not available to immediate experience. This opportunity allows us to reveal the extension of the complex subjective organization of any human action or activity.

It is important to state that the concept of subjective sense represents the complex social nature within which subjective experience is organized. Subjective senses never are a reflex or a copy of their social origins. Subjective senses are an indirect and distorted expression of the complex and simultaneous social elements that are relevant to any singular process of subjectivation, in which subjective repertories and configurations of the subject are completely involved. Subjective sense as a unity of subjectivity has five consequences for the ongoing construction of subjectivity.

First, individual subjectivity is a complex system of subjective configurations that define senses that are involved before, during, and after any human action or function. Therefore, human activities are understood from this perspective as processes of sense production, thus breaking down the traditional division between cognitive and affective activities. Within such a perspective, learning, like any function of the psychological subject, is a process of production of sense, and it should be theoretically constructed, taking into account this side of its subjective constitution.

Second, subjective organization is always a singular process, whose configuration has to be discovered in each particular case. For example, the subjective configuration of being sick would be quite different for different persons. This does not deny some common characteristics in persons who share certain objective conditions or positions, but these common characteristics should not be confounded with subjective sense.

Third, from this perspective, subjectivity represents a dynamic system involved in the subject's actions and activities. It does not represent any type of essential or static intrapsychical entity. It is a complex system that should be understood as a process and an organization, moments that continuously merge through human action and human development.

Fourth, subjectivity is not just an individual phenomenon, because social spaces and institutions also have a subjective character, taking part in a complex system of social subjectivity. Individual and social processes should not be completely understood through the subjective-objective dichotomy, because both of them are produced together in human life. Each of these elements is part of the objective condition of another. Subjective senses are a synthesis of objective conditions and lived situations, and they result from subjective factors involved in social scenarios within which the individual lives. At the same time, subjective expressions and individual production involve a person in a new system of objective conditions that become new sources of sense production all along human development. The best example of this is human culture: it is subjectively created but appears in each moment of a subject's life in an objective dimension.

Fifth, in this conception of subjectivity, the social context is always involved in a subject's actions, implying that the subject is both individual and social. Also, the historical character of subjectivity is present in any moment of sense production through a system of subjective configurations, a process that is common to individual and social subjectivity. Each of these levels of subjective organization depends on the other, and, at the same time, both of them are constituted by one another. An individual personality does not result from social influences; rather, it results as a moment within the process in which social facts are produced. The subject is an active agent of this production, because it is impossible to consider any social condition as external.

IMPLICATIONS OF SUBJECTIVITY FOR A THEORETICAL CONSTRUCTION OF HUMAN DEVELOPMENT

Accepting this conception of subjectivity leads us to consider the reciprocal and complex relation between communication and the production of senses.

This dialogical-subjective axis becomes important for considering human development in any area of life or human activity. Within this perspective, areas such as cognitive development, morality, and learning are understood as a process of subjective sense, integrating the topic of emotions in an organic way, which has been ignored in the study of these topics.

For a long time in Soviet psychology, particularly in activity theory, the concept of leading activities was crucial in understanding development. This concept was central in the periodization of development proposed by Elkonin. If we assume that human development is a process of subjective sense production, it is difficult to support this view on the basis of any kind of periodization. Vygotsky (1984) himself expressed this contradiction in different moments of his work, even though at times he could not avoid giving in to the temptation of elaborating a periodization of development. Vygotsky also introduced a concept that could be used in a different way in the comprehension of human development: the concept of the "social situation of development," later adopted by Bozhovich in Soviet psychology. By the social situation of development, Vygotsky understood the particular confrontation between new social demands and the child's available psychological resources in different moments of development. From this confrontation will emerge new qualitative moments in human development. This process could not be constrained to any rigid stage. In other words, according to Vygotsky, it would appear in any singular moment of life. So, for example, a social situation of development would not only be the beginning of school, a common experience to all children. A social situation of development for any child could also be loss of the mother, for example. The child's reaction to any of these events will be a singular production of subjective sense on which will depend the impact of the particular situation on his or her development.

In talking about development, one point should be taken into account: the difference between development and growth. Development has been understood according to the foregoing position in relation to subjectivity, as a holistic, qualitative change that involves different psychological processes and repertories. Development is a systemic change, and not the partial change of concrete psychological functions. On this subject, Vygotsky (1982b, p. 110) has written:

In the process of development, and especially in the historical development of behavior, changes do not take place in the functions we studied earlier (this is our mistake) or in their structure or in their system of movements; rather, in relations and interrelations between the functions, there appear new groups not known at the previous level. This is why the essential difference in transition from one developmental stage to another is often not a change in function, but between their functions, relations and structures.[1]

In this paragraph Vygotsky's view in relation to development is clear. Vygotsky supported the idea of stages, but these stages may be represented as qualitative moments of change and not necessarily as universal stages supported by universal criteria, such as age or leading activities. Behind periodization, understood as the regular sequences of stages, is the rejection of the singular, which has deep epistemological roots in the history of sciences. Retaking the concept of subjectivity has epistemological implications and may allow us to reintegrate singularity in scientific psychology (González Rey, 1995).

In my opinion, it is necessary to retake the concept of driving forces of development in order to advance the theoretical construction of this matter starting from subjectivity. The concept of the social situation of development could lead to two theoretical consequences:

First, the comprehension of development as a complex and contradictory process is characterized by a permanent tension between already formed psychological repertoires and configurations and new social scenarios in the subject's life. These contradictions become sources of subjective senses. These moments are not necessarily related to the same activity or social field or to the same temporal definition. As Wallon (1941) pointed out many years ago, the concept of the social situation of development supports the idea of considering the singular subject as the scenario of development.

Second, the dialectical relation between external and internal in the comprehension of development breaks down any idea of external determinants of this process, which suggests the idea of driving forces of development, understood as systemic and processual forces, enabling us to follow the process of development. Earlier (González Rey, 1995), I introduced the concept of the subjective unity of development, understanding it as that configuration able to integrate different changes in psychological repertoires and the subjective organization of personality. So, for example, swimming for a concrete young person could become a subjective unity of development, if, through this practice and the social processes involved in it, this youth produces new configurations related to new areas of his life, such as a profession, love relations, or social positions. In addition, he or she may develop new

---

[1] This quotation of Vygotsky was taken from Hakkarainen & Veresov (2001).

psychological resources leading to new systems of actions that enable him or her to get involved in new social spaces.

The importance of sense as a dimension of human development has been underlined by Hakkarainen and Veresov (2001, p. 137): "The divergence between the field of meaning and the field of sense within learning tasks constitutes a necessary precondition for the child's development in play and learning." This idea of considering the tension between sense and meaning addresses a driving force in concrete activity, one that was conspicuously lacking in the concept of leading activities, which was more a descriptive concept than a psychological conceptualization of the processes involved in development within activity.

References

Danziger, K. (1990). *Constructing the subject: Historical origins of psychological research.* Cambridge: Cambridge University Press.

González Rey, F. (1991). Personalidad, sujeto y subjetividad social. In M. Montero (Ed.), *Construcción y crítica de la psicología social.* Barcelona: Anthropos.

González Rey, F. (1995). *Comunicación, Personalidad y Desarrollo.* Havana: Editora pueblo y Educación.

González Rey, F., & Bratus, B. (1982). La tendencia orientadora de la personalidad y las formación del sentido. In *Algunas cuestiones teóricas y metodológicas sobre el estudio de la personalidad.* Havana: Editora Pueblo y Educación.

González Rey, F. L., & Chaiklin, S. (2002). Subjectivity in action: A reconstruction of activity theory. Paper presented at the Vth Congress of the International Society for Cultural Research and Activity Theory, Free University, Amsterdam.

Hakkarainen, P., & Veresov, N. (2001). Narrative learning: Developmental perspectives. In *Prienstvennocti stupeniei v sisteme rasvivaiusheva i pasvivaiushevaciia obrazabaniia.* Moscow: Isd "Gnom i D."

Koch, S. (1981). The nature and limits of psychological knowledge: Lesson of a century qua "science." *American Psychologist, 36* (3), 257–269.

Leontiev, A. A. (1992). Ecco Homo: Methodological problems of the activity theoretical approach. *Activity Theory,* nos. 11–12, 41–44.

Leontiev, A. N. (1978). *Activity, consciousness, and personality.* New York: Prentice-Hall.

Rogoff, B., Radzizewska, B., & Masiello, T. (1995). Analysis of developmental processes in sociocultural activity. In L. Martin, K. Nelson, & E. Tobach (Eds.), *Sociocultural psychology: Theory and practice of doing and knowing* (pp. 125–149). Cambridge: Cambridge University Press.

Vygotsky, L. (1982a). Myshlenie i rech. In *Sobranye sochinenya* (Vol. 2, pp. 6–361). Moscow: Pedagogika.

Vygotsky, L. (1982b). O psikhologiceskach sistemach. In *Sobranie socinenij* (Vol. 1, pp. 109–131). Moscow: Pedagogika.

Vygotsky, L. (1984). Problema vozrastnoj perioditsatsii destkovo razvitiia. In *Sobranye sochinenya* (Vol. 4, pp. 244–256). Moscow: Pedagogika.

Vygotsky, L. (1987a). *Thinking and speech.* In R. W. Rieber & A. S. Carton (Eds.), *The collected works of L. S. Vygotsky: Vol. 1. Problems of general psychology* (pp. 39–285). New York: Plenum Press.

Vygotsky, L. (1987b). Emotions and their development in childhood. In *Lectures on Psychology.* In R. W. Rieber and A. S. Carton (Eds.), *The collected works of L. S. Vygotsky: Vol. 1. Problems of general psychology* (pp. 325–338). New York: Plenum Press.

Wallon, H. (1941). *L' évolution psychologique de l'enfant.* Paris: Colin.

SECTION TWO

IDENTITY, DIVERSITY, AND INCLUSION

Introduction to Section Two

Identity, Diversity, and Inclusion

Wim Wardekker

In a recent publication, Kieran Egan (2002) has launched an attack on both "progressive" and "traditional" ideas about the goals of education: the first, because they depend on a wrong view of human development; the second, because they lead to a utilitarian view; and both, because ultimately they shortchange children's intellectual development. Egan also proposes an alternative (elaborated more fully in Egan, 1997):

The education of children today is a matter of ensuring that they make their minds most abundant by acquiring the fullest array of the cultural tools that can, through learning, be made into cognitive tools. I have drawn on Vygotsky in trying to make this argument, because he more than anyone seems to have had an understanding of the process whereby the cultural becomes cognitive and an understanding that it is the cognitive tools we acquire that most clearly and importantly established for us the character of our understanding. (2002, p. 184)

Although the expression "the fullest array of the cultural tools" raises the not unimportant question of the contents of curriculum, we will not concern ourselves with that here. Instead, our focus in this section of the present volume is inspired by what Egan calls the making of cultural tools into cognitive tools, or appropriation. Or, to be more precise, the issue is how to understand the human mind as it becomes progressively informed by cognitive tools. It clearly will not do to see the educated mind as a loose array of cognitive tools, to be invoked at will – if only because it would remain obscure who, in that case, is doing the invoking. All the chapters in this section, explicitly or implicitly, use and discuss the concept of "personal identity" as a way of thinking about that integration – and more than that, about the development and ways of acting of the whole person, as identity is not only about *cognitive* development or just about learning to use tools.

157

The first thing to be noted about identity is that it is itself understood as a cultural tool that has to be appropriated. And we do not just mean that psychologists and educators have to learn to use the *concept* of identity in understanding human minds. Every human being needs to learn to use "identity" as a cognitive tool, as the integrating principle for other cognitive tools, for feeling, thought, and action alike. Other mental tools, that is, can only function adequately if they become integrated into a person's identity – if that person learns to see himself or herself as able and willing to use that tool. This implies that identity is not something acquired once for all times; rather, it is in constant development as long as a person is learning. And as identity is a culturally developed and still developing tool, the quality of that individual development will be related both to the exigencies of the cultural situation a person finds himself or herself in, and the affordances a specific culture offers at a specific time. In a contemporary Western culture, identity has to be different from the identities of people, say, two hundred years ago, and to build their identities, people now have access to different possibilities. For instance, *national* identity is a less dominant ingredient than it was before. The "space of authoring" one's own identity is wider now for most people than it has ever been (Holland et al., 1998, p. 210), although this is not true for everybody, as the contribution of Solis to this section shows (see also Bauman, 2004, p. 38).

This leads to the second point we need to note: that identity (in our present cultures, at least) is predominantly language-based, or, rather, as several of the texts in this section explain, is based on (cultural) discourse. Perhaps the most eloquent description that makes this clear is that of Holland et al. (1998, p. 40): "Persons develop more or less conscious conceptions of themselves as actors in socially and culturally constructed worlds, and these senses of themselves, these identities, to the degree that they are conscious and objectified, permit these persons, through the kinds of semiotic mediation described by Vygotsky, at least a modicum of agency or control over their own behaviour."

Building a discursive identity, then, is (learning) to tell a story about ourselves to ourselves and to (significant) others, a story that can be the basis of what Edwards and Mackenzie (in this section) call agentic action. It is also clear, however, that identity does not work in a causal way and does not guarantee agency.

The stories about themselves that people (learn to) tell are not totally their own inventions. Other people expect them to incorporate some elements, such as gender and national or cultural identity, and, in at least some societies, some form of class identity. Positions, as Holland et al. emphasize, become dispositions; and Leontiev draws attention to the fact that one does not just choose an identity, but one relates to specific social positions expressed in specific meanings. (It may be important to note that Sennett [1998] points out that the positions one has to relate to themselves shift over time: he suggests that instead of race and gender, now age and good looks become more important as social classifiers.) Some elements, too, are derived from culturally available sources, as when a teenager models herself on a movie star, or on her mother (or does *not* want to be like her mother and assumes in that respect what Solis, in this section, calls a counteridentity). In that sense, identity can be seen as a *bricolage* of preexisting elements, which always reflects a social position. However, understanding identity as the mere occupying of an intersection of culturally available positions, as some structuralists have suggested, is to forget the important distinction Leontiev made between meaning and sense, or public and personal meaning: cultural elements and tools are not integrated into identity stories as they are, but as the person makes sense of them in the light of previous experiences, existing identity stories, and feelings about her own existence. A consequence of this is that people are not defined by, say, their class position: class as an element of identity is not an objective feature of a person but is a discursive construction of a person as she interacts with situations in which she lives. "We recognise the meanings valued in the cultures we inhabit through immersion in those cultures and the mediation, by others, of what is important. We then engage in a process of sense-making in which we make that knowledge our own and undergo a change in the way we think and act" (Edwards 2005).

It is clear from these descriptions that building identity stories is not just an intellectual game. It is, rather, about entering into long-term commitments to positions, persons, activity settings, and other objects one considers important. Sense giving rests on valuations and is thus an emotionally grounded process with moral implications. Both Sennett and Holland et al. emphasize this point in relation to becoming a member of a social practice: Sennett (1998, p. 146) points to the *feeling* of being needed, that is, of being accepted as a member, as a necessary element in building an identity as a member; likewise, Holland et al. (1998, p. 119) state that identifying yourself as an agent in the system (and being identified by others as such) is a necessary precursor to mastering the system. One has to develop a concept of oneself in the activity and to *want* to either realize that self or avoid it. However, both Sennett and Bauman are concerned that in modern Western societies, the possibilities for engaging in long-term commitments are diminishing. Bauman (2004, p. 66) sees this as a consequence of consumerism, which emphasizes instant satisfaction: any long-term commitment lasts longer than the satisfaction experienced and is thus felt to be dreary and inflexible. As a consequence, especially young persons, according to Bauman (p. 30), are at risk of having only superficial commitments to mass-produced identities (thus forming what he calls "cloakroom communities") and consequently lack the skills to engage in secure and safe attachments.

Other qualities of identity are elaborated or at least hinted at in several texts in this section: it is related to the concept of reason (Wegerif), it has a moral dimension (Edwards & Mackenzie), it includes self-efficacy (of which Edwards and Mackenzie say that it may generalize to situations other than those in which a person saw herself to be an effective agent). Most importantly, however, many of the chapters are concerned with how identity develops discursively, each pointing out relevant features of the specific cultural situations in which that development has been studied. Foremost in these analyses is the importance of differences between people as a source of development. In itself this is not surprising, because the very concept of identity implies both identifying yourself with and distancing yourself from specific images of people and groups. Wenger (1998) drew attention to the implications for identity constitution of participation in culturally and institutionally defined forms of activities (practices). It is evident from Wenger's argument and related studies that the focus on identity also implies the necessity of accepting diversity as a resource for development (rather than as a hindrance or just as statistical variance).

It is, however, how this process works in specific instances that is the topic of a number of research projects described here. Thus, using Habermas's concept of communicative understanding as a guideline (as do Macías et al.), Wegerif shows how trying to understand the other "across differences" is a creative act based in an exploratory attitude, an act that "is a more essential characteristic of human reason than explicit reasoning" (the latter representing a monological model of reason). Edwards and Mackenzie indicate how identity shifts occur as people dis- and reidentify with others or with groups, a process that "may involve reflective comparisons between oneself and one's neighbors or friends." Macías et al. describe how identity shifts occur as people move from one social milieu to another: "Cultural identity emerges in contrast with a cultural 'other,' an 'other' that enables an 'alien' view to look into us," they say. At the same time, they emphasize that not only the content of identity changes but also the discursive means by which the identity story is told. Edwards and Mackenzie, too, look at the process of identity formation and point out that it is not a unidirectional or straightforward process: depending on context, identity shifts may take place for one "public" but not for another, and (at least for a time) regression is possible as well as progress.

In a recent argument, Tharp and his colleagues (Tharp et al., 2000) proposed that this focus on identity and diversity brings new challenges to our schools and asks for a transformation of teaching. In particular, the issue of inclusion must be given high priority, both for social reasons (justice) and for reasons of optimizing learning through diverse inputs and interactions. This gradual transformation of the notion of learning inevitably has far-reaching consequences for the organization of the teaching-learning process in schools. However, it would be shortsighted to think of diversity *only* in terms of the benefits for identity development it can entail. Where there are differences between people or groups, there is also very often a question of power and inequality involved. Wegerif, Macías et al., and Edwards and Mackenzie do not pay much attention to this and thus give a rather "benign" account of the importance of dialogue. However, inequality between cultural groups is a central theme in the chapters by de Haan and Elbers, Solis, and Collins.

In the classroom processes investigated by de Haan and Elbers, the presence of a participant from the dominant culture in a discussion group of students influences the process in such a way that "exploratory talk," in the sense Wegerif uses that concept, is inhibited or at least structurally altered, with consequences for the identity processes of the students involved. Solis (who, by the way, uses a concept of identity that seems more inspired by structuralism than that of the other authors in that the role of personal sense giving seems rather diminished) looks at the way identity processes are formed and sustained in discourse that is definitely antihegemonic. Her analysis may have profound implications for education, as it shows how difficult it is to get people to think about themselves in a new way when the system (be it state or school) continuously tries to confirm their "old" identities (cf. Ten Dam, Volman, & Wardekker, 2004). Lastly, Collins exemplifies how power-dominated discourses can distort and inhibit identity processes at the group and system level. Incidentally, his analysis demonstrates how an activity theory model (using the work of Engeström) provides us with some essential viewpoints for the understandings of learning and development that are lacking in some other competing theories.

References

Bauman, Z. (2004). *Identity: Conversations with Benedetto Vecchi*. Cambridge: Polity Press.

Edwards, A. (2005). Understanding mind in world: The Vygotskian legacy. Paper produced for ESRC TLRP Thematic Seminar Series: Contexts, communities, network:

Mobilising learners' resources and relationships in different domains, February 2005 Glasgow Caledonian University.

Egan, K. (2002). *Getting it wrong from the beginning: Our progressivist inheritance from Herbert Spencer, John Dewey, and Jean Piaget.* New Haven, CT: Yale University Press.

Egan, K. (1997). *The educated mind: How cognitive tools shape our understanding.* Chicago: University of Chicago Press.

Holland, D., Lachicotte, W., Skinner, D., & Cain, C. (1998). *Identity and agency in cultural worlds.* Cambridge, MA: Harvard University Press.

Sennett, R. (1998). *The corrosion of character: The personal consequences of work in the new capitalism.* New York: W. W. Norton.

Ten Dam, G., Volman, M., & Wardekker, W. (2004). Making sense through participation: Social differences in learning and identity development. In J. v.d. Linden & P. Renshaw (Eds.), *Dialogic learning: Shifting perspectives to learning, instruction, and teaching* (pp. 63–85). Dordrecht: Kluwer.

Tharp, R., Estrada, P., Dalton, S. S., & Yamauchi, L. (2000). *Teaching transformed: Achieving excellence, fairness, inclusion, and harmony.* Boulder, CO: Westview Press.

Wenger, E. (1998). *Communities of practice: Learning, meaning, and identity.* Cambridge: Cambridge University Press.

9

Identity Shifts in Informal Learning Trajectories

Anne Edwards and Lin Mackenzie

The English government is currently exercised by a breakdown in social cohesion, which is evidenced in the number of citizens who find themselves at risk of social exclusion, that is, disconnected from those networks which bind people into socially beneficial systems. One strand of the policy response is aimed at enhancing local social capital in order to support the participation of individuals in opportunities to be made available to them. This policy line is a sophisticated and complex response. It aims to intervene in the lives of individuals, their families, and their communities in order to disrupt patterns of social exclusion and to offer new pathways of participation, while helping to develop the wherewithal of individuals to engage with these opportunities. The argument therefore runs that if one is to change lives, one needs to change the environments that shape and are shaped by those lives.

This approach therefore appears to have much in common with socio-cultural and activity theory (SAT) interpretations of the extent to which the social and cultural are incorporated in the individual. However, SAT analyses are usually strong in their drive from the social or cultural to the individual (Chaiklin, 2001; Engeström, 1987, 1999), but are arguably less well-developed when focussing on how individuals interpret and act in their social worlds. The individual, for example, appears curiously absent in the following accounts.

What we learn and what we know, and what our culture knows for us in the form of the structure of artefacts and social organisation are those chunks of mediating structure. Thinking consists of bringing these structures into co-ordination with each other such that they can shape (and be shaped by) each other. *The thinker*

The research team involved in the study described in this chapter consisted of Anne Edwards, Lin Mackenzie, Stewart Ranson, and Heather Rutledge, and the project was funded by the Joseph Rowntree Foundation.

in this world is a very special medium that can provide co-ordination among many structured media, some internal, some external, some embodied in artefacts, some in ideas, and some in social relationships. (Hutchins, 1986, p. 57, emphasis added)

Human actions and their psychological aspects must be grasped as particular parts of social practices. (Dreier, 1999, p. 7)

The concrete location of individual subjects in social practice remains strangely implicit or ambiguous. (Dreier, 1999, p. 6)

When we turn to activity theory, the lack of connection between the individual and collective is acknowledged as a difficulty (Engeström, 1999). Here the individual seems to be only a bit player and appears almost by default, perhaps when she is faced with something unexpected and is in a context that allows her to respond to it. Jay Lemke (2001) calls this phenomenon "slippage." (A slippage in a system allows the individual to emerge.)

In our recent work we have been looking at the learning trajectories of adults who are vulnerable to social exclusion and who have participated in the community-based provision, loosely termed Family Learning Centres. These centres aim at enhancing the capabilities of participants, thereby building their resilience and enabling their participation in socially beneficial systems. In this study we have been challenging SAT to pay more attention to the processes of the incorporation of the collective in the individual.

We suggest that SAT could then make a useful contribution to understanding how trajectories of exclusion might be disrupted. For example, analyses of learning trajectories in both formal and informal learning during adulthood (Antikainen, 1998; Gorard et al., 1998) have suggested that patterns of participation in learning opportunities owe much to existing patterns within families. That is, families in which there is a history of participation are more likely to produce individuals who take up opportunities to learn. If we are to understand how these patterns of nonparticipation are disrupted and such disruptions are provoked in order to widen participation and increase social cohesion, we need a stronger and forward-looking understanding of how the individual connects with the social and collective than is arguably currently available.

LEARNING AND IDENTITY IN OUR STUDY
OF LEARNING TRAJECTORIES

We are working with a situated notion of learning, to the extent that we see mind and action produced in participation in sets of practices. We acknowledge that the discursive practices of settings produce specific forms of subjectivities within those settings (Cubero and de la Mata, 2001; Walkerdine, 1997). Yet we are also interested in how the subjectivities, of those whose trajectories of exclusion are disrupted, are formed and transformed. Dreier's (1999, 2000) analyses of socially sustained pathways of participation offer a useful starting point, but they do not attend sufficiently closely to the personal sense making of participants to meet our concerns. Instead, we want to gain some purchase on what can be done at a microlevel to enable those who are vulnerable to social exclusion to move towards the opportunities for inclusion that are made available to them.

When examining identity formation within settings such as Family Learning Centres, we have focussed on the extent to which the settings are providing flexible client-centred learning zones for participants, encouraging participants to expand their interpretations of the resources available to support their actions, and enabling them to reposition themselves as capable actors in their worlds. We make little distinction, therefore, between learning and shifts in identity. For us, identity is closely aligned with a capacity for particular forms of action and hence a capacity to interpret and use environmental affordances to support action. We, thus, follow both Harré (1983) and Luckmann (1982) in their views that identity operates as an organising principle for action and that people intentionally direct their actions towards projects they believe they can realise. However, we pay more attention to contextual affordances for action and how they are interpreted than Harré and Luckmann appeared to be doing at the time. We also recognise that individual learning trajectories need to be traced over time and across locations if we are to capture how individuals' spiralling in and out of different settings shape their interpretations of and responses to the action potential in each setting.

THE STUDY

The study consisted of two phases. The first involved a mapping of family learning provision across England through a questionnaire to managers of Education Action Zones, that is, areas of specific economic deprivation that were receiving additional educational funding. The questionnaire was followed up by interviews with a purposive sample in order to identify strong themes in terms of funding, location, and purpose. The second stage consisted of a set of case studies (n = 6), which between them represented the broad themes that emerged in the first phase.

In this chapter we focus on the findings from one of the case studies: a drop-in centre that is used primarily but not exclusively by women and

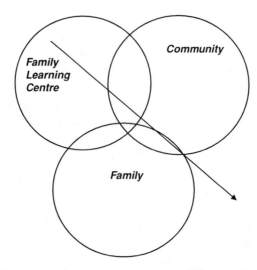

Figure 9.1. A learning trajectory across different settings.

is situated near the middle of a large city. In our analysis, we have used a framework derived from activity theory (Engeström, 1999). This has allowed us to explore the dynamics that are found within the setting, between the histories of the services and the workers who run it, the division of labour within it, the communities that inform its goals, the activities that take place, and how they are interpreted and their outcomes.

When looking at how participants were developing their identities as participants in those settings and were operating in other settings including their families, we needed a conceptual framework that recognised their trajectories across settings, with or without support from professionals within the Family Learning Centres. The framework is shown in outline in Figure 9.1. Using this framework as a heuristic, we examined the overlaps between services and the practices that occurred within them as a result of closer partnerships among service providers in communities and analysed how they supported consistent forms of participation across settings (Edwards et al., 2002).

We are now turning to the trajectories of individuals in order to explore how they developed as learners and how practices in the drop-in centre were supporting that learning. The conceptual framework indicated in Figure 9.1 meant that in individual trajectories we were alert to differences between settings in how individuals saw and therefore positioned themselves and their capacity to transform their worlds as they participated in them. That is, we were looking for what Nederveen Pieterse refers to as "signs of empowerment" in life histories (Nederveen Pieterse, 1992). However, we preferred to talk of seeking signs of agentic action, where agency is recognised as a capacity to act on and transform the object of activity and to be able to evaluate what one has done.

THE SUPPORT OF INDIVIDUAL TRAJECTORIES

When examining learning and the conditions in which it occurs, we have worked with parallel but different notions of the zone of proximal development (ZPD). Firstly, in exploring the practices that shape identities in the family learning centres, our focus was on the extent to which these centres as activity systems operated as learning or development zones (Engeström, 1987). We were, for example, interested in whether they were responsive to the needs and strengths of participants and were flexible enough to accommodate their dynamic identity development. That is, our gaze was directed at the capacity for responsive slippage evident in the work of the centres.

When examining the identity trajectories of individual participants in these settings, we have worked with a more relational version of the ZPD, which owes much to notions of assisted performance (Schaffer, 1992). Here, our concern has been with how individuals, in both formal and informal environments, are able to engage with others in order to approach, assess, and respond to the possibilities for action available to them in a situation – that is, in activity theory terms, how they are able to expand the object of the activity together. We are calling this capacity relational agency, where such agency is evident in the ability to both give and seek support.

We are, of course, not the first to attempt to look at joint action and mutual support within the sociocultural field. For example, van Oers and Hännikäinen (2001), looking at early education, have described the concept of "togetherness" in which they drew on Vygotskian concerns with affect. They argued for more attention to group processes in the study of learning in the early years of education and particularly to how intersubjectivity, as mutual understanding, is created and maintained. Their analysis focused on group belonging, however, and not on how relational agency is generated and sustained in interaction with another. Goldstein (1999), also working in an educational setting, similarly examined the affective nature of the ZPD. Using the work of Noddings (1984) on the ethics of care, she augmented what she described as current understandings of the ZPD as an interpsychological dimension with an understanding of it as an interrelational one. Her emphasis was on teachers' connections with learners' standpoints and engrossment in and receptivity to learners' positions in order to struggle jointly to make sense.

We also find support for our attention to the relational from Hicks (2000), who has suggested that moral projects are curiously absent from discussions of social learning. For Hicks, in such projects self is placed in relation to the intentions of others. She argued that a shift in emphasis to a stronger recognition of the moral elements involved in recognising others' sense making and goals can enrich existing dialogic accounts of learning. This notion of self-in-relation also resonates with Taylor's (1991) concern with responsible engagement with others, with Shotter (1993) in his call for relational ethics, and with Benhabib (1991) on discursive rationality. Arguably by engaging with the motives of others and, in Bruner's (1996) terms, considering how those relate to cultural "proprieties," people become included in practices that support the well-being of others and ultimately of themselves. This argument again echoes Noddings on the ethics of care.

We do not see the two interpretations of ZPD as incompatible. We find support for this suggestion in Valsiner's fine-grained analyses of the connections between a ZPD and the contexts in which it is enacted, where, for example, the zone of freedom of movement internalised by those working within a ZPD may differ between settings (Valsiner, 1998). Consequently, we recognise that different settings allow for different forms of relationship within a ZPD.

Here, given the focus on individual trajectories, we pay more attention to the relational assisted performance version of the ZPD than to the idea of centres as learning or development zones. We are particularly interested in how trajectories of exclusion are disrupted, how new trajectories are supported, and how they change over time. In listening to the accounts of their own learning given by Tracey, Maggie, and the other women we have interviewed and met with in focus groups, we have been struck by a common pattern of modes of participation as learners and associated identity shifts.

These modes can be captured in broad terms in the Vygotskian analyses of emergent identity offered by Rom Harré (1983). The attractions of this model, shown in Figure 9.2, include its capacity to show change over time, its ability to capture Vygotskian distinctions between the intermental and the intramental (or the collective and the individual), and the opportunity to consider how individuals contribute to the social or intermental plane and shift understandings within it. The model assumes that in the process of learning and identity development, individuals move from quadrant 1 through 2 and 3 to 4. Harré acknowledges that it is merely a heuristic and that distinctions between quadrants are not clear-cut. For example, there is a dynamic going to and fro between 1 and 2, and he notes that, at the time he produced the model, too little was known about movement between 2 and 3. The model is enriched by subsequent sociocultural analyses. For example, Lave and Wenger's (1991) descriptions of learning, identity, and knowledge use and production mean that we are now more likely to attend to movement between 3 and 4 than did Harré. In addition, enhanced understandings of

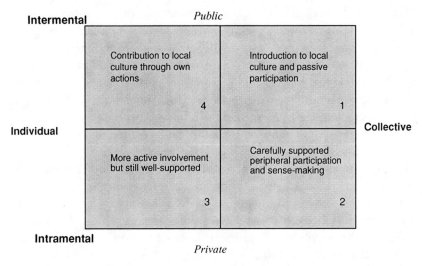

Figure 9.2. Steps in a pathway of participation.

the conversational bases of learning and intersubjectivity – see, for example Shotter (1993) – suggest that quadrants 2 and 3 are sites of relational support for individual interpretations and actions. That is, the other is always in some way part of our learning trajectory. Nonetheless, the model, together with the more recent insights just outlined, has proved a useful framework for raising questions about and informing our analyses of individual learning trajectories.

In exploring these trajectories, we have asked three broad questions.

- Is there a pattern of participation over time, which suggests that there may be stages in modes of participation? That is, what are the identity shifts?
- How are these identity shifts and any associated learning supported?
- Are there differences in modes of participation between settings?

LOOKING AT THE INDIVIDUAL STORIES

In addition to gathering background information in interviews with centre workers, we have gathered evidence on individual learning trajectories in three ways:

- Observations in the centre and on visits, that is, "trips" with users of the centre
- Focus group interviews with users of the centre
- Individual interviews with people who use the centre

Evidence from all three sources has informed our analyses and our across-case comparisons. However, the data presented here come mainly from interviews with individual users in the Hollybush drop-in centre carried out once people had become accustomed to our participation in centre events. In tracing the trajectories of Tracey and Maggie, whom we have taken as exemplars, we have explored with them their entry into the centre, why they stayed, what and how they have learnt there, what and how they have learnt elsewhere, how they related currently to the centre, and what their future plans as learners were. But first some background on the Hollybush Centre.

Hollybush had an established history of engagement with the community it served and a primary focus on the needs of women. The workers, who are all women, offered, in addition to the drop-in facility, a range of services that included support for mental health problems, financial advice, childcare, and short-term learning projects in collaboration with, for example, adult education and community arts services. Its work within its inner-city community had evolved over fifteen years. Workers in the centre came from social services, housing, and financial advice and volunteer backgrounds, but worked fluidly and collaboratively across roles and responsibilities.

Although the centre aimed at helping women to reposition themselves within their worlds so that they were able to deal with the complex demands of relationships, childcare, and economic viability, it did not have as a primary concern either the creation of good mothers or the production of a capable work force. Workers refused to intervene with children if their mothers were present, and adult education opportunities were a far lower priority than short "trips," which enabled participants to see the world beyond the confines of their housing estate. Rather, the centre aimed at helping participants to deal with breakdowns in social networks and to build up new networks of social support by encouraging mutually supportive relationships within the centre. The workers liked to see themselves as friends to users and aimed at creating an open and accepting family ethos.

> WORKER 1: It's the same for every individual. If you've got a friend who doesn't judge you and you know is supportive, then that can make a big difference.

The importance of nonjudgmental support resonated throughout our interviews, as shown in a centre worker's comments about the "drop-in" element characteristic of the centre:

> WORKER 2: I think that purpose is having somewhere to go that is open, you can go in at any level really. Go in for a cup of coffee. Go in for

advice. You don't need a reason to step over the door, you know in terms of using the professionals here. . . . you might be meeting your friend, seeing what is going on for the kids, somewhere where you can take the kids and we don't mind if they make a mess.

The development of this capacity to support each other was also evident in our focus group discussions and interviews with individual participants. As we have already indicated, a capacity to use the resources available does not simply apply to making use of physical resources, such as how to get a loan from the financial advice service. It also involves a capacity to offer support to and ask for support from others. This attribute is an important aspect of relational agency, where one's ability to engage with the world is enhanced through doing so alongside others. What the centre was doing was creating a relatively open system for that kind of fluid form of relational agency to emerge. The fluidity of such relationships is important, as it was clear that what was being encouraged was not dependency but a capacity to both seek and give help when engaging with the world. We can see the impact of those strategies on both Tracey and Maggie.

Tracey's Trajectory

Tracey was in her mid-thirties and was the single parent of three children. Her mother left home when she was ten, and Tracey left school with no formal qualifications. Her self description captures how she has changed over time and why she thinks she has changed:

TRACEY: I'm a bit wild, but I'm very mature. And it is nice because if I had stayed the way I was when I was younger I wouldn't be able to give the kids the knowledge of what I know now and how to behave.

She started to attend the centre because it is located within the local community centre building, and she was familiar with that through using it frequently with her sister. She then became a regular visitor to the centre.

TRACEY: All the staff are very friendly and helpful. It is a nice place to go if you need support and advice.

She was, however, becoming frustrated with other users of Hollybush.

TRACEY: Not enough people turn up for classes so they don't run.

TRACEY: Last year I wanted to do a play for Christmas. And because I couldn't get no support I didn't bother.

TRACEY: Some people in the drop-in aren't friendly to new ones.

When she discussed learning, both familiarity and emotional support remained strong features of her descriptions. For example, her art class run within the centre was

TRACEY: a nice group of women and we all supported each other.

Relationships were also important in her Internet class, which was not run by Hollybush.

TRACEY: I'm able to mix with different people. I like that. I never used to like to talk to people. But I like talking to people now.

When considering learning to drive at the centre, she assessed the alternatives:

TRACEY: I'd have to go to a private instructor, and if I don't like them, then I've got no chance.

Supporting and not supporting seem to be a salient construct for Tracey. When describing her friendships, she explained:

TRACEY: There is a lot of support. I get a lot of support because I give a lot of support. But there's lots round here that don't give any support. So it makes it awkward to live here. But I don't take no notice of them ones.

She has three close friends who help each other out in specific ways.

TRACEY: I help Jade out and I go shopping for her. And she helps me and she baby sits for me with the kids.

She saw herself as very different from her sisters, as someone who is doing something.

TRACEY: I'm the only one who has got any get up and go in my family... and I've done it on my own back

She explained the importance of this degree of independence and difference from other women in her world in terms of being a role model for her daughters. Most of her attempts at engaging with more formal modes of learning such as an Internet class were given the rationale that they would help her to help her children. She became reflective about her own learning when considering its impact on her children. Her father did not give her educational support.

> TRACEY: Dad never said you must do this or you must do that. He never came to a parents' evening (at her school). So we didn't have a really good childhood . . . that's why I'm trying to better myself.

Tracey placed great emphasis on the support she gave her children. But there was no sign that she was helping them to become supportive of others. Again the roots of this strategy could be found in her own history.

> TRACEY: I had to look after me Dad. How to wash clothes and cook, go shopping. Stuff I shouldn't have had to learn about until I was older really. It was really stressful.

Her own agentic action in terms of deliberative action was revealed in her support of her children.

> TRACEY: It [learning Internet skills] is very hard. . . . I found it really frustrating. But I'm doing it because we've got a computer here and I need to learn it for the kids and help them.

> TRACEY: Having children you can't be shy. You have to go out and meet people. . . . you've got to go to school, see the teachers.

But her capacity for deliberative action was nonetheless limited. She was easily dissuaded from pursuing actions such as supporting new people in the drop in or the Christmas play. She was also unwilling to undertake more formal education. Even here, however, her ambition or dream was guided by the salience of support as a life-directing construct for her.

> TRACEY: I'd like to do social work or something like that. Where you can help and advise. I'd like that type of thing. But I haven't got the qualifications and it takes about three to five years to qualify.

Tracey's trajectory appears to have achieved its impetus from a reflective desire to be different from her sisters, many of her neighbours, and the person she was obliged to become when her mother left home. Here she echoed what Hodges (1998) has described as a process of disidentification with the mores of one's community in order to enable oneself to move on.

That impetus was sustained through a number of relationships within which she was variously supported or supporting. Hollybush offered her a new family and a new way of being. Her initial engagement in the activities of the centre was relatively passive (quadrant 1) (Figure 9.2). And even after

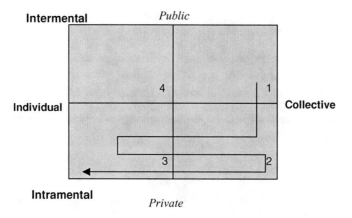

Figure 9.3. Tracey's steps towards participation in the drop-in centre.

seven years she did not appear to be making a contribution to its collective life. That is, she was not operating in quadrant 4. But she was operating in quadrants 2 and 3 and engaging in forms of relational agency both inside and outside the centre, and particularly within her family she was operating as a supporter in quadrant 3.

The support she gained from centre workers led her to take art classes in the centre and Internet classes outside it. It gave validity to her reflections on her own education and that of her children and encouraged the help she gave them as learners. The centre, by emphasising mutual support, helped her develop her capacity to use local resources so that she moved from the in-centre art classes to the external Internet class. There were signs in the interview of the beginnings of her disidentification with Hollybush in her frustrations with users of the drop-in and her new identifications with other learners in her art and Internet classes.

Importantly, we are not tracing a linear trajectory of individual learning and mastery over environmental constraints. Rather we are seeing learning as a capacity to recognise and use what is available to support one's actions and an ability to acknowledge the purposes and direction of those actions. The trajectory is therefore not a simple one of steady progress through the quadrants. (It appears, though, that as she became more actively in control of her life, recursive loops taking her back to quadrant 1 became less necessary.) Tracey had reflected on her own identity shifts, felt pride in her capacity to make them, and recognised how they were supported in relationships in which she was variously the supporter and the supported. If we look at Figure 9.3 we can see that Tracey has made enough movement to be able to operate in quadrant 3 in active ways within the fairly safe private or semiprivate arena of friendly classes, immediate family, and friendships.

Maggie's Trajectory

Maggie was in her late twenties and lived with the father of her two children. Her mother was a single parent, who returned to Jamaica to run her own business. Maggie left school with a low-grade-leaving certificate and undertook a chef's training course. When interviewed, she was a part-time silver service waitress and was taking courses in early-childhood education in a nondegree program, with a view to eventually becoming a teacher. Both of these were relatively recent developments for her and marked a growing confidence. Currently, because of her studying she saw herself as different from friends and neighbours and had started to identify with the teachers in her son's school where she helped out one day a week.

> MAGGIE: Yeah, I think I am a lot different from the people I hang around with. . . . she [a friend] doesn't really understand my need to study.

> MAGGIE: I'm there [at the school] 24/7. They all call me Maggie. I know all the teachers. I'm always invited to all the teachers' meals. I've been to the pub with the teachers.

Maggie started to attend Hollybush eight years ago because she needed the support it offered her. She was still attending regularly but was aware of how far she had moved on and how she could help others.

> MAGGIE: [When you see someone there who is continuously depressed], you think to yourself, well I was lower than that and I've come to this stage now. . . . you have to approach them first, because they won't approach you. . . . you know that because you have been there.

She still got support from the centre.

> MAGGIE: I walk straight into the kitchen . . . and it's nice, they give you a hug and you know it like a proper hug as Luke [her son] does. I am really close to at least five of the women here and probably closer because of that common ground thing [i.e., have all at times had considerable problems].

Her view on successful initial entry into the centre was the ability to "humble yourself" (i.e., accept that you won't be integrated immediately). People were in established supportive relationships with each other. It would take time to integrate (i.e., participation in quadrant 1 was bound to be peripheral). Her role currently extended beyond mutual support to include work on the management committee and joining in painting the centre and scrubbing the kitchen. She told us that "You appreciate places once you contribute to them," and it remained her "safety net."

Her analysis of what Hollybush meant to her echoed Figure 9.1. Although disidentification in order to see herself as a serious learner was important, she recognised the support she got from it. In her case, there was no expectation that the overlaps will be managed by others. Instead, it was her choice that she sustained the connections.

> MAGGIE: You can get isolated by going to Uni[versity] because you have this circle of people doing the same circle of things. . . . this means there is this overlap. It's like me, I've got the centre and I've got the family and it means you are more independent because it actually gives you the confidence to be more independent.

Maggie's childhood was very different from that of Tracey. She was "pushed" by her mother to attend ballet, tap dancing, and karate classes. She visited museums, used the library, attended church. Maggie felt that her mother "invested" in her, and she wanted her mother to "be proud" of her. The motivation for becoming a teacher was to be able to join her mother in Jamaica. She was more "laid back" with her own children, but she was encouraging her older child to support the younger one in, for example, her reading. Maggie arguably had more cultural capital than Tracey and had a supportive brother and aunt and a partner. Nonetheless the social capital engendered in the centre was an important part of what supported her as an actor in her world.

In the centre she no longer operated in quadrant 1 but still benefited from the supportive relationships that are features of quadrants 2 and 3. In addition, she also operated in quadrant 4 and contributed to the collective life of Hollybush. Again, as with Tracey, we are not observing a linear trajectory even in the modes of operation within the centre. Instead, her work in quadrant 4 is sustained by the support she gets and gives in 2 and 3. We can see the pattern in Figure 9.4.

In Figure 9.5 we can see Maggie's parallel trajectories and can observe how situation-specific they are in terms of their development. Outside the centre in, for example, the school where she helps, Maggie is arguably operating in quadrant 1 with some movement into 2, while as a waitress, where she is older than the others and usually team leader, she is again operating in 2, 3, and 4. The school and the club where she is a waitress are very different environments for Maggie in terms of her own history and sense of self-efficacy.

Intermental *Public*

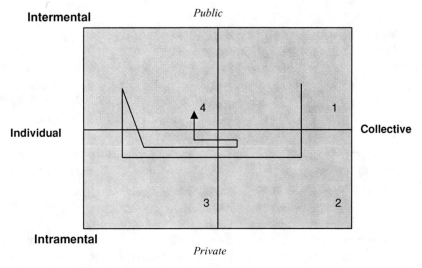

Individual **Collective**

Intramental
Private

Figure 9.4. Maggie's steps towards participation in the drop-in centre.

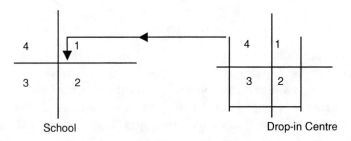

School Drop-in Centre

Figure 9.5. Maggie's parallel trajectories.

But the disruption of her social exclusion and her entrance into these two activity systems seem to have been supported and sustained by the reciprocity of the relationships she continues to experience at Hollybush.

DISCUSSION OF THE TRAJECTORIES

Is there a pattern of participation over time? What are the identity shifts? It does seem that there is a pattern of progression between the four quadrants shown in Figure 9.2. But that progression is not linear; rather there is a movement back and forth in order to gather resources for action in a more advanced mode of participation. Identity shifts do seem to involve a process of disidentification and reidentification. But these processes are not necessarily a discarding of family patterns. They may also involve reflective comparisons between oneself and one's neighbours or friends.

How are these identity shifts and associated learning supported? There does seem to be a recursive movement through the quadrants with forms of generally supported peripheral participation in 1 and forms of relational agency in operation in 2 and 3, which allow for shared expansion of the objects of activity and joint use of the resources that allow a response to these interpretations.

Are there differences in modes of participation between settings? This seems to depend on continuity of identity across settings. In Tracey's case there is continuity in both identity and mode of participation. Maggie's trajectory shows a recent reidentification as a would-be teacher, which does not noticeably impinge on her identity in the centre. But her capacity to operate in quadrant 4, that is, to demonstrate agentic action and empowerment, is evident across settings, including her family, and has arguably given her the confidence to pursue her ambition to become a teacher and enter another cycle of reidentification.

SOME IMPLICATIONS FOR POLICY

The Hollybush Centre has provided both Tracey and Maggie (and many others) with the opportunity for a range of modes of participation, from peripheral or passive participation through sets of supportive relationships to the opportunity to contribute to its collective life through deliberative action, which enhances the resources available to others. Its practices offered enough flexibility for movement through the four quadrants in either direction. Its success warns against too strong an emphasis on learning as a matter of individual and sustained mastery and for the need to attend to the affective and dialogic aspects of learning and identity development. The disruption of trajectories of exclusion is necessarily an affective process. At the very least, such disruptions to existing identity trajectories require emotional support. However, we are saying more than that. We are, in addition, arguing that such disruptions are likely to be achieved through joint action, where agentic action aimed at transforming the object of activity is given support. We are aware that all our examples are women and recognise that our small evidence base needs augmenting before we can generalise.

The two trajectories discussed here do support current policy, which is aimed at the enhancing of social capital. We hope that our analyses have enabled us to examine social capital at a microlevel. Where cultural capital is low, as in the case of Tracey, relational support is a vital resource, but it is also important for the culturally rich Maggie. Relational support needs to be seen as a responsive resource that can be accessed flexibly. Vulnerable people may need to learn how to both seek and offer it. As Antikainen (1998) has observed, the family is the significant mediating institution and learning community. Enhancing the capacity of families and family members to seek and offer forms of relational agency seems likely to build resilience and disrupt trajectories of exclusion.

SOME IMPLICATIONS FOR SAT

The elements of the study discussed here raise two questions for SAT. Both relate to how SAT deals with the incorporation of the collective into the individual. Firstly, we have seen that individuals operate across a number of activity systems. In some settings, the cultural capital they have accrued previously is valued and participation is therefore only briefly peripheral, and some settings are more open to new forms of cultural capital (Holland and Lave, 2001). But it does seem that a capacity for effective contributions to one setting connects with a wider sense of self-efficacy and confidence in an ability to select settings where one's capital is recognised and useful and to move into them. That an ability to act on and transform the object of one's activities, at the very least, gives impetus to identity trajectories. A capacity for deliberative transformative action may be learnt in some settings but not others and may be more easily exercised in some environments. But it is a capacity, and individual learning trajectories within the same settings differ as a result of that capacity. SAT arguably needs to give individual differences the attention it gives to individual settings.

The second point returns to the importance of relationships with others in the identity trajectories described here. Throughout the chapter, reference has been made to relational agency. We have described it as people's ability to seek and use help that expands their interpretations and supports their responsive actions, where agency is a capacity (perhaps emergent rather than actual) to undertake deliberative action. Our analyses across the case studies and amply illustrated in the two trajectories here tell us strongly that a capacity for relational agency both as the supported and the supporter is a crucial factor in the development of purposive identities. We know that intersubjectivity enhances individual performance. Yet SAT analyses of how that operates in different ways at different points in learning trajectories still require some development.

A major attraction of the field initiated by Vygotsky is the importance he placed on the need to develop theory in iteration with the field, by undertaking close examination of the field. Although we cannot claim in our study to have developed theory, we hope that by exploring individual learning trajectories we have at least raised some questions about how SAT deals with individuals.

References

Antikainen, A. (1998). Between structure and subjectivity: Life-histories and lifelong learning. *International Review of Education, 44* (2–3), 215–234.

Benhabib, S. (1991). *Situating the self.* London: Routledge.

Bruner, J. (1996). *The culture of education.* Cambridge, MA: Harvard University Press.

Chaiklin, S. (2001). The category of personality in cultural-historical psychology. In S. Chaiklin (Ed.), *The Theory and practice of cultural-historical psychology* (pp. 238–259). Aarhus: Aarhus University Press.

Cubero, M., & de la Mata, M. (2001). Activity settings, ways of thinking and discourse modes: An empirical investigation of the heterogeneity of verbal thinking. In S. Chaiklin (Ed.), *The theory and practice of cultural-historical psychology* (pp. 218–237). Aarhus: Aarhus University Press.

Dreier, O. (1999). Personal trajectories of participation across contexts of social practice. *Outlines, Critical Social Studies, 1* (1), 5–32.

Dreier, O. (2000). Psychotherapy in clients' trajectories across contexts. In C. Mattingly & L. Garro (Eds.), *Narratives and the cultural construction of illness and healing* (pp. 237–258). Berkeley: University of California Press.

Edwards, A., Mackenzie, L., Ranson, S., & Rutledge, H. (2002). Disruption and disposition in lifelong learning. *Outlines, Critical Social Studies, 4* (1), 49–58.

Engeström. Y. (1987). *Learning by expanding.* Helsinki: Orienta-Konsultit.

Engeström, Y. (1999). Activity theory and individual and social transformation. In Y. Engeström et al. (Eds.), *Perspectives on activity theory* (pp. 19–38). Cambridge: Cambridge University Press.

Goldstein, L. (1999). The relational zone: The role of caring relationships in the co-construction of mind. *American Educational Research Journal, 36* (3), 647–673.

Gorard, S., Rees, G., Renold, E., & Fevre, R. (1998). Patterns of participation in adult education and training. Working Paper 15. School of Education, Cardiff University.

Harré, R. (1983). *Personal being.* Oxford: Blackwell.

Hicks, D. (2000). Self and other in Bakhtin's early philosophical essays: Prelude to prose consciousness. *Mind, Culture, and Activity, 7* (3), 227–242.

Hodges, D. (1998). Participation as dis-identification with/in a community of practice. *Mind, Culture, and Activity, 5* (4), 272–290.

Holland, D., & Lave, J. (Eds.). (2001). *History in person.* Oxford: James Currey.

Hutchins, E. (1986). Mediation and automatization. *Quarterly Newsletter of the Laboratory of Comparative Human Cognition, 8* (2), 47–58.

Lave, J., & Wenger, E. (1991). *Situated learning: Legitimate peripheral participation.* Cambridge: Cambridge University Press.

Lemke, J. (2001). Re: horizontal/vertical/dialogue/dialectic. XMCA discussion archive, April 2001, http://lchc.ucsd.edu/histarch/index.hmtl.

Luckmann, T. (1982). Individual action and social knowledge. In M. von Cranach & R. Harré (Eds.), *The analysis of action*. Cambridge: Cambridge University Press.

Nederveen Pieterse, J. (1992). Emancipations, modern and postmodern. In J. Nederveen Pieterse (Ed.), *Emancipations, modern and postmodern* (pp. 5–43). London: Sage.

Noddings, N. (1984). *Caring*. Berkeley: University of California Press.

Schaffer, R. (1992). Joint involvement episodes as contexts for cognitive development. In H. McGurk (Ed.), *Childhood social development: Contemporary perspectives* (pp. 99–129). Hove: Lawrence Erlbaum.

Shotter, J. (1993). *Cultural politics of everyday life*. Buckingham: Open University Press.

Taylor, C. (1991). *The Ethics of authenticity*. Cambridge, MA: Harvard University Press.

Valsiner, J. (1998). *The guided mind*. Cambridge, MA: Harvard University Press.

van Oers, B., & Hännikäinen, M. (2001). Some thoughts about togetherness: An introduction. *International Journal of Early Years Education, 9* (2), 101–108.

Walkerdine, V. (1997). Redefining the subject in situated cognition theory. In D. Kirshner & J. Whitson (Eds.), *Situated cognition: Social, semiotic and psychological perspectives* (pp. 57–70). Mahwah, NJ: Lawrence Erlbaum.

10

No Human Being Is Illegal

Counteridentities in a Community of Undocumented Mexican Immigrants and Children

Jocelyn Solis

Mexico's close proximity to the United States has historically been a source of both tension and political and economic resourcefulness. While the study of globalization and economic expansion has been an important component of immigration and politics between both countries (Suarez-Orozco, 1998), little attention has been paid to the concurrent personal life and changes in immigrants themselves. This chapter attempts to illustrate how Mexican immigrants and their children in New York undergo psychological trans-formations in the context of their institutional and personal histories and actions. Using Vygotskian sociohistorical theory, I investigate how Mexican immigrants create tools to appropriate and transform their surrounding social context as they concurrently define and transform themselves. This chapter specifically illustrates how "undocumented" Mexican immigrants and children develop their own identities through interactions with the challenges and pressures of society. My purpose is also to understand the psychological functions of identity in material ways: how undocumented Mexican immigrants identify themselves and what this allows them to do, think, and know at particular times and places. In this sense, identity is used as an overarching cultural frame for knowledge, thought, and action, rather than as one component of human development.

MEXICANS IN NEW YORK

By focusing on the dialectical tension between individuals and society, this chapter considers the emergence of illegality as one possible historically situated identity. Issues of immigration are often controversial and politically charged, raising concerns about the extent to which the presence of newcomers affects the country on a societal (social, cultural, economic) and institutional level. Illegal immigration, in particular, has been an ongoing focus of public discussion in the United States, reemerging especially strongly during times of economic recession and presidential campaigning. Due to geographic proximity, Mexican nationals are often at the center of debates on illegal immigration and the object of xenophobic discourse when represented in the media as a threat to the country's stability in terms of economic, linguistic, and cultural homogeneity (e.g., Wolfe, 1997). In spite of such disapproval, Mexican migration to the United States has increased at great speed, especially to geographic sectors that were not formerly receiving sites. New York City has become such a receiving region as a result of economic policies and crises in Mexico since 1982 (Smith, 1996); activists estimate that the Mexican population in New York currently numbers more than 500,000 people. While an understanding of the social, political, historical, and economic conditions that exist in both Mexico and the United States is necessary to make sense of undocumented immigration, this chapter focuses on the societal level through individual migrants' experiences and organized actions.

THEORETICAL BASIS

According to Scribner (1985), Vygotsky divides the study of psychological phenomena along several levels of history. In Scribner's modified version, they include four simultaneously occurring levels: the history of the species, the history of individual societies, the life history of the individual, and the history of a particular psychological system. I base my analysis along this multidevelopmental organization, especially along the last three levels of history in a heuristic sense. That is, this organization allows me to identify important levels of analysis as one way of conceptualizing the problem of illegal identity with the understanding that such separation is really a theoretical tool to understand how each level is present in an integrated way when the problem is studied empirically. Thus, societal history comprises the wider, large-scale, institutional situation of illegal immigration, whereas individual history (ontogeny) represents the more local practices associated with undocumented immigrants; the third level of history is the development of identity as a psychological system. Illegality as an identity is theorized as the integration of societal and individual histories, rather than as separate, hierarchical, or linear progressions. Therefore, society and individual are dialectal dimensions of the history of identity as a psychological system.

Identity is a psychological system that integrates the individual's external-material activities with mental activity. My argument is that external structures (e.g., legal status, race or ethnicity, gender) are adopted by individuals through activities to identify themselves in certain ways. In other words, identity is a developmental process, continuous and malleable according to the surrounding context, the material and social conditions (Deaux, 1993; Moscovici, 2001). The formation of illegality as an identity can be thought to have its origins in external conditions, outside of the individual. I have argued elsewhere that the world is arranged according to ownership of territories enforced by structures of protection and control; they presuppose the fact that borders can be crossed either legally or illegally (Solis, 2001). The identity category "legal/illegal immigrant" is already available to Mexican immigrants before they cross the U.S.-Mexico border. Therefore, I argue that "illegal immigrant" is an available identity that preexists individual people. It comes to function as an identity when it is adopted by individual people for a purpose, such as to understand the organization of U.S. society and their own place of silence and invisibility in it.

Illegality as an identity serves as a political and moral divider, one that validates some as insiders, or people who "belong" in the United States, while identifying others as outsiders who have committed an illicit act. It also serves as a racial divider because illegal immigration is generally associated with nonwhites. The development of illegality as an identity in an individual's history thus has its origins in the broader, societal history and social structures that set up categories of membership and nonmembership. As a psychological system, personal identity is a phenomenon that is constructed historically, politically, and culturally.

A related body of research has investigated the sociocultural formation of the self from the perspective of the social psychology of identity (Deaux & Philogène, 2001) and social cognition. For instance, Leahy and Shirk (1985) argue that, through social interactions, children come to distinguish between themselves and others; over time, their sense of self becomes less dependent on interaction with others. Similarly, Hart and Damon (1985) argue that children's sense of self as an entity separate from other people becomes increasingly integrated and synthesized as children move from one developmental stage to another. Although these researchers and others (e.g., Smollar & Youniss, 1985) suggest that the formation of a self-concept comes out of one's participation in interpersonal relations and events, their methods fail to look directly to such activities by relying on interviews and scales that cannot describe the developmental process in a contextually rich manner. Moreover, their theoretical perspective stresses the developmental sequencing of self-formation and fails to question its teleological assumptions and cultural relativity. Such research leaves little room to understand the origins of developmental diversity, variability, and multiplicity in the formation of selves.

Social representation theory also states that the formation of cognitive phenomena is rooted in social interaction and communication between individuals and groups of people forming a dialectical relationship between individual thought and social conventions (Augoustinos & Walker, 1995). Moscovici (2001) defines social representations as the everyday thoughts and common knowledge or assumptions constructed by a collectivity and shared by individuals. Within a similar perspective, Jones et al. (1984) examine the way in which self-concepts are formed through social comparison. Making the political context explicit, they discuss the effects of stigmatization by others on the formation of the self that result in low self-esteem and social withdrawal. They also mention the potential individuals have to form alternative social comparison groups that resist stigmas imposed by those in power as might be the case in the formation of an "undocumented" identity. However, much of this work is theoretical, requiring examination of the activities through which social comparisons become available to individuals and analysis of multiple, simultaneous, and contradictory social comparisons that give rise to concepts of oneself. Social psychological theories of self or identity formation also tend to leave unquestioned the function of this development, another indication that identity has become a naturalized given in psychological literature. Thus, *deconstruction* of the self as a method of postmodern and poststructuralist psychology (Gergen, 1990; Henriques et al., 1984) is a primordial step in critically analyzing the sociopersonal functions of illegality as an identity.

Taking political function into account further, it is not surprising that much of the Mexican American and Chicano literature takes issue with the development of racial or ethnic identity in adults and children (García & Hurtado, 1995; Hurtado, 1996; Matute-Bianchi, 1991; Meier & Ribera, 1993; Sánchez, 1993). As race or ethnicity is a critical divider or organizing social structure of U.S. society, the existence of a Mexican identity to be studied and affirmed functions as a vehicle for political existence and representation. People are grouped according to racial or ethnic identities as a way of becoming visible and being acknowledged by those in power.

The formation of ethnic or racial identity has also been conceptualized as a psychological reaction to racism and discrimination. Cross (1995) states that a primary, defensive function of African American youths' "oppositional" identities is to protect them against racism and psychological stress. He argues that a fully developed black identity also offers a sense of purpose and affiliation and serves as a mechanism to facilitate interaction with nonblacks. In other words, racial identity emerges as a reaction to societal prejudice against racial minorities.

Although politically relevant, much of this literature examines the functions of racial identity in its own right. This chapter characterizes some ways in which immigration status intersects with the formation of identity for Mexican children and adults in the United States. Therefore, it is necessary to understand how illegality acts as one way of organizing the Mexican community in New York within particular political, social, historical, and personal contexts. It is important to keep in mind, however, how other social structures are embedded within the complex development of identity of Mexican immigrants and their children. Illegality as an identity is thus multifaceted, encompassing not only immigration status but also race, ethnicity, language, and geographic location. Physical proximity and close interaction with linguistically and racially diverse groups in the city creates multiple possibilities and sites for the formation of identity. Hence, I argue that the activities (mental and material) in which undocumented immigrants and children engage serve as grounds for the formation of an illegal or undocumented identity at particular moments and places.

Social constructionism offers a method to denaturalize psychological phenomena by *deconstructing* objects of study, such as identity, and locating their basis in history, culture, and politics. Postmodernism (Lyotard, 1984) and poststructuralist views (Poster, 1989) also question the teleological, unitary, and hegemonic stances taken by social theories. Unlike traditional theories that essentialize people as one personality category or identity, Henriques et al. (1984) posit that the "positionalities" of subjects of theory and research must be considered in contexts of power and multiplicity, where assumptions and values are politically created and contested. Rather than study identity, then, as a hegemonic and progressively cohesive, naturally occurring entity, it must be redefined and studied through multiple and simultaneous subject positions (e.g., "illegal" immigrant; parent; worker) occupied or transformed by individuals in complex, continuous, and changing relationships.

The formation of identity, thus, cannot be studied here in a teleological fashion, where identity changes in age-related increments until it reaches some fully developed form. Rather, identity is understood as a psychological form that emerges under simultaneous, intersecting societal and individual dimensions of history through goal-directed actions. Thus, studies of racial or ethnic identity serve to counter predominant ideologies and to create the possibility for multiple identities to exist for investigation. This poststructuralist, cultural-historical stance views identity formation and human development in general as variable and multiple. In other words, my objective is to discover some of the contextual and cultural conditions that make illegality as an identity possible in the psychological formation of Mexican immigrants and their children.

Central to this discussion is the notion of cultural activity. Developmental theories have placed a great emphasis on defining the role of activity to explain psychological change (Brandtstädter, 1998). While some have emphasized the individual's key psychological activities to lie in internal, self-regulatory mechanisms and cognitive operations, others have also emphasized the physical and material actions of the individual on the environment in a number of ways. I borrow the Vygotskian notion of activity captured in the dialectical relationship between the outer, social world and the individual's inner consciousness through the use of cultural tools. Vygotsky tells us that human mental functioning is never solely habitual or solely cognitive but is always developing in this dialectal relationship. Practical activity, or human goal-directed behavior, is mediated by the creation of cultural tools that function to reorient one's activity, transforming it from material activity to mental activity, which is then exercised on the material, social world (Vygotsky & Luria, 1994). Vygotsky's explanation of the development of thought exemplifies these principles best. As the child is exposed to and participates in language (which is culturally created), she comes to acquire the language of her world in a functional sense; that is, external speech becomes egocentric, allowing the child to "think aloud" and plan future actions when involved in practical activity; in time, egocentric speech is transformed into inner speech or thought, yet serves a similar purpose: to plan and coordinate actions in the world (Vygotsky, 1986). In this way, language is a cultural tool transformed into signs, a symbol system developed from the actual social practices and interpersonal relationships through which its meanings are *scaffolded* by more expert partners; eventually, signs mediate between the individual's outer social world and inner consciousness through practical, meaningful, and intentional activity.

In order to understand the place of interaction between individual and societal histories, there needs to be an appropriate unit of analysis: cultural activity that comprises both the resources and structures already available in society, and the individual's participation and employment of them as tools that help achieve a particular goal. Discourse was one cultural activity that was examined in this study, using Vygotsky's explanation of the relationship between language and thinking. Leont'ev (1978, p. 59) states that Vygotsky "isolated two principal interrelated features that must be considered basic to psychological science. These are the equipped ('instrumented') structure of human activity and its incorporation into the system of interrelationships with other people." In this framework, discourse is understood to encompass not only structural aspects of language but also a broader system of communication and understanding. Discourse is a preexisting semiotic system, a cultural resource, that can reflect, construct, and change social reality. As adopted by the individual for practical action, discourse becomes constitutive of the mind. Thus, self-identity can be one outcome of discourse, where discourse is both a societal condition and a personal resource (Daiute, 1998; Guerra, 1998).

Discourse psychology has offered a more contextualized and dynamic account of psychological phenomena than have traditional studies of identity that view identity as a composite of traits inherent to the individual (Parker, 1997). Falling within the rubric of social constructionism, it posits that psychological phenomena such as identity emerge from discourses present in social institutions, embedded in relations of power. Social constructionism provides a lens with which to critically scrutinize structuralist views of the self by examining the cultural and political basis of its formation (Gergen, 1990). Rather than being assumed to be an essential entity or a natural given, identity is the individual's variable occupation of a social position within a system of available locations of power (Harré & Gillett, 1994; Parker, 1997). In this sense, identity is constructed through language activities that produce one's social positions; thus, identity is a point of convergence of both societal and individual development (Gergen, 1991; Parker, 1997).

National discourses on illegal immigration take the form of societal, institutional responses (e.g., by way of the media or the law) that presume to maintain the ideals of American liberal democracy, such as justice to all law-abiding citizens. This type of discourse makes it possible for undocumented immigrants to be denounced, at both an institutional and individual dimension, as unsolicited individuals, undeserving of jobs and social services that pertain to others. Public, social institutions present discourses of national homogeneity and stability, characteristics to be defended by combating the invasion of "illegal" immigrants (Edstrom, 1993). Such discourses by institutions become available to U.S. citizens to use as a means of understanding one's position within the problem. Institutions in general are social structures governed by certain ideological premises that set up markers of inclusion and exclusion. Discourses, as the language of institutions, convey certain messages formalized by guiding ideologies that they are designed to maintain; some have called such discourses "speech genres" (Bakhtin, 1986) or society's "grand narratives" (Lyotard, 1984). By the same token, however, institutions are made up of individual people who represent the whole.

This study understands the psychological formation of illegality as an identity to be situated in networks of Mexican immigrants, members of institutions whose activities give meaning to this identity. Moreover, their identity functions as an overarching framework through which knowledge, thought, and goal-directed actions are formed. In this way, it is important to understand how Mexican families negotiate multiple societal values, opinions, and attitudes toward undocumented immigrants with their own experience and understanding of what it means to be undocumented, and what they do with this understanding. Again, this must be viewed within the individual's discursive participation, cultural activities, and social positions within certain institutions.

THE STUDY

The site of my research was a grass-roots Mexican immigrant organization in New York City that I call *La Organización Guadalupana.* Specifically, I theorize that community organizing has been one instrument for undocumented immigrants to adopt a publicly recognizable position, a rather uncommon stance taken by a population that generally needs to remain hidden. Here, I draw a theoretical distinction between an "illegal" identity as that preexisting social position adopted by Mexican immigrants and an "undocumented" identity, a *counterposition* constructed by Mexican immigrants specifically to contest predominant discourses about them. Based on ethnographic participant observation I conducted over two years, I conclude that community organizing, especially at the grass-roots level, serves as a cultural-psychological tool for contestation of an illegal identity and for the emergence of an undocumented identity. My findings on the organization's institutional position were based on an analysis of public documents I collected and that I triangulated with conversations and written texts produced in a writing workshop I conducted with Mexican children and with interviews with their mothers. This chapter focuses on the activities of the children's writing workshop in which they were asked to write and illustrate a booklet about their lives for future immigrant children and families. However, I should first note what the organization of which they are a part claims. Essentially, I found that the organization's critical counterdiscourse on illegality emerges strongly in a series of texts published monthly in an information bulletin, as well as interpersonally in community meetings and during immigrants' rights protests. For instance, placards commonly read "no human being is illegal."

Examples of how the institutional counterdiscourse of the organization serves the psychological development and critical consciousness of individuals can be found in texts produced separately by mothers and children.

For instance, the women I interviewed claimed significant changes to their self-esteem and self-confidence were the result of having engaged in a range of activities of the organization. They claimed to have achieved a new sense of empowerment as a result of speaking, reading, and writing activities in which their subjectivities were pronounceable and critical of predominant views of "illegal" immigrants. They learned to see themselves as individuals who are part of larger social forces in which they partake and of global politics that disregard their welfare. The women claimed, moreover, that their sense of empowerment transferred to other situations outside of the organization. As they described them, these changes were part of a process that did not take place overnight but were the result of their participation in a number of activities fomented institutionally by the organization. Their personal transformation into communicators and activists points to the psychological importance of the speaking and writing tools provided by the organization. Under a common framework where goals in support of one's rights are shared, these cultural activities became psychological tools, significant in the women's personal development.

As for their children, all of those who participated consistently in the project (a total of five children between five and fourteen years of age) were bilingual to varying degrees, although its five core participants were English-dominant. For example, when we first met, Marcos, who was nine years old, claimed he could not write in Spanish at all and often checked his spelling with me when he wrote texts in English. He also stated repeatedly that he could not speak Spanish well and preferred to speak English. By the end of the project, however, he did learn to decode texts in Spanish even though he never attempted to write in it. No doubt, his contact with other Mexican children who were raised in New York and who had developed language skills in both English and Spanish was a source of inspiration for Marcos, even though English usage dominated all of our sessions. In spite of his own hesitation about the quality of his Spanish, Marcos displayed throughout the course of our project a range of oral Spanish usage, including the ability to retell jokes he had heard on Spanish-language television. Apart from his linguistic transformation, he seemed to begin to undergo a transformation of consciousness as well. His mother testified to a development I had also witnessed: by the end of our workshop, Marcos was beginning to embrace an antiassimilationist stance that contradicted his earlier position of anti-Mexican affiliation. One could theorize that his involvement in the workshop had served to "counterscaffold" him into an ideology that allowed him to better understand, participate, and identify with his peers, family, and community.

ACTIVITIES LEADING TO CRITICAL CONSCIOUSNESS IN CHILDREN

Key discourse activities engaging the children were revising and editing texts. These activities provided the children with a special forum for the display of their language and literacy skills, as well as for cultural knowledge to be encoded. A content analysis revealed that revising was an activity that allowed the group to display cultural knowledge and to develop culturally shared meanings. In addition, such literacy practices allowed the children to counterscaffold themselves by defying and correcting me and each other. In the following exchange, for example, the group collectively revised a text I had compiled from children's responses to a peer interview. The section they revised in this example included responses to a question about how Mexican immigrants come to New York. The text I drafted was a transcription of the group's responses, ranging from flying in on an airplane to crossing the border illegally. One of the youngest girls, Ariel, whom I had interviewed myself and who had difficulty responding to this question, finally replied that people do not fly but walk here. In this excerpt, the older children and I discussed whether this information provided by the five-year-old was accurate:

KAR: [*reading aloud*] *otras personas llegan caminando* [other people get here walking] [*pause*]. *Cruzan la frontera y es un viaje difícil* [They cross the border and it is a difficult journey]

DAV: aw, I thought you meant walking

KAR: I don't think they walk. I think they run across

JOC: should we change it? . . .

JOR: . . . they run?

DAV: yeah

JOR: you mean they're being chased or what?

DAV: yeah, most of the time

KAR: yeah! Because the, the, the–, the American guards, they–, they be chasin' them! [*reading*] *Cruzan la frontera y es un viaje MUY difícil* [They cross the border and it is a VERY difficult journey].

After twelve-year-old Karina's objection that some people run, rather than walk across the border, she further evaluated illegal migration as a "very difficult journey." Thus, revising texts aloud served as opportunities to determine what knowledge about illegal immigration was shared. By the end of the ten meetings, it was clear that fourteen-year-old David and his sister Karina's shared perspectives about illegality were closest to that advocated by the organization. Marcos, Margarita, and Ariel, the youngest of the group, on the other hand, shared less of the older children's knowledge, although they were exposed to our conversations, as well as their families' involvement in the organization's political manifestations. Through such goal-directed activities, the youngest children were beginning to be counterscaffolded into an ideology different from that posed by society, as their own knowledge was revised and reconstructed. On the other hand, the youngest children were more familiar with the organization's public activities through direct experience when they accompanied their parents. Although the meaning of particular words was still to be developed by the youngest children, these events were often coded in Spanish. For example, Margarita, Marcos, and Ariel once recounted a time when they accompanied their mothers to Washington, D.C., for a march for general amnesty; narrating their participation in the event in English, all three children used the word *amnistía* when I questioned them about what the purpose had been. The elicitation of bilingual and bicultural knowledge positioned the children as experts who could use their diverse knowledge and skills to mediate or counterscaffold the expectations of future Mexican immigrants and their consequent integration into life in New York City.

In a content analysis of the children's texts and illustrations, the children did not define themselves in terms of immigration status (being legal or undocumented), although the older children generally did align themselves overtly in favor of undocumented Mexican immigrants. Instead, the children generally used other characteristics to identify themselves or others. For example, Karina produced a comic strip in which a Mexican girl was harassed by another student. In this situation, the social structure of language status became an identifying tool; the Mexican girl is identified as a non-English speaker as well as a person searching for a means of defense. Interestingly, her defense comes from the intervention of a bilingual teacher, an adult authority figure who can mediate between an English-speaking oppressor and a Spanish-speaking oppressed character to redraw relations of power between the two girls. Karina portrayed the learning of English as a necessary means of defense for Mexican immigrant children.

In other illustrations, Karina and the younger children identified themselves relationally by including family members in their drawings. Indirectly, all of the children also identified themselves as inhabitants of New York, often depicting quotidian characteristics of the city such as subways, yellow taxis, and tall buildings with many windows, or places they frequented such as their school or church. When I asked the children to write personal letters describing themselves to our booklet's potential readers, they also described themselves according to place of residence (New York City), age, and physical characteristics such as hair color. Consider Karina's letter, in which she also warned readers about misconceptions about New York City. Such warnings were also deemed important in texts of the organization's bulletins and by the mothers I interviewed later.

Hi! I live in New York City. I have chocolate brown hair. I am twelve years old. I was born in January, 1988. Here in New York there's a lot of pollution and cars and buildings. It's not like in the movies all nice and goody-goody. It's practically the same as Mexico. Karina

When I asked Margarita and Ariel to draw illustrations about themselves instead of writing letters, Margarita drew herself standing next to her parish, which she identified by name in her illustration. This is the same parish that her family frequents and that serves as a neighborhood locale of the *Organización Guadalupana*. Ariel, on the other hand, identified herself according to something she liked: a chocolate ice cream standing outdoors next to her house and her sister. Thus, the children's illustrations also served as tools for the production of graphic texts of identity, although not necessarily in terms of illegality or immigration status. Although the children displayed a wide range of knowledge about undocumented immigrants and generally positioned themselves as their advocates, their social positioning in the context of the writing workshop invoked identifying criteria that came forth moment by moment, interpersonally, in discourse strategies that were pertinent to the goals of the immediate activity. In general, all of this serves as evidence that the children were counterscaffolding their potential audience in terms of their conceptions of life in New York.

CHILDREN'S CONCEPTIONS OF ILLEGALITY AND CITIZENSHIP

In order to test further whether children and youth involved in the organization share similar notions of illegality and citizenship, I examined one session when I had asked my core group of participants to interview each other about other people's beliefs about immigrants and about what they, themselves, believed about immigrants. On this occasion, Karina tried to define the word "immigrant" for Marcos whom she was interviewing and who did not understand my question. Upon learning that Marcos did not know what an immigrant was, I asked Karina to explain this to him so that he would be able to answer the question. To my surprise, she affirmed that an immigrant was a person who had not lived more than ten years in the United

States "'cause in order not to be an immigrant you gotta have at least ten years here, then you could become a citizen. Right?" At this moment, her older brother David began to counter this claim even after Karina insisted that you could "make the papers [file an application], and after ten years you could be a citizen." Karina was alluding to the legal conditions needed for amnesty according to the 1986 Immigrant Reform and Control Act in which legal residency was granted to undocumented immigrants who could demonstrate that they had lived continuously in the United States since 1982. The cutoff date for this last amnesty does not apply to immigrants who entered the U.S. illegally after that date. This includes most Mexicans currently residing in New York, such as Karina and her family.

Karina demonstrated that she understood citizenship in the societal-historical context of immigration as dictated by dominant power structures. In this situation, she defined citizenship as an outcome following from immigration. A citizen is a nonimmigrant, but an immigrant is a potential citizen depending on time lived in the United States according to Karina's understanding. Perhaps recognizing his sister's partial understanding, David challenged her notion of citizenship as a goal of immigrants contingent on time. In their conversation, immigrants were also understood implicitly to be undocumented. David contested Karina's definition by proposing that one has to be born in the United States in order to be a citizen. I also attempted to clarify our definition of immigrants and citizens by asking in a confirmatory way, "Citizens are people who are born here, right?" In this sense, we were introducing a new definition of citizen in relation to immigrant, not based on legal status or human rights, as the organization posits, or on length of stay in the United States, as Karina proposed, but on birthplace. David further argued in favor of this new definition of citizenship as birthright and offered that his U.S.-born, youngest sister is a U.S. citizen and a potential Mexican immigrant.

David, however, later reorganized our shared societal understanding of citizenship, stating that he was also a citizen simply because he lived in the United States. This, again, stirred a debate between him and Karina who reverted to her original understanding: "No, that's not a citizen! ... A[n] immigrant is a person who doesn't have ten years over here who came from another country." David finally ended this discussion by countering societal definitions of U.S. citizens by integrating both legality and residence criteria as a means of identifying citizens. He stated, "Karina, I didn't say I was a *legal* citizen!" Suggesting that he identifies himself as a citizen as a result of residing in the United States, David could also be qualified as an "illegal" citizen, a contradictory term according to predominant societal beliefs.

Through such discourse strategies as defining, challenging, and offering counterarguments, children's understanding of legal or illegal categorizations and citizenship in the context of producing a children's booklet is counter-scaffolded in a direction alternative to that offered by society. Karina and David's responses to the questions with which this session began revealed that their identification of immigrants was expressed not only in terms of illegality or citizenship but also on other social structures of power. Being an immigrant, aside from being a noncitizen, was also understood by these children in terms of class and language inequalities. When questioned about what other people thought about immigrants, Karina identified the other in "other people" as Americans. Specifically, she referred to employers and other adults and children who arrived in the United States prior to Mexican immigrants, describing them as people who think they are better than immigrants because they mistakenly think of immigrants as "different" or unequal. In her response, Karina positioned immigrants as those who are treated unfairly by "Americans" as defined by a social order based on power and time of arrival. She stated, "Some people think that they're different... like they're disrespectful, like, people feel better than them but they're not. They're just the same.... Some Americans, like, when immigrants are working for them... they treat them bad." Because her response assumed immigrants of a working class, I asked her:

JOC: Can kids be immigrants?

KAR: yeah

JOC: so, what do people think about those immigrants? 'Cause they're not working

KAR: um kids? They treat them bad because since they're immigrants, they come here after them [Americans] so they don't know English and they make fun of them.

In her responses, Karina made a distinction between adult immigrants, who are oppressed as a result of their social class, and child immigrants, who are oppressed as a result of their language status. As Stevens (1999) argues, assimilationist ideologies generally assume that one cannot speak a language other than English and be considered American and that one needs to speak English in order to be American. Knowledge of such disparities with which immigrants are faced was retaken when I asked Karina about what she, herself, thought of immigrants. She repeated that people are "just the same," meaning equal, and that immigrants "come here to make a better life, but sometimes it doesn't turn out the way they want it to... 'cause some immigrants, they come here to get a better job, but they, they sometimes don't. They get a worse job sometimes 'cause the bosses treat them badly."

She completed her thought with a piece of advice for parents of immigrant children based on her own experience:

> KAR: About the kids, it's difficult for them cause it's hard learning English.... I think that's hard for them cause, like, I know this girl, she came [from] Mexico, and she's supposed to be in third grade, and she has trouble speaking English, so if parents are gonna bring their children from Mexico they gotta bring them young like me 'cause... me and David were brought young and we learned English with no trouble.

While the youngest children in the group had not yet developed an explicit understanding of immigrants to be able to respond to my questions, Karina and David did add other criteria for citizenship that went beyond the inclusion of legal and human rights as advocated by the *Organización Guadalupana*. In our interactions, the children also included birthplace and place of residence, as well as social class and language status as the preexisting social structures of power upon which immigrants and citizens are identified in U.S. society. On the other hand, they did demonstrate an important commonality with the larger community discourse in that they were capable of articulating their own and others' immigrant identities in terms of power and social injustice in ways that countered predominant societal perspectives. This is done in their immediate interactions and through written texts compiled, edited, and revised in their booklet. In this sense, one can argue that the older children were scaffolding their less expert peers, those directly in front of them, as well as their potential audience into a particular critical consciousness that counters societal discourses.

Eventually, Karina's and David's own opinions about immigrants as expressed in this interaction took the form of a text that we included in the booklet for other children under the heading "*Los inmigrantes*/Immigrants," whose clarifying subtitle was "the people who come from Mexico to live in the United States." Other counterdiscursive texts included advice columns. Although David and Karina were the only participants to discuss illegality explicitly, the younger children also demonstrated a developing awareness on the subject, such as knowledge that people move from one place to another and that the actual move is quite difficult. Karina and David discussed explicitly on other occasions their knowledge about how migrants are persecuted and die on the border, and what families can do to retain their U.S.-born children if an undocumented parent is deported. In their separate advice columns to children, teenagers, and adults, they addressed illegality only in their advice to adults, who were warned about abuses on the part of employers and were encouraged to demand a minimum wage. David and Karina even considered naming the children's booklet "Illegal in New York," but decided that illegality was not the only topic covered in their texts about life in the city, an authentic reflection of their interactions during this project. I argue that the children's developing understanding of illegality was closely related to a particular kind of dialectal, personal-institutional history.

During the group interview with the children's mothers, I asked them whether they shared their reading of the organization's monthly bulletin with their children. I was already aware that David and Karina were literate in Spanish and that they were, in fact, familiar with the bulletin, remarking that they especially liked its illustrations. Marcos, as I mentioned earlier, was beginning to read in Spanish, and, according to his mother, made attempts at home to read the monthly bulletin aloud. Mercedes and Lucía, mothers of the youngest children (Marcos, Ariel, and Margarita), stated that they did not actually discuss the readings of the bulletin directly with their children, but recognized that they were exposed to adult conversations about the issues that emerged in the bulletins, as well as their own reasons for participating in the organization's activities. Based on what the mothers discussed and on what the children themselves had to say in our meetings, it was clear that even the youngest children, although not fully conscious or articulate of the meanings of immigration and illegality, were being counterscaffolded by their family's and the organization's practices through exposure to their conversations and activities, such as accompanying their mothers to meetings, demonstrations, and other events.

CONCLUDING THOUGHTS

Although the children were involved in the organization's practices and exposed to their own parents' active participation and reflection about it, they identified Mexican immigrants in relation to legal status to varying degrees. They were capable of this as a result of their involvement ranging from participating peripherally in political socialization practices to explicitly advocating for Mexican immigrants' rights. The children of Mexican immigrants, especially those who are born in the United States, will have access to more mainstream political rights and will carry significant voting power. It is important to consider that an important segment of the population is being socialized into an ideology of citizenship based on civic activism and family and community values. As U.S. citizens, they will be able to solicit their parents' legalization in time. Therefore, the permanent settlement of these children and their families in the United States, as well as the way that these families identify themselves, their communities, and their cultural and legal rights have long-term implications for their power to bring about social change through citizenship, including both direct political involvement and community organization practices. As such, it is critical to identify how these children are counterscaffolded to be able to consider the potential directions of changes to society. In this sense, cultural-historical activity theory and deconstructionist methods can serve profound political functions through the identification of cultural goals and tools in communities seeking empowerment.

References

Augoustinos, M., & Walker, I. (1995). *Social cognition: An integrated approach.* Thousand Oaks, CA: Sage.

Bakhtin, M. M. (1986). *Speech genres and other late essays* (V. W. McGee, Trans.). Austin: University of Texas Press.

Brandtstädter, J. (1998). Action perspectives on human development. In W. Damon & R. M. Lerner (Eds.), *The handbook of child psychology: Theoretical models of human development* (5th ed., Vol. 1, pp. 807–863). New York: John Wiley & Sons.

Cross, W. E. (1995). Oppositional identity and African American youth: Issues and prospects. In W. Hawley & A. Jackson (Eds.), *Toward a common destiny: Improving race and ethnic relations in America* (pp. 185–204). San Francisco: Jossey-Bass.

Daiute, C. (1998). Points of view in children's writing. *Language Arts, 75* (2), 138–149.

Deaux, K. (1993). Reconstructing social identity. *Personality and Social Psychology Bulletin, 19* (1), 4–12.

Deaux, K., & Philogène, G. (Eds.). (2001). *Representations of the social.* Oxford: Blackwell.

Edstrom, M. (1993). La imagen de México en Estados Unidos: La inmigración mexicana en los medios impresos estadounidenses, 1980–1988. *Revista Mexicana de Sociología, 54* (4), 21–65.

García, E. E., & Hurtado, A. (1995). Becoming American: A review of current research on the development of racial and ethnic identity in children. In W. Hawley & A. Jackson (Eds.), *Toward a common destiny: Improving race and ethnic relations in America* (pp. 163–184). San Francisco: Jossey-Bass.

Gergen, K. J. (1990). Social understanding and the inscription of self. In J. W. Stigler, R. A. Shweder, & G. Herdt (Eds.), *Cultural psychology: Essays on comparative human development* (pp. 569–606). Cambridge: Cambridge University Press.

Gergen, K. J. (1991). *The saturated self: Dilemmas of identity in contemporary life.* New York: Basic Books.

Guerra, J. C. (1998). *Close to home: Oral and literate practices in a transnational Mexicano community.* New York: Teachers College Press.

Harré, R., & Gillett, G. (1994). *The discursive mind.* Thousand Oaks, CA: Sage.

Hart, D., & Damon, W. (1985). Contrasts between understanding self and understanding others. In R. L. Leahy (Ed.), *The development of the self* (pp. 151–178). New York: Academic Press.

Henriques, J., Hollway, W., Urwin, C., Venn, C., & Walkerdine, V. (Eds.). (1984). *Changing the subject: Psychology, social regulation and subjectivity.* London: Methuen.

Hurtado, A. (1996). *The color of privilege: Three blasphemies on race and feminism.* Ann Arbor: University of Michigan Press.

Jones, E. E., Farina, A., Hastorf, A. H., Markus, H., Miller, D. T., Scott, R. A., & French, R. de S. (1984). *Social stigma: The psychology of marked relationships.* New York: W. H. Freeman.

Leahy, R. L., & Shirk, S. R. (1985). Social cognition and the development of the self. In R. L. Leahy (Ed.), *The development of the self* (pp. 123–149). New York: Academic Press.

Leont'ev, A. N. (1978). *Activity, consciousness, and personality.* Englewood Cliffs, NJ: Prentice-Hall.

Lyotard, J.-F. (1984). *The postmodern condition: A report on knowledge.* Minneapolis: University of Minnesota Press.

Matute-Bianchi, M. E. (1991). Situational ethnicity and patterns of school performance among 15 immigrant and nonimmigrant Mexican-descent students. In M. A. Gibson & J. U. Ogbu (Eds.), *Minority status and schooling: A comparative study of immigrant and involuntary minorities* (pp. 205–247). New York: Garland Publishing.

Meier, M. S., & Ribera, F. (1993). *Mexican Americans/American Mexicans: From conquistadors to Chicanos.* Rev. ed. New York: Hill and Wang.

Moscovici, S. (2001). Why a theory of social representations? In K. Deaux & G. Philogène (Eds.), *Representations of the social* (pp. 8–36). Oxford: Blackwell.

Parker, I. (1997). Discursive psychology. In D. Fox & I. Frillektensky (Eds.), *Critical psychology: An introduction* (pp. 284–298). London: Sage.

Poster, M. (1989). *Critical theory and poststructuralism: In search of a context.* Ithaca: Cornell University Press.

Sánchez, G. J. (1993). *Becoming Mexican American: Ethnicity, culture and identity in Chicano Los Angeles, 1900–1945.* New York: Oxford University Press.

Scribner, S. (1985). Vygotsky's uses of history. In J. Wertsch (Ed.), *Culture, communication, and cognition* (pp. 119–145). Cambridge: Cambridge University Press.

Smith, R. C. (1996). Mexicans in New York: Membership and incorporation in a new immigrant community. In S. Baver & G. Haslip-Viera (Eds.), *Latinos in New York: Communities in transition* (pp. 57–103). Notre Dame, IN: University of Notre Dame Press.

Smollar, J., & Youniss, J. (1985). Adolescent self-concept development. In R. L. Leahy (Ed.), *The development of the self* (pp. 247–266). New York: Academic Press.

Solis, J. (2001). Immigration status and identity: Undocumented Mexicans in New York. In *Mambo montage: The latinization of New York* (pp. 337–361). New York: Columbia University Press.

Stevens, G. (1999). Age at immigration and second language proficiency among foreign-born adults. *Language in Society, 28* (4), 555–578.

Suárez-Orozco, M. M. (Ed.). (1998). *Crossings: Mexican immigration in interdisciplinary perspective.* Cambridge, MA: Harvard University Press.

Vygotsky, L. (1986). *Thought and language* (A. Kozulin, Trans.). Cambridge, MA: MIT Press.

Vygotsky, L., & Luria, A. (1994). Tool and symbol in child development. In R. van der Veer & J. Valsiner (Eds.), *The Vygotsky reader* (pp. 99–174). Oxford: Blackwell.

Wolfe, A. (1997). Immigration angst. *New York Times*, July 23, p. A21.

11

Cultural Identity and Emigration

*A Study of the Construction of Discourse about Identity
from Historical-Cultural Psychology*

Beatriz Macías Gómez Estern, Josué García Amián,
and José Antonio Sánchez Medina

In this chapter we try to offer both a conceptual and a methodological proposal for the study of cultural identity from historical-cultural psychology.
First, we develop a conceptual framework in which we define acts of identification as a suitable unit of analysis for cultural identity. Acts of identification dynamically integrate social and individual components, both of which
are necessary in the explanation of cultural identity. Second, we present an
empirical research project based on these conceptual ideas. In this project we
analyze the acts of identification performed by various groups of Andalusian
people from southern Spain that differ in their experience of migration. We
study how this experience of "otherness" shapes their acts of identification
when talking about Andalusia as a cultural group.

CONCEPTUAL AND METHODOLOGICAL APPROACHES

The study of cultural identity connects concepts that concern the individual
and the social planes in psychological functions. The first problem in the
study of cultural identity is whether it should be attributed to the individual
or to the group (Ferdman, 1990). Different answers have been given to this
question. For instance, some works in the social sciences attribute the concept of identity to the group and consider that the individual assumes this
cultural identity as a member of that group (Ball, Giles, & Hewstone, 1984).
When talking about a collective identity in a given social group, these scholars
search for a set of constant traits possessed by all individuals in the group.
From this perspective, the role of individual agency is underestimated in the
process of constructing one's own cultural identity. On the other hand, psychological approaches, especially those from social psychology, have stressed
individual elaboration of group categories. The role of social factors in the

construction of social identity is consigned to that of an explanatory variable. Social identity is considered as an individual self-assignment in a set of descriptive categories that are infused with personal meaning. The issue is whether there is continuity between personal and social identity, or if they each refer to different realities (Brewer, 1991; Brewer & Gardner, 1996; Deaux, 1993; Hoog & Abrams, 1987).

This dichotomy between culture and individual makes the study of cultural identity extraordinarily difficult, because the two poles of the dichotomy are based on different explicative principles: group dynamics and individual psychological processes. Related to this theoretical problem is a methodological one. Research in social psychology has the aim of searching for and reflecting the organized scheme of the different identities to which a person can be assigned. To obtain that information, researchers study social identities in artificial laboratory environments, where the subject has to answer questions about his or her social ascriptions in a categorical fashion.

The main problem with the method described is that when researchers understand social identity as a categorically structured entity, they search for categories and, by doing so, do not allow subjects to express themselves about their identities as they would in their everyday life. Everyday expressions of cultural identity may not fit the researchers' theoretical criteria and methods. The consequence of this is a disintegrated and fragmented idea of identity.

We think that other ways of studying identity are possible without renouncing empirical research. To overcome these theoretical and methodological problems, we need a theoretical framework that allows us to link culture and individual (Penuel & Wertsch, 1995a, 1995b). We also need a methodology that does not denaturalize our object of analysis by using artificial categorizations in laboratory research. We propose to approach cultural identity from a historical-cultural perspective. From this point of view we understand that:

1. *Identity is created through social interactions.* Identity mechanisms and construction processes (not only identity contents) must be sought in the social processes through which they are created.
2. *Identity is mediated by cultural tools.* The construction of cultural identity, like other higher psychological functions, is mediated by cultural tools, mainly by semiotic tools such as symbols, myths, and social languages. The use of a given set of tools configures identity itself and its functions (Wertsch, 1985, 1994, 1998).
3. *Identity is situated, linked to institutions of practice and cultural activity settings.* Cultural identity is a socially situated process. To understand

that process, we must analyze the social settings in which it takes place. To consider the institution as an essential piece in the understanding of cultural identity means to accept that it is in these cultural settings where not only contents but also the functional organization of cultural identity are created, regulated, and transformed. It is more than a simple influence of social variables on individual psychological processes.

These theoretical assumptions have methodological implications for the study of cultural identity. The first methodological issue is the unit of analysis. As noted previously, sociocultural processes and individual functioning are conceptualized as two poles of an irreducible tension. This dynamic process of tension between these two forces is reflected in human action. Human action offers the possibility of studying all the elements involved in this tension as human agency, psychological tools, and institutions. Taking into account the concept of identity we have developed from a cultural-historical psychology, we consider *mediated action* as the unit of analysis. In Penuel and Wertsch's (1995b, p. 84) words,

We must examine how, for example, identity as a self-chosen description of the person takes place within action. Identity formation must be viewed as shaped by and shaping forms of action, involving a complex interplay among cultural tools employed in the action, the institutional context of the action and the purposes embedded in the action.

We understand identity as an action that aims to define or characterize, in some way, a person's belonging to a group. Mediated action is a unit of analysis that allows the inclusion and coordination of both individual and social factors. Mediated action, understood within cultural-historical psychology, becomes in this sense a powerful analytical tool because action is not confined to the individual level but transcends it, allowing us to analyze identity at the social level. This characteristic makes action-mediated-by-tools a resource that allows overcoming the methodological individualism found in many human science works in the Western tradition. By definition, action allows considering simultaneously the agent that performs it and the cultural instruments used. Mediational tools configure a subject's acts of identification. We can suppose that studying the mediational means that individuals use to perform their actions provides a way to analyze how they build their identity.

This concept of action facilitates the study of cultural identity construction because it allows investigation at an interpsychological level. Considering identity as an action also implies thinking of this concept as a dynamic one that may change from activity to activity, depending on the different ways of coordination that could be established between cultural tools, purposes, and contexts.

As already emphasized, cultural identity acts are principally mediated by symbolic cultural instruments, such as language, and are constituted in social interactions. In this sense, it is especially useful to consider acts of identity as actions developed in the frame of communicative facts with a rhetorical nature. We are going to center on Habermas's (1984) theory of action and a rhetorical perspective of discourse to develop these ideas. Both of these perspectives extend and enrich the concept of identity with which we are dealing.

Acts of identity can be understood as communicative actions. According to Habermas, there are three kinds of action that, when coordinated jointly, make up the communicative action: teleological, dramaturgical, and normative.

Teleological action consists of strategic action directed toward some objectives and goals. With this kind of action, the actor tries to achieve some given aims depending on the interpretation they make of the situation. When a person performs a cultural identification act, his aim is to reflect on the traits that define themselves in relation to his cultural group in relation to other people. This means that in a communicative process people's actions have the purpose of making the audience identify in some way with their arguments.

In dramaturgical action, the agent tries, intentionally or not, to make the audience identify with his state of consciousness, his private world. The actor gives the audience access to his subjectivity. Dramaturgical action has a special value when we talk about cultural identity, because it is part of the tapestry that, together with other identities, constitutes our private personal world. When we talk about our cultural identity, we are performing a manifestation of our thinking that refers to a part of ourselves, a part of how we perceive ourselves, and a part of our subjective world.

Normative or rule-governed action (linked to sociocultural settings of practice) points to the socially situated component of cultural identity. In this sense, a social group can demand that a given actor behave in a given way, depending on the agreements that regulate interpersonal relations in that social group.

We can also approach identity as a rhetorical action. We have regarded cultural identity as actions generated in communicative social interactions. However, we cannot understand these actions as simply informative ones. Acts of identity are arguments (i.e., rhetorical actions) created to persuade and convince our audience about which traits define us in relation to our cultural group. Cultural identity is configured and developed in the rhetorical act. In fact, we become conscious of our cultural identity when we speak to an interlocutor or an audience. But rhetoric not only refers to persuasion of others; rhetoric action is also addressed simultaneously to others and to oneself. Identity implies arguing about oneself or about a perceived belonging to a group (i.e., cultural, ethnic, and professional). Acts of identity can also be considered as rhetorical actions aimed at persuading the audience in the framework of a communicative event. The individual performs an argument in order to persuade his or her audience, but simultaneously the argument influences and modifies the individual's own point of view. In the process of individual deliberation, we use the same arguments that we employ when we try to persuade others (Billig, 1987).

From the approach we have defended in this chapter, cultural identity can be considered as a rhetorical discourse that develops in the frame of a communicative event. But how can we analyze this discourse?

The scenario in which we are going to analyze acts of identification is the discussion group. Discussion groups are useful for the cultural-historical researcher because of their socio-interactive nature. This feature allows the researcher to study the origin of psychological processes in the interpsychological plane of functioning. For the same reason, they provide an excellent arena for analyzing how cultural identity grows from the close interaction that takes place in social institutions, such as schools. Discussion groups require and permit the expression, discussion, and negotiation of points of view and experience, in which the participants create shared realities through rhetorical communicative actions. They permit access to new ideas, arguments and counterarguments, and the search for agreements, as the participants put forward opinions and try to persuade each other. These actions lead to new ways of understanding both oneself and others. When identity becomes the discussion issue, it is possible to analyze the appropriation process and the discussants' use of cultural tools in argumentation and reflection about themselves and their belonging to a certain cultural group. The discussion group gives us a setting to study the participants' acquisition, use, and mastering of new tools to construct their personal or cultural identity. It provides a view not only of how participants' identity actions create opinions among the people in the audience and simultaneously build and reveal their own image but also of how that personal and/or cultural identity is being reconstructed externally and internally in the course of discussion.

The other question that emerges is, How can we identify acts of identification in the flux of discourse that takes place in a discussion group? We use Bakhtin's theory to differentiate several aspects of discourse. Bakhtin (1981) suggests utterance as the empirical unit of analysis of communication because discourse takes reality only in the concrete moment and context in which it is performed – that is, in the concrete utterances that people use to talk.

Following Bakhtin, we can study several dimensions of utterances. We can study the *generic form* of utterance. This refers to an utterance's formal aspects, that is, its compositive structure. In this sense, we can distinguish two different elements. On the one hand, we can study the dimension particularization-generalization. Billig's (1987) contributions about two opposite processes such as particularization and generalization seem very useful from a rhetoric perspective. On the other hand, from psycholinguistic contributions we can establish different discursive styles, such as the explicative, the expositive, and the narrative one.

We can also analyze the *semantic referential content* of utterances. All utterances are constructed from elements that participants use to build their act of identity, and in front of which they take a position. In this sense, we are interested in analyzing the topics used to construct acts of identification and the position a speaker takes referring to identification, that is, the utterance's orientation. In the case of cultural identity, the orientation shows whether a person considers the trait characterized in the utterance about a cultural group's identity a differential feature for this group.

From this methodological perspective, different strands of empirical research can be carried out. We can raise the question of how our participation in different scenarios promotes the use of new mediated tools that will shape new acts of identity. In this sense, we have studied the influence of several experiences and social settings (like the migrating experience) in the development of cultural identity.

Therefore, our methodological proposal is to study cultural identity through communicative, rhetorical, and mediated acts of identification that people perform to define themselves.

CULTURAL IDENTITY AND EMIGRATION: AN EMPIRICAL STUDY

The conceptual ideas described in the first section of this chapter will be illustrated in the empirical research carried out with groups of migrants and nonmigrant people in the region of Andalusia in southern Spain. This empirical study examines the relationship between "otherness" and the construction of cultural identity from a cultural-historical perspective. The concepts of identity and difference form a dialectical tandem. They complement and nourish each other (Woodward, 1997). Cultural identity emerges in contrast with a cultural "other," an "other" that enables an "alien" view to look at us. From this perspective, cultural identity emerges and shapes itself in different ways, depending on whom we are contrasting ourselves with.

Among a broad variety of sociocultural experiences, a large tradition in different social sciences gives evidence of the experience of contrast with a cultural "other," as a meaningful person in the construction of cultural identity. As many anthropologists and social psychologists point out, when a contrast with other cultures is produced, people become conscious of their own cultural identity (Barth, 1976; Lotman, 1996). These authors show that in the process of constructing cultural identity, we first construct the border between "us" and "they" and then fill it with selected features or contents (narratives, history, myths, etc.). This experience of "otherness" can be studied through the experience of emigration, in which people who have lived or live this experience have had the opportunity of contrasting their cultural "me" with a cultural "other" (Labrador, 2001).

We are not interested in how identities are defined or what contents they include without taking into account the people who construct them or the cultural contexts in which they do this. Rather, we are interested in why, with what instruments, and for what reason they construct a perceived coherent image of themselves and their cultural group – that is, their cultural identity (Castells, 1997). Thus, our aim is not to make an objective analysis of a given community but to find out what are the instruments that community members use to build up a relatively coherent discourse about their affiliation to a group and what situations may affect the suitability of a given instrument. Specifically, our research aim is how the migration experience influences the structure and contents of the acts of identification performed by Andalusian people participating in a focus group task. Our working hypothesis is that both structure and contents of the acts of identification will vary depending on the emigration experience of our study's participants.

Research Design and Sample

Our *explanatory variable* is the emigration experience, with three levels (nonemigrants, emigrants, and returned emigrants), and our *outcome variable* is the structure and contents of the acts of identification (Table 11.1).

The sample was composed of thirty-four Andalusian adults (sixteen women and eighteen men), equally distributed into the three levels of emigration experience (Table 11.2).

Procedure

Acts of identification were studied through discourse analysis in a group discussion. A video recording was made of each debate. The video camera was located in a place were it did not disturb the participants. Two debates were

Table 11.1. Research project design

Explanatory variable	Outcome variable
Emigration experience	Acts of identification
Nonemigrants	Structure
Returned emigrants	Contents
Emigrants	

Table 11.2. Sample of participants, ages 24–73

Emigration experience	Distribution
Nonemigrants	12
Returned emigrants	11
Emigrants	11

set for each category. The number of participants for each of them was five to six people. Participants were asked to discuss (without taking into account the researcher) Andalusian identity. The question leading the discussion was in each of the cases: Is there an Andalusian identity? Participants should give their opinion and argue about whether there are differential features that make an Andalusian people and region. The researcher presented two opposite positions about the discussion topic, in order to animate the talk. Each debate had a duration of between twenty and sixty minutes. The first one hundred utterances per debate were analyzed. Debates were transcribed and codified in a category system. The unit of analysis was the utterance (act of identification), understood as each participant's turn-taking, with each participant's talk allowed to continue without interruption. This unit of analysis is taken from Bakhtin's theory (1981). A reliability rating was calculated on 10 percent of the utterances selected randomly. Data were statistically analyzed using high log linear procedures.

Category System

The function of the category system is to analyze the structure and contents of the identification acts performed by our debate participants. It is divided into three main sections. In the first one, formal aspects of language are analyzed, in the second, the speaker perspective, and in the third, the discourse contents (Table 11.3). In this section we describe the different categories used in our analysis (Figure 11.1).

Table 11.3. Category system: Acts of identification

Structure: Discursive genres		Structure: Speaker's perspective	Semantic referential content	
Decontextualization level	Speech genres	Comparison	Topic	Identity orientation
Theoretical argument	Narratives	Comparative	Psychological features	"Identitarian"
Practical argument	Expositions	Noncomparative	Close interactions	Non-"Identitarian"
Practical generalized argument	Explanations		Macrosocial factors	Ambiguous/ contradictory
Mixed utterances			Geographical features	

RESULTS AND DISCUSSION

In general terms, we can say that the results obtained in this study correspond to our aims and hypotheses. We expected to find differences between the acts of identification of nonemigrants, returned emigrants, and emigrants.

We reflect first about how the experience of emigration affects the way cultural identity is constructed. We do this by comparing emigrants' with nonemigrants' acts of identification. Afterward, to analyze how that relationship between emigration and cultural identity is shaped, we compare emigrants' and returned emigrants' acts of identification.

Our data show that the identification acts change in our sample depending on the debate participants' migration experience. The structure and the contents of the identification act are different in emigrants and nonemigrants. In the following paragraphs, we describe how each of these groups constructed their utterances about Andalusian cultural identity.

Our analyses show that the nonemigrants group uses mainly theoretical arguments as discursive tools. These general utterances do not have a concrete experience as reference but a "universal" of cases and agents. These generalities constitute descriptions or assertions about Andalusia or about psychological traits of the Andalusian people. These utterances are not elements of comparison with other communities, but they just reveal how Andalusians are.

On the other hand, people who have lived a migration experience base their arguments on their own particular experiences. This particular discourse

STRUCTURE: Discursive Genres

Decontextualization Level

1. Theoretical argument: Subjects talk about an abstract situation or fact; it is not a personal experience but a categorization.

"We are different and they can envy us in our way of life, of acting, we are generally more happy people."

2. Practical generalized argument: Reference is made to a people group doing a concrete action.

"Pepe, what happens is that our life is lived like this. Working during the day and living during the night. That's the change."

3. Practical argument: Subjects talk about their own experience or related situations with those close to them (friends, family, etc.).

"In my neighborhood, I go out from home in my neighborhood and they say to me 'Loly, only listening to you talking. . . .' . . . they know me. Everybody say 'Bye Loly, bye Loly.'"

4. Mixed: Levels just described appear in a single utterance.

"About culture we are behind them, we must tell the truth. Catalans, I can talk about Catalonia because I lived there, because I have been there, and I see that they are at a higher cultural level."

Discursive Style

1. Narratives: Reference is made to a story or a concrete event that happened to someone.

"We are six brothers and sisters, we are from [name of a village] in Cordoba, and we came to Montoro with my parents when we were little children, and from there we went to work to Cordoba. And there I met my husband, who is from El Campo de la Verdad."

2. Expositions: Subjects make a neutral assertion or a negation of features or events.

"We are much more open."

3. Explanation: Subjects relate a situation to another fact. Usually the relation is established as a cause-effect relation.

"I see that we are different. . . . I mean to other areas, because, sure, perhaps climate and because habits are different too."

STRUCTURE: Speaker Perspective

Comparison

1. Comparisons: Subjects use another group or person as referent.

"We are as good workers as them, and we also know how to have fun."

2. Noncomparisons: Subjects do not use another group or person as a referent.

SEMANTIC REFERENTIAL CONTENT
Topic
1. Psychological features: Subjects refer to an individual's or a group's personal features. Those features commonly imply abstractions about ways of being and of behaving. In any case, the weight of those features referred to falls on how those individuals are described.

"Catalans are very nice/we are very open."

2. Close interactions. Subjects refer to how people behave, ways of life, habits, and close relations between individuals and between groups (microsocial level).

"What happens here is that we know how to have fun, not as in other places."

3. Macrosocial level: Subjects talk about social institutions, such as language, economy, educational systems, stereotypes, and folkloric manifestations.

"The economy in Andalucia doesn't work, because they carry everything to the north."

4. Geographical features: Subjects refer to the material conditions of a territory, including geography, climate, and environment, and also family roots.

"When I passed Despeñaperros and I saw that light, I said to myself, 'Now I'm at home.'"

Orientation
1. Identitary: Subjects characterize the group or territory of belonging.

"We are different, neither better nor worse but different."

2. Nonidentitarian: Subjects do not characterize themselves as belonging to a group or territory that is seen as a differentiated entity.

"I don't believe what they say about how lazy Andalusian people are."

3. Ambiguous or contradictory: Subjects' orientation is not clear or contradictions appear in different parts of the utterance.

"I have a daughter studying journalism and she pays her tuition fee every year."

Figure 11.1. Category definition.

is usually organized as narratives. These utterances are in most cases comparisons with the receiving community, where they contrast Andalusian traits with those of the host community.

The excerpts in Figures 11.2, 11.3, and 11.4 are some standard utterances extracted from our debates that exemplify the results described. The excerpts

"And also...perhaps tolerance has been more stimulated than in other places. Because here different cultures have coexisted. There have been Muslims, Jews, Christians, and they have coexisted without problems."

"It's mentality. The Andalusian has a kind of different personality.... People who can, for example..., we take life a bit less dramatically, but then we have our things. And they say that [we are] less serious, but no, the Andalusian is serious."

"But he is also more open, the Andalusian is more open. He gets to all cultures."

Figure 11.2. Nonemigrant standard utterances.

"Then I was a very happy person, we were four in the family, my parents, my brother and I. My father was a born worker, and for life circumstances my brother came to live to Madrid, and well, incredibly mad about all of us coming. I didn't want to come, but well, that illusion about the capital of Spain.... I feel immigrant, but with a very big pain because I am Andalusian by my four sides. Then, if I go back again with my roots, well, I'd go to the village with my eyes closed. And in fact my husband is from Madrid, and he, it's not even that I have persuaded him but... he would go, to Cordoba, he says that not to the village, but..." [laughs]

Figure 11.3. Emigrants' standard utterance.

"But I think that, for certain reasons an Andalusian identity doesn't exist. The main one is..., well, we first should discuss what we mean by Andalusian identity, but I think that if we had it, we'd defend it like other communities as Catalonia or the Basque Country.... I think that there might be some details, which shortly differentiate us from Spain. However, I don't think that such an identity exists."

Figure 11.4. Returned emigrants' standard utterance.

in Figure 11.2 begin with the utterances of nonemigrants. In the first utterance the speaker uses Andalusian history to argue that Andalusia is idiosyncratic. He defines Andalusia as a place whose people are tolerant because of Andalusia's history of ethnic and religious mixture. The utterance's strength is in the description of a situation in a generic, decontextualized way and in the establishment of causal links between traits and circumstances. We can observe general assertions also in the two following utterances. Another characteristic of these utterances is that they do not use comparisons as a resource in their expositions. When they do, they do not name a specific alter (other) as a referent but a "generalized other" as in "other places, other people."

We find a completely different portrait in the emigrants' discourse, presented in Figure 11.3. We can observe how Andalusian emigrants, when given the instruction to argue about their cultural identity, draw upon their personal experience of migration, which is detailed and narrated as a story. They build their cultural identity constantly by comparing their homeland with the place to which they have emigrated. The strong emotional dimension of their discourse accompanies this subjectivity, and it can be seen in utterances such as: "I'm Andalusian by my four sides."

How can we explain the differences in the persuasive instruments used by emigrants and nonemigrants to construct their cultural identity? Why, answering the same question about their cultural identity, do they display such a different set of discursive tools to persuade their audience?

We can use the concepts of "activity setting" and "semiotic choice" (Wertsch, 1998) and "motive of the activity" (Leontiev, 1981) to answer these questions. We think that the prompt function of identity changes with the experience of emigration and other historical-cultural experiences, and that makes people participating in a focus group choose different semiotic tools (Wertsch, 1998) to construct their acts of identification. Emigrants and nonemigrants interpret the focus group situation in two different ways, and that confers to the setting two different motives. Whereas nonemigrants interpret the setting as a formal task, and search for *rational persuasion* using *theoretical arguments*, emigrants interpret the same situation as an occasion for sharing personal experiences. They do not have the purpose of convincing the audience of the truth of their assertions but of exposing dramaturgically and sharing their personal experience with the rest of the emigrants in the group. Their purpose is then searching for the audience's empathy and involving it. But, even if their purpose is not persuading, they also reach that second aim: in that situation, *practical arguments* are more useful than theoretical ones because they have an effect on *affective persuasion* (Perelman & Olbrechts-Tyteca, 1994). The utterance is loaded with a high emotional force related to its capacity to involve the audience's empathy, in the dimension of dramaturgical actions described by Habermas.

Nonemigrants and emigrants use different semiotic instruments (or make a different semiotic choice) to reach different goals. Whereas nonemigrants search for rational persuasion of their audience through theoretical arguments, emigrants use practical arguments to reach affective persuasion of an audience composed of other emigrants.

This means that the function of identity can change depending on sociocultural variables, such as emigrational experience, and that different discursive tools are used to reach different goals or functions. Then we are answering the question we pointed out at the beginning of our exposition, namely, Why, for what reason, and with what instruments do people construct a given cultural identity?

EMIGRANTS VERSUS RETURNED EMIGRANTS

The first difference between emigrants and returned emigrants is the reference to the physical geographical topic. Although emigrants use this topic very often, returned emigrants do not use it to construct their acts of identification. Let us return to the example we showed previously to observe how emigrants refer to physical geographical issues (see Figure 11.3).

As we can notice in the utterance in Figure 11.3, the content referring to the attachment to land is very strong. It seems that the speaker delights in talking about her lost land and is proud to show how much she misses it. Andalusia's physical geographical traits are always positively valued, even in the cases when they are "objectively" disturbing, like the hot weather in summer. In our example, the speaker claims her Andalusian roots and admits her pain for having to live in a different land. We should also notice the use of the word "land" instead of other more institutionalized categories like "autonomous community" or region. "Land" refers to the direct bond between the person and the place he or she occupies, as a natural belonging. From the distance, land provokes nostalgia, which is one of the most outstanding signs of an emigrant's debate in our study. These debates are loaded with expressions with an enormous affective charge, like "I am Andalusian by my four sides."

In contrast with emigrants' acts of identification, returned emigrants' utterances are interesting because they do not refer to the physical geographical topic (see Figure 11.4).

The different use of physical geographical topics between emigrants and nonemigrants connects with our next category: the discourse orientation. We must remember that in this category the orientation is identitarian when the speaker is defending the existence of a differential trait in Andalusian culture or identity. It is nonidentitarian when the speaker is defending the opposite. When the utterance defends and neglects at the same time an Andalusian identity, we call it ambiguous or contradictory.

The results obtained in this category indicate that identitarian utterances are mostly found in emigrants. Emigrants have no doubt about the existence of Andalusian identity, which is defined, as we have already observed, based on differences with the receiving culture.

On the other hand, returned emigrants are more ambiguous than the rest of the groups in their discourse orientation. Returned emigrants blend their definition of Andalusia and Andalusians, subordinating it to different criteria and criticizing the unconditional acceptance of emigrants. Let us consider the returned emigrant's utterance in Figure 11.4. In this utterance, the speaker is negating the existence of an Andalusian identity, because there is not a claim for a political autonomy in the Andalusian community. She accepts that there is a certain bond to the land in Andalusia, but that does not justify a cultural identity. Her position is then ambiguous or contradictory in some sense, because she is taking different perspectives to analyze the situation.

How do we explain this difference between emigrants and returned emigrants? We can consider emigrants and returned emigrants as two stages of the same emigrational experience. In these stages returned emigrants have already passed the stage of idealizing their original area during their emigration period. They have "suffered" during the emigrational period some kind of "acculturation" or integration in their receiving culture system. They have been socialized into a different culture, in a way that enables them to turn back to their vernacular culture with the "other" point of view internalized. During the emigration period, two different processes take place: idealization of the original culture – in many cases anchored in the past culture – and socialization and learning of a new way of life. Therefore, when these people came back to Andalusia, they clashed with the real image of this area, in part because of their idealization, in part because they were looking at it from a new point of view, usually a more critical one. These people who start belonging to a nobody's (or nowhere) space, or a border space, have "flying roots."

The speakers in the emigrant group show an "unconditional acceptance" of all the Andalusian features they name. The positive and in many cases exalted valuation is an outstanding characteristic of their utterances. These utterances about Andalusia frequently have a strong emotional charge. Probably these emigrants have already experienced the enculturation shown in returned emigrants. At the debate moment, however, this dimension seems to be less important than the idealization of the "lost land" when they are abroad. This hierarchy is shown in both the reference to physical and geographical topics and the identitarian orientation. When this idealization disappears, as it happens in the returned emigrants, their "biculturalism" condition is highlighted. Again, we find the relation between cognitive and affective components of cultural identity an interesting subject for further analysis.

Thus, two parallel but not neutralizing processes take place. On a cognitive level emigrants in some way adopt the receiving community perspective and become skilled in the use of other instruments different from those of their original community. Then, in some way they become bicultural, with all the implications it has (in their everyday practices and in their perspective about their own community). On an emotional level, some radicalization about their original community identification takes places when people are far from their own land (Eriksen, 1988).

The debate situation causes an emotional radicalization of their own identity to emerge in the emigrants, because of the distance from their "lost land." That radicalization takes the form of an unconditional acceptance of any Andalusian trait and has a high affective charge (referring to the emotional dimension). We gather that emigrants are as bicultural as returned emigrants in their everyday practices, but the nostalgia issue is made more immediate for them by the discussion group session, so that is what emerges in it. On the other side, returned emigrants have already overcome that period, and so a moment of disillusionment can occur. As emigrants, they "suffered" a certain acculturation and were socialized in the new culture. Therefore, having adopted a new viewpoint, they now observe their own culture from an outsider's perspective. That makes them more critical in regard to Andalusia.

CONCLUSION

The results of our study show that there is a clear influence of the experience of emigration in the construction of cultural identity. Nonemigrants' utterances constitute theoretical arguments. They refer to a universe of cases and use descriptions or assertions as speech genre. This decontextualized discourse is related to the topic they name the most – psychological features of the Andalusian people – which requires a certain abstraction of practices to characterize a group's psychological features. Emigrants usually talk about their own experience, using practical arguments, by doing narrative life stories referring to their emigrational experience. Very often, they use comparisons to define themselves as Andalusian people and talk about their Motherland with a very emotional charge, idealizing it and missing it. Returned emigrants use theoretical arguments, because they combine different decontextualization levels in their discourse. They also use many narratives, as many as emigrants do, but those narratives are included in a broader argument that constructs the explanation. It is important to underline their ambiguous or contradictory orientation toward the "reality" of Andalusian cultural identity. They look at this reality from a more critical point of view, because they have interiorized another culture's practices.

We can conclude that the experience of emigration influences not only the contents to which the acts of identification refer but also the function these identification acts perform. With this research study, we have tried to illustrate how we can study cultural identity as a mediated, communicative, and rhetorical action.

References

Bakhtin, M. (1981). *The dialogic imagination: Four Essays by M. M. Bakhtin* (M. Holquist, Ed.). Austin: University of Texas Press.

Ball, P., Giles, H., & Hewstone, M. (1984). Second language acquisition: The intergroup theory with catastrophic dimensions. In H. Tajfel, C. Fraser, & J. Jaspars (Eds.), *The social dimension: European developments in social psychology* (Vol. 2, pp. 668–694). Cambridge: Cambridge University Press.

Barth, F. (1976). *Los grupos étnicos y sus fronteras.* Mexico City: F.C.E.

Billig, M. (1987). *Arguing and thinking.* Cambridge: Cambridge University Press.

Brewer, M. B. (1991). The social self: On being the same and different at the same time. *Personal and Social Psychology Bulletin, 17*, 475–482.

Brewer, M. B., & Gardner, W. (1996). Who is this "we"? Levels of collective identity and self representations. *Journal of Personality and Social Psychology, 71*, 83–93.

Castells, M. (1997). *Information age: The power of identity.* Malden, MA: Blackwell.

Deaux, K. (1993). Reconstructing social identity. *Personal and Social Psychology Bulletin, 19*, 4–12.

Eriksen, T. H. (1988). *Ethnicity and nacionalism: Anthropological perspectives.* London: Pluto Press.

Ferdman, B. (1990). Literacy and cultural identity. *Harvard Educational Review, 60* (2), 181–204.

Habermas, J. (1984). *The theory of communicative action: Vol. 1. Reason and the rationalization of society.* Boston: Beacon Press.

Hogg, M. A., & Abrams, D. (1987). *Social identifications.* London: Routledge & Kegan Paul.

Labrador, J. (2001). *Identidad e inmigración. Un estudio cualitativo con emigrantes peruanos en Madrid.* Madrid: Servicio de Publicaciones de Universidad Pontificia de Comillas.

Leontiev, A. N. (1981). The problem of activity in psychology. In J. Wertsch (Ed.), *The concept of activity in Soviet psychology* (pp. 37–71). New York: Sharpe.

Lotman, I. M. (1996). *La semiosfera. Semiótica de la cultura y del texto.* Frónesis, Cátedra: Universidad de Valencia.

Penuel, W. R., & Wertsch, J. V. (1995a). Dynamics of negation in the identity politics of cultural other and cultural self. *Culture & Psychology, 1*, 343–359.

Penuel, W. R., & Wertsch, J. V. (1995b). Vygotsky and identity formation: A sociocultural approach. *Educational Psychology, 30* (2), 83–92.

Perelman, C., & Olbrechts-Tyteca, L. (1994). *Tratado de argumentación. La nueva retórica*. Madrid: Gredos.

Wertsch, J. V. (1985). *Vygotsky and the social formation of mind*. Cambridge, MA: Harvard University Press.

Wertsch, J. V. (1994). The need for action in sociocultural research. In J. V. Wertsch, P. del Rio, & A. Alvarez (Eds.), *Sociocultural studies of mind* (pp. 56–74). Cambridge: Cambridge University Press.

Wertsch, J. V. (1998). *Mind as action*. New York: Oxford University Press.

Woodward, K. (1997). *Identity and difference*. London: Sage.

12

Diversity in the Construction of Modes of Collaboration in Multiethnic Classrooms

Continuity and Discontinuity of Cultural Scripts

Mariëtte de Haan and Ed Elbers

If students from different ethnic groups or cultural backgrounds join together in one classroom and construct a "common" practice, can they still be described as different? Given this "common" classroom practice that they share (which is the result of both classroom traditions of the past and the day-by-day sharing of experiences leading to a common history and tradition as a group), and the reshuffling of the variety brought along given the particular dynamics of this classroom, how is this difference to be perceived or conceptualized?

Furthermore, if we are able to describe this variety, how do we describe it in terms of its effect for the construction of knowledge or learning? Do we see variety as a problem or as fruitful input? For instance, do we see this as productive or counterproductive? (Compare the classic discontinuity thesis in which diversity is seen as disadvantageous for the culturally "deviant" groups versus seeing heterogeneity in the classroom, by using the Bakhtinian term social heteroglossia, as a potential that is able to foster learning – e.g., Gutierrez, Rymes, & Larson, 1995, pp. 447, 453.)

In this chapter we consider different conceptualizations of (cultural) variety in classrooms from a sociocultural activity theory perspective and related approaches, especially those concepts that answer the question how this variety is related to the differential participation of students in past or present out-of-school contexts. The chapter focuses on differences found along ethnic lines in collaborative learning situations and evaluates these findings against the different theoretical claims on how classroom cultures are or are not connected to the outer world. In particular it will deal with differences found in peer learning situations with respect to the use of role division models and norms on how to establish joint knowledge in small groups. We take up the so-called discontinuity thesis based on differences in past socialization experiences between students and its recent reformulations based on the ongoing production of identities in classrooms. We claim that both elements of this "classic" (dis)continuity concept and more recent insights should be used to explain variety in the classroom. We show how past socialization experiences are continued in the classroom but at the same time are reconstructed when they are strategically used to stress ethnic differences and power relationships in the classroom.

This search for theoretical concepts that can explain both the continuity or resistance of certain (cultural) patterns or norms (based on a common history) and the fluid context-bound aspect of variety found in classroom life is placed in a more general search for theoretical concepts that explain the migration of scripts, patterns, or forms of activity across contexts.

We would like to discuss different theoretical possibilities that explain this migration of forms of activity through contexts and show the relatedness as well as the changing character of these forms of activity as they move from context to context. What is needed is a concept or notion of culture, context (or activity and activity system) and its relatedness that explains both change and continuity, fluidity and stability, and moment-by-moment construction and historical formation. This would help us to address the issue of diversity and sameness both as specific contextual constructions and as carrying the traces of activities of the past or other significant socializing contexts into the present.

SOME NOTIONS ON (DIS)CONTINUITY AND DIVERSITY OF CLASSROOM LIFE

In order to be able to make the claim "that elements of this 'classic' (dis)continuity concept and more recent insights should both be used to explain variety in the classroom," we give a short overview of how this concept is differently used in classroom studies as we perceive it.

Classic Discontinuity

The "classic" studies (e.g., Heath, 1983; Philips, 1972, 1983) revealed that the adaptation process that all students have to undergo to become accustomed to the culture of the classroom turned out differently for different cultural groups. For some groups this adaptation is more successful than for others, depending on the distance between their home culture and the classroom culture. In this kind of study, different interaction patterns in the classroom are directly linked with interaction patterns in the home context of particular groups (for overviews, see Cazden, 1986; Gallego & Cole, 2001; Mehan, 1998).

Here discontinuity is the mismatch between different cultural contexts, seen as relatively coherent and distinctive patterns associated with a particular group.

Secondary Discontinuity

More or less in response to these classic studies, Ogbu pointed out that the relative gap between school culture and minority cultures could not explain the differences between the variation in school success of minority groups. The nature of the integration process of the minority group in the guest country is seen as more relevant than the distance between cultural patterns per se. Ogbu's (1992) distinction between primary cultural patterns (those which exist before contact with dominant culture in the guest country) and secondary cultural patterns (those which develop as a response to contact with the culture of the guest country – e.g., resistance patterns) is revealing here. It is not the difference or distance between the culture of the minority group and the dominant culture of the guest country that is relevant. It is how minorities act in response to (or how others act toward them with respect to) normative patterns that foster school success. Perceived status, patterns of (selective) assimilation, and processes of resistance are considered relevant in this respect (Gibson, 1997; Portes, 1995).

Here, the *reconstruction* of cultural differences is stressed, as well as the fact that cultural patterns do not exist as such but are always a reaction (resistance, adaptation) to and exist in particular social structures in which minority groups take certain positions.

Discontinuity within the Classroom

Another group of classroom studies focuses on the reconstructions of identities in the classroom context. In these identity construction studies, discontinuity is not between the school context and home context but between the different identities formed within the school. Cultural backgrounds are translated in terms of identity construction from the view that culture is not static but constantly reconstructed in response to specific contextual circumstances. Here past experiences from students' home backgrounds are relatively unimportant.

Group differences in these studies are not always or only linked to differences in the home communities. School-related identities are sometimes shared by groups that do not share a common social or cultural history (Holland & Eisenhart, 1990). These identities are worked out in the school context as a reaction to the specific school or classroom environment. The focus is on the manipulation of what is offered in the classroom context. New configurations of difference come into being by regrouping opposed identities based on distinct home cultures, for instance, based on the notion of the "educated person" (Levinson, 1996).

In particular these studies show how conflict and resistance characterize the relations between teachers and students from low-income and ethnic- or linguistic-minority backgrounds (see, e.g., Gee, 1992, on the cultural dimension and Wilcox, 1982, on the socioeconomical dimension).

(Dis)Continuity in the Present: Multiple Cultural Identities

In postmodern conceptions of culture, cultural discontinuity is the point of departure rather than the diagnosis of a problematic situation (school failure). Multiple identity formation and flexibility to move across different cultural contexts are said to be characteristic of postmodern individuals, irrespective of their cultural background. This approach is only scarcely represented in classroom studies or educational studies in general. Eisenhart (2002) argues that this postmodern conception of culture, influenced by features of contemporary life – such as migration and the possibility of frequent traveling – has not always influenced educational research enough. Eisenhart uses the term "cultural productions," suggesting that we look at cultural identities not as given but as ongoing expressions of identity, stressing more the present position in ongoing social relations than previous socialization experiences both inside and outside school.

This approach is of course similar to the identity studies but differs with respect to the importance given to the interconnections between different cultural contexts. Instead of looking at identity construction in the classroom only, it is important to trace the connection between multiple cultural contexts. Eisenhart concludes that ethnographic research should collect data that stretch across time and place, because observation in situ is not enough. Ethnographers should follow patterns of affiliation in numerous networks of different spaces and times and delineate technological means and sources of communication (Heath, 1996, pp. 370–372, cited in Eisenhart, 2002). Multisite ethnography (Marcus, 1995, cited in Eisenhart, 2002) is one possibility; analyzing discourses among distinct but related groups would be another.

In the interpretation of the findings of our study, we show that we need explaining principles raised in all these traditions to understand diversity in classrooms, and in learning situations in particular, as part of a larger sociohistorical and sociocultural whole. Then we take a closer look at these approaches from the perspective of their underlying notions of culture and context, or activity and activity system.

THE STUDY

The analysis presented here is part of a larger project of which the main goal is to understand collaboration patterns between students in multiethnic classrooms from both the classroom and out-of-school contexts. In particular, we are interested in the kind of activities students create in order to facilitate the joint construction of knowledge or skills in these contexts (what role divisions they set up, what norms on how knowledge should be constructed are used, etc.). We focus on group work situations in math lessons according to the philosophy of realistic math (see, e.g., Gravemeijer, 1994), in which, apart from starting from realistic everyday contexts, the exchange of ideas and the joint construction of knowledge between students are important principles. In this chapter we use a data set that we collected in the seventh grade in one multiethnic primary school in a large city in The Netherlands. In this school 80 percent of the students are of an ethnic minority background, mainly Moroccan. We selected an analysis of four math lessons in which five different groups collaborated on math problems. The lessons were videotaped to give an overall view of the classroom activity, and audiorecorders were placed on the tables of each of the five groups. The audiotaped material was transcribed, and the analysis is based on twenty hours of this transcribed material. The classroom consisted of twenty-two students: five are native Dutch and seventeen from other backgrounds (twelve Moroccan, three Turkish, one from Yugoslavia, and one from Ghana). There were two minority-only groups and three mixed groups with both Dutch and minority students. For the composition of the groups, see the appendix table. The analysis consisted of two parts.

First, qualitative descriptions of each case focused on how students organize their activity to share knowledge and the kind of social context that is created in their attempt to share knowledge (norms and patterns with respect to collaboration and participation).

Second, a quantitative analysis based on patterns found in the qualitative descriptions measured differences between the Dutch and minority students in modes of collaboration and ways of sharing knowledge that went together with specific power relationships between the students. In particular, we identified two different modes of collaboration in which knowledge was exchanged: the teacher-student model (based on a more asymmetric relationship) and the activity-based exchange model (based on a more symmetric relationship). The two different modes of collaboration differed with respect to various aspects, which all together represented a totally different script or kind of activity. Typical for the teacher-student model was that the student who took on the teacher role would structure the activity for the other students, ask questions, evaluate answers, take responsibility for the learning of the other students, be careful to not give the solution right away, and refrain from answering questions or doing tasks while he or she would be explaining. Typical for the activity-based exchange model is that the student who is explaining would do so while he or she is doing the task, accepting solutions of fellow students as solutions to the problem at hand (and not as answers to a test); the solutions of all participants are of the same nature, and questions posed are not to elicit a known answer but serve to inform. In both models, status differences between explainers and the ones being explained to exist, but they have a different quality.

Each episode of collaborative interaction was scored into one of these two categories. Furthermore, we scored who was explaining to whom, using the following categories (depending on the composition of the group, some categories are not relevant):

- Dutch student explains to minority student(s).
- Dutch student explains to Dutch student(s).
- Minority student explains to Dutch student(s).
- Minority student explains to minority student(s).

RESULTS

Classroom Norms on Collaboration and Sharing Knowledge as Represented by the Teacher

In the school where we collected our data, collaboration between the students is stimulated as a means for effective learning. The team has received a training in collaborative learning from an advice center for schools (SAC) and, since then, has incorporated collaboration between students as a regular strategy in the higher grades (more specifically from the sixth grade on, because students are considered to need particular skills in order to collaborate effectively). Students are seated in groups of four, five, or six and the groups are composed so that positive work attitudes and order will be maximized. During classroom activity the teacher encourages the students to collaborate by explicitly telling them that they are expected to find solutions together, that they are expected to talk and think together, and that in case one student does not know or understand, she expects the other students to help or explain. She is not specific about the role division model that they should use (in the sense that she tells students to play teacher or something), but she does encourage arriving at solutions together and sharing solutions, and she corrects students who work by themselves and regularly checks if students have reached a certain conclusion together or by themselves, while encouraging the first strategy. Also, she encourages students to explain solutions to other students when she discovers that one student has and another has not yet found the right procedure. In all five groups, students are clearly aware of the teacher's norms and expectations in this respect as they regularly correct fellow students who want to work alone and remind them that they are expected to arrive at solutions as a group. Still, they work out different ways of collaborating with respect to how they actually are to arrive at common solutions.

Differences between Groups: Results of Quantitative Analysis

The quantitative analysis showed that there were significant differences between the collaboration patterns in the mixed groups (the groups with both Dutch and minority children) and in the groups with only minority children. Although in all groups the activity-based collaboration is the most frequent, the teacher-student mode is far more frequent in the mixed groups. In these groups, the Dutch students exclusively take on the role of the teacher, and the minority students take on the student position.

Table 12.1 shows that the teacher-student model is most frequent in the mixed groups. Table 12.2 focuses on who is playing the teacher, showing that, in the relationship between Dutch and minority students, the Dutch student always takes on the teacher role. This relationship is not once reversed, that is, minority students do not teach Dutch students using that mode. Table 12.3 shows the distribution of the teacher-student mode in each group. Although most frequent in group 3, in group 2 the teacher-student mode is used relatively frequently too. A qualitative analysis shows that this is a special case in which one Moroccan girl parodies the teacher role.

These results show that there are systematic differences in collaboration patterns between the groups. However, a qualitative analysis of typical examples of these patterns can help us understand the nature of these differences. We give examples here of episodes that we consider typical for the mixed groups and the groups with only minority children. For each group we present both a case that is typical for their collaboration as scored in the quantitative analysis and a counterexample that apparently challenges but finally confirms the typical case.

Table 12.1. Number (percentage) of collaborative learning episodes in teacher-student and peer-based modes of minority groups (groups 1 and 2) and mixed groups (groups 3, 4, and 5)

	Teacher-student mode	Peer-based mode
Minority groups (1 and 2)	8 (6.2%)	121 (93.8%)
Mixed groups (3, 4, and 5)	33 (23.9%)	105 (76.1%)
TOTAL	41 (15.4%)	226 (84.6%)

Note: Total number of collaborative learning episodes is 267. Chi-square = 16.09, df = 1, p < .00.

Table 12.2. Percentages of collaborative learning episodes in the teacher-student and peer-based collaboration modes, classified according to direction of explanation ("who explains to whom") in the mixed groups (groups 3, 4, and 5)

Who explains to whom/Mode of collaboration	Teacher-student collaboration mode	Peer-based collaboration mode	Total
Dutch to minority student	22.4	49.3	71.8
Dutch to Dutch student	0.7	10.1	10.9
Minority to minority student	0.7	12.3	13.0
Minority to Dutch student	0	4.3	4.3

Note: Number of collaborative learning episodes in the mixed groups is 138 (= 100%).

Table 12.3. Collaborative learning episodes in the teacher-student collaboration mode, classified according to direction of explanation ("who explains to whom") in the five groups

Who explains to whom/ Group	Group					Total
	1	2	3	4	5	
Dutch to minority student	-	-	24	2	5	31
Dutch to Dutch student	-	-	1	0	0	1
Minority to minority student	0	8	1	0	0	9
Minority to Dutch student	-	-	0	0	0	0

Note: Number of collaborative learning episodes in the asymmetric collaboration mode is 41.

Adoption of Classroom Norms on Collaboration in Mixed Groups

Case 1: A Dutch Student Adopting a Teacher's Role

The students are working on a task that requires them to calculate how many small boxes can be put into a larger box. The task involves going to a store where sweets can be bought, either in small regular packets or in a big family-size pack. Fragment 1 is the beginning of the interaction of group 3, immediately after the teacher introduced the task and told the children to start working together.[1]

Fragment 1: Group 3 (5/6/00)

ANNELIES: >Oké<, >so:m vie:r<, hoe <u>vaak</u> past het <u>gewone</u> doosje in het ge<u>zins</u>pakket?(.) Nou?, reken uit?

ANNELIES: >Okay<, >problem 4<, how many <u>times</u> does a standard packet fit into the family pack? Well? Work it out.

MAKTOUB: Een, twee drie?

MAKTOUB: One, two, three?

ANNELIES: Wat?

ANNELIES: What?

MAKTOUB: Drie keer?

MAKTOUB: Three times?

ANNELIES: Nee:, (..) <u>Lo:::gisch</u> nadenken=.

ANNELIES: No: (..) Think lo:::gically=.

GORAN: ((leest)) =Hoe vaak past=

GORAN: ((reads)) = How many times goes =

ANNELIES: =**Kijk?**

ANNELIES: =Look.

GORAN: Hoe<u>vee:l.</u>

GORAN: How <u>many</u> times

ANNELIES: (..)<Ja:>, (.) kijk? (..) <u>Gewone</u> pakje,(.) past drie:keer zo (.)

ANNELIES: (..) >Yes<, (.) Look. Standard packet, three times like this (.)

MAKTOUB: en drie [keer

MAKTOUB: and three [times

ANNELIES: [keer <u>zo</u>, dan heb je op da-, gewoo:n opeen pakje heb al ne:gen. En dan moet je die: <u>drie</u> keer doen, want die drie: die <u>zo</u> zit:, zit <u>ook</u> hie:r.=,

ANNELIES: [times like <u>this</u>. There you already have, just one packet you have already nine. And then you should take that <u>three</u> times because the three, that is <u>there</u>, is also here. =

MAKTOUB: °Ja°.

MAKTOUB: °Yes°.

ANNELIES: en drie: (.) past drie keer in de <u>negen</u>, dus moet je drie: keer doen. Is drie: keer negen is zevenentwi:ntig.

ANNELIES: and three goes three times nine, so you should take it three times. Three times nine is twenty-seven.

(..)

(..)

---

[1] For transcript notation, see Gail Jefferson, "Preliminary notes on a possible metric which provides for a 'standard maximum' silence of approximately one second in conversation," in *Conversation*, ed. Derek Roger and Peter Bull (Clevedon: Multilingual Matters, 1989), pp. 166–196.

GORAN: **Zevenentwintig kee:r.=**   GORAN: Twenty-seven times.=

ANNELIES: =Snappen jullie der wat   ANNELIES: =Do you understand?
van?

BEREND: ((lacht)) Ja.   BEREND: ((laughs)) Yes.

This episode shows how Annelies takes on a teacher role, taking responsibility for the learning of Maktoub and Goran, both minority students, giving them assignments, giving feedback, and checking their understanding. Annelies is the typical example of the Dutch student who eagerly adopts (or responds to) the explanation model. Throughout the study she does not give up this position and holds on to her superior status (only lending it to Berend, the other Dutch student when she does not understand something herself). Repeatedly she confirms her teacher role through putting herself into or defending the teacher's position. For instance, she tells the others to write neatly so that the teacher will be able to read it, or she remarks "that's the way schoolbooks are organized" in an attempt to make her fellow students accept the sometimes confusing numbering of the tasks. Also, she takes over the discourse of the teacher with respect to focusing on understanding the task rather than just doing the task.

Case 2: A Dutch Student Refusing a Teacher's Role
In order to show the pattern of role taking in this classroom, we selected a counterexample. Although a Dutch student, Lonneke, does the majority of the explaining in this group, she does not take on a teacher's role. However, she still seems to have a mediating role as she explains unknown words from the tasks in the textbook or the meaning of certain mathematical signs.

We have selected a few fragments that show how the only Dutch student in this group has a difficult time in denying her teacher role and receiving criticism for not being a (good) teacher.

In fragment 2 one can see how the Dutch girl Lonneke is criticized for not being smart enough (to be the teacher of the group). Also, they criticize copying behavior (in favor of explaining to others), although this seems a more general statement.

Fragment 2: Group 4 (26–5–00–A79)

LONNEKE: Kijk hier,   LONNEKE: Look, here, hundred and
honderdzeventig, uh honderd?   seventy, uh.. hundred?

IKRAM: Wel waar.   IKRAM: Yes it is.

( ): Vier.   ( ): Four.

FAHD: Ze <u>ken</u> het gewoon niet. Ze doet gewoon wat . . . (. . .)

( ): 1,2,3,4,5,6,7.

ABDEL: Ze zijn toch z<u>o</u>: <u>dom</u>!

LONNEKE: <u>Jij</u> bent dom!

FAHD: Ja.

ABDEL: >Ja en zij zegt alles tegen jou voor<.

FAHD: Ja::. Maar daarna doet ze d<u>o</u>:m.

IKRAM: Hall<u>o</u>:: Maar je hoeft niet <u>alles</u> voor te zeggen.

FRANÇOISE: Ja en jij (. . .) Je hoeft niet alles voor te zeggen. Gisteren heb je <u>alles</u> uh opgeschreven wat ze ((Lonneke)) zei.

IKRAM: Kan ook wel ehh . . . Je ken 't beter <u>uit</u>leggen.

LONNEKE: Ja.

FAHD: She just does not know how. She is just doing something (. . .)

( ): 1,2,3,4,5,6,7.

ABDEL: **They are so <u>stupid.</u>**

LONNEKE: **<u>You</u> are stupid.**

FAHD: Yeah.

ABDEL: >Yeah, and she ((meaning Lonneke)) gives you all the answers<.

FAHD: Ye:::s. But after that she acts stu:pid.

IKRAM: Hell<u>o</u>:: But you don't have to give <u>all</u> the answers.

FRANÇOISE: Yes and you (. . .) You don't have to give all the answers. Yesterday you wrote down all the answers she ((Lonneke)) gave you.

IKRAM: You could also (. . .) ehh (..) it's better to ex<u>plain</u>.

LONNEKE: Yes.

In fragment 3, one sees that Lonneke is both invited to explain and criticized for not explaining. Lonneke defends herself, saying that the group does not give her a chance.

Fragment 3: Group 4 (25–5–00–A56)

FAHD: Vier. (..) Hoe moet je dat ( ).

LONNEKE: Bij <u>deze</u> heb ik gewoon vijfentwintig en tien<u>dui:zend</u> gedaan.

( )

LONNEKE: >Hier staat-<, hier staat ((leest voor)) hoeveel <u>bo</u>men passen er dan nog op de perceel A, B en C?

( )

ABDEL: Wat moet je nou o:pschrijven, ik wee<u>:t</u> dat, dat niet.

FAHD: Four. (..) How do you do that?

LONNEKE: With <u>this</u> one, I just have done twenty-five and ten thousand.

( )

LONNEKE: >Here it says<, here it says ((reads)) how many trees fit on the parcels A, B and C?

( )

ABDEL: What do you have to write down, I don't. don't know that.

( ): **A, B̲ en C.**

LONNEKE: **Jij hebt deze.**

( ): Maar hoe wil je dat uitleggen?

IKRAM: °Zij legt helemaal geen reet uit°.

( ): ( )

LONNEKE: Ik (.) le::g (.) nie:t (.) u::it, dat doe ik pas als ik het, (.hh) als ik het zelf gemaa::kt heb. E:cht goe::d. En iemand vraa::gt het aan mij:.

( ): A, B and C.

LONNEKE: Yes, you have this one.

( ): But how do you intend to explain that?

IKRAM: °She does not explain a fuck° ((literally she says 'not an ass')).

( ): ( )

LONNEKE: I(.) do (.) no:t (.) explain, I will explain only when I, when I have finished (the work) myself. Real good. And no one asks me (to explain it).

This counterexample shows that the teacher role is somehow expected from Dutch students but can be accepted only under certain conditions (the explanation must have certain qualities, and the status of the Dutch student with respect to her knowledge must be recognized). The example clearly shows that this role-taking pattern has two sides: the attribution of the teacher role to the Dutch student by the minority students, and the acceptance of it by the Dutch student. The example suggests that although there seems to be a strong normative tendency that Dutch students take on teacher roles, this is not always put into practice.

Conclusion

In the mixed groups (Dutch and minority), the norms on collaboration put forward by the teacher are translated into a teacher-student model. Although the role division model that is inherent in this collaboration mode is not explicitly promoted by the teacher for group work, it is an adoption of the teacher's way of explaining to the students in the sense of taking responsibility for the learning of the students, asking known-answer questions, evaluating answers, and so on. This is confirmed by statements in which the Dutch students identify with the teacher's task or "translate" the language of the textbooks (as if they serve as the representatives of the books, the school, and the teachers more than the minority students do). From the data, we concluded that this role pattern in which the Dutch students take on a teacher's role was evoked both by the Dutch students themselves (e.g., when they say "I'll explain it to you") and by the minority students (e.g., when they ask for an explanation or expect the Dutch student to have more knowledge or play the teacher's role). If we compare this teacher-student model (on the base how it is practiced in, e.g., group 3) with the model put forward by the teacher in her instruction for group work, we can say that these mixed groups focus particularly on the explanation part of her model and not so much on the "think and work together" part of it. They seem to rely on a more "traditional" teaching model that most likely is modeled by the teacher in her own explanations.

Adoption of Classroom Norms on Collaboration for the Migrant Groups

Case 3: A Migrant Student in an Egalitarian Leader's Role

We present a fragment from group 1 with only minority children (three Moroccan, one Turkish student). The fragment shows a contrast with group 3 in case 1 in that, although there is explanation going on, no one adopts a teacher's position. These students work on the same task as in case 1.

Fragment 4: Group 1 (5/6/00)

HASSAN: Een, twee, drie:

ASSAD: Drie keer drie, is wat?

SAMIRA: Hier ben i:k

ASSAD: Een, twee, drie:(.), vier, vijf ze:s (.) zeven, acht ne:gen (...)

ASSAD: ((telt door tot 27))

HASSAN: Wa::nt, <hie:r>(.) dit-, is (.) twaalf centimeter, en hier past drie keer in, dus drie doosjes passen hier zo in, e::n=

SAMIRA: =Drie doosjes passen zo-=

HASSAN: =E:n (.), omhoo:g, omhoo:g passen er ook drie doosjes in, toch?=

SAMIRA: =Ja, want drie keer drie is [negen, vier keer drie is twaa:lf

HASSAN: [hier drie, hier drie en hier drie en hier zevenentwintig, en tweeëntwintig en tweeëntwintig doosjes.

SAMIRA: Hoe doen jullie dat dan?

HASSAN: One, two, three

ASSAD: Three times three, is what?

SAMIRA: I am here

ASSAD: One, two, three, four, five, six, seven, eight, nine. (...)

ASSAD: ((counts up to twenty-seven))

HASSAN: For, here, is (.) twelve centimetres, and here it fits three times, so three boxes fit here like this, and =

SAMIRA: =Three boxes fit like this=

HASSAN: =And (.) going up three boxes also fit, isn't that right?=

SAMIRA: =Yes, because three times three is [nine, four times three is twelve.

HASSAN: [Here three, here three, and here three, and here twenty-seven, twenty two, twenty-two boxes.

SAMIRA: How do you do that?

HASSAN: Gewoon.

(Hasan zit tegenover Samira. Nu loopt hij naar Samira's kant van de tafel)

HASSAN: Kij:k, hie:r, twaalf centimeter ( ) drie keer, dus, drie (.), drie doosjes zo, >en dan gaan we naar hoogte kijken<, hier past ook drie keer, drie doosjes naar boven, drie doo:sjes >zo<, en hier ook drie: keer, dus drie doosjes naar boven, en hier drie doosjes, zeg (.), zeg maar.

HASSAN: Just like that.

(. . .)(Hassan sits opposite Samira. He now walks to Samira's side of the table.))

HASSAN: Look here, twelve centimetres. ( ) Three times, so, three, (.) three boxes like this > and then we look at the height<. Here it also fits three times, so three boxes up, three boxes like this, and here also three times, so three boxes up, here three.

What we see is that Hassan clearly is the leader in this interaction, having more knowledge of the task than the others. He uses a demonstrating mode, based on an egalitarian leadership model (evidenced, for instance, through the fact that all participants can take initiative, adopt leading roles, and are consulted for their knowledge). He does not ask the other students known answer questions or evaluate their responses, typical for teachers. Equal participation in a variety of aspects (turn taking, exposing knowledge, taking the lead) seems a crucial value in this group as fragment 5 from the same group shows, in which Feliz wants to compare her answer but is criticized by Hassan, Samira, and Assad.

Fragment 5: Group 1 (5/6/00)

SAMIRA: Dus de eerste is tweeduizend tweeho::nderd ( ) tweeduizend...

SAMIRA: So the first is two thousand, two hu::ndred, two thousand

FELIZ: Is de eerste tweeduizend?

FELIZ: Is the first one two thousand?

HASSAN: ((geïrriteerd)) A:ch ma:n.

HASSAN: ((irritated)) Hey man.

SAMIRA: ((geïrriteerd))> Ja, je zit alleen maar af te kijken<, hallo↑

SAMIRA: ((irritated))>You only want to copy it<, come on↑.

FELIZ: ((geïrriteerd))>Ik ↑begrijp het niet! Jullie ↑begrijpen<-

FELIZ: ((irritated)) >I don't under↑stand, you understand<-.

SAMIRA: Ja, jij doet ook niet mee:

SAMIRA: Yes, you don't work with us.

HASSAN: Tweeduizend.

HASSAN: Two thousand.

FELIZ: Helemaa:l we:l Maar jullie zeggen niks aan mij.

FELIZ: I do. But you don't tell me anything.

HASSAN: Wij zeggen niks, wij, jij doet niks.

HASSAN: We say nothing. You do nothing.

SAMIRA: Omdat je ook niet <u>mee</u>doet.

SAMIRA: Because you don't work with us.

(...)

(...)

HASSAN: Weet je waarom dat we niks <u>ze:ggen</u> , want je moet ook eigen ( )

HASSAN: Do you know why we say nothing, because you should have your own ( ).

FELIZ: Leg het dan ui:t↑ Leg dan ui:t↑ Leg dan ui:t↑

FELIZ: Explain it, explain it to me.

ASSAD: Waarom moet je <u>ui:</u>tleggen? Je moet gewoon meedoen.

ASSAD: Why do we have to explain? You should work with us.

The fragment shows how equal participation is favored over playing a student's role. This is in sharp contrast with the norms in group 3, case 1, in which Annelies does not expect this kind of participation: the adoption of a (in a sense passive) student role is sufficient for her.

Case 4: A Migrant Student Parodying a Teacher's Role
In fragment 6 we see how a minority student adopts a teacher's role in a group with only minority students. We argue, however, that she is parodying this role.

Fragment 6: Group 2 (5/6/00)

LEERKRACHT: ((aan Fouzia)) Overleg- Leg het eens even uit aan jouw groepje. Dat zij dat <u>ook</u> snappen? ((Leerkracht loopt weg))

TEACHER: ((addressing Fouzia)) Explain it to your group, so that they understand <u>too</u>.((Teacher leaves))

FOUZIA: ((tegen medeleerlingen)) Snappen jullie sommetjes? (hhh) ((lacht))

FOUZIA: ((addressing the other students)) Do you understand the problems? (hhh) ((laughs))

( ): Nee

( ): No

FOUZIA: Nee?

FOUZIA: You don't?

( ): Nee.

( ): No.

FOUZIA: Ok. Uhm, <u>ja:</u>. Ok. Uh, <u>ja:</u> OK, u:h. ((lacht)) u::hm, nou weet ik het niet meer. >Oh jawe:l<. Kijk, <u>hier</u>boven, hoeveel passen daar?

FOUZIA: O.k., Hmm, yes, O.k. Uh, yes, O.k., uh ((laughs)). U::hm, I don't know it either. >Oh yes<. Look, at <u>this</u> part. How many fit in there?

ILHAM: Drie, drie, drie.

ILHAM: Three, three, three.

FOUZIA: Nee, sa↑men. Kijk ((lacht))

FOUZIA: No, take them toge↑ther. Look ((laughs)).

ILAM: Negen?

FOUZIA: Negen, ja.

ILAM: Nine?

FOUZIA: Nine, yes.

The interaction continues, and the students, led by Fouzia, solve part A of the problem. Later, in the same lesson, they start part B.

Fragment 7: Group 2 (5/6/00)

FOUZIA: Kijk, je doet gewoon de le::ngte, Ok. eerst rekenen wij de lengte uit. >Als je het maar stapje voor stapje doet dan we zijn zo klaar-< ((lacht)).

FOUZIA: Look, you do the le::ngth. O.k., first we calculate the length. If you do it step by step, we will be finished in no time ((laughs)).

((andere leerlingen lachen))

((Other students laugh))

FOUZIA: Ok, uh, de le::ngte, wat is de le:ngte? ((lacht))

FOUZIA: O.k., uh, the length, what is the length? ((laughs))

STUDENT: Drie centimeter.

STUDENT: Three centimetres

FOUZIA: Hoe↑veel is het naar boven? ((lacht))

FOUZIA: How much is it upwards? ((laughs))

ZAKARIA: Vier centimeter.

ZAKARIA: Four centimetres.

FOUZIA: ((lachend)) Hoeveel le::ngte is het?

FOUZIA: ((laughing)) How lo:ng is it?

ILHAM: Drie centimeter.

ILHAM: Three centimetres.

FERITL: Drie centimeter.

FERITL: Three centimetres.

ILHAM: Je moet deze doen.

ILHAM: You should take this one.

STUDENT: Ok., Hier drie centimeter.

STUDENT: O.k., here three centimetres.

ILHAM: Drie.

ILHAM: Three

FOUZIA: Goed zo, en uh, bree:dte?

FOUZIA: Well done, and uh, what about the width?

Ilham: Ja, uh, vijftien.

ILHAM: Yes, uh, fifteen.

FOUZIA: Ja, hoe weet je dat?

FOUZIA: Yes, how do you know?

STUDENT: Ja, hoe weet je dat?

STUDENT: Yes, how do you know?

FOUZIA: ((lacht)) Dat is ook uitkomst.

FOUZIA: ((laughs)) That is the solution.

The fragments show that Fouzia is taking on a teacher's role; however, she clearly is not at ease in this role. It is not so much that she is not familiar with this role, as she does not have much trouble performing it (although her identification with the teacher's role does not go as far as Annelies). But this role taking has an extraordinary position, as if parodying the role. This is affirmed by the fact that she performs this role on command, that she does this while all participants laugh a lot, that she does this only in the present lesson, and that she is criticized by the other students after a while when they say "don't talk like this."

Conclusion

Case 3 shows that the adoption of the classroom norms on collaboration takes up various aspect of the model set by the teacher. In particular these students take up the "think and work together" aspect of how the teacher stimulates group work. The minority students in these groups took this model up as an activity-based knowledge sharing in which the traditional teacher role is not included. The norms related to working together and sharing solutions are adopted and are perhaps even more elaborated in this group than the model the teacher herself was able to expose (with respect to taking turns, bringing in knowledge). Furthermore, case 4 shows that the minority students know how to adopt the more traditional teacher role but somehow do not consider this appropriate or the most "natural" way of organizing group work.

DISCUSSION AND CONCLUSION

How do we explain the differential adoption of the norms of collaboration set by the teacher and/or the role division and knowledge-sharing practice she models in the classroom by the different groups?

One possible explanation is that the minority students, in particular the Moroccan students, prefer egalitarian positions in group work as a consequence of their home socialization. We have evidence (see Pels, 1991, 1998) that socialization among peers is a relatively important and independent domain in Moroccan culture in which adults are relatively absent. Peer socialization is recognized as a qualitatively different domain of upbringing where specific skills are taught that are more difficult to learn in the presence of adults, given the asymmetry in status between adults and children (Pels & de Haan, in preparation). This would explain the rejection of an adult-child model in peer-peer interaction. In contrast, Dutch students might model adult-child relationships in their peer-interaction as a consequence of the frequent interference of adults in their social world. We refer here to what is called the creation of a so-called child world separated from the adults' world (see, e.g., Ariès, 1962; Rogoff, 1990) but also heavily influenced by adults. This influence is, for instance, evident in speech modes of middle-class mothers in which they adapt their speech to the child and fill in the "gaps" in the communicative skills of children through filling in missing information or interpreting the intended message. Thus middle-class mothers mediate between the child and the adult world through creating specific speech modes for children. In both cases there is a relative gap between the child or the peer world and the adult world. In the case of the Moroccans, however, this peer world or domain is created and held intact by children, and in the case of the middle-class milieu the child world is more constructed and supported by adults who interfere regularly. This explanation would agree with what we have called "classic" discontinuity between school and home.

The data show, however, that differences in past socialization experience are not a sufficient explanation, given the fact that minority students (in minority-only groups) do apply the teacher-student mode occasionally (in this study, they parodied this role). Also, they show familiarity with this mode by taking on the student position in the mixed groups. This is no doubt a consequence of their socialization in the classroom in which they have become familiar with this role division model and pattern of sharing knowledge. Still, the minority students seem to be reluctant to apply the teacher-student mode as a standard for group interaction and put forward strong norms on equal participation and symmetry in role taking, and they seem to have a strong preference for "explanation-in-activity" in favor of the teacher-student model. But they are able to switch between different role division models and knowledge-sharing procedures according to the situation at hand. Their use of these different models cannot be understood without looking at the specific context of this classroom in which these students were socialized for a considerable amount of time (the model of collaboration fostered by the teacher, the kind of teaching she herself models, and the specific position the minority students have in this group).

The differences found can also be understood by referring to the relative status attributed to both groups in this classroom. Representing the teacher role is obviously higher in status than representing the student role. Given the higher social status of the Dutch students in this classroom (particularly with respect to school matters), is it likely that they seek to express and confirm this status through adopting a teacher's role? This explanation was confirmed in a conversation with the teacher in which she said that she often heard Dutch students claim that they would not have a Moroccan student explain something to them. Interestingly, she pointed out that the status of some Moroccan (male) students was entirely different in the school yard during school breaks in which they represented a high status based on their social skills and appeal.

This points partly to what has been called "school-related identities," that is, a reshuffling of identities depending on the specific school context. Also it points to the reconstruction of ethnic differences in the classroom that exist outside the classroom, given the relatively low-social-status position of Moroccan citizens compared to Dutch citizens in the Dutch society.

Yet another interpretation that seems valid here is that the Dutch students identify more with the school system and its norms (in this case, with a teacher's role that clearly controls and designs the student's learning) than the minority students do. This might be related to both their familiarity with the system and their perceived possibilities with respect to their school career.

Taking this all together, and given the fact that these explanations do not exclude each other but on the contrary reinforce each other, we conclude that:

1. "Differences" between students are not to be studied as a simple, uni-dimensional phenomenon but as one that has different layers or can be looked at from various angles (it can be seen in terms of status relationships based on ethnicity but also in terms of a different response to institutional rules on how to construct common knowledge based on a different history with peer socialization).
2. Perceived differences between students should be looked upon both from the perspective of how these differences take form in other contexts (in time and place) *and* from the perspective of how these differences have taken form as a consequence of the students' being a member of a (particular) classroom culture with its own mostly rather dominant and robust communicative practices (e.g., interactive rules, patterns of role taking). Thus, the differences found are a result of the reconstruction of differences found in other contexts but take a specific form as a consequence of their reconstruction in the context of formal schooling, which has itself a strong and compelling structure (compare the notion of the contestation of the dominant discourse in Gutierrez et al., 1995, p. 451).

In our interpretations of the data, we have made use of the different versions of the (dis)continuity thesis that have developed using both continuity of past socialization experiences and school-based reconstruction of identities. These data show that both are, in important ways, related, given that past socialization experiences are a relevant "input" for school-based identity construction, and in that sense these experiences are both continued and reconstructed.

In searching for theoretical concepts that can underpin these claims – that is, a concept or notion of culture, a context (or activity and activity system) that explains both change and continuity, fluidity and stability, and moment-by-moment construction and historical formation – we may need to borrow from different traditions. This research would take into account:

- The active appropriation and manipulation of cultural differences and sameness in specific contexts (considering the consequences of the "inter-pretative turn" in anthropology): Students' (different) identities are con-structed as a result of their interactions in the school context.
- The dynamic and complex character of "webs of meaning" when they travel through different contexts and the mutual effect these have on each other (e.g., secondary acculturation): Differences between students are not "absolute" but specific to the context of the classroom and are specific responses to that classroom.
- The different historical time scales in which changes (and resistance to changes) take place, and how and when these time scales influence each other (Lemke, 2000; Ohnuki-Tierney, 1990) (the same would be true for scales of place).
- The (what some scholars call) structural dimension of cultural differences and sameness and the power relationships inherent to them (Ogbu 1992): Students produce a cultural frame of reference or a culture of resistance in response to the school culture, which is related to more structural factors (power relations between social classes or ethnic groups).
- The resistant, persisting, stable aspects of culture in contexts of change (such as migration) in relation to changing aspects.
- Individual aspects of identity formation but not leaving out the collec-tivities, the common histories of groups of people that form points of reference for individuals.

Our search for the dynamics between continuity and change in the context of multiethnic classrooms, and the fact that we are dealing with multiple, interacting systems of meaning, raises a number of interesting questions. For example, when would we expect differences between students to emerge? Do we need a particular kind of contrast or a critical mass of members who represent a certain pattern of behavior? That is, do you need a minimal amount of competent participants for a certain cultural pattern to come into being? Holland and Cole (1995) suggest that cultural artifacts come into being when there is enough "critical mass."

When would we expect cultural patterns to change (or to be put in a dif-ferent perspective or to be extended) as a consequence of the exposure to specific cultural contexts such as classrooms? For instance, Ohnuki-Tierny

(1990) mentions factors that prevent historical change, such as ambiguity in the interpretation of cultural meanings (paradoxes are not seen or communicated), routinization of meaning (a meaning is taken for granted and is not consciously "tested"), or factors that do foster change (including "symbolic marginality" and the ability to traverse category boundaries and to stand outside the system in order to comment critically on it). Applying these ideas to multiethnic classrooms, one could say that a particular "clash" between cultural patterns is needed in order to bring about change and permit an outsider's perspective of the system.

To conclude, our experience in this research project suggests that combining different approaches to cultural differences is useful in creating a rich or "thick" understanding of them. These different approaches in the interpretation process do not contradict but rather serve to reinforce each other.

Appendix Table. Composition of the groups

Group 1	Group 2	Group 3
Feliz (Turkish girl)	Ferit (Moroccan boy)	Annelies (Dutch girl)
Samira (Moroccan girl)	Fouzia (Moroccan girl)	Berend (Dutch boy)
Assad (Moroccan boy)	Ilham (Moroccan girl)	Goran (Yugoslavian boy)
Hassan (Moroccan boy)	Zakaria (Moroccan boy)	Maktoub (Moroccan boy)
Group 4	Group 5	
Abdel (Moroccan boy)	Chantal (Dutch girl)	
Fahd (Turkish boy)	Danielle (Dutch/Czech girl)	
Ikram (Moroccan girl)	Farouk (Moroccan boy)	
Françoise (Ghanaian girl)	Mimoun (Moroccan boy)	
Lonneke (Dutch girl)	Yalcin (Turkish boy)	

References

Ariès, P. (1962). L'enfant et la vie familiale sous l'ancien régime [The child and family life under the ancient regime]. Paris: Plon.

Cazden, C. B. (1986). Classroom discourse. In M. C. Wittrock (Ed.), *Handbook of research on teaching* (pp. 432–463). New York: Macmillan.

Eisenhart, M. (2002). Changing conceptions of culture and ethnographic methodology: Recent thematic shifts and their implications of research on teaching. In V. Richardson (Ed.), *The handbook of research on teaching* (4th ed., pp. 209–225). New York: Macmillan.

Gallego, M. A., & Cole, M. (2001). Classroom culture and cultures in the classroom. In V. Richardson (Ed.), The handbook of research on teaching (4th ed., pp. 951–997). Washington, DC: American Educational Research Association.

Gee, J. P. (1992). The social mind: Language, ideology, and social practice. New York: Bergin and Garvey.

Gibson, M. A. (1997). Conclusion: Complicating the immigrant/involuntary minority typology. *Anthropology & Education Quarterly, 28* (3), 431–454.

Gravemeijer, K. P. E. (1994). *Developing realistic mathematics education*. Utrecht: CD-B Press.

Gutierrez, K., Rymes, B., & Larson, J. (1995). Script, counterscript, and underlife in the classroom: James Brown versus Brown v. Board of Education. *Harvard Educational Review, 65* (3), 445–471.

Heath, S. B. (1983). *Ways with words: Language, life and work in communities and classrooms*. Cambridge: Cambridge University Press.

Holland, D., & Cole, M. (1995). Between discourse and schema: Reformulating a cultural-historical approach to culture and mind. *Anthropology & Education Quarterly, 26* (4), 475–489.

Holland, D., & Eisenhart, M. A. (1990). *Educated in romance*. Chicago: University of Chicago Press.

Lemke, J. (2000). The long and the short of it: Comments on multiple timescale studies of human activity. *Journal of the Learning Sciences 10* (1–2): 193–202.

Levinson, B. (1996). Social difference and schooled identity at a mexican secundaria. In B. Levinson, D. Foley, & D. Holland (Eds.), *The cultural production of the educated person: Critical ethnographies of schooling and local practice* (pp. 211–237). Albany: State University of New York Press.

Mehan, H. (1998). The study of social interaction in educational settings: Accomplishments and unresolved issues. *Human Development, 41*, 245–269.

Ogbu, J. U. (1992). Cultural discontinuities and schooling. *Anthropology & Education Quarterly, 13*, 290–307.

Ohnuki-Tierney, E. (1990). *Culture through time: Anthropological approaches*. Stanford: Stanford University Press.

Pels, T. (1991). *Marokkaanse kleuters en hun culturele kapitaal: Opvoeden en leren in het gezin en op school* [Moroccan preschool children and their cultural capital: Child rearing and learning in the family and at school]. Amsterdam/Lisse: Swets & Zeitlinger.

Pels, T. (1998). *Opvoeding in marokkaanse gezinnen in nederland. De creatie van een nieuw bestaan* [Child rearing in Moroccan families in the Netherlands: The creation of a new existence]. Assen: Van Gorcum.

Pels, T., & de Haan, M. (In preparation). Continuity and change in patterns of upbringing. A review of the literature on Moroccan socialization in Morocco and in the Netherlands (working title).

Philips, S. U. (1972). Participant structures and communicative competence: Warm Spring children in community and classroom. In C. B. Cazden, V. P. John, & D. Hymes (Eds.), *Functions of language in the classroom*. New York: Teachers College Press.

Philips, S. U. (1983). *The invisible culture: Communication in the classroom and community on the Warm Spring Reservation*. New York: Longman.

Portes, A. (1995). Segmented assimilation among new immigrant youth: A conceptual framework. In R. G. Rumbaut & W. A. Cornelius (Eds.), *California's immigrant children: Theory, research, and implications for educational policy* (pp. 71–76). La Jolla, CA: Centre for U.S. Mexican Studies.

Rogoff, B. (1990). *Apprenticeship in thinking: Cognitive development in social context.* New York: Oxford University Press.

Wilcox, K. (1982). Differential socialization in the classroom: Implications for equal opportunity. In G. D. Spindler (Ed.), *Doing the ethnography of schooling* (pp. 133–174). New York: Holt, Rinehart & Winston.

13

"Discourse" in Cultural-Historical Perspective

Critical Discourse Analysis, CHAT, and the Study of Social Change

Chik Collins

What part does discourse play in significant social events and processes of social change? This question is very important for social scientists in general, but it seems particularly significant for the cultural-historical tradition. Cultural-historical activity theory (CHAT) is, after all, profoundly marked by discussions about the importance of "semiotic mediation," and of linguistic mediation in particular, in the development of human communities. Yet, in terms of seeking to address the role of language use in processes of social change, it seems that the cultural-historical tradition has lagged behind other schools of social science. Perhaps then, it might be suggested, cultural-historical researchers should be looking to learn from these other schools and to use their tools and insights. The principal school that might come to mind here is the school of critical linguistics and critical discourse analysis (CL-CDA), originating in the work of Roger Fowler and his colleagues at the University of East Anglia in the later 1970s, and represented today in particular by the well-known works of Norman Fairclough (esp. 1989, 1992, 1995, 2000, 2001). Yet, as contributors such as Jones (2004) and Engeström (1999a) have argued, and as I have argued myself elsewhere (Collins, 1999), close scrutiny of the CL-CDA tradition in general, and the work of Fairclough in particular, reveals serious difficulties with the idea of complementing CHAT with CDA.

Perhaps, then, CHAT researchers might seek instead to build more effectively on the bases to be found within the CHAT tradition itself. In this chapter I seek to contribute something to this latter course of action. The chapter begins with a brief discussion of some of the principal problems with CL-CDA, focusing in particular on its "problem of context"; highlights the difference between CDA and the cultural-historical tradition on this crucial question; and provides a case study of social change in the west of Scotland, which takes the form of an account of a major, central government–led, urban policy intervention in a poverty-stricken housing estate in the town of Paisley. An attempt will be made to show how analysis of language-use in this process, conducted along the lines of CHAT, can help us both to understand this process of social change better than we otherwise would and to demonstrate, much more clearly than CDA has ever managed to do, the vital role that linguistic processes can play in such processes.

CDA AND THE PROBLEM OF CONTEXT

The CL-CDA lineage has sought to assert the crucial importance of ideology in the reproduction of power relations in contemporary liberal capitalist societies. Authors have emphasised that ideological meanings, conveyed in language, are seldom transparent to the ordinary subject, and they have set out to develop techniques of linguistic and discursive analysis that can be used to reveal ideological meanings that would otherwise remain hidden. Moreover, it has been argued, particularly by Fairclough (esp. 1992), that such ideological uses of language play a vital role in processes of social change. Social change in contemporary liberal capitalist societies is, he maintains, substantially, if not primarily, a matter of discursive change. Discursive change produces social change. Thus, those who are in the position to shape discursive change ("orders of discourse") are able to shape processes of social change in conformity with their own intentions and interests. This makes the task of critically analysing discourse all the more vital – for it seems even more clearly to become a necessary part of any struggle to bring about *desirable* social change. As Fairclough puts it, CDA "is nothing if it is not a resource for struggle against domination." In particular, CDA can be a resource to "those in struggle" against the current, and massively damaging, hegemony of neoliberalism. On this basis CDA "can make a considerable contribution on issues which are vitally important for the future of humankind" (Fairclough, 2001, pp. 216, 204–205).

These are highly admirable aspirations for social science which many, if not most, cultural-historical researchers will share. On inspection, however, we find a very significant gap between these aspirations and what has actually been delivered by the CL-CDA lineage across some twenty-five years. For one finds very little in the way of genuine and novel insights that can be shown to have been, actually or potentially, a significant resource for people involved in struggle. Indeed, one will find a virtual absence of the kind of "struggle" that Fairclough seems to be referring to in his own work. Instead, one finds a marked tendency to assume that ideological uses of language produce their intended effects on acting subjects. And, as Jones (2004) has noted, the conclusions of some of his more recent work are addressed not to what he calls "those in struggle" but to the New Labour government, which has itself been actively promulgating the neoliberalism that is being struggled against.

So why do we find this problematic and worrying gap in the CL-CDA lineage? There are a number of reasons, but the most important for present purposes reflects a fundamental problem of the lineage – one that is usually discussed as "the problem of context." Relatively early in the development of the lineage, it was recognised that the initial contributors had tended strongly to conduct their analyses as if meanings could simply be "read off" from linguistic forms (Fowler et al., 1979; Hodge and Kress, 1979; Thompson, 1984, pp. 125–126). What was being neglected was the inherent connection between meanings and contexts, and this, it was recognised, would have to be rectified. Nonetheless, within a few years Roger Fowler himself was bemoaning the continuing failure of researchers to provide the kind of concrete studies that "would allow the critical linguist to specify historical context in detail" and to indicate "relevant historical, economic and institutional circumstances" and their "implications for beliefs and relationships." In future, he insisted, critical linguists would have to be seen to take "a *professionally responsible attitude* towards the analysis of context," and in this light, he suggested, it would be useful for them to approach their work as "a form of history-writing" (1996, pp. 9–10). These comments were first published in 1987. In 1996 they were republished – and it would seem that this was because their relevance to the CL-CDA tradition had not diminished. Fairclough, who had major works published in 1989 and 1992, was given no exemption from the charges levelled – and rightly so (Fowler, 1996, esp. pp. 9–10).

Why then should the CL-CDA tradition have failed to address the problem that was identified and accepted by leading exponents some years ago? The explanation seems to be something other than the failure of professional responsibility suggested by Fowler. It seems to reflect the deep influence of linguistic idealism in the development of the CL-CDA lineage. In the early works, this came in the form of Sapir-Whorf, and in the work of Fairclough it has continued with the influence of Foucault's theory of discourse (see esp. Fairclough, 1989, 1992; Fowler et al., 1979; Hodge and Kress, 1979). This deep and continuing connection with linguistic idealism helps to explain what Engeström has described as CDA's "insistence on discourse as a privileged and more-or-less self-sufficient modality of social conduct and interaction" (1999a, p. 169). The failure to address the "problem of context" seems to reflect influences built into the basic assumptions of the lineage. And this is vital in explaining the gap between aspiration and actuality we find within it. To actually provide some resources for "those in struggle," and indeed to demonstrate that discourse genuinely is of real significance in processes of social change, it would be necessary to engage with discourse in all its concrete interconnections, perhaps even as "a form of history-writing." Yet such a course is radically undermined by assumptions that underlie the CL-CDA tradition and militate against the treatment of context as anything more than "discursive context."

DISCOURSE IN CULTURAL-HISTORICAL PERSPECTIVE

The rootedness of CHAT in materialism points towards something radically different. This means that when writers in the cultural-historical tradition tell us about the intimate connections between meanings and contexts, then we should not expect to find inherent impediments to acting on what they have told us.

We can see this clearly in foundational CHAT writings such as Vygotsky's *Thinking and Speech* and Leont'ev's *Activity, Consciousness and Personality*. Thus, in a way that seems to parallel the invocation that meaning cannot simply be "read off" from discursive forms, Leont'ev (1978, p. 85) reminds us that while "language appears to be the carrier of meaning, yet language is not its demiurge." But, as the quotation continues, we find a perspective radically different from that of CL-CDA.

Behind linguistic meanings hide socially developed methods of action (operations) in the process of which people change and perceive objective reality. In other words, meanings represent an ideal form of the existence of the objective world, its properties, connections, and relationships, disclosed by co-operative social practice, transformed and hidden in the material of language. For this reason meanings in themselves, that is in abstraction from their functioning in individual consciousness, are not so "psychological" as the socially recognized reality that lies behind them.

Similarly Vygotsky (1987, p. 50), in discussing the relation between thinking and speech, warns against separating thinking from "the full vitality of life, from the motives, interests and inclinations of the thinking individual." This separation can make meaning appear like "an independent and autonomous primeval force." In the same way, in a cultural-historical perspective, the study of discourse needs to attempt to grasp the life, in all its vitality, that has given rise to that discourse – and failing this we may well indeed end by making discourse appear as demiurge. But for Vygotsky, as Leont'ev reminds us, "an opposite thesis remained unshakeable: Not meaning, not consciousness lies behind life, but life lies behind consciousness." Meanings become "the subject of psychology" only when studied concretely, in the "internal relations of the system of activity and consciousness," and in the movement of that system. Indeed, Leont'ev notes that it is only "functioning *in the process of activity and consciousness of concrete individuals . . .* that meanings can exist" (1978, pp. 60, 87, 89; emphasis added).

All of this points towards a radically different conception of discursive meanings from that which characterises CL-CDA. In the CL-CDA framework the problem is presented as one of situating, or embedding, discourse in its wider context – as if the relation between the two were one of "interaction." Yet, in a CHAT perspective, the problem appears as one of grasping an internal relation. Discourse is not to be "contextualised" after the event, so to speak, because its internal relations to concretely interacting phenomena in the generative process of social existence should not be broken apart in the first place. At root, this is what it means to treat discourse as a sociocultural and historical phenomenon, as "produced from within, out of, and as driven by the logic of evolving activity that connects individuals to the world, to other people and to themselves" (Stetsenko and Arievitch, 2004a, p. 486).[1]

"THE CONDITIONS OF CLASS SOCIETY AND THE STRUGGLE FOR IDEOLOGY"

Leont'ev's account of the movement of meaning in the process of activity of consciousness has a particular relevance to the concerns of this chapter because he addresses himself to "the conditions of class society" and "the struggle in society for the consciousness of the people" (1978, pp. 93–94). Drawing on Marx, he argues that the historical emergence of class relationships brings with it a breakdown of the "commonness of motives of activity among the participators in collective work." With this there emerges a particular duality in meaning: "socially developed meanings begin to live in the consciousness of individuals as if with a double life" (1978, pp. 87–88). Here he draws on Vygotsky's discussion of meaning and sense. In living speech, abstract word meanings take on a sense that derives from the circumstances in which they are articulated. The spoken word "absorbs intellectual and affective content from the entire context in which it is intertwined" (Vygotsky, 1987, p. 276). This "noncomformity" of meaning and sense is inherent in human life, but particularly in capitalist society it assumes the special character of an "opposition" (Leont'ev, 1978, p. 91). Functioning "in the

---

[1] Stetsenko and Arievitch are discussing "The Self in Cultural-Historical Activity Theory," but their words are equally applicable to the phenomenon of discourse.

process of activity and consciousness of concrete individuals," socially given meanings take on a *"personal sense,"* which reflects much more than just their contextual "enrichment." It reflects, more particularly, "the 'alienation' of human life" and the consequent "disparity between the objective result of man's activity on the one hand, and its motive on the other" (Leont'ev, 1981, p. 252). As meanings are forced into internal connections with the realities of the individual's life, and its socially determined motives, they are "individualized and 'subjectivized'" and take on a "partiality": "Personal sense *also creates the partiality of human consciousness*" (Leont'ev, 1978, p. 93).

Here, moreover, Leont'ev's discussion seems to connect not just with Vygotsky but also with the account of language given by Vološinov and Bakhtin. The meanings that individuals must use in the concrete circumstances of their lives do not come from a dictionary. Individuals must assimilate "ready" meanings, which come bearing all the traces of their previous uses (cf. Bakhtin, 1981, pp. 293–294). Leont'ev acknowledges Vygotsky's point that this can be an extremely difficult process. But in the "conditions of class society and struggle for ideology," it becomes still more problematic and still more "full of dramatic effect" (1978, pp. 93–94). Here he seems to echo Vološinov. For the latter, meaning "becomes an arena of the class struggle." The ruling class "strives to impart a supraclass, eternal character to the ideological sign" and "to drive inward the struggle between social value judgements which occurs in it." This means that the inherent "inner dialectic quality" of meaning "comes out fully in the open only in times of social crises or revolutionary changes" (1986, p. 23). And, according to Leont'ev (1978, p. 93; cf. Vološinov, 1986, pp. 17–24),

In its most naked forms the process about which we are speaking appears in the conditions of class society and the struggle for ideology. Under these conditions personal meanings reflecting motives engendered by actions of life relationships of man may not adequately embody their objective meanings, and then they begin to live as if in someone else's garments. It is necessary to imagine the major contradiction that gives rise to this phenomenon. As is known, as distinct from the life of society . . . the life of the individual does not "speak for itself " . . . perception by him of phenomena of reality may take place only through his assimilation of externally "ready" meanings – meanings, perceptions, views that he obtains from contact with one or another form of individual or mass communication. This makes it possible to introduce into the individual's consciousness and impose on him distorted or fantastic representations and ideas . . . [which] only serious real life confrontations can dispel.

Leont'ev goes on to argue that dispelling such "distorted" meanings is not in itself sufficient. For "subjective personal meanings" are not *adequate* meanings, and need "reshaping." He insists, in a way that again seems very similar to Vološinov and Bakhtin, that any such reshaping "takes place under conditions of the struggle in society for the consciousness of the people," and this makes it a decidedly *collective* process.

Here I want to say that the individual does not simply "stand" before a certain window displaying meanings among which he has but to make a choice, that these meanings – representations, concepts, ideas – do not passively wait for his choice but energetically dig themselves into his connections with people forming the real circle of his contacts. If the individual in given life circumstances is forced to make a choice, then that choice is not between meanings but between colliding social positions that are recognized and expressed through these meanings. (Leont'ev, 1978, p. 94)

DISCOURSE AND SOCIAL CHANGE

The preceding discussion highlights the basic incompatibility between the CL-CDA lineage and the root assumptions of the cultural-historical tradition. It also highlights that the cultural-historical tradition, perhaps especially when linked to the contributions of Vološinov and Bakhtin, contains some significant resources that can be brought to bear in addressing the relationship between discourse and social change. Indeed, it would appear that these resources could allow us to address this relationship in ways that mirror some of the best intentions of CL-CDA – by perhaps engaging with real processes of struggle and seeking to conduct our work in ways that allow for some contribution to these and other struggles for positive change. The remainder of this chapter deals with an attempt to do something along these lines in the author's own locality – the town of Paisley in the west of Scotland.

Treating discourse as a sociocultural and historical phenomenon means grasping its production "from within, out of, and as driven by the logic of evolving activity that connects individuals to the world, to other people and to themselves" (Stetsenko and Arievitch, 2004a, p. 486). One way of approaching this task would be along the following lines. Precisely because discourse is produced by the logic of evolving activity, its analysis will tend to reveal traces of that historical evolution and of its twists and turns, moments of reconstitution and realignment. These traces provide vital prompts to the researcher, who can begin from there to investigate, to reconstruct, and hopefully also concretely to grasp the historical evolution of the human activity from within, and out of, which particular uses of language emerged. In this way, the research begins from discursive processes in order to generate an account of a larger pattern of sociohistorical development, which is in turn the key to the *comprehension* of those same discursive processes – and also of their role in the ongoing changing of the active human communities that produce them.

In such an approach there will be some tendency for the method of the study not to be closely mirrored in the order of the presentation. The latter will tend not to reproduce the "preliminary" phase of discursive analysis and to begin instead with the reconstruction of the historical evolution of the object of the study. So it is with what follows – the discursive materials with which the investigation began appear in the presentation only after much of this reconstruction has been provided. Suffice it to say at this stage that these discursive processes appeared at the time somewhat curious. They involved an impoverished community in the west of Scotland, which had suffered very badly through the neoliberal policies of the Conservative governments of Margaret Thatcher during the 1980s. This community was struggling to make "sense" of a major central-government intervention in its neighbourhood that promised to bring about a local "renaissance." This intervention was encapsulated in a new discourse of "partnership." In struggling to make sense of the intervention, the community simultaneously struggled to make sense of this discourse.

FERGUSLIE PARK

The community in question was Ferguslie Park – a housing estate on the outskirts of Paisley, built mostly in the 1930s and owned and managed by the local government (or "council"). By the first half of 1991, it housed 10,000 people – around a tenth of Paisley's population. This housing consisted mostly of tenemental flats built for those being cleared from the town's inner slums. These people were generally the families of unskilled manual workers in low-paid and irregular employment. They lived in poverty and were very often regarded as a feckless and dangerous social element requiring supervision and control. Symptomatically, the scheme was located between two railway lines, which virtually sealed it off from the rest of the town. In 1942 part of the estate was set aside for supervised housing for "known and proven incorrigible tenants, who have persistently neglected their duties as tenants and citizens" (Emsley and Innes, 1942). Ferguslie's reputation has always borne the stigma associated with these origins. But the stigma has intensified. When, in the 1960s, industrial decline brought increasing poverty and unemployment to Paisley, the combination of the estate's dependency on unskilled industrial jobs, its "undesirable" reputation, and the operation

of the council's allocations policy meant that the victims were dispropor-
tionately located in Ferguslie. Subsequently, further economic decline in the
town, combined with more poor management, low investment, failed policy
experiments, and the myriad social problems associated with poor housing
estates all deepened the problems of the local community. Ferguslie achieved
"notoriety."

Ironically, a major factor that fuelled this notoriety was the high profile
given to it by a stream of urban policy projects and experiments from the
late 1960s onwards. In terms of their ostensible remit – tackling deprivation
and reversing the decline of the area – these projects failed. In the mid-1960s
Ferguslie had around 13,500 people living in some 3,500 units of housing. By
the later 1980s the population had fallen to 5,000, and 1,000 units of housing had been cleared and demolished. Unemployment, housing problems,
poverty and its attendant problems of family breakdown, crime, and drug
abuse, and the wider stigmatisation of the area had all become substantially
worse.

In the wake of the 1987 U.K. General Election, things seemed set to get
worse still. Labour lost decisively, and Thatcher embarked on a third term
that promised a radical deepening of her government's neoliberal project.
One of the flagships for this third term was the now infamous "poll tax."
This was a highly regressive form of local taxation designed to undermine
the power of local government – seen as a base for continuing collectivism.
While better-off areas would pay less under this system, working-class areas
would pay much more. The poorest sections of society, hitherto exempted
from local tax payments, were to be made to pay a minimum of 20 percent
of the applicable charge for their households. The new regime was to be
implemented in Scotland one year ahead of the rest of Britain. This seemed
to bode very badly for Ferguslie Park. Yet it was in this same moment that
a basis for great new optimism seemed to emerge. Ferguslie Park was going
to participate in a radical new central government initiative to transform the
area and the prospects of its inhabitants. It would see the creation of new
"partnerships" in four estates across Scotland. These "partnerships" were to
be high profile, of ten years in duration, and generously funded. The initiative
was called *New Life for Urban Scotland* (1988) and it was encapsulated in a
new discourse of "partnership."

THE DISCOURSE OF "PARTNERSHIP"

According to this discourse of "partnership," "community participation"
would provide the key impetus for change and improvement in each of

these estates. It would be supported by the full gamut of organizations and agencies that had a role to play in the life of the community. All of these would, in their role as "partners," work – and indeed "be seen to work" – in harmony with the local community in generating "new life" in the area. The curious nature of this discourse should already be apparent. Promises to deepen neoliberal projects do not typically entail such apparent care for social harmony and generosity towards poor communities. So how do we account for this discourse? As has already been said, we account for it as "produced from within, out of, and as driven by the logic of evolving activity" – the activity of the Conservatives in pursuing their neoliberal project in Scotland.

The late 1980s was the period of Thatcherite triumphalism in England – heralding a new era of neoliberalism. But Scotland opposed, and voted against, all of this, and in 1987 it did so even more decisively than previously. The Thatcherites saw this as a consequence of the Scots' "dependency culture," which made them inherently unsympathetic to the emerging "enterprise culture." So the government set out to remedy this affliction – to redefine the culture and character of the nation by reengineering the balance of the public and private spheres in the life of the nation (a commendably materialistic approach!). Thus, Scottish society found itself facing a substantially new and concerted policy agenda – in housing, urban policy, economic development, and training (Kemp, 1993). *New Life for Urban Scotland* was central to this. It was to direct the attack on the "dependency culture" where it was at its worst. This was in some of the poorest council estates, which were owned almost entirely by local government, and which had very high levels of dependence on state welfare benefits. Four of these areas would become, in effect, laboratories where policy ideas could be piloted before being generalised much more widely.

The areas were carefully chosen to maximise viability. Ferguslie's appeal was its location – one mile from the growing Glasgow Airport, with almost immediate access to the motorway that links Glasgow and the west to Edinburgh, and only six miles from the centre of Glasgow itself. It was also immediately adjacent to one of the largest property developments in Scotland on the site of a former car plant and had developable land both within the estate and in its immediate environs. To the government it seemed that this potential might be harnessed to a long-term strategy to bring about change. More affluent groups would be attracted in and the deprivation statistics would be transformed. In ten years the Conservatives and the private sector would solve the worst problems bequeathed to the locality by postwar social democracy.

Yet, there remained a clear problem of *legitimacy*. The Scots had voted against all of this, and so it tended to look worryingly like another Thatcherite imposition. *And in the logic of this situation lies the key to the logic of the discourse of "partnership."* It was necessary to represent the whole exercise as something *other* than an imposition, as a model of harmony, consensus, and stable and enduring relations of "partnership." Similarly, because the elected local authorities in Scotland were controlled by the Labour Party, their role would have to be minimised.[2] They were to play only an "enabling role." The resulting deficit in terms of *representative* democracy would be remedied by a special emphasis on *direct* democracy and "community participation." Local communities would also be "partners." Thus, out of the dissensus and representational deficit of Scotland in the late 1980s was generated a discourse of consensus and popular legitimacy. It very clearly emerged "under conditions of the struggle in society for the consciousness of the people," and it equally clearly involved an attempt "to introduce into the individual's consciousness and impose on him distorted... representations and ideas" that had little "basis in... real life experience" (Leont'ev, 1978, pp. 93–94).

Connecting to the work of Bakhtin and Vološinov, we could conceptualise the generation of this discourse as an attempt by the government to "organize speech," to introduce a certain typical form of construction for the utterances of all those who were to be involved in the "partnership" process. The government was seeking to create a substantially new framework of social relations in its "partnership areas," and this required a specific kind of *speech genre* – one that would reflect the "conditions and goals" of this activity (Bakhtin, 1986, p. 60). Its use would help to ensure that participants "theorized" their contribution to this system as the government wanted them to – not as a government attempt to deepen the application of neoliberal policies, but as the working of colleagues in a harmonious partnership to transform the fortunes of a hitherto impoverished community.

It is not difficult to understand the potential appeal of this speech genre. Would not many people like to be able to think of their daily work in such a positive way? But here the precise language of Leont'ev's discussion about processes of meaning in the conditions of "struggle for ideology" is important. In these conditions the "externally 'ready' meanings" that individuals must assimilate are not only "introduced" but also "imposed" (1978, p. 93). How is this possible? In the case of the *New Life* "partnerships," it was made possible by the power of government to decide, in Lasswell's (1936) phrase,

---

[2] Between the mid-1970s and 1996 Scotland had two tiers of local government – district and regional. For the town of Paisley, these were Renfrew District Council and Strathclyde Regional Council.

"who gets what, when, how." Local authorities desperately needed resources from the central government to spend in their most deprived areas, and other "partners" were susceptible to similar pressures and incentives – whether direct or indirect. This added a "discipline" to the speech genre, which could enforce a certain adherence – a stick to add to the carrot of its undoubted emotional appeal. Those who "wanted in" on *New Life* would have to be seen to be willing to conform to the government's "representation" of it, and one important aspect of this would be that they should "talk the talk."

THE FERGUSLIE PARK PARTNERSHIP

The Ferguslie Park Partnership (FPP) was formally established in June 1988. It was led by a Partnership Board composed of representatives of the various "partner" organizations.[3] The board finalized its strategy for the area by the end of the year, and devolved its implementation to five thematic subgroups (Scottish Office, 1989). The latter were serviced by members of an implementation team who moved into purpose-built offices in the estate.

The local community was to be represented at board level by two members of a body called the Ferguslie League of Action Groups (FLAG). FLAG emerged in the mid-1970s as the body through which local people voiced their grievances and pursued "social justice." It rapidly acquired a "Scotland-wide" reputation as an effective organ of assertive, and at times quite militant, "community action" (Gaster et al., 1995, p. 7; see also Kintrea 1996). In the mid-1980s, however, the organisation was persuaded to make a significant tactical change and began to enter into collaboration with the Labour Party–controlled local authorities. Between 1984 and 1988 it participated with these authorities in an "Area Initiative," which sought to offset the worst effects of the government's neoliberal policies. The "pragmatism and adaptability" that

---

[3] Representatives of central government took four seats on its board – including the chair and another for a seconder who acted as the "chief executive" of the local implementation team. Also represented were "quangos," such as the Scottish Development Agency, the Training Agency and the Housing Corporation in Scotland, the government's Department of Employment, the local Health Board and the local Enterprise Trust. (Quangos are quasi-autonomous nongovernmental organizations. In reality they are not very autonomous at all. The Conservative government merged the SDA and the Training Agency into Scottish Enterprise in 1990. The Housing Corporation in Scotland was incorporated into a new body called Scottish Homes in 1989. Both of the new bodies displayed strong privatizing and marketizing agendas.) The two local authorities, Strathclyde Regional Council and Renfrew District Council, were represented, but by one official in each case rather than by elected politicians. (This reflected the deprioritizing of the mechanisms of *representative* democracy.) Some months later these were joined by two members from a newly formed "Business Support Group" representing private sector interests – including those involved in nearby property developments.

FLAG had shown in these years subsequently led the government to believe that it would "buy into" its "philosophy" of "partnership" (William Roe Associates, 1994, p. 10). This was a very important consideration in selecting the four areas for "partnership" status. If local residents were not willing to work as "partners," then the legitimacy of what the government was doing would begin to look highly tenuous. The whole *New Life* programme, and indeed the government's broader agenda, might begin to look like another Thatcherite imposition and become more open to conscious reflection than the government might like.

In Ferguslie, the initial stages were not straightforward. To the community activists within FLAG, things seemed just *too* incongruous. FLAG had, in the Area Initiative, worked in something like a "partnership" with the local authorities. But this partnership was conceived in opposition to the Conservative government. Now FLAG was being asked to form a "partnership" with the Conservatives themselves. This led to concerns about the *motive* for this emerging activity, and to an early crisis. As consultant researchers were later to note, "Initially . . . mistrust of the government's motives fuelled suspicion about what lay behind the initiative. The community feared that the collaboration which had been established with the local authorities might be hijacked for wider political purposes" (William Roe Associates, 1994, p. iii).

The government set about assuaging these fears. It did so in two main ways. Firstly, the extent and nature of community representation on the Partnership Board were altered. FLAG's direct participation was increased from two to four people, and two local politicians – the regional councillor (RC) and one of the two district councillors for the area – were given seats as additional "community representatives." These councillors had played a prominent role in the previous Area Initiative and were generally trusted by FLAG. Secondly, a key FLAG member was identified for the position of "community development executive" (CDE) in the Partnership's implementation team. This person was to be responsible for developing the relationship between the Partnership and the local community.

These changes provided reassurance to FLAG. But this was to prove ephemeral, for the changes also effected a significant realignment in local relations. Henceforth, the RC and the new CDE were to play a key role in *managing FLAG on behalf of the FPP*. They were to use their authority to seek to ensure that FLAG would work within the prescribed "partnership" framework – and that it would not be seen to challenge it in a way that could undermine the basis of the government's claims to legitimacy for the *New Life* programme. And this was to mean also defending and enforcing the authenticity of the speech genre of "partnership." This realignment was to prove crucial to the subsequent development of the FPP. From the perspective of FLAG, it set the scene for a process of learning about the nature of that project – a process that was driven by the logic of their collective engagement in it. Was it actually a "partnership," one that sought to include the community in a consensual process in order to transform its life? Or was it perhaps what they had initially feared it might be – an attempt to use the community "for wider political purposes"?

This learning process seemed set for a time to bring about some positive change – both in Ferguslie Park and beyond. However, this was to lead to a special intervention aimed at halting that process. The result was not just that learning was not realised, and positive change prevented, but that the FPP itself failed and then seemed to implode.

THE DIALOGICS OF PARTNERSHIP

Analysis of discourse conducted along the lines of CHAT as previously outlined (and from which the reconstruction just provided was begun) gives some significant insight into how these processes unfolded. This is not, of course, to claim that they were determined by language. Rather, it is to suggest that because language was an integral aspect in a system of internal relations of activity and consciousness, discursive processes offer us a window on the movement of the system as a whole. Again, the linkages to Vološinov and Bakhtin are clear. For the former, processes of language use provide us with an "index of social changes":

The word is implicated in literally each and every act or contact between people – in collaboration on the job, in ideological exchanges, in the contacts of ordinary life, in political relationships, and so on. Countless ideological threads running through all areas of social intercourse register effect in the word. It stands to reason then, that the word is the most sensitive *index of social changes*, and what is more, of changes still in the process of growth, still without definitive shape.... The word has the capacity to register all the transitory, delicate, momentary phases of social change. (Bakhtin, 1986, p. 19)

For Bakhtin, too, language registers social processes – in particular, the conflicts between social groups. In this connection, he points to the special importance of *speech genres*. The characteristic forms of construction of utterances reflect determinate sets of social relations. When the latter shift or change, then so too do the genres they produce. As Bakhtin (1986, p. 65) puts it, "Utterances and their types, that is, speech genres, are the drive belts from the history of society to the history of language."

On this basis, let us proceed to pay special attention to the way the members of FLAG responded to the attempt to defend the authority of the speech genre of "partnership" in their locality. This provides a certain "window" on FLAG's collective learning process. But because the question of the role of the local community was so vital to the legitimacy of the Partnership, these linguistic processes also provide a way in to begin to address broader questions about the FPP as a process of social change.

"Partnership" and "Poll Tax"

While the changes to the board and the promise to appoint the new CDE had reassured the FLAG activists, the wider political discord that had fuelled their scepticism remained in place. As a result, FLAG was soon again raising doubts and suspicions about the nature of its local "partnership." We get a good insight into this in key participants' accounts of arguments about how FLAG should respond to the issue of the poll tax (explained earlier). In the early period of the FPP, communities across Scotland were campaigning against the implementation of the tax, and a mass movement for nonpayment – ultimately successful – was taking shape. In the past, FLAG, in its pursuit of social justice, would have been involved. But in the framework of "partnership," participation became problematic. Its implementers were now FLAG's "partners," and any action on the issue would challenge the "partnership" ethos. FLAG was persuaded to take no action. There follow two extracts from interviews carried out with individuals involved – the first with the Partnership's CDE, and the second with a FLAG activist.[4] Each has been asked about FLAG's failure to campaign against the poll tax.

> CDE: whether they realise it or not. the FLAG organisation then moves, from the traditional role it has been doin' up into what you can maybe say is startin' to get near the politics with a big P, and we know all the lines that certain . . . politicians take and stuff like that, so to keep that nucleus going, maybe there have to be some hard decisions taken, by saying well, if we're lookin' for, somethin', or, to do a bit of . . . lobbyin'

---

[4] In an approach informed by the works of Bakhtin and Vološinov, transcriptions should seek to be as faithful to the "voice" of the speaker as is reasonably possible. But this is not always the most sympathetic way to approach an international readership. For this reason the transcription here is rendered close to standard English. Some observations on emphasis and intonation/expression are added in square brackets. Otherwise, a comma indicates a short pause in the utterance, a full stop a longer pause, and ellipsis stops indicate that a part of the utterance as transcribed has been omitted. Collins (1999) provides a more "voice-faithful" transcription.

at some stage to get a result for what this community needs right now then maybe we're going to have to sort of give up two or three things at that particular stage because they don't have a go, at the politician right, while we're actually you know sittin' there and they're a part of the organisation . . . but it is a personal decision of their's, if they know that certain campaigns will have . . . [*very quickly*] repercussions, so they've got to make an informed decision, "what is best fur this community, me gettin' involved in that campaign, or me playin' along with this game to get an extra resource comin' in here?"

ACTIVIST 1: FLAG was told not to . . . by their regional councillor.

COLLINS: Why?

ACTIVIST 1: [*long pause, then in a "matter of fact" manner*] Because the Partnership is in Ferguslie. I mean that's the only way to explain it. because the Partnership is here FLAG cannot be if you like be the great activist group it was in the past. . . . because the partnership is here our hands are tied in certain aspects, of local government, things that you would petition against in the past, you just [*emphatically*] don't do it now because, the partnership is here. you know what I mean? I mean we used to go . . . on demonstrations . . . against all different things, poll tax included, before the partnership [*suppressed nervous laughter*] came, but it doesn't happen now.

In these extracts, we can see how the attempt of the CDE and RC to defend and enforce the authenticity of the "speech genre" of "partnership" was being stretched and tested in the dialogical flow of utterances. The CDE attempts to answer the question by invoking the genre. But this proves difficult, and he ends by portraying the "partnership" process as a "game" to extract resources from potentially unforgiving adversaries. Moreover, throughout the utterance one detects echoes of other voices who do not accept this logic and who have expressed an opposing view. The activist, on the other hand, cannot use the genre to account for FLAG's inaction. The attempt to do so is faltering and hesitant, and this in itself is articulate – in that it testifies to the difficulty the FLAG activists faced in using the genre as their own.

The tensions here, however, are not simply discursive. They testify to the inherent tensions in logic of the evolving activity. As an "acting subject" of this activity, FLAG was learning about the nature of "partnership" – in particular, the limitations that the status of "partners" placed upon its action. But the activists found it difficult to accept those limitations. FLAG had been born as an agency of "community action" and social justice, and though it had latterly worked collaboratively with the local authorities, it had done so in order to *offset* the impact of Thatcherism in its area. Now it was finding out that it was required to abandon any idea of community action in the face of one of the most unjust social measures in living memory – in order not to offend Thatcher's Scottish ministers. More specifically, it was being informed of this by people to whom it had recently been very close. FLAG was beginning to face the prospect that it might have to make a choice between "partnership" and protest – not simply as meanings, but as "colliding social positions... recognized and expressed through these meanings" (Leont'ev, 1978, p. 94).

Other conflicts in the early period that generated a stretching and testing of the speech genre of partnership brought forth an attempt to defend its authenticity. Throughout 1989 and the first half of 1990, the Partnership was able to manage this process and prevent any outright breakdown. In mid-1990, however, an important event changed this situation. Thatcher's leading Scottish minister[5] made a visit to the estate for the official opening of the new FPP offices. Groups from across the wider locality mounted a demonstration against the poll tax to coincide with his visit. The FLAG activists were duly reminded of their role as "partners" and advised not to participate. They decided to comply with this advice. As a result, a group of FLAG activists, in their capacity as members of the Partnership Board, attended a reception for the minister (dining on quails' eggs!), while their erstwhile allies from the broader Paisley district protested outside. For this they later faced stinging criticism, led by the one FLAG activist who did join the protest. The following extracts from an interview I conducted with this activist some months later give an indication of how this criticism was voiced:

> ACTIVIST 1: From the day that Partnership came in, FLAG as a pressure group ceased to exist, and they had all the sort of leadin' activists in Ferguslie tied up quite neatly, meetings at nine o'clock in the mornin'... I believe it was on the advice of [the RC and CDE] that the other FLAG activists just let the poll tax thing die... [*emphatically*] don't rock the boat keep everythin' quiet forget the fuckin' poll tax we don't want to upset anybody.... if they've got any problems that's where [the CDE] comes in,... he knows the people in Ferguslie Park and he knows how to deal with them.

Here FLAG stood accused of failing to represent the interests and grievances of the people of Ferguslie Park, and of allowing itself to be led and manipulated

---

[5]   Malcolm Rifind, then secretary of state for Scotland.

by the Partnership – particularly through the RC and the CDE. This line of criticism gained a significant currency within the estate. Clearly, the form of construction of utterances like these was quite alien to the speech genre of partnership, and as a result they constituted a direct challenge to the government's intervention.

FLAG's subsequent action was framed by the dialogics of this situation. It was responding to two sets of voices – one set exhorting it to work within the framework of partnership, and the other criticising it for doing that. Its response was to seek, from the second half of 1990, to continue within the Partnership, but to distance itself from the CDE and the RC, and henceforth, in the interests of the people of Ferguslie Park, to demand the status of "full partners." This was to prove significant in terms of the subsequent development. For FLAG was now setting out quite consciously to compare "rhetoric with reality." Henceforth, the limits of the speech genre of partnership would be probed and tested in a much more focussed and coherent way. The activists, in measuring the extent to which they were in practice allowed to participate as "full partners," would simultaneously test out the applicability and appropriateness of the speech genre to their own experience.

By the end of 1990 their experience had led them to conclude that they were not being accorded the status of "full partners." Instead, it seemed that the Partnership was transferring housing and land out of the public sector and promoting private property development in ways, and at a rate, that FLAG was not at all comfortable with. FLAG's own attempt to get issues of poverty onto the agenda brought little success. Moreover, the activists were stung by the response of the Partnership when they tried to raise these concerns. They were told that by becoming "negative" in their attitude and "obstructive" of the efforts being made by the other "partners," they were increasingly "losing their credibility" within the FPP. Jeopardising the success of the Partnership would only work against the interests of local people.

Increasingly concerned by all of this, FLAG sought, at the end of 1990, to find a way to get its concerns onto the agenda. The chair and secretary of the organisation approached the author of this chapter and requested a research report on the problems they were experiencing. The research was carried out in the first quarter of 1991. It involved, among other things, tape-recorded interviews with the FLAG activists and others involved in the Partnership.

The Disintegration of "Partnership"

The interviews with FLAG members show a further stage in the developing relationship between FLAG and the Partnership. Two main factors seem to have been at work. Firstly, the sharpness of the Partnership's riposte to FLAG's prior attempt to voice its concerns had led the activists to formulate these concerns even more pointedly. It seems to have heightened an existing dissatisfaction into a sense of moral indignation, which then fuelled the sharpening of the antagonism (cf. Scott, 1990, pp. 111–115). Secondly, FLAG's participation in the research project itself seemed, in a way that brings the thinking of Paolo Freire to mind, to oblige the activists more systematically to confront the problematic gap between the discourse of "partnership" and its practice (Freire, 1972a, 1972b; see also John-Steiner and Souberman, 1978; Stetsenko and Arievitch, 2004b). As a result, at this stage the discourse shows much more of the "dramatic effect" (Leont'ev) or "inner dialectic quality" (Vološinov) in the movement of meanings.

In theorising such movement of meanings, Vološinov emphasises the great importance of "evaluation" (see esp. 1986, pp. 70, 103–105). Leont'ev also uses this term when discussing the relationships between meaning, motive, and personal sense (1978, p. 91). For Vološinov, anything significant to the life of a social group is subject to its evaluation. Whenever such topics are spoken about, they are evaluated from the group's perspective – from its "social purview." In this process, utterances and the terms deployed within them are given an "evaluative accent" that reflects the attitudes and judgements struck by the group. This whole question of evaluation, moreover, is seen to be inseparable from questions of meaning and how they change. Here, he suggests that "it is precisely evaluation that plays the creative role. A change in meaning is, essentially, always a *re-evaluation*: the transposition of one particular word from one evaluative context to another" (Vološinov, 1986, p. 105).

Returning now to developments within FLAG, we can see that by the early part of 1991 a much clearer "take" on the meaning of "partnership" was crystallizing. The earlier (personal) sense of incongruity about the meaning of "partnership" was giving way, through a collective process of engagement, to the fashioning of an alternative – and, as Leont'ev might have said, "more adequate" – meaning. The following two extracts show how this process was animated by the Partnership's earlier allegation that FLAG was "losing credibility" with the other "partners" because of its increasingly "negative" approach.

COLLINS: you said that you're seen as bein' negative.

ACTIVIST 2: [*emphatically*] negative.

COLLINS: what do you mean by that?

ACTIVIST 2: …I always ask them that, what do you mean by I'm [*emphatically*] negative?, and they say that I'm just questionin' everything, and I'll I'll do that till doomsday. and if that's what they call "negative," I'm quite happy to go along bein' called negative, but I see it as [*emphatically*] a positive, a positive way,...because at the final analysis...its the people in Ferguslie Park who have got to live with it.

ACTIVIST 3: we don't think our credibility nosedived, we think our cred-ibility in the eyes of the people of Ferguslie Park actually went up a wee bit, you know I mean it has actually got a wee bit better, because, we [*emphatically*] stood up, to the officialdom in here, we stood up to them and we said to them "hey wait a minute, you are not passing this through until we've had time to discuss it,"...for him to say that our credibility fell, was totally wrong. Our credibility actually went up, our credibility in the eyes of Ferguslie Park people went up. and that's more important to us, than to have...his credibility. we don't care what he thinks of our credibility.

If, with Vološinov and Bakhtin, we see the government as attempting to impart an "authoritative" character to the meaning of "partnership," then in these utterances we see this in quite an advanced stage of breakdown. They show a quite clear separation of "social purviews" and a very stark transposition of word meanings between the evaluative contexts provided by these purviews – so stark that a "negative" becomes a "positive" and a "loss" becomes a "gain." This is particularly clear also in a contrast drawn by another member, labelled activist 4, between what FLAG "see the partnership doin' and...what the partnership see, which is two totally different things." Increasingly, it was emerging that speakers in different positions in the net-work of social relations evaluated the same social processes in quite anta-gonistic ways.

All of this also meant that the speech genre of partnership was under heightened strain – to the point where the activists were quite explicitly rejecting its appropriateness to their needs. This can be seen in the following three interview extracts where the activists are engaging with the ideas of community participation, partnership, and consensual working, which were central to that genre.

ACTIVIST 4: we've just been overrun by, what the [government] say we need...in the strategy document I think its quoted there "to enable the people of Ferguslie Park to take...more control of their lives"...[*contemptuously*] that is crap. [*long pause*] I mean it really is...that quote, I would just take straight back out...I would remove that because I mean I really don't believe that's what it's about.

ACTIVIST 1: at the end of the day the Partnership is goin' to do what they want, and to be quite blunt to hell with the community, and that's' bein' serious....[its a] tokenistic, a tokenistic role, they're [the community] there when it suits the Partnership for them to be there. you know it's . . . alright, when . . . the Partnership need us to be there, that's when, everythin's goody goody. but I mean there's a lot of meetings go on behind closed doors where we're not involved, where decisions are taken, about Ferguslie Park, and the community is not involved in them. . . . the decisions are made before we go into meetings . . . because if you like wheels within wheels in the partnership, you know . . . its not if you like community involvement, it definitely is not.

ACTIVIST 2: once the [*laughing*] Partnership had its offices, in Ferguslie Park, the ball game changed. the whole ball game changed . . . all of a sudden there were meetings goin' on that the community knew nothing about. consultation process, well they'll deny this, the consultation process, is out the window in my opinion . . . I mean . . . we're wanting in (at) the embryo, to be there when the ideas come out, we're actually going to have a community that's sittin' back and waitin' with baited breath, (for) what's comin' next.

The reevaluations here are very stark indeed. They demonstrate how the main themes of the speech genre of partnership were being rejected as inappropriate to the context of Ferguslie Park – not by an isolated voice, but by the main body of the FLAG activists. Symptomatically, at this point the word "partnership" itself seemed to become "a dirty word" in the mouths of the FLAG activists. The activists seemed not so much to speak as to "spit" the word – as if all of the evaluative connotations that expressed their grievances were distilled and conveyed in the intonation of this one word. Here what Bakhtin calls the "particular typical expression" that adhered to the word "partnership" was shifting significantly.[6] This shift, in turn, was a clear indication that the activists were starting to invoke a quite different social form for the construction of their utterances – the characteristic themes of which were not those of consensus and partnership, but those of struggle and protest. This can be seen in the following two extracts from the interviews:

ACTIVIST 3: the way I would see FLAG, . . . is [as] an equal partner of the partnership. obviously you've got four main members of the

---

[6] "Genres correspond to typical situations of speech communication, typical themes, and, consequently, also to particular contacts between the *meanings* of words and actual concrete reality under certain typical circumstances. Hence also the possibility of typical expressions that seem to adhere to words. . . . This typical (generic) expression . . . belongs not to the word of language as such but to that genre in which the word usually functions. It is an echo of the generic whole that resounds in the word" (Bakhtin, 1986, pp. 87–88).

Partnership you've got [the government] ... the regional council the district council and you've got us, the community. if we're not there, then they've nothin' ... if we withdraw from there, you've got those three, plus the private sector if ye want tae say the private sector, you've got those three, who cannot do anything without our say so, I mean because, they will destruct, and I mean this we will disrupt, every single meetin', that happens in that partnership, ... we will go back to [*emphatically*] demonstratin'. we will demonstrate outside the offices, ... wherever, ... and we'll show them that the Ferguslie Park people are no pushover, they are no pushover the people down here, take pride, in what they're doin', the people of FLAG take pride in what they're doin', they take a sense of achievement when they get somethin' at the end of it. they feel ... the work that they're doin' is well worth while because if it wasn't none of us would be here, there would be no FLAG there would be no need for flag, if we didn't feel that our work, ... was worthwhile, the partnership, on the other hand, feels, that FLAG. is, a thorn in its side, that it has got to get rid of.

ACTIVIST 2: FLAG was so strong before, with the previous activists, who set up the procedures where the councillors an they all were together, 'n' they didn't have to batter doors down, now. [*slowly/seriously*] the days of that may have to, be relooked at ... we may have to go back to that situation.

These utterances register the fact that the Partnership was increasingly unable to manage the conflicts that had been testing and stretching the speech genre of partnership. The activists seemed to be in the process of tearing apart the very fabric of the genre, criticising its inappropriateness and moving on to something else. More precisely, they seemed to be moving *back* to something else – to a speech genre of "community action," which had been the product of an earlier period in the organization's development. The utterance of activist 3 shows again the animating effect of the Partnership's evaluation of FLAG as "negative" and lacking in "credibility" in all of this. The activist encapsulates this in the notion that the Partnership sees FLAG as "a thorn in its side." Against this is posed a counterevaluation – stressing the pride and the sense of achievement that the activists feel in their work, the conviction that this requires that they be accorded the status of "full partners," and their willingness, if necessary, to use quite confrontational methods to achieve it. The expectation is that if something is not to change soon, then there will be no "partnership." Activist 2 poses essentially the same scenario. Against the model of consensual working, which first began to emerge during the earlier

Area Initiative, the activist poses the prospect that it may well be necessary once more to "batter doors down." Crucially, the utterances – particularly the first – also show a perception that the legitimacy of the Partnership rested on the consent and participation of the community and that this gave FLAG real scope to publicly challenge that legitimacy.

Forbidden Learning

It is on this basis that I suggest that FLAG's learning process was one that held out some promise for positive change. The linguistic analysis offers us a kind of window on the movement of a system of internal relations of activity and consciousness in which FLAG seems to have identified the key contradiction of the government's intervention in its estate. Although its legitimacy rested on claims to the status of the community as "full participants," this commitment could not be adhered to in practice. The reality was that there could be no dissent from, or even meaningful discussion of, the imposition of a predetermined neoliberal agenda – which the people of Scotland had decisively rejected. Not only was FLAG identifying this contradiction; it was on the verge of implementing an alternative model for its activity – an action that would fundamentally undermine the legitimacy of the FPP.

This process was local, but its significance was much wider. For the contradiction at the heart of the FPP was also at the heart of the whole system of governance in Scotland in the late 1980s. The danger for the government was that, because of the high profile given to Ferguslie Park in piloting its wider agenda, the local process might also have an impact on the public perception of its wider legitimacy. On the broader canvas, this danger was more than theoretical. For in each of the other three "partnership areas," community groups were voicing similar feelings. In one of the areas, the community had begun a public boycott. If FLAG were to do likewise, the other two areas might well have drawn similar conclusions and followed suit. FLAG's learning process could, in this light, have had serious implications for the whole project of "thatcherising" Scottish society and culture. It could have helped to create a broader collectivity of learning across the four "partnership areas" and beyond and to shine a light on the government's fundamental problem of legitimacy.

The response of the FPP to this emergent learning process was to intervene in haste to shut it down. This was a kind of "forbidden learning." Its prevention, they decided, meant that FLAG, as its key agency, should be first neutralised and then eliminated. Its historic identity as an agency of community action, and the apparent propensity for this identity to reemerge in the present, meant that it was not a "safe bet" in the new framework of "partnership." The task of fashioning an alternative body was entrusted to the RC and the CDE. During the summer of 1991, they hastily initiated the creation of a "Community Forum." They did this with the support of *some* of the FLAG activists who had in the recent past been very critical of the Partnership. Yet the latter provided support, having been told that the new structure would increase the scope for activists to find paid employment in servicing it and its related projects. Subsequently, each of these activists secured such employment. In doing so, they were more or less "recanting" on their previous learning. Those who would not recant were marginalised and soon left the estate to live elsewhere. FLAG itself was duly wound up completely. The ostensible reason for this reengineering of community representation was to *improve* community participation in the Partnership. In practice, it was to mean the end of any prospect of such participation for the near future. For in the coming years it was the time-consuming work of fashioning the new Community Forum (with the former CDE in the role of its chief executive), rather than the work of representing the community in the functioning of the Partnership itself, which was to consume almost all of the energies of the local community (see Gaster et al., 1995; William Roe Associates, 1994).

The Consequent Implosion

The Scottish poet Robert Burns famously remarks that "the best laid plans" often go awry. If this is true, then what of poorly laid plans, enacted in haste, in communities that are known to be deeply troubled through the complex impact of poverty? What would be the consequence of this hasty intervention to close down FLAG's learning process? In something less than four years, this was to become apparent through the interaction between Ferguslie Park and the Labour Party in the Paisley area. The two were linked in particular through the prominent role played in each by the RC and the CDE. The labyrinthine politics of this cannot detain us here. The important fact is that they led to Irene Adams, member of the UK Parliament for Paisley North, raising widely reported concerns about developments in Ferguslie Park.

Ferguslie's "Community Business"

Here it is necessary to return to the community infrastructure as it developed in the mid-1980s – during the Area Initiative. In this period FLAG acquired a "community business" counterpart, called Ferguslie Park Community Holdings (FPCH). The latter had been one of the pioneers of "community business" in Scotland. It was very much a *community* business, with a strong *social* mission, and quite a strong sense of community "ownership" developed around this. It was governed by a board of twelve – all of them community representatives – and was dependent on subsidy from both central and local government. But when the FPP was created, FPCH was seen as too reminiscent of the "dependency culture," which the government wanted to break. The outcome was the creation, with start-up funding from both central and local government, of Ferguslie Community Business Enterprise (FCB). Around three-quarters of the employees were no longer required, and the old board was replaced. The new board comprised four members of the Business Support Group and two local councillors – the regional councillor and a district councillor. There were now only three community representatives – one of whom was the CDE. Writing in 1991, Kintrea (1992: 63) was to report to Scottish Homes that the community business now operated at "arm's length" from the rest of the community: "community involvement these days in the local community business is minimal."

A major element of FCB's subsequent activities involved developing a security company – FCB Enterprise Security Limited. This was based on protecting the various development sites in and around the estate and on picking up work in the wider locality. Irene Adams (the MP for neighbouring Paisley North) alleged, however, that this company was deeply implicated in a very vicious drugs war that was going on in and around Paisley, and which had seen a number of "cold-blooded executions" (*The Scotsman*, April 18, 1995). The MP herself was soon reported to be under police protection, and local councillors were said to be in fear of their lives. Soon the chief constable of Strathclyde was offering "to give witnesses new identities and a new life in a foreign country if necessary" (*The Scotsman*, May 5, 1995). Ferguslie was hugely tarnished – local property prices collapsed – but so too was the reputation of the town of Paisley as a whole.

Understanding the Implosion

This outcome cannot be disentangled from the reengineering carried out by the FPP. An enterprise culture was what the government wanted to create, and the irony is that it clearly did help to do that. Of course there were problems with drugs and criminality in the estate prior to the arrival of the Partnership, but it seems clear that the Partnership's intervention interacted with the pre-existing problems in a highly adverse way. Firstly, the community business was all but detached from the scrutiny of the broader community. The directors drawn from the Business Support Group seem to have been "absentee" directors, and the district councillor seems to have taken a somewhat "hands off" position. So in practice the active membership of the board of the community business amounted to the CDE and the RC. Secondly, the capacity of the broader community to exercise any meaningful control or influence over the community business was further reduced by the elimination of FLAG and the marginalizing of some of its more assertive individuals.

Our analysis of discourse also helps us to explain how these two aspects were linked and emerged out of "the logic of evolving activity." It was the need to "manage" FLAG that led to the strategic importance of the CDE and the RC in the FPP. Only people with detailed local knowledge and connections could attempt to do this. The linguistic analysis shows quite clearly their attempts to achieve it and allows us to chart their failure – which was in turn to lead to the elimination of FLAG. But grasping this strategic importance of the CDE and RC in this respect allows us also to understand their capacity to empower themselves in the structures of the FPP. Analyses of the structure and operation of the Partnership up until 1995 reported concerns about their recurring presence at a number of key points and nodes across its structures (see Gaster et al., 1995; William Roe Associates 1994). Yet, such concentrations of power can be dangerously susceptible to the power of those who play according to rules even harsher than those of "partnership." One anonymous company director was quoted in a prominent newspaper as follows: "We are all afraid; after all, we are talking about people walking around and shooting other people" (*The Herald*, April 18, 1995). A councillor was quoted in a similar vein: "I have a suitcase packed and waiting behind my front door because I'm scared. These are heavy people. They shoot folk in broad daylight" (*The Scotsman*, April 18, 1995). Here the simultaneity between the destruction of FLAG with its long-standing commitment to positive social action and the burgeoning of a negative and antisocial element is very striking. It evidences the consequences that flowed, concretely, from the closing down of FLAG's learning process – the virtual implosion of the FPP itself.

PARTNERSHIP, CULTURE, AND POLITICS

This implosion, we find, emerged from the contradictory nature of the evolving activity. Yet, from the perspective of the implementation of the Conservative's "partnership" agenda, the implosion was ultimately less problematic than it might have been to allow FLAG's learning process to continue and to "expand." The rootedness of the implosion in the dynamic of the "partnership" intervention could be ignored or denied. The problem could be portrayed as the activities of "a few bad eggs." And with no effective community voice to say anything different, the damage could be minimised.

For, by this time, relations with community groups in the other three areas had also been "stabilised" in various ways – generally less brutally than in Ferguslie Park. The logic of "partnership" was being widely disseminated to other areas, and to the operation of local government and other organizations and agencies more generally. Resistance to this process had been undermined by the election of the Conservatives for a fourth term of government in 1992. Increasingly, conformity to the concept of "partnership" was required by government initiatives and directives, with funding allocated to those who could demonstrate it. "Enterprise" was becoming "a word of praise" (Vološinov, 1986, p. 23). The logic of "partnership" began to become part of the landscape – taken for granted, common sense. Who could conceivably be opposed to the idea of "working in partnership" to deliver improvement and change for Scotland – especially in its most troubled communities? There seemed to take place a kind of "collective forgetting" of the origins and nature of "partnership" – and of the damage that its substantive (neoliberal) content had done, and was doing, particularly to those troubled communities. The momentum behind all of this was now too strong for the revelations to do more than temporarily slow it.

Two years later, in 1997, the Conservatives lost the General Election. In Scotland they failed to win a single seat in Parliament. The Labour Party won – as "New Labour." It was pledged to address the fundamental problem of the Tory years in Scotland – its democratic deficit. It was to create a devolved Scottish Parliament, which would henceforth be an expression of the will of the Scottish people. Yet, even before it was created, "New Labour" pledged that it would continue with the "partnership" agenda inherited from its predecessors. This agenda had indeed become a matter of very significant consensus across Scotland. In due course, it was adopted by the new Parliament, and it continues to underpin policy across key areas – housing, local government, urban policy, economic development and labour markets, and training and education.

The great irony in all of this seems to be that the Conservatives' post-1987 "partnership" agenda did in significant ways achieve its aims – when we remember that it was intended to achieve a change in the culture and character of the nation through shifting the balance of the public and private realms. For now a neoliberal agenda was being embraced in Scotland – even by the erstwhile proponents of left-wing social democracy in the Labour Party. The irony is that while this was supposed to revitalise the fortunes of the Conservative Party in Scotland, it in fact led to its virtual destruction. The beneficiaries were ultimately to be "New Labour" – who would now promote neoliberal policies even further.

What, then, of the more immediate objectives of *New Life for Urban Scotland* – the radical improvement of the four areas and the creation of a model that would then bring similar improvements in other areas? These objectives were not at all met – even in those four initial areas, where very large resources were deployed. Indeed, with the continuance of neoliberal policies at national level, problems in poor communities intensified. Yet, again, such "unhelpful" evidence was managed carefully and "spun" positively (Cambridge Policy Consultants, 1999; cf. Collins, 2001). Again, it seemed that, even under the new government, it was "forbidden" to learn about the real impact of neoliberalism on communities.

As if to prove the point, a new generation of partnerships was created in 1999 – Social Inclusion Partnerships – built on "the key planks of the *New Life* approach" (Scottish Office, 1999, paras. 7.21–7.22). These too have failed – and have "officially" been seen to fail (Cambridge Economic Associates, 2003). Their failure, however, is attributed to problems with *implementation* rather than policy content. The answer? Another generation of partnerships – now called Community Planning Partnerships. The broader economic policy context for these is the pursuit of "entrepreneurial dynamism" (Scottish Executive, 2004a, 2004b). And just as all of this is being announced, the newspapers report that males born in Ferguslie Park and similar areas of poverty "are more likely to spend time in prison than a black man in America – the population commonly associated with one of the highest levels of imprisonment in the world" (*The Herald*, January 2005).

CONCLUSION

CHAT is very conscious of the relationship between micro- and macrolevel social processes. Engeström (1999b) proposes a methodology of "radical localism" in which researchers seek to grasp the concrete interconnections between the two and determine how local interventions can have significance on a much wider canvas. The research here reported might be seen to bear some similarities to this idea. It shows how the logic of the partnership intervention in Ferguslie derived concretely from the political logic of the Conservative's neoliberal project in Scotland. It shows, in turn, the acute significance of the microlevel processes in this one community for the development of that wider project, the consequent attempt to manage these processes, and the results that ultimately emerged – again in concrete terms. Of course, it is not possible to say precisely what might have transpired had FLAG's learning process not been closed down in the summer of 1991 and had that process continued and connected to other areas to create a broader collectivity of learning. But what does seem apparent is that had the latter happened, problems would have been posed for the implementation of the partnership agenda in Scotland, which could have affected the subsequent development at the national level – perhaps quite significantly.

What has allowed the research to demonstrate this is its focus on *discourse*. But, more specifically, it has been its focus on *discourse in cultural-historical perspective*. It is at best doubtful that such insights as it has been able to offer would have been generated through the application of the tools of CL-CDA. Indeed, it seems to be the approach to discourse as "produced from within, out of, and as driven by the logic of evolving activity that connects individuals to the world, to other people and to themselves" (Stetsenko and Arievitch, 2004a, p. 486) that allows us to give some effective demonstration of the most central claims of the CL-CDA lineage.

Firstly, it allows us to show that discourse actually can be of great significance in social change. In the case of Ferguslie, but also in the other three *New Life* partnerships, the discourse of "partnership" helped to provide the initial justification for the interventions, allowing these to become established and to develop the kind of momentum that was required for the broader "partnership" agenda across Scotland. Its effectiveness was not that it was ideologically inscrutable – and even less that it was scrutable only through the tools of CL-CDA. Rather it was that the process of "expropriating" was, as Bakhtin might tell us, "complex and difficult" and dependent on concrete experience and active learning. Ultimately this particular process took too long to crystallize. By the time it was doing that, the power and momentum of the FPP was already too great for the resources of FLAG.

Secondly, the cultural-historical approach allows us to show that discourse can indeed be a significant component of a useful method for the study of social change. But this method is based on an approach that seeks not just to situate, or embed, discourse in its "context," but rather to grasp it concretely, in its development and in its internal relations to the movement of a system of activity and consciousness.

References

Bakhtin, M. M. (1981). Discourse in the novel. In *The dialogic imagination: Four essays by M. M. Bakhtin* (pp. 259–422) (Michael Holquist, Ed.; Caryl Emerson and Michael Holquist, Trans.). Austin: University of Texas Press.

Bakhtin, M. M. (1986). The problem of speech genres. In *Speech genres and other late essays* (pp. 60–102). Austin: University of Texas Press.

Cambridge Economic Associates. (2003). *Developing a transition framework for social inclusion partnerships: Interim programme review.* Research from Communities Scotland, Report 19. www.communitiesscotland.gov.uk.

Cambridge Policy Consultants. (1999). *An evaluation of the New Life for Urban Scotland initiative.* Edinburgh: Scottish Executive Central Research Unit.

Collins, C. (1999). *Language, ideology and social consciousness: Developing a sociohistorical approach.* Aldershot: Ashgate.

Collins, C. (2001). From new life to new labour: The mythology of partnership. *Concept, 11* (2), 3–7.

Emsley, D., & Innes, J. (1942). *Housing management and unsatisfactory tenants,* Paisley: Paisley Town Council (cited extensively in *Paisley and Renfrewshire Gazette,* May 16, 1942).

Engeström, Y. (1999a). Communication, discourse and activity. *Communication Review, 3* (1–2), 165–185.

Engeström, Y. (1999b). Activity theory and individual and social transformation. In Y. Engeström et al., *Perspectives on activity theory* (pp. 19–38). Cambridge: Cambridge University Press.

Fairclough, N. (1989). *Language and power.* London: Longman.

Fairclough, N. (1992). *Discourse and social change.* Cambridge: Polity Press.

Fairclough, N. (1995). *Critical discourse analysis.* London: Longman.

Fairclough, N. (2000). *New labour, new language?* London: Routledge.

Fairclough, N. (2001). *Language and power* (2nd ed.). London: Longman.

Fowler, R. (1996). On critical linguistics. In C. R. Caldas Coulthard & M. Coulthard (Eds.), *Texts and practices: Readings in critical discourse analysis* (pp. 3–14). London: Routledge.

Fowler, R., et al. (1979). *Language and control.* London: Routledge and Kegan Paul.

Freire, P. (1972a). *The pedagogy of the oppressed.* Harmondsworth: Penguin.

Freire, P. (1972b). *Cultural action for freedom.* Harmondsworth: Penguin.

Gaster, L., et al. (1995). *Interim evaluation of the Ferguslie Park Partnership.* Edinburgh: Scottish Office Central Research Unit.

Hodge, R., & Kress, G. (1979). *Language as ideology.* London: Routledge and Kegan Paul.

John-Steiner, V., & Souberman, E. (1978). Afterword to Vygotsky (1978, pp 121–133).

Jones, P. E. (2004). Discourse and the materialist conception of history: Critical comments on critical discourse analysis. *Historical Materialism, 12* (1): 97–125.

Kemp, A. (1993). *The hollow drum.* Edinburgh: Mainstream.

Kintrea, K. (1992). Ferguslie Park case study. In A. McGregor et al., *Community participation in areas of urban regeneration: A report to Scottish Homes.* Edinburgh: Scottish Homes (Research Report No. 23).

Kintrea, K. (1996). Whose partnership? Community interests in the regeneration of a Scottish housing scheme. *Housing Studies, 11* (2): 287–306.

Lasswell, H. (1936). *Politics: Who gets what, when, how.* New York: McGraw-Hill.

Leont'ev, A. N. (1978). *Activity, consciousness, and personality.* Englewood Cliffs, NJ: Prentice-Hall.

Leont'ev, A. N. (1981). *Problems of the development of the mind*. Moscow: Progress.

Scott, J. C. (1990). *Domination and the arts of resistance*. New Haven, CT: Yale University Press.

Scottish Executive. (2004a). *The framework for economic development in Scotland*. Edinburgh: Scottish Executive.

Scottish Executive. (2004b). *A smart, successful Scotland: Strategic direction to the enterprise networks and an enterprise strategy for Scotland*. Edinburgh: Scottish Executive.

Scottish Office. (1988). *New life for urban Scotland*. Edinburgh: HMSO.

Scottish Office. (1989). *A pattern for new life: Strategy for the regeneration of Ferguslie Park*. Edinburgh: HMSO.

Scottish Office. (1999). *Social inclusion: Opening the door to a better Scotland*. Edinburgh: Scottish Office.

Stetsenko, A., & Arievitch, I. M. (2004a). The self in cultural-historical activity theory. *Theory and Psychology, 14* (4): 475–503.

Stetsenko, A., & Arievitch, I. M. (2004b). Vygotskian collaborative project of social transformation: History, politics and practice in knowledge construction. *International Journal of Critical Psychology, 72*, 58–80.

Thompson, J. B. (1984). *Studies in the theory of ideology*. Cambridge: Polity Press.

Vološinov, V. N. (1986). *Marxism and the philosophy of language*. Cambridge, MA: Harvard University Press.

Vygotsky, L. S. (1978). *Mind in society: The development of the higher psychological processes*. Cambridge, MA: Harvard University Press.

Vygotsky, L. S. (1987). *Thinking and speech*. In R. W. Rieber & A. S. Carton (Eds.), *The collected works of L. S. Vygotsky: Vol. 1. Problems of general psychology* (pp. 39–285). New York: Plenum.

William Roe Associates (1994). *An evaluation of community involvement in the Ferguslie Park Partnership*. Edinburgh: Scottish Office Central Research Unit.

14

Reason and Dialogue in Education

Rupert Wegerif

A concern with reason has always been at the heart of European educational theory. For the ancient Greeks, reason was considered the defining characteristic of humanity. Both Aristotle and Plato argued that the promotion of reason should be a central aim of education. The movement for universal education that began in eighteenth-century France was at least in part inspired by the belief that education for all would expand the influence of reason in society and therefore fuel social progress. Harvey Siegel (1997) argues that thinking skills programmes are a continuation of this Enlightenment project to promote reason by means of education. Some "postmodernist" thinkers, such as Lyotard and Foucault, have strongly criticised this Enlightenment project. However most postmodern theory applied to education, when examined closely, does not involve a rejection of the ideal of reason so much as a redefinition of reason in terms of local dialogues (e.g., Parker, 1997). The important question is not so much, should education promote reason but, rather, which model of reason should it promote. In this chapter I tentatively put forward the suggestion that the idea of "dialogue across difference" (Burbules, 1993) offers a coherent model of reason that could serve as an ideal within education.

THE DIALOGIC TURN

Recently there has been an increasing number of studies in education and psychology informed by dialogical rather than monological theoretical assumptions. In the area of cognition and learning this "dialogical turn" implies a move away from explanation in terms of underlying cognitive structure and toward descriptions of the dynamic construction of meaning in conversations (e.g., Edwards & Potter, 1992; Wells, 1999). Those who use the term "dialogical" often refer to the Russian writers Bakhtin and Volosinov.

273

Volosinov (1929/1986, pp. 102–103) puts the dialogical position very clearly when he writes that "meaning is like an electric spark that occurs only when two different terminals are hooked together" and further: "In essence meaning belongs to a word in its position between speakers; that is, meaning is realised only in the process of active, responsive, understanding."

The claim being made is that meaning is never simply given but is always created out of the interaction between different voices and different perspectives. This implies the further claim that, when people understand or know something, they do so dynamically in a communicative act and not statically in a structure (Wells, 1999, p. 77).

To understand the significance of the dialogical turn, it is necessary to consider the contrasting monological paradigm that can still probably be said to represent the mainstream in psychology. The monological paradigm in science generally seeks to find the universal laws and structures underlying surface phenomena. The ideal motivating this endeavour is to produce a single logically coherent model of everything independent of perspective. The monological paradigm is often accused of overlooking the fact that knowledge is never independent of social, historical, and biological contexts that give it meaning. One aspect of the contextual background required to interpret knowledge claims is their position within conversations, including what could be described as the long-term conversations of a culture. The dialogical claim from Bakhtin and Volosinov is that any utterance needs to be seen as a link in a chain of communication (Bakhtin, 1986, p. 69). Dialogicality means not merely that participants in interactions respond to what other participants do, but that they respond in a way that takes into account how they think other people are going to respond to them. Rommetveit (1992), quoting Barwise and Perry, calls this circularity "atunement to the atunement of the other" and points out, firstly, that it influences most human behaviour and, secondly, that it is impossible to understand the effects of this circularity using monological representations. Monological models assume closed systems with regular, and therefore discoverable, relationships between inputs and outputs. If human behaviour has to be understood in much the same way as we interpret meaning in a continuing dialogue, then, as Rommetveit claims, monological models are inappropriate.

In the monological paradigm, it is normal to see models as a way of getting a handle on reality, which we can use to inform interventions that change things. For those who adopt the assumptions of the dialogical paradigm, on the other hand, the role of models is not so straightforward. Often the emphasis is more on the critique of monological models than on their replacement with useful dialogical alternatives. In what follows I will take "reason" as a paradigmatic case to argue that dialogical models of cognition are possible and can be applied as a useful tool for changing reality.

THE CONCEPT OF A DIALOGICAL MODEL OF REASON

Intersubjective Orientations

Models of reason in psychology that refer to logical structures in the mind reflect a strong tradition in the philosophy of rationality (or reason) originating with Plato that links human reason to formal logic and mathematics. The social philosopher Jürgen Habermas challenges this monological tradition in accounts of reason and proposes an alternative dialogical account of reason that he calls "communicative rationality." I do not intend to outline his argument here but merely to draw from it features that I claim can be used to characterise dialogical models of cognition in general. Habermas (1991, p. 286) begins his account of communicative rationality by drawing a distinction between "a success-oriented attitude" and "an attitude oriented to reaching understanding." Although he does not dismiss the strategic or profit-maximising rationality that issues from a success-oriented attitude, he argues that this kind of rationality is a parasitic derivative of the more fundamental communicative rationality issuing from an attitude oriented to reaching understanding. Use of the word "attitude" carries with it the danger of being interpreted as referring only to individual states, whereas Habermas makes it clear that he is referring to ways in which participants in a dialogue can orient themselves to each other. He refers to this as the "structural properties" of intersubjectivity. To emphasise this, I use the term "intersubjective orientation" in place of attitude.

Habermas's claim about the centrality of intersubjective orientations connects his later work to the very different tradition of Jewish writer and theologian, Martin Buber. In his seminal work, *I and Thou* (1923/1958), Buber draws a distinction between the "I-thou" type of relationship, characterised by mutual responsiveness, and "I-it" relationships, in which an active subject confronts and dominates a passive object.

A similar distinction is found later in the work of Bakhtin (1981, p. 343), who contrasts the "authoritative" voice to the "persuasive" voice. The authoritative voice "demands that we acknowledge it, that we make it our own; it binds us quite independent of any power it might have to persuade us internally." This is the voice of literal meanings with "no play with its borders, no gradual and flexible transitions, no spontaneously creative stylising variants on it." Bakhtin contrasts this to what he calls "the internally persuasive word" that "is half-ours and half-someone else's. Its creativity and productiveness consist precisely in the fact that such a word awakens new and independent words, that it organises masses of our words from within, and does not remain in an isolated and static condition" (ibid.).

Buber's distinction between "I-thou" and "I-it" modes was explicitly taken up and developed by Immanuel Lévinas (1989, pp. 59–74). Lévinas (1990, p. 223) claims that the "encounter with the face of the other" is an opening of meaning that underlies the possibility of reason, or what he called, "la pensée raisonable." Levinas's thought had a considerable influence on Jacques Derrida, who was his student at the Sorbonne, and so he could perhaps be considered one of the sources of contemporary poststructuralist theory. Monological reason, or what he called "the Western tradition of reason," is, Levinas claims, a retreat into what he called a position of "self-sovereignty" in which the other is kept at a distance precisely by "representations" of it. Real reason or "wisdom" begins, he claimed, with a response to "the call of the other." This projects the self into relationships of "responsibility." Again, as with Habermas, Buber, and Bakhtin, reason is seen as rooted in fundamental intersubjective orientation between people in a dialogue.

Evidence confirming the significance of intersubjective orientations for the development of thinking has recently been offered by Peter Hobson (2002). A developmental psychopathologist, Hobson studied the difference between the development of thinking in autistic children and in normal children. He demonstrated, using experiments as well as case studies, that the normal development of thinking crucially depends on the quality of the relationships formed in the first eighteen months of life. He describes relationships in which different perspectives are brought together as motivating initial symbol use and opening up "a mental space" between the participants, which then becomes internalised in individual consciousness. Autism is the result, he claims, of a failure, for whatever cause, to form such relationships. It is interesting that while autistic children can sometimes do the kind of fast and accurate calculations that computers can also do, they lack a capacity for creative thought. Hobson's focus is the development of reason, in the ancient Greek sense, as that faculty that distinguishes normal human thinking. His work supports, at an ontogenetic level of analysis, Habermas's more phylogenetic claim that reason emerges out of an orientation towards mutual understanding.

These varied sources suggest the significance of an account of "intersubjective orientation" to any dialogical model of cognition.

Interaction Rules

Buber's "I-thou" relationship might be a precondition for the emergence of reason, as Hobson claims, but it is not, in itself, reasoning. For Habermas, the possibility of rationality is always implicit in successful communication. One of his claims is that when the consensus assumed by communicative action is broken, then the options are coercion of one side by the other (strategic action) or a move into explicit reasoning about different viewpoints. Over time, reason presumably emerges as the least costly option (it is worth noting that this may be a slow historical process of which we are only at the beginning!). In Habermas's account of communicative rationality, a second level of description of reason is often referred to as the social rules governing what he calls an "ideal speech situation." He never actually gives details of what these rules are. At one point, however, he quotes approvingly an account by Alexy of the procedural rules that might be used to structure a speech situation in which unforced agreement could be achieved. These are rules such as, Every participant has an equal right to participate and to question claims (Habermas, 1990, p. 92). Habermas's insight here is that we need shared social rules to open up a space for thinking between the Scylla of coercion and the Charybdis of unreflective consensus.

Computer simulations of complex adaptive systems provide an interesting metaphor for thinking about the significance to cognition of following rules. Whereas computer models of cognition based on the information-processing metaphor embody monological assumptions, computer simulations of complex adaptive systems are based on a computer implementation of the complex feedback loops used by Rommetveit to characterise dialogicality. Casti (1997) argues that such simulations represent a new scientific method distinct from methods of experiment and linear mathematical modelling that were developed in the study of closed and relatively noncomplex systems. A complex adaptive system is any system in which several agents reciprocally adapt to each other (Holland, 1992). Once agents reciprocally adapt to each other, the circular feedback loops involved produce a level of complexity that makes reduction to a monological model impossible.

One solution adopted to studying complex adaptive systems is to simulate them with programmes in which multiple agents are each given a set of rules of behaviour, and possibly also rules on how to adapt those rules, and then set loose to interact. Such studies have found that the interaction of many agents, each following simple rules, can result in the "emergence" of new self-organising systems that can not be predicted or explained by the rules that the agents are following. One striking example is the simulation of flocking behaviour, which was achieved by giving virtual birds three simple rules to guide their flight: keep a minimum distance from neighbours, fly at about the same speed as neighbours, and always fly towards the perceived centre of the mass of birds. Understanding flocking had been seen as a hard problem until this simulation clarified how it might work (Waldrop, 1992, pp. 241–243). An illustration of "emergence" in complex adaptive systems closer to dialogues is provided by Robert Axelrod's (1997) various demonstrations of the emergence of apparently cooperative behaviour and even values such as "loyalty" in simulations of social interaction. Some have applied the theory of complex adaptive systems to the tricky question of the emergence of consciousness and cognition (e.g., Edmonds, 1997; Juarrero, 1999).

Although dialogues are undoubtedly complex adaptive systems (Holland, 1992), I am not suggesting that they can be modelled perfectly by a computer simulation. This would be just another variety of the computer metaphor of mind. Meanings in dialogues are very different from defined series of computer bits. But, nonetheless, as a metaphor for dialogues, simulations of complex adaptive systems can teach us something – namely, that complex and unpredictable behaviour can be modelled by using multiple agents following simple rules of interaction. This kind of model is not a monological model. There can be no "identity" or equals sign in such a model, and so it cannot predict or explain in the same way or with the same accuracy as a monological model. However, the success of various computer simulations in providing insights into how reality works shows that this kind of dialogical model can be useful and certainly deserves to be part of the eclectic tool box of methods called "scientific" because they reliably help add to the sum of shared knowledge and capability.

Exploratory Talk as a Dialogical Model

Another chapter in this volume, by Sylvia Rojas-Drummond et al., makes use of the concept of "exploratory talk." The concept of exploratory talk, as used by Mercer (1995), emerged in the context of a characterisation of three "types of talk" found empirically in collaborative learning in classrooms. The three "types of talk" described by Mercer can also, as a later article made clear (Wegerif & Mercer, 1997a), be seen as reflecting orientations of the kind that Habermas referred to as "structural properties of intersubjectivity":

- Cumulative talk, reflecting an orientation towards a group identity with sharing and a desire to understand each other but without any critical challenges

- Disputational talk, reflecting an orientation towards individualised identity so that argument is seen as a competition that each seeks to win
- Exploratory talk, which is oriented beyond group or individual identity towards the process of shared inquiry so it allows critical challenges and explicit reasoning within a cooperative framework

Of these three intersubjective orientations, the one found most educationally desirable by teachers was obviously exploratory talk. This combines features of cumulative talk, being a kind of cooperation, with features of disputational talk, because it includes challenges and competition. However, the competition in exploratory talk is between ideas, not between people. A key indicator of an exploratory orientation is that participants are able to change their minds in response to good arguments. In the light of the previous discussion of intersubjective orientations, it seems that an exploratory orientation is a development from a communicative orientation in which social ground rules support shared inquiry within a relationship of trust and cooperation.

To turn this idea of exploratory talk into a useful model that could be applied in a classroom, the research team needed to specify it more closely in terms of social ground rules. Lists of social ground rules for exploratory talk are given in the chapter in this volume by Rojas Drummond et al. I will not repeat them here, save that any list must include such rules as responding to challenges with reasons and asking others for their views.

Encouraging children to take an exploratory orientation and to use these ground rules meant working with teachers to "teach" these ground rules and to turn the classroom into a social and physical environment that supported and rewarded their use. The ground rules displayed on the wall were important for this, as were the seating arrangements and the frequent reminders from the teacher that the way groups talked together was as important and valued as the answers that they came to. Equally important was the way that the teacher talked with the class. Using our talk lessons led the talk of the teachers to change almost as much as the talk of the children.

The chapter by Rojas-Drummond et al. confirms the earlier findings reported by Mercer, Wegerif, and Dawes (1999) and by Wegerif, Mercer, and Dawes (1999) that teaching primary age children to use exploratory talk leads to an improvement in their individual test scores on standard tests of nonverbal reasoning. These findings support the claim that children learn to reason better as individuals through personally appropriating strategies used first in dialogue with others. This finding fits well with Vygotsky's (1991, p. 36) claim that, as he put it, "all that is internal in the higher mental functions was at one time external," meaning that the ability to perform cognitive tasks when acting alone stems from a prior socialisation process when the same or similar tasks are performed with the help of others. More qualitative analyses of the talk of children solving reasoning test problems also support the claim that the exploratory orientation and the ground rules of exploratory talk worked as a dialogical model of reason (Wegerif & Mercer, 2000).

EXPANDING THE MODEL OF REASON

While the concept of exploratory talk represents one dialogical model of reason, it is not the only possible one. The emphasis on explicit reasoning in its definition appears to exclude much that might also be called reason. To consider how to produce an understanding of dialogical reason that goes beyond a reduction in the process of explicit verbal reasoning, I use the analysis of an example of thinking in the talk of seven- and eight-year-old children engaged in a "philosophy for children" session.

The children are thinking together with a teacher about issues raised by a picture book that they all have in front of them. The book is *Where the Wild Things Are* by Maurice Sendak (1963). When we join them, they have just read aloud about how the bedroom of the story's hero turns into a forest and the bedroom walls "become the whole world." The teacher, Mark Prentice, then encourages them to think about imagination and the meaning of the word "world." Presented here is a slightly edited version of the talk that follows:

HELEN: [You can just start] staring at things and make it into your picture.

HELEN: It can be about twenty things in one place.

TEACHER: Say that again Helen because it's interesting.

HELEN: There's about twenty things in one place.

TEACHER: That you can just look at and stare?

HELEN: Yeh, there are also lines on the curtains they could turn into loads of green leaves.

EMMA: Yeh or bamboo stalks.

TEACHER: So you can stare at something and get a different picture?

EMMA: Yeh, you could change it into a leopard or something.

TEACHER: Have you ever done that? Stared at something and looked at all the shapes that are inside it?

ALEX: Yeh, you could turn that into a big bone or something.

TEACHER: This radiator here – so we have power to change things don't we. How do we do that?

EMMA: I was in my room the other day and I closed my eyes nearly shut and my rocking horse I thought it was this kind of a pot – a shaking pot.

[...]

TEACHER: Can you create your own world?

SEVERAL: Yes.

TEACHER: How can you create your own world?

SEVERAL: Imagining, dreaming.

TEACHER: That's interesting so you can create your own world by imagining – did Helen create a world when she started to talk about the curtains up there?

HELEN: There's about a thousand worlds all in one person's head, all in one place.

[...]

TEACHER: What do you think – Alex?

ALEX: Well one time I invented my own country which I called Alexland 'cos I became my bedroom a whole country and I pretend all my toys are alive.

TEACHER: So you created a world.

ALEX: Yes.

TEACHER: Now is that a real world?

ALEX: Well sometimes I feel like it's really real but then when I've found something like a catalogue, which I pretend you couldn't get catalogues and stuff like that, then the world just disappears.

TEACHER: So it disappears when you look at something else.

ALEX: Yeh when I look at something – when I go downstairs it just disappears, because my bedroom's the best place – because my toys are up there.

The teacher's role is very interesting here. He is not giving them ideas but facilitating the group thinking by repeating key points and asking prompting questions.

Here, there are few challenges or explicit reasons. Instead, the children seem to build on each other's comments with similar memories and ideas. Helen's idea that things can seem to be different as if "there were about twenty things in one place" is picked up by Emma and Alex, who share examples of this. This is what has been called cumulative talk because there is a sharing of experience and ideas without challenges or critical grounding. But it is nonetheless apparent that some serious thinking is going on. This leads up to the realisation, articulated by Alex, that there can be two different worlds, his own world and the adult world, and that objects from the adult world, found in his world, can make his world dissolve. Someone could say that this is not reasoning but just a description of his experience. However, reasoning is implicit in the description. This way of describing experience is a way of seeking to understand it, and these descriptions reveal the world in a new way. This is perhaps what Wittgenstein (1967) calls a "perspicuous representation." He describes his experience but with insight into its general structure.

This description of how his world can dissolve in the face of anomalous objects is given in response to a prompt by the teacher that could be taken as a challenge. "Is it really real?" But Alex does not reply to this with any explicit reasoning of the kind, "yes, it is because" or "no, it isn't because" – he replies with a description that is a kind of anecdote: "Well sometimes I feel like it's really real but then when I've found something like a catalogue, which I pretend you couldn't get catalogues and stuff like that, then the world just disappears." We could say that Alex offers a reason why Alexland is not really real. However, the whole utterance here is much more than just a piece of explicit reasoning, it is also a sharing of his experience in a way that invites us inside that experience.

For me, Alex's understanding that one world can be dissolved by the presence of an artefact from another world is a powerful piece of thinking. However, I understand this through the similar ideas that it evokes for me but probably not for Alex. I am thinking of the role of catalysts in chemistry, which turn one kind of thing almost instantly into a very different kind of thing. I am also led to the idea of a paradigm shift in the development of science that has been described by Thomas Kuhn as a radical shift to a different worldview sometimes sparked by anomalies thrown up by the original paradigm.

My response to what Alex says takes me beyond what is given, not through explicit reasoning but through a kind of resonance in which the structure of his narrative account connects for me with similar structures in events that I have read about or experienced. It is precisely through this kind of resonance that the children seem to be building on each others ideas. One child sees a forest of green leaves emerging from the shapes in the curtain; another sees the radiator on the wall as the spinal bone of an animal; a third sees her rocking chair as a "shaking pot." And so they share and build the idea of different worlds and the factors that influence how these different worlds form and dissolve. Alex's very clear statement of a powerful idea does not come on its own but is a product of this dialogue. It is probably as new for him as for the others in the group.

Creative play with words and ideas assumes an orientation of mutual trust and support, a sense in which each participant knows that what he or she says will be accepted. In the exploratory talk around reasoning tests, the children frequently rejected suggestions, saying something like: "No, I don't agree because of x, y, z." In the preceding example, it would be unlikely that anyone would reply to Alex's claim that you can see the radiator as a big bone by saying "No, I don't agree because . . . " Instead the participants try to make the best sense they can of a different perspective, and this effort seems to open up a space of reflection in which ideas can resonate together.

REFLECTION

According to Bakhtin, understanding another's speech involves producing one's own answering-words, and these words are inevitably shaped by different histories and backgrounds. Any understanding across the difference between people in a dialogue is necessarily a creative act. However, conversations can be more or less creative. Normally language is used to do things in the world without much reflection. If someone says "pass the salt," they do not expect a reflection on the meaning of "pass" or "salt." In this kind of interaction, consensus is assumed, and the creative space between people is small. This space can be opened up by turning language back upon itself in the form of questions. Any open question asking "What?" or "Why?" involves a shift from a cumulative attitude of acceptance to a more exploratory attitude. Reflection means not assuming that we know the answer or that we know what things are, but stepping back from certainty to allow things to present themselves in new ways.

While reflection is not the same thing as creativity, it seems that the reflective use of language can open up a space between people allowing creativity to occur. However, the kind of intersubjectivity that results, the attitude of shared exploration, is not dependent in itself on particular forms of language. Language can be used to promote and maintain relationships, but ultimately relationships are not reducible to language. An exploratory silence is different from a disputational silence or a cumulative silence.

In my view, the talk in the transcript extract illustrates an episode of dialogical reason. This dialogical reason is not reducible to reasoning. Dialogical reason is the broader concept of all talk that helps people reach shared understandings. The exact ground rules that define the best kind of talk or knowledge construction depend on the task and the social context. If the task is solving reasoning tests, then explicit reasoning is, understandably, likely to be appropriate. If the task were understanding a different culture, as in ethnography, then the ground rules should probably emphasise listening and open reflection more than the critical assessment of reasons. Although there are many different types and instances of dialogical reason, all can be characterised as forms of dialogue across difference. The difference may be small, as in the difference between two possible solutions to a reasoning test question, or large, as in the difference between two culturally based worldviews. However, it is this interanimation of different perspectives that produces a creative space of reflection.

CONCLUSION

Thinking about reason from a dialogical perspective shifts the focus of attention away from abstract cognitive structures and towards the ways that people respond to each other in dialogues. Some research described by others (see, e.g., Rojas-Drummond, Chapter 16 in this volume) applied what I would claim is a dialogical model of cognition consisting of an intersubjective orientation called "exploratory" and a set of ground rules specifically designed to support collaboration in the classroom. This model has proved an effective support for teachers. Its implementation resulted in a significant improvement in the quality of collaborative learning and reasoning. However, while exploratory talk is a dialogical model of a kind of reason, the focus on explicit reasoning makes it a limited model. It is clearly a useful pedagogical device or "scaffolding," but it should not be taken to limit the possibilities of reason. Through the analysis of a transcript of young children thinking together with a teacher, I have argued that dialogical reason is characterised by the creation of a space of reflection between participants in which resonance between ideas and images can occur. To put this idea more simply: creativity is a more essential characteristic of human reason than explicit reasoning.

The understanding of dialogical reason that I am arguing for is very broad. It includes all thinking in which reflection and creativity are opened up by the interanimation of different perspectives. The example of "exploratory talk" shows that dialogical models of reason can be a useful tool in education. In principle, it should be possible to produce different pedagogical models of this kind for different contexts and different tasks.

The Enlightenment project of applying reason to every area of social life has achieved great things, but many argue that it has become hijacked by too narrow a conception of reason. If we replace monological models of reason with a model of reason as "dialogue across difference," could we then restore this original Enlightenment project? Could we move from a situation where we are using dialogues in classrooms as a tool to help children learn prespecified nuggets of knowledge towards a situation where induction into dialogue is itself the main aim of education?

References

Axelrod, R. (1997). *The complexity of cooperation: Agent-based models of competition and collaboration.* Princeton, NJ: Princeton University Press.

Bakhtin, M. (1981). *The dialogic imagination.* Austin: University of Texas Press.

Bakhtin, M. (1986). *Speech genres and other late essays.* Austin: University of Texas.

Buber, M. (1923/1958). *I and thou* (2nd ed.) (R. Gregory Smith, Trans.). Edinburgh: T. & T. Clark.

Burbules, N. (1993). *Dialogue in teaching.* New York: Teachers College Press.

Casti, J. (1997). *Would be worlds.* New York: Wiley.

Edmonds, B. (1997). Modelling socially intelligent agents. Paper presented at the AAAI fall symposium on Socially Intelligent Agents, Cambridge, MA, November.

Edwards, D., & Potter, J. (1992). *Discursive psychology.* London: Sage.

Habermas, J. (1990). *Moral consciousness and communicative action.* Cambridge: Polity Press.

Habermas, J. (1991). *The theory of communicative action* (Vol. 1). Cambridge: Polity Press.

Hobson, P. (2002). *The cradle of thought: Exploring the origins of thinking.* London: Macmillan.

Holland, J. (1992). Complex adaptive systems. *Daedalus, 121* (Winter), 17–30.

Juarrero, A. (1999). *Dynamics in action.* Cambridge, MA: MIT Press.

Lévinas, E. (1989). Martin Buber and the theory of knowledge. In S. Hand (Ed.), *The Lévinas Reader* (pp. 59–74). Oxford: Blackwell.

Lévinas, E. (1990). *Totalité et infini: Essai sur l'extériorité.* Paris: Le Livre de Poche.

Mercer, N. (1995). *The guided construction of knowledge: Talk amongst teachers and learners.* Clevedon: Multilingual Matters.

Mercer, N., Wegerif, R., & Dawes, L. (1999). Children's talk and the development of reasoning in the classroom. *British Educational Research Journal, 25* (1), 95–111.

Parker, S. (1997). *Reflective teaching in the postmodern world: A manifesto for education in postmodernity.* Buckingham: Open University Press.

Rommetveit, R. (1992). Outlines of a dialogically based social-cognitive approach to human cognition and communication. In A. Wold (Ed.), *The dialogical alternative: Towards a theory of language and mind* (pp. 19–45). Oslo: Scandanavian Press.

Sendak, M. (1963). *Where the wild things are.* Harmondsworth: Puffin Books.

Siegel, H. (1997). *Rationality redeemed? Further dialogues on an educational ideal.* New York: Routledge.

Volosinov, V. N. (1929/1986). *Marxism and the philosophy of language.* Cambridge, MA: Harvard University Press.

Vygotsky, L. (1991). The genesis of higher mental functions. In P. Light, S. Sheldon, & B. Woodhead (Eds.), *Learning to think* (pp. 34–63). London: Routledge.

Waldrop, M. (1992). *Complexity: The emerging science at the edge of order and chaos.* London: Penguin.

Wegerif, R., & Mercer, N. (1997). A dialogical framework for researching peer talk. In R. Wegerif & P. Scrimshaw (Eds.), *Computers and talk in the primary classroom* (pp. 49–65). Clevedon: Multilingual Matters.

Wegerif, R., & Mercer, N. (2000). Language for Thinking. In H. Cowie, D. van Aalsvoort, & N. Mercer (Eds.), *New perspectives in collaborative learning.* Oxford: Elsevier.

Wegerif, R., Mercer, N., & Dawes, L. (1999). From social interaction to individual reasoning: An empirical investigation of a possible socio-cultural model of cognitive development. *Learning and Instruction, 9* (5), 493–516.

Wells, G. (1999). *Dialogic inquiry: Toward a sociocultural practice and theory of education.* Cambridge: Cambridge University Press.

Wittgenstein, L. (1967). *Philosophical investigations.* Oxford: Blackwell.

SECTION THREE

DYNAMICS OF ACTIVITY AND THE VARIATIONS OF LEARNING

Introduction to Section Three

Learning in Social Settings: Challenges for Sociocultural and Activity Theory

Ed Elbers

Section III presents six studies performed in a variety of learning contexts. De Groot Kim, van Oers, and Japiassu discuss diverse forms of children's play and their significance for development. Hedegaard, Rahm and her colleagues, and Rojas-Drummond and her colleagues deal with children's learning in formal contexts. The authors of the six chapters in this section differ in their approach to learning, in the scale of their presentation, the methods adopted, and the way they relate to sociocultural theory and activity theory. Despite their differences, however, the authors appear to share a commitment to further developing sociocultural and activity theory – in two respects. Firstly, they express a need to understand how children contribute to their own development. Children learn by participating in cultural activities; that means that children contribute to these activities and consequently to the creation of the conditions of their learning. A view on learning and instruction that considers adult-child relationships merely as a site for the transmission of culture seems to have been abandoned by the authors a long time ago. Learning, in contrast, is a constructive activity, in which children create something new. The challenge is to make this creative process visible. The second issue relates to the first one: if children contribute to the creation of the conditions of their learning, how does this influence their identity and their relationships with others? Because sociocultural theory has traditionally privileged relationships between children and more experienced members of the culture, the question arises: How should relationships between children and adults be conceptualised, if they encompass more than a tutor-tutee relationship within a zone of proximal development? The authors of the chapters in this section present interesting thoughts and observations on these two themes.

Chapter 15, by Mariane Hedegaard, combines the presentation of a model of learning with observations in the classroom. Hitherto, Hedegaard argues, theories of learning have mostly emphasised the mental side of learning. Learning, however, is not just about a change of mind, but also encompasses practices and products of practical, even manual activity. Her model makes visible how shared activities of participants in the classroom lead to both mental and material products. She borrows her examples from a teaching experiment in a school, using a "double move approach" to teaching that is using exploratory and constructive activities of children as a central element in the curriculum. Children are encouraged to construct models, drawings, and plays as tools for representing and elaborating their conceptual knowledge. The products, and the discussions in the classroom leading up to the products, are important conditions for learning as well as motivating factors. The productive side of teaching and learning makes visible that knowledge is not independent from contexts. Concepts become meaningful only in their connection to practices and institutions – hence, Hedegaard's interest in the differences between learning contexts. Both the family and the school present a multitude of learning opportunities, but when the distance between home and school becomes too vast, the differences can work out disadvantageously. The school has as an important task to provide bridges between home and school, and it can do so by recognising each child's competencies and home experience as an input into the joint activities in the classroom.

In Chapter 16, Sylvia Rojas-Drummond, Laura Gómez, and Maricela Vélez present results of a programme used in Mexican primary schools for teaching reasoning skills and exploratory talk. The programme, Thinking Together, originally introduced by Dawes, Mercer, and Wegerif (2000), was adapted for use in Mexican schools. By teaching the ground rules of exploratory talk and by practicing these with materials such as games, texts, software, and activity cards, the teachers created a zone of proximal development for the students. The children then practiced the reasoning skills during their work in small groups. Interestingly, the authors show that the intervention program improved not only children's collaborative reasoning but also individual problem-solving skills. By emphasising the importance of language as a tool for both reasoning and communication, these authors relate themselves firmly to sociocultural psychology. However, by placing particular value on the way children learn from each other, they go beyond the idea of a zone of proximal development as created on behalf of the child by an adult. Talk during collaborative work makes children's reasoning visible; by criticising and commenting on each other, children influence their peers. Rojas et al. borrow the concept of an "intermental development zone" from Mercer (2000), extending the concept of zone of proximal development to peer interactions and to the mutual support children give each other through effective communication.

Chapter 17 by Jrène Rahm, Wendy Naughton, and John C. Moore reports on a student-scientist partnership program involving seventeen- to eighteen-year-old students from underrepresented groups. The authors are particularly interested in students' interpretations of these partnerships. Some of the projects were teacher-led, with students participating in existing research, for instance, on ecology or the effects of drug use. These projects were well defined and left little space for students to contribute their own ideas. Other projects led to partnerships dealing with scientific questions that were new for both the student and the teacher. Here, the students could play a more active role. The students, working on the empirical and conceptual contents of the projects, also acquired an insight into the perseverance that science demands. The students learned multiple lessons at the same time, not only enlarging their conceptual and technical knowledge but also gaining an understanding of the social aspects of scientific work. The authors observed how motivated students were and how much they profited from the learning opportunities offered, especially as the project was not organised as a typical course but envisaged forms of guidance that would help students to gain confidence in their talents. The authors advocate a dynamic view on guidance. They argue that guidance is best understood as a form of collaboration in which not only the expertise of the student and mentor are important but also the participants' perception of their roles and contribution in the project.

Sonja de Groot Kim, in Chapter 18, presents parts of an observational study, carried out over an extended period, of two- and three-year-old children in preschool classrooms. Her position as observer, yet an outsider, allowed her to appreciate the importance of nonverbal activities and meanings that contributed to the creation of a gendered culture, in which boys had more and easier access to outdoor activities and to the teachers' attention than girls. The boys' nonverbal behaviour (rough and tumble play and playful aggressive behaviour) led, without anybody's intention, to certain benefits. These activities did not have a specific purpose until the teacher began to interpret them in certain ways. Because of the overt behaviour of the boys, the teacher allowed them out into the playground sooner than girls or permitted them rather than the girls to play with certain play devices. Over time, this resulted in a tacit rule that the boys could go out first for playing or outdoor activities, whereas girls were expected to wait. This rule benefitted the boys, and it was a disadvantage for girls, who could play less than the boys. With her chapter, de Groot Kim contributes to a recognition of the role of nonverbal communication and activity in the creation of cultural expectancies and children's understanding of themselves. Her contribution sheds more light on nonverbal factors in the creation of joint understanding – factors that are sometimes undervalued in sociocultural theory.

Bert van Oers's contribution (Chapter 19) deals with the question of how children in their play participate in the construction of new meanings. Referring to the Dutch historian Huizinga (1938), he considers play an essential contribution to human cultural development and innovation. The idea of innovation has always been fundamental to Vygotsky's theory of play, but van Oers proposes concepts that go beyond Vygotsky's (1978, chap. 7) famous text on play. In order to better understand how the construction of new meanings is carried out by children in their play, van Oers conceptualises play as a process involving three planes. The first plane consists of the common perspective that children have created and which, once they have agreed on it, is taken for granted. The second plane is formed by the stream of actions and talk that creates the pretend play from moment to moment, and which deals with the division of roles and the sequence of events in the play. Vygotsky has described this plane as encompassing the introduction of new qualities into play, which he called "predicates." As van Oers argues, however, the process does not end here. The new qualities are materialised in the form of signs. That is the third plane. Whereas the new qualities are restricted to the actual play situation, the signs that children produce to express them go beyond the play situation and can be used in a variety of future situations. The signs, van Oers writes, are "inscripted" on the situation. By making inscriptions, children create symbolic tools that transcend the particular play context. Van Oers shows how the particularities and fantasies of children give rise to new cultural tools; though at first developed to coordinate play, these tools also can be applied to other situations. These new meanings may even come into conflict with existing significations and interpretations of the culture and, in this way, contribute to cultural innovation. By proposing the concept of inscripting, van Oers connects children's play, on the one hand, with children's future development and, on the other, with the wider development of the culture. His chapter brings together understandings of Vygotsky and Huizinga.

In Chapter 20, Ricardo Japiassu also deals with the construction of novel meanings in children's play. Borrowing from activity theory, he conceptualises play as the organising activity of children's behaviour, which leads to psychological neoformations in the form of new representational tools and activities. Whereas van Oers connects play to the future culture, Japiassu places the origins of pretend play in the historical development of material production. The use of tools and the social relations demanded by the production process were too complicated for children. Pretend play then has the function of preparing children for social life. Play allows children to preexercise cultural skills and roles that they need as future competent members of the society. Children vary and experiment with the meaning of objects and social roles, at first by imitation, but gradually they go beyond the superficial meaning of objects and situations by imposing new meanings on them. The process culminates in the phase of fantasy play and creative imagination. This sequence amounts to what Japiassu calls a process of decontextualisation, involving an increasing ability to impose new perspectives on the world. Using this perspective, Japiassu extends Vygotsky's theory of play by proposing an ontogenetic sequence of phases of play and compares this sequence with other research on pretend play.

By reflecting on a variety of learning situations, the authors contribute to the two themes mentioned earlier: the contribution of children to their development and the nature of social relationships and identities. The chapters by Hedegaard and van Oers appear to be relevant, particularly, to the first theme: Hedegaard, with her "double move in teaching," connects children's exploratory activity with the curriculum of the school. Van Oers, introducing his idea of "inscriptions," conceptualises play as a process that allows children to create meanings that transcend the circumstances of the play situation. The other authors, in various ways, explore the second theme: Rojas-Drummond and colleagues with their notion of an "intermental development zone" between peers, Japiassu with his elaboration of the educational significance of play, de Groot Kim with her emphasis on the importance of nonverbal activities during play in the preschool, and Rahm and colleagues with their notion of learning partnerships and a multiplicity of learning experiences.

References

Dawes, L., Mercer, N., & Wegerif, R. (2000). *Thinking together: A programme of activities for developing thinking skills at KS2*. Birmingham: Questions Publishing.

Huizinga, J. (1938). *Homo ludens*. Groningen: Tjeenk Willink.

Mercer, N. (2000). *Words and minds: How we use language to think together*. London: Routledge.

Vygotsky, L. S. (1978). *Mind in society: The development of higher psychological processes*. Cambridge, MA: Harvard University Press.

15

Children's Learning through Participation in Institutional Practice

A Model from the Perspective of Cultural-Historical Psychology

Mariane Hedegaard

A child learns through participation with others in institutionalised activities. Learning takes place through the tasks and expectations that the child meets in these activities. But the child also contributes to the creation, change, and development of the activities and thereby to his own surroundings and learning conditions. The child is not only adapting to tasks and demands. Each person, whether a schoolchild, a teacher, or a parent, contributes to the activities in which he or she takes part and thereby, as a collective, creates the conditions for each other's activity.

In traditional classroom teaching, learning is seen as an individualised activity promoted by the teacher's lectures and formulation of questions and the students' answers and work with exercise material. Classmates are seen as interfering with the single child's learning process. In the more modern teaching types, where children can work together, teaching is still expected to relate to and measure each student's competence, and thereby learning is still conceptualised as a change in the child (Hedegaard, 2006). In these approaches, the product of the children's activity is not seen as important; what is conceptualised is the process of learning as change in the children's minds. This conceptualisation, by itself, gives a too-narrow perspective on learning activity, as I argue in this chapter.

Alternative approaches to teaching include those based on activity theory: Davydov's approach (1982, 1990) of "developmental teaching," Lompscher's approach (1984, 1999) of "ascending from the abstract to the concrete," and my own approach (Hedegaard, 2002) of "the double move in teaching." Here, the content of the subject matter, the students' collaborative research activity by using models, and the product of student activity are considered significant. But there has not been a theory of learning that differs from the "change of mind" conceptualisation of learning in school that can integrate the collective practice and object-related aspect of teaching in these approaches into a general theory of learning. To address this problem, I discuss a theory of learning that is appropriate for these teaching approaches.

The objective of learning within activity theory, though, is not conceptualised as transcending the change of personal competencies to include the student's products of the learning activity. This has been contrasted to the objective of work activity, where the products are seen as central in maintaining a shared social practice. The product has to be understood in relation to the collective in which the activity takes place. Both aspects of learning activity, its relation to the community and the production of material, have to be conceptualised as central for learning, although these aspects have qualities in learning that are different from those in work activity. These aspects have to be integrated in the social settings that are created in schools and other institutions that promote learning activity.

I formulate a model of learning activity here that relates schoolchildren's learning to practice in school, where learning is seen as being connected to the children's and the teacher's classroom community and where the products of the learning activity are considered as important.

The model of learning activity departs from Vygotsky's concepts of the instrumental and mental act, which I use as "a germ-cell model for human learning."[1] When this "germ cell" is combined with Vygotsky's different conceptions of development, it becomes possible to transcend the idea of learning as a transformation of "the mind." The germ cell of the instrumental and mental act will be elaborated to encompass different forms of learning as situated and local practices in different institutions. To do this, I draw upon and extend Sylvia Scribner's (1985) interpretation of Vygotsky's formulation of the different historical levels of human learning and development.

Inspired by Vygotsky, Scribner identifies four levels of learning activity and development: the phylogenetic–species-specific level; the societal-historical level; the institutional-ontogenetic level; and the psychological-functional level. These four levels can be seen as conditions for each other in a hierarchical-interactive connection, where each level becomes the context for the analyses on the subsequent level with its specific content.

The first level contains the epistemological considerations of what characterises humans at the phylogenetical level – namely, that humans produce tools and appropriate procedures for tool use through learning. At the societal level, the analyses focus on the genesis of tool production and its connected procedures as they relate to the evolution of the different institutions in a

---

[1] A germ cell is the initial relation from which the logic of the concepts of a subject area develops (Davydov, 1982, 1990).

society. At the ontogenetic level, the focus is on the development of children's appropriation of competence with tools through their participation over time within societal practice in different institutions. The level of personality in Scribner's interpretation focusses on the psychological function. I prefer to interpret this level as an individual's development within institutional traditions, which can be followed through a person's concrete appropriation of specific practice traditions, both situated and local, and which can be analysed as related to the person's change in his or her social situation.

THE PHYLOGENETIC LEVEL: THE INSTRUMENTAL ACT

Vygotsky (1997a, p. 87) focussed on tool use as the key characteristic of human mental activity and characterised the process that combines persons, tools, and the world as "the instrumental act."

The inclusion of a tool in the behavioural process, first, sets to work a number of new functions connected with the use and control of the given tool; second, abolishes and makes unnecessary a number of natural processes, whose work is [now] done by the tool; third, modifies the course and the various aspects (intensity, duration, order, etc.) of all mental processes included in the instrumental act, replacing some functions with others, i.e., it recreates and reconstructs the whole structure of behaviour just like a technical tool recreates the entire system of labour operations.

Vygotsky's main interest in this connection was how the instrumental act was transformed and became a *mental act*, and thereby influenced the subject's learning and development.

Vygotsky's theoretical focus was primarily on humans' *psychological* functioning with mental tools (i.e., oral and written language, models, blueprints, number systems) (see Figure 15.1). It is the mediation of these mental tools that especially influences humans' psychological relation to the world.

The most essential feature distinguishing the psychological tool from the technical tool, is that it is meant to act upon mind and behaviour, whereas the technical tool, which is also inserted as a middle term between the activity of man and the external object, is meant to cause changes in the object itself. The psychological tool changes nothing in the object. It is a means of influencing one's own mind or behaviour or another's. It is not a means of influencing the object. Therefore, in the instrumental act we see activity towards oneself, and not toward the object. (1997a, p. 87)

Vygotsky's focus on the mental act and psychological tools has drawn attention away from the importance of the instrumental act and the change

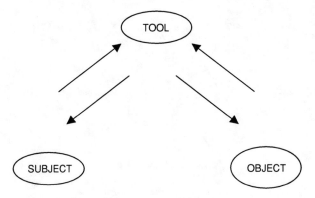

Figure 15.1. The model of the mental act.

in the object as part of learning activity; however, a model of learning activity should encompass both. A clear distinction between material or technical tools and mental tools is not possible because all artefacts and tools have a mental as well as a material aspect. The unity of the mental and material aspects in the act is important for understanding humans as cultural beings, taking part in cultural practices to which they contribute and by which they are influenced. The subject's acting on the object by using tools is just as important and should be included in a theory of learning activity. The conceptualisation of the fundamental relation between humans and the world as mediated by both instrumental and mental procedures is significant.

THE SOCIETAL LEVEL: THE INSTRUMENTAL ACT AND ITS LOCATION WITHIN INSTITUTIONAL TRADITIONS

The necessity to locate human instrumental and mental acts in cultural practices is one of Leontiev's (1972, pp. 54–58) main points and is the basis for the dialectic between the internal and external aspects of human activity. Leontiev also ascribes this aspect to Vygotsky's theory and cites Vygotsky's claim that "all activity is initially social in nature" (p. 55).

Vygotsky identified two main, interconnected features [of activity] that are necessarily fundamental for psychology: its tool-like ("instrumental") structure, and its inclusion in a system of interrelations with other people. It is these features that define the nature of human psychological processes. The tool mediates activity and thus connects humans not only with the world of objects but also with other people. Because of this humans' activity *assimilates the experience of mankind*. (Leontiev, 1972, pp. 55–56)

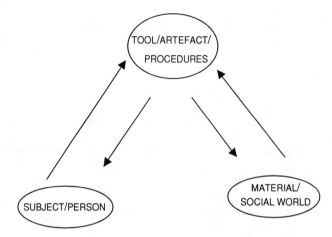

Figure 15.2. Extension of Vygotsky's model of the instrumental act to include procedures with artefact as mediating between the person and the social and material world.

Therefore, the processes of how humans' interact and regulate the
object/world as well as their own mental processes cannot be separated in
our attempts to understand human learning (see Figure 15.2). This point
is also clearly demonstrated in Wartofsky's theory that advances a cultural-
historical approach to an epistemology of human learning and development.
Like Vygotsky, he uses the concept of tool as mediating between the person
and the world, but he extends the concept of tool to include all kinds of
artefacts and extends the understanding of acting to include perception as
well. His main point in this connection is that cultural artefacts influence
the way humans perceive their environment and, thereby, how they act and
transform the environment. Furthermore, Wartofsky (1979, p. 204) describes
artefacts as "objectification of human needs and intentions already invested
with cognitive and affective content" and thus, in agreement with Leontiev,
he unites both the material and the mental aspects of tools and artefacts and
their procedures.

Wartofsky's explication of artefact as the objectification of human needs
and intentions is very important for understanding learning not only as a
cognitive phenomenon of changing persons' minds and capacities but also
as a phenomenon that includes change in the "objects" so that the objects
attain both cognitive and affective content. We cannot experience and act on
the objects in the world as objects in themselves; our experience is always
influenced by cultural artefacts. This leads to the conception that both object
and tool in Vygotsky's model are artefacts (i.e., cultural phenomena).

But why do some artefacts become objects that we acquire, or influence, or try to understand, or learn to handle, whereas others become tools for a specific person in a given situation? Why are some artefacts objects for learning activity, whereas others function as tools in this activity?

- First, for each person what have become tools have once been objects for the instrumental act.
- Second, artefacts that become objects are connected with Wartofsky's idea that artefacts are objectifications of human needs and intentions.
- Third, there has to be some social practice that helps the single person to learn which objects can relate to his actual needs and motives.

The third point introduces an important factor in understanding a person's learning of instrumental and mental acts – namely, institutional traditions and practices that specify both the objects of activities and the means of activities (e.g., at home, in school, at work). How a person's needs and intentions can be directed to specific object domains and why some artefacts become objects for learning are connected to institutional practices.

In his description of learning activity, Davydov (1999, p. 124) directly stresses the object of activity as the central aspect: "One important feature of activity is the fact that it is always, whether explicitly or implicitly, object related. This implies that all its components have some object-related contents and that the activity itself is necessarily directed toward the creation of some material or spiritual product."

Schooling has evolved as an institutional practice in which humans concentrate especially on the appropriation of mental tools and procedures in the form of theoretical knowledge. Learning as an outcome of the students' own experimentation does not seem to be as important as the students' appropriation of theoretical knowledge. But theoretical knowledge by definition contains the concrete aspect of production, so it will not be very difficult to include this as a central element of teaching.

It should be noted that, in logical science, knowledge about the interrelation between general and specific core aspects – is referred to as theoretical knowledge. Children's need in learning consists then in their striving to obtain knowledge of general aspects of an object, that is theoretical knowledge through experimentation and exploration. Making experimentation and transformation with objects necessarily involves creativity. (Davydov, 1999, p. 125)

The productive aspect in the students' appropriation of knowledge has to be more central within a cultural-historical approach in which activity is central. Children's own creativity in producing models and activities that can encompass their knowledge should be appreciated more directly, as I will demonstrate in the example later.

Tool mediation can be seen as activities with artefacts; and subjects acquire competence with procedures connected to different types of artefacts. Because everyday activities with artefacts are quite different in the home, daycare, school, higher education, professional education, and work, it is important to differentiate between the types of learning in these institutions. Both the kinds of knowledge and the methods of learning differ between home, school, and work (see Figure 15.3).

Everyday Knowledge, Subject Matter Knowledge, and Professional Knowledge

To be able to understand how learning takes place for children in school, one should distinguish between everyday knowledge that children have appropriated and use in their daily activities in the home and community and the special subject matter or scientific knowledge that children come in contact with in school. Examples of everyday knowledge connected to practical activities at home are cooking, cleaning, and "cozy activities." In everyday knowledge, procedures and content are intertwined, and can be characterised as "silent" knowledge. In school, knowledge is based on teaching traditions with subject matter knowledge and procedures (i.e., language learning with reading and writing procedures, mathematical learning with the four basic operations for calculating, geography with map reading, and history with the time line). Vygotsky ascribes scientific knowledge to the school tradition. It is important, however, to differentiate between subject matter knowledge and scientific knowledge. Subject matter knowledge is connected to specific, explicitly defined domains in school, where there is some form of systematicity. But in subject matter, the methods, and content are usually not integrated and do not define each other in a reflected way as they do in science. In subject matter teaching in school, methods are seldom taught as integrated with the content of the subject matter, though this would be the ideal.

Knowledge connected to craftsmanship and professional work is related to knowledge domains that are quite different from science and subject matters in school. Here, content and procedures have developed through work traditions. For the professional persons, knowledge has become embodied

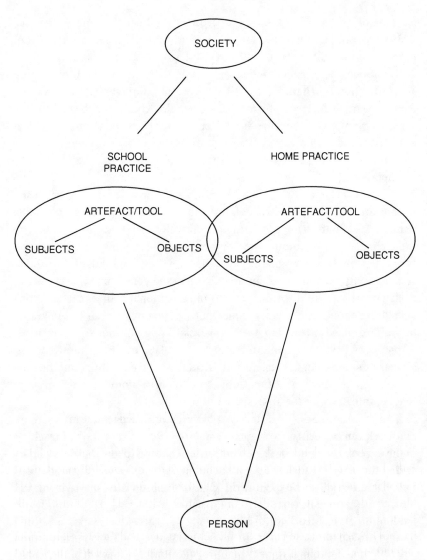

Figure 15.3. Vygotsky's model of the instrumental act transformed into traditions for practice.

in procedures and methods, similar to everyday knowledge, but with the difference that in work traditions, professionals can become conscious of and reflect upon procedures and methods if they do not fit the task.

The different ways of practice that one can find in the home, school, higher education, and the workplace create different conditions for children's learning of concepts and practice procedures. Scribner (Scribner & Stevens, 1989), for example, has shown that mathematics is learned and used in school in ways that are different from those at the workplace. She studied American milkmen's delivering practices and found that their methods of keeping account of how much milk they had delivered and the payment they received were done quite differently from what one would expect from the basic arithmetical operations learned in school. Her research showed that mathematical knowledge and skills are not abstract entities but are combined with the concrete institutional practices in the workplace (see also Lave, 1988, for other examples).

The knowledge and skill a child acquires at home and in daycare institutions are still relevant in school, but subject matter knowledge and skills come to dominate school teaching and the child's activity in school. The same change can be found when apprenticeship learning and preparation for professional life takes place. Then, the knowledge and skill of the professional activity become dominant in relation to subject matter knowledge and skill. This relationship is what we find in educational courses that are connected to apprenticeship education, where subject matter can be integrated but subordinated to teaching professional skills (e.g., methods of carpentry). Apprentices have to be able to read and calculate and have knowledge in several subject matters to benefit from a professional education, but the profession, and not the logic of the subject matter area, dominates the subjects that are integrated in the apprenticeship schools.

The implication of the differences between knowledge at home, school, and work can be related to Vygotsky's advice (1982) about ways of teaching in the different institutions: teaching at home should follow the child's logic, and in the school it should follow the subject matter logic.[2] To these two, I add that at work it should follow the logic of the professional activity and of

---

[2]   There is no agreement in general in school politics about this, and the fight is between dominant positions in the cultural fields that recommend different educational methods. What children find in school is not that teaching should follow the logic of the material and prepare the child for life in other institutions, but a mixture of conflicting demands related to the positions of parents, teachers, school leaders, politicians, and researchers that have a general connection to schools in society as well as the specific parents and teachers in a specific school, so the children who enter the activities of school meet these built-in conflicts through the educational practice. An example from the Danish school is the discussion in general about when and how the child should learn to read. The practice differs from one kindergarten class to another. Many parents expect that their child learns to read when the child enters kindergarten class at five or six years of age in Denmark, but the dominating political /pedagogical tradition recommends that the child wait until first grade. So value positions in the cultural field influence the activities in the traditions for practice in school (see Figure 15.5).

the work tasks. The differences between activities in the different institutions are related to the content, the methods, and the context in which teaching takes place.

Variation in Practice Traditions within the Same Type of Institution

In the learning theory presented here, cultural traditions for practice are given a central place in the explanation of both content and direction of teaching and learning in the different educational institutions of society. Inside the different educational institutions, such as home, daycare, school, and after-school institutions (i.e., clubs and scout organizations), there are different traditions for practice; in the same society, however, these different traditions are also connected through shared societal and historical contexts. Practice in the same type of institutions (e.g., home and school) can be different between nations and even within the same country (see Rogoff, 2003, for examples on variation in practices that include children at home and in schools in different societies) and also can change in the same institutions over time. Within the same type of institution, such as schools, different traditions for classroom teaching can be found. In some countries, drill learning and repetition still dominate. In other countries, book teaching has been supplemented or replaced by project-oriented teaching (i.e., in the Scandinavian countries).

One can differentiate between aspects that influence the same type of institutional practice. Aspects that each contribute to specific practice are *ideal practice* (practice in theory), *formal practice* (practice that is formulated into laws and regulations), and *actual practice* (shared activities of the participants in a specific institution).

The model depicted in Figure 15.4 can illustrate these key relations for institutional practices in a specific society that together create conditions for children's learning. The relations between children, society, and institutions are mediated by the three kinds of cultural practice. Practice traditions include the three mentioned aspects of practice, and these aspects are conditions for the one aspect in focus; in actual practice, the three aspects are interwoven, so they are difficult to differentiate.

The first and most important institution for a child is the family. The actual practice in the family is usually unwritten and often unspoken. These practices include both traditions that are unique for a specific family, though at the same time they are founded in traditions common for several generations of family practices in a specific society or nation. The shared family practice in a society can also be seen as a kind of idealised or theoretical family

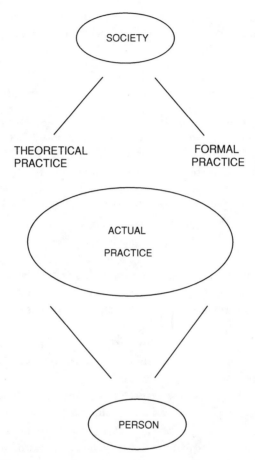

Figure 15.4. Different aspects of practice traditions as mediating factors between society and person, society and institution, and institution and person.

practice when it becomes formulated as norms. The formal practice of the family is defined through family laws (i.e., legacy, divorce, birthright) and bureaucratic regulations (children's school attendance).

Most school traditions for practice are much more explicit than family traditions, and they exist as ideal or theoretical practices. The idealised types of school practice are formulated as educational theories and proposals for school didactics. The most explicit traditions are formalised in policy papers, curriculum plans, and instructional plans; they have become formal practice. The formal practices can be seen as the societal conditions for the school as an institution. Both the formal and the idealised school practices (traditions) are realised and turn into actual practice, both in the daily activities in a specific school and through the activities of the individual schoolchildren, teachers, and parents.

The difference between family and school in actual practice can be found in how societal practice traditions (the formal practice) are incorporated in the actual practice. Because governmental institutions determine school conditions through economic support, exams, and control, the formalised and idealised traditions for school practice regulates the actual practice of a single school more directly than is the case for family practice.

For some children the discrepancy in the tradition for practice of home and school are so great that children develop attitudes of failure, disappointment, and opposition instead of motives for learning and acquiring the skill and knowledge offered in school. This is what we found in a research project with Puerto Rican children. To overcome this discrepancy, this research project explored in an after-school program how home and community traditions can be connected with subject matter teaching (Hedegaard and Chaiklin, 2005).

An after-school setting can be an ideal place to bridge the gap between family practices characteristic of a community tradition and the subject matter practices of school traditions. One of the aims with the after-school project with Puerto Rican children was to use their motivation from home and community life to introduce educational activities that combined the knowledge they have acquired at home and in the community with the skills and knowledge needed for the subject matter of history and literacy in school. It is easier for a teacher to become sensitive to her pupils in an after-school program than in a school class because there is not a fixed curriculum. The instruction in an after-school activity is an offer to the pupils and their parents instead of an obligation like school. Most after-school institutions are based on children's choice and their desire to attend in contrast to children's involvement in school and family. Therefore, an after-school program has the strength that children attending this type of institution are less opposed to instruction than they are when attending school.

From this brief analysis, I contend that the educational task in schools is to build bridges between the tradition for learning practice at home and in school. Connecting traditions of practice at home with traditions of practice in school and after-school institutions can become a motive-creating experience. A way to do this is to use knowledge, thinking modes, and motives that children have acquired at home as a foundation for the subject matter concepts and activities offered in school.

THE FORMATION OF PERSONALITY: DEVELOPMENT OF
CONCEPTS, THINKING PROCEDURES, AND MOTIVES

Children are born with individual differences, but they are not born as personalities. Through upbringing and education, the child becomes a person. The acquisition of cultural motives, skills, and knowledge is central to becoming a person who can participate in family life, work, and community life.

The institutionalised practices in which children participate and learn are not static. Everyone who participates in an institution's social practice contributes to this practice and leaves his or her mark on the activities. A family, a daycare institution, and a school will be marked by the children who are engaged in the activities, just as the children will be marked by the institution's activities. By participating in the daily activities in an institution, the children appropriate as well as contribute to ways of being together and the social-historical experiences that are accumulated in these practices, emotionally, motivationally, and cognitively.

Trajectories through Institutional Traditions for Practice

The different activities that characterise the different institutions in which children participate, in different periods of their life, lead to qualitatively different periods in their development. El'konin (1999) has presented a theory according to which the different periods in a child's development parallel the different institutions that dominate the child's life. The first period is dependent on practice at home and in daycare and deals with the child's development and direct emotional contact with other human beings. The second period is related to practice in school and deals with the child's development of roles in relation to other human beings. The third period is related to peer group activity and professional education as preparation for work and deals with the close personal relationship and work relationships.

Development of Motives

In El'konin's theory, changes in the child's social relations are hypothesized as the central aspect in the child's psychic development. Change in a child's social relations happens when the child is introduced to a new kind of institutional life, as when he is introduced to a daycare, kindergarten, school, or after-school setting (club). This introduction to new activities changes, elaborates, and extends the child's activities and influences the child's orientation to the world. This change also implies a change in what is important for the child – a change in his dominant motives. This does not imply that a child's earlier dominant motive disappears. Rather, it gets another position in the child's motive hierarchy (see Figure 15.5).

In all activity, in learning activity in the comprehensive school as well as in after-school or club activity, children produce or reproduce the object of their activity through their tool use. So the motive and their cognition actually have a material aspect that is the product of their learning activity.

Because the motive is bound to the object of activity, the object of activity is crucial also in learning activity, and the material aspect of this object and how the child produces the object through using tools are the basis for the child's appropriation of motives as well as knowledge and skills.

A. N. Leontiev's (1972, 47–48, 49–50) comments are useful in clarifying the relation between the object of the activity and children's development of motives and cognition:

Humans do not simply find external conditions to which they must adapt their activity. Rather these social conditions bear with them the motives and goals of their activity, its means and modes.

Mental reflection of the object world is not produced directly by external influences (including "reverse" influence), but by processes through which the subject enters into practical contact with the object world. . . . In connection with the analyses of activity, it is sufficient to point out that its objective produces not only the objective character of images but also object-orientation of desires and emotions.

Everyday Knowledge and Conceived Knowledge Transformed into Active Knowledge

According to Vygotsky (1982), the acquisition of subject matter knowledge in school extends the meaning of everyday knowledge; at the same time, subject matter concepts can be understood and become functional for the child only if they build on the child's everyday knowledge. If teaching succeeds in creating this relation, the child will be able to use the learned subject matter knowledge as tools for analyzing and reflecting on his everyday activities. The subject matter knowledge thereby becomes integrated with the child's everyday knowledge and can develop into functional concepts for the child where content and form define each other.

The child's concept formation takes place through the child's participation in cultural activities. Here, the child acquires tradition for practice in the form

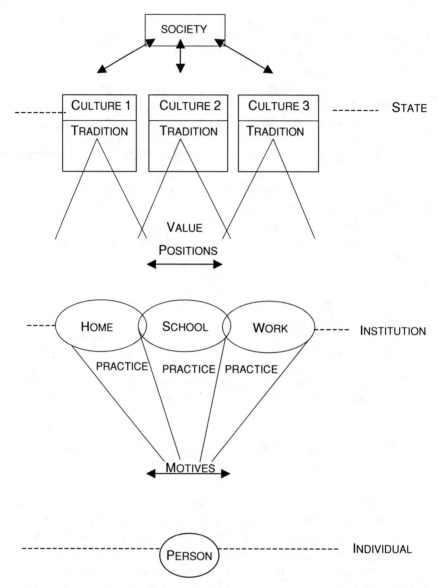

Figure 15.5. A model of children's learning and development through participation in institutionalised practice.

of both manual and cognitive skills and knowledge. According to Vygotsky, the child has acquired and can use concepts when knowledge is organised into a reciprocal system of conceptual relations.[3]

The interdependence between concepts and their inner connection in a reciprocal system is the main device for systematisation of a person's concepts about the world. It is also the main device for understanding how historically produced social experiences become acquired. Vygotsky writes that through the acquisition of conceptual systems that relate to the social, societal, and political aspects of life, the young person for the first time can be conscious of the societal ideologies and of himself as a person in society – that is, his self-consciousness develops.

One of the important aspects of concept formation that Vygotsky puts forward is that the concepts symbolise both abstract and concrete aspects of the subject area conceptualised. He characterises the child's cognitive development as an increase in the complexity of the relations between the concrete and abstract aspects of the conceptualised area.

AN EXAMPLE

To illustrate the interconnections between the different theoretical levels in learning activity in children's concrete learning activity, I provide an example from a three-year teaching experiment based on the ideas of the double move in teaching (see Hedegaard, 2002). The approach is characterised by the children's construction of their own models of central concepts. These models extended over time as a result of children's explorative activity.

In the teaching project, these models were developed through tasks that created oppositions and conflicts so that new concepts had to become formulated and earlier concepts had to be reformulated. This led to a transition from the first formulated general relation – the germ cell – that there is a relation between animals and the natural setting in which they live: the adaptation

---

[3] Vygotsky's theory has often been misunderstood on this point based on interpretation of his book *Language and Thought*, 1963, and revised edition, 1987. Vygotsky's theory of children's conceptual development is interpreted as a development directed toward a hierarchical organization with "everyday concepts" at the bottom and abstract concepts at the top. Vygotsky (1997b) criticized such misunderstandings of idealizing the form of concepts independent of the content. The problem of separating between form and content of concepts arises according to Vygotsky from the condition that the contents are seen as culturally developed and socially and historically determined, while the thinking forms mostly have been seen as biological processes determined by organic maturation, running parallel to the brain's organic development. But the interdependence between form and content characterizes both the historical evolution of mankind and the development of the single person (Hedegaard, 2007).

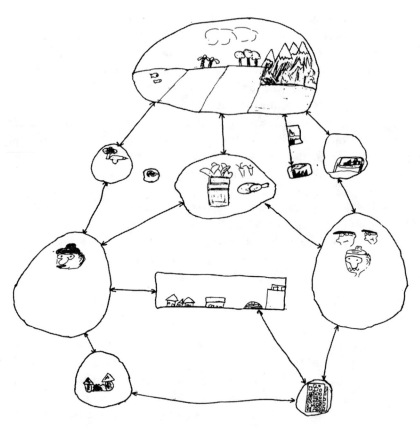

Figure 15.6. Morten's and Loke's model of the historical changes in a society from the start of fifth grade.

of animals to nature. This germ cell was then unfolded into the models of evolution of animals, the origin of humans, and the historical change of animals. In the children's models, one could follow this transformation from the first to the last models; and, as in Morten's and Loke's model (Figure 15.6), reminiscences from the earlier version of the model could be found in later models.

Experimental Teaching Where Children Construct and Use Models to Guide Their Learning Activity

The concrete example is from the fifth-grade history teaching. The children have individually and collectively constructed a model of central concepts of society. They have had different tasks for which they have used this model to construct activities that are based on the general relations depicted in their model. Through class discussion, the model has been adapted to the different historical periods with which they have worked: the Stone Age, the Iron Age, the Viking age, the Middle Ages, and the Age of Enlightenment. The last version of their model (from the nineteenth session) is the one that guides the children in the teaching session that in this chapter will exemplify the project (the twenty-sixth session). The activities that dominate the period that includes this session (the nineteenth to the thirtieth session) were the discussion of which factors promoted the social change from the Middle Ages to the Age of Enlightenment; and writing scripts and performing plays that illustrate these factors.

The learning objectives were the extension of the germ-cell model (see Figure 15.7) with the concepts:

- Religion to include power
- Tools to include knowledge
- Division of labour to include classes in society

The learning activities include:

- Watching film about the voyages of discovery
- Planning and performing plays about central events in the Age of Enlightenment based on the concepts of the model

To illustrate the change of the children's models over time, Morten's and Loke's initial model in fifth grade (the third teaching session) is shown (Figure 15.6), followed by a later version (nineteenth session) of the model that the teacher put up at the black board based on the children's discussion of the changes from the Middle Ages to the Age of Enlightenment (Figure 15.7).

The different signs in Figure 15.6 illustrated (from the top) the concept of nature (to the left), tools, person, and society, with the change in society's conditions over time illustrated (at the bottom) with the three different signs with buildings. The three persons (to the right) illustrate that humans have to live together, and the sign in the middle of the figure illustrates that they need food. The city sign (to the right) illustrates that people who live in society need some regulations. The last symbols are signs for pollution and one that illustrates that factories and people pollute nature, and thereby damage nature, which is shown by the other symbol of a bird smeared in oil.

After this model there have been several versions (e.g., there have been several models of the society of the Middle Ages, made by the children both individually and collectively at the blackboard).

In this model the students have incorporated different forms of knowledge together with tools; between human's way of living and between ways of living and society, they have incorporated division of labour with its concrete

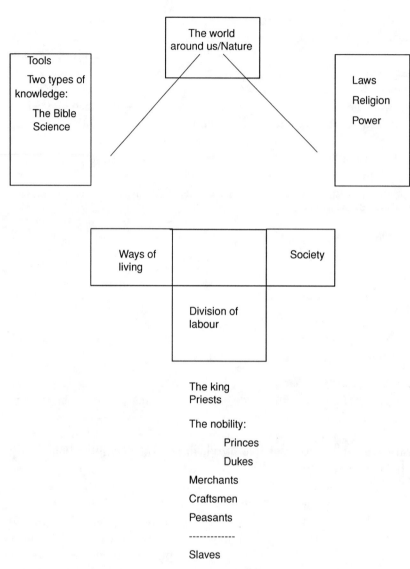

Figure 15.7. The extended model for the Age of Enlightenment.

examples from the Age of Enlightenment. The last part is how the relation between society and nature is regulated through law, religion, and power.

Creating and Rehearsing a Play (Twenty-sixth Session)

The children were divided into four groups, each group being asked to produce a play about the Age of Enlightenment. The group in focus has five children, Morten, Allan, Jørgen, Juliane, and Lisbeth. Morten is extremely active in the planning phase for his group, putting forward ideas about the theme and the content of the play. He gets into an argument with Juliane, who also wants to contribute ideas.

The teacher introduces the idea of writing a script. "You have to choose a theme that illustrates the most important aspects of the Age of Enlightenment. For example, some of you talked about the great explorers. Write down key ideas about your theme: permission from the king, dangers at sea, arriving home. Once the key words are ready, you have to decide which characters are to appear in the play."

MORTEN: I have an idea. We'll show a man who persuades the king to give him some ships. He gets them and then he takes some slaves.

JULIANE: [*objects*] But first we have to write down some key ideas.

MORTEN: [*defends himself*] Well, that's just an idea – do any of you have other ideas?

ALLAN: Yeah, something about Columbus sailing to India.

MORTEN: Or what if he got caught up in a storm and ended up in America and take some slaves.

ALLAN: Yes, and sold them and got some spices.

MORTEN: Or is it silver and coffee that they have? [*The other children join in now.*]

JØRGEN: [*says that they can take loads of silver*]

JULIANE: [*says that the black slaves want to have the goods; they take everything and sail away*]

MORTEN: Oh do shut up.

JULIANE: [*affronted*] I'm allowed to say something about the play too, you know.

MORTEN: Why should the black slaves steal?

JULIANE: Because they are poor.

MORTEN: [*feels provoked and decides to put it to a vote*] Who votes for Juliane's idea and who votes for mine?

JULIANE: The slaves might be able to sail a big ship you know. They have sailed with slave ships.

MORTEN: [*sarcastically*] No, they just walked across the water on a big bridge. Don't you see that they were below deck and couldn't see how the ship was sailed?

LISBETH: [*makes a mild attempt to back up Juliane and says they perhaps have had their own boat*]

MORTEN: [*asks Jørgen*] What do you vote? [*He doesn't know.*]

ALLAN: Let's just say that they sail round Africa and find America. It's just typical that we can't make our minds up.

MORTEN: What should we do, then?

JULIANE: [*sulkily*] I don't know. It's always the boys who decide every-thing.

ALLAN: [*defends Morten*] Your idea would take ages.

MORTEN: What happens in your story, Juliane?

JULIANE: [*says that it involves a slave boy called Zacha*] He's really clever and had learned on the slave ship how to sail. He manages to slip away with the ship and they are trying to catch him all over Europe.

TEACHER: [*arrives and asks them what their theme is*]

MORTEN: We have two ideas.

ALLAN: The first one is that they want to go over and trade with the Arabs. They get caught in a storm and end up in America where they sell all their things.

TEACHER: What's wrong with that?

MORTEN: Nothing, but Juliane has another idea. [*He makes fun of her idea.*]

LISBETH: We could do both.

MORTEN: Yes, we could put Juliane's in at the end.

JULIANE: Well, you'd better get yours written down then.

Allan starts writing down some key words. Morten goes up to the front of the classroom and pulls down the map of the world to find out where they get shipwrecked. Later during the class discussion, Morten describes the group project to the rest of the class. "Some people go round South Africa, they get shipwrecked, they meet some blacks, and they don't know where they are. They steal their jewellery and take some slaves, and then they go to Central America."

They perform the play for their classmates and a parallel class. The play goes as planned. In the class discussion during the thirtieth session, they discuss what they have learnt from putting on the play, by using the categories in their model. During the class discussion, the children became aware of a new idea, in terms of the model, dealing with the concepts of the division of labour.

They formulate that this division, besides indicating level of power, also can be related to the idea that different kinds of labour cover various needs.

INTERPRETATION OF A CHILD'S LEARNING ACTIVITY

Morten's Social Activity and Motivation

There is little doubt that Morten was the leading force in working out a theme, deciding on the roles, and ensuring that there was a unity in the planning of the play; he was also the key figure in carrying it out. Morten's motivation to work with the group and his motivation to put together a good play within the framework of the subjects they had been studying were interconnected. He used the teamwork with his classmates to carry out the class assignments, jointly resolving both social and academic problems. For example, Juliane had irritated him, putting forward what was in his opinion a historically illogical idea – that the black slaves in the play should steal a ship. But he was so interested in making the group work as a team that he used a procedure that involved asking each member of the group what he or she thought. He also asked Juliane what she proposed they should do. He then went on to formulate a story that preserved group unity.

Morten's Thinking and Concept Formation

Morten's idea for the group play was not very original – it was very close to the ideas they have heard from the teacher – but he was nevertheless able to put coherence and cohesion into the group's idea, and could also integrate Juliane's idea. This illustrates his ability to bring together apparently contradictory story lines and work out and argue for a solution that combines both stories to create an entity. At first, it was not clear where they are to sail to, but once they have agreed on the story line, Morten solved that problem by pulling down the classroom's map of the world and finding out where the various places were located.

CONCLUSION: IDENTIFYING THE FOUR LEVELS OF LEARNING ACTIVITY

The case illustrates how the material production as a result of the children's activity is a very important condition for their learning. The play performance and the video recording of the play became a significant motivating factor for the children. The production of the play and the recording materialised the children's concepts as well as developed their motives for their work, both for the content of history and for the general conceptual system that the teacher promoted through the teaching.

A very central product that the children created was their personal models depicting key conceptual relations within the theme of the teaching: the evolution of animals, the origin of man, and the historical changes of society.

How can this case illustrate the different levels of learning activity?

The level of mankind can be found in the children's dependence of tools; they both use and produce their own conceptual tools in the form of visual models. They made models that hang in the classroom, which also evolve into new versions through their use in the class activity. The models had both a conceptual and a material aspect. This material aspect was very important for the children, as can be seen from the following event. The librarian at one point asked if the models could be exhibited in the school library, but the children voted no, because they were afraid that other children would not show respect to their products and spoil them.

In the session presented here, the activities had both material and conceptual products. The models were visualised in different versions, but the models were also consulted when planning the activities of the play. This planning was written down as well as realised in the performance of the play.

The societal level can be found in the concrete project in how it is located within the cultural traditions in the Danish comprehensive school, that is, in the time schedule for the classroom activities as well as through the teacher's guiding, correcting, and controlling activity. It is also demonstrated by the way a teaching project transcends the tradition in the Danish comprehensive school, where it took place.

The institutional level in the experimental teaching project as planning and analyses of the social practice was primarily within the school activities. But the teachers and researchers knowledge of the children's experience from home and community was a foundation for the activities in the classroom. Learning as children's trajectories through different institutional practice and interaction between the different institutions in creating conditions for the children's learning cannot be demonstrated in this example.

The personal level can be illustrated by focusing on a child's development of social learning and development of motives, as well as a way of thinking and concept appropriation.

DISCUSSION

With this contribution, my aim has been to outline a theory of learning activity that can promote a teaching practice in school that integrates the child's explorative activity with subject matter concepts – "the double move approach." Vygotsky's conception of the instrumental and mental act has been the departure for my theoretical analyses that has centred on social practice as the key concept.

A person's relation to the world is mediated by the social practice in which a person participates. It is through this participation in institutionalised social practice that a person acquires new motives and competencies. Thereby, learning basically becomes a change in the person's motive relation to the world through changes in the person's relation to other persons and in the person's contribution to shared practice.

The child, through his learning activity in school, will appropriate competencies with tools or artefacts that have both an intellectual and a manual dimension. The relations that the child enters into are depicted in Figure 15.5. Activities in institutional practice are the focus in this model. As demonstrated in Figure 15.4, there are two aspects that influence the child's activity in concrete institutional practice: a formal (law governed) aspect, and the theoretical (norm governed) aspect of practice.

A child's competencies and development of motives are a joint concern between several participants in the social practice in which the child participates. The interactions in this practice have to be seen as an engaged and intentional interaction, where the specific child's motives (the child in focus) as well as other children's and/or adults' contribute to the improvement of the competencies that are realised in the interaction.

The motives and competencies the child learns in school are dependent on two factors: the conditions for participation in activities, where the artefacts and tools (concepts and methods) of a subject matter area are presented so that the child can use them in his or her own activity; and the child's participation, which gives room for his or her competencies to create products that he or she finds interesting and that are recognised socially.

References

Davydov, V. V. (1982). Ausbildung der Lerntätigkeit [Development of learning activity]. In V. V. Davydov, J. Lompscher, & A. K. Markova (Eds.), *Ausbildung der Lerntätigkeit bei Schülern* (pp. 37–44). Berlin: Volk und Wissen.

Davydov, V. V. (1990). *Types of generalization in instruction: Logical and psychological problems in the structuring of school curricula* (Soviet studies in mathematics education, Vol. 2) (J. Kilpatrick, Ed.; J. Teller, Trans.). Reston, VA: National Council of Teachers of Mathematics. (Original work published 1972).

Davydov, V. V. (1999). What is real learning activity. In M. Hedegaard & J. Lompscher (Eds.), *Learning activity and development* (pp. 123–138). Aarhus: Aarhus University Press.

El'konin, D. B. (1999). Toward the problem of stages in the mental development of children. *Journal of Russian and East European Psychology, 37* (6), 11–30.

Hedegaard, M. (2002). *Learning and child development.* Aarhus: Aarhus University Press.

Hedegaard, M. (2006). Undervisning i klasser med mange børn fra indvandrerfamilier. In B. Elle, K. Nielsen, & M. Nissen (Eds.), *Pædagogisk psykologi* [Pedagogical psychology] (pp. 123–145). Roskilde: Roskilde Universitetsforlag.

Hedegaard, M. (2007). The development of children's conceptual relation to the world, with focus on concept formation in pre-school children's activity. In H. Daniels, M. Cole, & J. Wertsch (Eds.), *The Cambridge Companion to Vygotsky* (pp. 246–275). Cambridge: Cambridge University Press.

Hedegaard, M., & Chaiklin, S. (2005). *Radical local teaching and learning.* Aarhus: Aarhus University Press.

Lave, J. (1988). *Cognition in practice: Mind, mathematics, and culture in everyday life.* Cambridge: Cambridge University Press.

Leontiev, A. N. (1972). The problem of activity in psychology. In J. W. Wertsch (Ed.), *Culture, communication and cognition: A Vygotskian perspective* (pp. 37–69). Cambridge: Cambridge University Press.

Lompscher, J. (1984). Problems and results of experimental research on the formation of theoretical thinking through instruction. In M. Hedegaard, P. Hakkarainen, & Y. Engeström (Eds.), *Learning and teaching on a scientific basis* (pp. 293–356). Aarhus: Aarhus University, Institute of Psychology.

Lompscher, J. (1999). Learning activity and its formation: Ascending from the abstract to the concrete. In M. Hedegaard & J. Lompscher (Eds.), *Learning activity and development* (pp. 139–168). Aarhus: Aarhus University Press.

Rogoff, B. (2003). *The cultural nature of human development.* Oxford: Oxford University Press.

Scribner, S. (1985). Vygotsky's use of history. In J. V. Wertsch (Ed.), *Culture, communication, and cognition: A Vygotskian perspective* (pp. 119–145). Cambridge: Cambridge University Press.

Scribner, S., & Stevens, J. (1989). *Experimental studies on the relationship of school math and work math.* Technical Paper Series No. 4. New York: Teachers College, Columbia University.

Wartofsky, M. (1979). *Models – Representations and the scientific understanding.* Dordrecht: D. Reidel.

Vygotsky, L. S. (1982). *Om barnets psykiske udvikling* [About the child's psychic development]. Copenhagen: Nyt Nordisk Forlag.

Vygotsky, L. S. (1987). *Thinking and speech.* In R. W. Rieber & A. S. Carton (Eds.), *The collected works of L. S. Vygotsky: Vol. 1. Problems of general psychology* (pp. 39–285). New York: Plenum Press.

Vygotsky, L. S. (1997a). The instrumental method in psychology. *The collected works of L. S. Vygotsky: Vol. 3. Problems of the theory and history of psychology* (pp. 85–89). New York: Plenum Press.

Vygotsky, L. S. (1997b). *Educational psychology.* Boca Raton, FL: St Lucie Press.

16

Dialogue for Reasoning

Promoting Exploratory Talk and Problem Solving in the Primary Classroom

Sylvia Rojas-Drummond, Laura Gómez, and Maricela Vélez

INTRODUCTION

In this chapter, we present a study based on previous investigations carried out through a nine-year collaboration between the Open University, in the United Kingdom, and the National Autonomous University of Mexico. In this endeavour, we seek to understand as well as to promote diverse cognitive, discursive, and cultural processes involved in the social construction of knowledge in Mexican and British primary school children. The data reported here address the development and promotion of a particularly effective type of talk, called "exploratory talk," as a discursive tool to facilitate social and individual reasoning in Mexican children.

Our research follows a sociocultural perspective, whose fundamentals are rooted on the seminal ideas of Lev S. Vygotsky (e.g., 1962, 1978), and which have given rise to several and varied developments that can be included in this approach, in spite of their heterogeneity (e.g., Brown and Reeve, 1987; Cole, 1985, 1996; Coll, 1990; Coll, Palacios, & Marchesi, 2001; Elbers et al., 1992; Lave, 1991; Light & Butterworth, 1992; Mercer, 1995, 2000; Newman, Griffin, & Coll, 1989; Rogoff, 1990; Wertsch, 1985a, 1985b, 1991). This perspective has produced a great number of theoretical and methodological contributions, including particularly fruitful applications to understanding development and learning, as well as promoting social and educational processes.

The research reported here was funded by grants C01–1 of the Secretaría de Educación Pública (SEP) and the Consejo Nacional de Ciencia y Tecnología (CONACyT) – National Council for Science and Technology – and grant 306–303 from the Dirección General de Asuntos del Personal Académico-DGAPA, UNAM, Mexico. We are also grateful to Hugh Drummond and Ed Elbers for comments on different versions of the manuscript. Omar Torreblanca and Jose Luis Lara supervised and carried out all the technical work related to filming. We also appreciate all the support given by the schools' directors, teachers, and children for carrying out the research.

319

The sociocultural perspective assumes that cognition and other psychological phenomena are situated in and take their meaning from the social and cultural practices in which individuals participate. At the same time, it argues that reality, knowledge, and meaning are constructed by individuals in interaction with others in a shared social context (Bruner, 1990; Cole, 1996; Vygotsky, 1978). Research following this perspective considers units of analysis centred on human action and interaction mediated through a variety of cultural artefacts, which take place in particular sociocultural milieus (Bronckart, 1992; Mercer, 1995, 2000; Wertsch, 1998).

This perspective emphasises the central role played by language, among all the cultural artefacts that mediate human action in the form of tools and signs (Bronckart, 1992; Cole, 1996; Coll et al., 2001; Feinman, 1992; Gergen, 1992; Mercer, 1995, 2000; Rabinow & Sullivan, 1979; Vygotsky, 1962, 1978; Wertsch, 1991; Wertsch, Del Rio, & Alvarez, 1995). Throughout development, language functions as a key mediator of activity at both the interpsychological and intrapsychological planes. Thus, during dialogical exchanges, individuals negotiate meanings and construct knowledge jointly, gradually increasing their intersubjectivity. These interactions in turn create "zones of proximal development" (Vygotsky, 1978), or "intermental development zones" (Mercer, 2000), in a process that facilitates the appropriation of diverse cultural artefacts and practices by individuals (Rogoff, 1990). Likewise, social communication is gradually reconstructed as internal speech or "voices of the mind" (Wertsch, 1991, 1998), contributing significantly to reasoning, problem solving, knowledge construction, and self-regulation, among other important psychological functions (Rojas-Drummond & Alatorre, 1994; Rojas-Drummond et al., 1998).

Particularly, research on the analysis of interaction and discourse in various cultural and educational contexts has been inspired especially in the sociocultural approach, given its emphasis on language. This research has included detailed analyses of the role of social interaction, discourse, and artefact mediation in influencing the course and outcome of diverse educational practices (e.g., Candela, 1999; Coll, 1990; Coll & Edwards, 1996; Coll et al., 2001; Edwards & Mercer, 1987; Forman & Cazden, 1985; Hicks, 1996; Jadallah, 2000; Lemke, 1993; Mercer, 1995, 2000; Solomon, 1993; Spears, 1996; Wells, 1999; Wertsch et al., 995). These studies have also contributed to understanding the dynamics of interaction and knowledge construction, identifying factors that encourage and constrain communication in the classroom. In this respect, they include analysis of how language can support the learning process (Coll et al., 2001; Edwards & Mercer, 1987; Forman & Cazden, 1985; Mercer, 1995).

Within this approach, research assumes that education is essentially a communicative process in which participants negotiate personal perspectives in order to construct new shared meanings and understandings. For example, Edwards and Mercer (1987) assert that learning is the process whereby two people know now what only one of them knew before. These authors have carried out a line of research over several years in order to understand how teachers and pupils share their understanding to achieve "common knowledge" through language; their work as pioneers in this field in British classrooms has provided thorough and enlightening contributions to the fields of psychology, discourse analysis, and education. Similarly, these researchers have analysed how language works as a "social mode of thinking" to guide the construction of knowledge in schools (Mercer, 1995).

Researchers of discourse in educational settings have analysed interactions between experts and novices, as well as among peers. Regarding peer groups, Mercer and Wegerif (e.g., Mercer, 1995; Wegerif & Mercer, 1996; Wegerif & Scrimshaw, 1997) have studied the different types of talk that children use when they work together in small groups to solve problems. They have identified the following types:

1. Disputational talk, which is characterised by disagreements among participants: Decisions are taken individually and they are expressed by short statements and counter-statements.
2. Cumulative talk, which consists of a sum of opinions and ideas that are exposed without arguing: Group members propose one opinion after another without explaining the reasons for exposing them, and every participant intends to please the rest of the group or at least avoid confrontation.
3. Exploratory talk, which is characterized by the critical but constructive engagement of participants with each other's ideas: Suggestions are offered for joint consideration which may be challenged and counterchallenged, but challenges are justified and alternative hypotheses are offered, making reasoning visible in the talk.

Each type of talk presupposes the use of certain "ground rules," a concept introduced by Mercer and Edwards (1981) to refer to particular rules of interpretation that define the sort of answer that is appropriate in a particular situation. In this case, the ground rules for exploratory talk, the objective of our study, encourage children to work collectively so they can take turns, present, explore and negotiate alternatives for solving various problems, argue their points of view making their reasoning visible to others, ask others for justifications, and try to reach consensus.

According to Mercer (1995), exploratory talk is essential to achieve effective communication, grounded in accountable and visible reasoning. Therefore, exploratory talk is privileged in science, academia, the law, politics, and many other social contexts. Thus, its understanding and promotion become particularly relevant in diverse educational settings inside and outside of school. For this reason, in the present study, we analysed how language mediates the way knowledge is jointly constructed by shared understandings among primary students, and particularly the role played by exploratory talk in this process.

It is important to underline that a central aspect of exploratory talk is the use of arguments as a discursive strategy to identify and resolve differences of opinion, as well as to persuade by defending points of view. These actions can in turn give rise to the construction of shared meanings and the eventual reaching of agreements among participants, allowing for collective problem solving. In our study we consider argumentation as the act of providing reasons to make admissible a certain position, opinion, or conclusion, or to confront others' perspectives (see Billig, 1987). Related to argumentation is the concept of argument, which we define as the combination of an assertion plus one or more supporting statements (see van Eemeren et al., 2000). Such support can refer to different types of reasons, including tests, justifications, contextual demonstrations, examples, analogies, and beliefs. At the same time, an argument may contain, besides supporting statements, a conclusion.

Argumentation has become a topic of interest and research in the recent decade, and there are good reasons for this. One of them is that a series of studies has demonstrated the positive effects of discussing ideas upon learning (Barnes, Britton, & Torbe, 1990; Candela, 1999; Edwards & Mercer, 1987; King, 1994, 1995). Another reason is that, as Habermas (1984) argues, many communicative practices are oriented towards reaching, maintaining, and renovating consensus. An important characteristic of argumentation is that it emerges from the need to solve a difference of opinion through exploration of the justification of competing points of view; therefore, everyday communication includes argumentation. As Habermas claims, learning processes by which we acquire knowledge of the world, by which we overcome our difficulties in comprehension, and by which we renovate and extend our language are all supported in argumentation. For these reasons, a wealth of studies on argumentation has recently emerged in English-speaking countries (for a review, see Andrews, 1995; Andrews, Clarke, & Costello, 1993; Freedman & Pringle, 1984; Kraf, 1975; Wilkinson, 1986). For the Spanish language, there are far fewer studies on argumentation (e.g., Candela, 1990, 1995, 1997; Serra et al., 2000). Given this scarcity of studies, in this report we also analysed Mexican primary school children's capacity for argumentation.

One of the findings of research on talk among peers refers to the fact that students do not necessarily engage automatically in the construction of relevant knowledge when they work jointly to solve educational tasks. For example, Jadallah (2000) argues that it is essential that learning experiences involve students in exploration, analysis, evaluation, and/or synthesis of knowledge. Similarly, Maybin (1994) suggests that children need guidance into how to use language effectively. Given this state of affairs, Mercer, Wegerif, and Dawes have developed and tested educational programs to train explicitly exploratory styles of interaction among British primary school children in a series of studies (Mercer, 1996; Mercer, Wegerif, & Dawes, 1999; Wegerif, 1996; Wegerif & Mercer, 2000). In general, these authors have found that exploratory talk can be promoted successfully in primary school children; and the use of exploratory talk can greatly improve their reasoning abilities, which in turn enable them to solve problems more effectively in groups and individually. Similarly, their findings demonstrate that children who participate in these training programs offer more arguments for their opinions, consider diverse alternatives before arriving at a decision, look for agreements, give more elaborate explanations, and provide hypotheses for ideas. Thus, exploratory talk needs to be promoted in primary school children so that they can be endowed with a very powerful tool to enhance communication, reasoning, and knowledge construction.

In a preliminary study carried out by our team in Mexico, Rojas-Drummond, Fernández, and Vélez (2000) analysed and promoted exploratory talk in primary school children. We found that, in accordance with the British results, although children did not initially use much exploratory talk, those who underwent training improved significantly in group problem solving; however, we did not find significant effects for individual problem solving. As a result, we assumed that children might have needed a longer and more intensive training programme to achieve individual appropriation of exploratory talk.

For the reasons stated previously, in the present study we developed a more intensive and longer training program, making the study as a whole, and the training procedures in particular, more equivalent to those carried out by our British colleagues. Therefore, we adapted the original procedures to our culture, language, and educational context. In particular, we wanted to investigate whether appropriation of exploratory talk could be induced in a group of Mexican primary school children; whether this appropriation resulted in a better use of language and particularly in children's capacity for argumentation; and whether an improvement in exploratory talk resulted in better group and/or individual problem-solving abilities in the children.

Finally, we share with our British colleagues some theoretical assumptions that guided our research, based on a sociocultural perspective. Among these are: (a) language can represent a powerful tool to facilitate effective communication, as well as collective and individual reasoning; (b) primary school children have not necessarily developed fully the ability to use this tool effectively to reason and solve problems; (c) education should provide opportunities for children to develop competent use of this tool; and (d) although sometimes educational experiences are not optimal for fostering this capacity, it can be promoted with appropriate teaching and learning experiences. In the present study, we tested some of these assumptions.

METHOD

Participants

Eighty-four children of fifth and sixth grades (ten to twelve years old) from two public primary schools in Mexico City, Mexico, participated in the study; forty-six were male and thirty-eight were female. Schools were in the same neighbourhood and pertained to the same socioeconomic status (low to middle-class). One school was assigned to an experimental, and the other to a control condition (with forty-two children in each). We subsequently selected randomly eighteen children, nine each from the experimental and control groups (six triads), in order to carry out a finer, microgenetic analysis of some of the changes occurring during the process of appropriation, by the children, of the discursive tools under study.

Setting

For the control school, the study took place in the children's respective classrooms. For the experimental school, tests were administered also in the children's classrooms, while the intervention programme was implemented in a multipurpose room. This room was adapted especially to suit the needs of the intervention programme and was fitted with modular furniture, educational materials, computers, and a small library.

Materials

All participants were administered an adapted version of the Raven's Test of Progressive Matrices. The adaptation was made following Wegerif (1996) and consists of creating two shorter formats from the original one by distributing half of the problems to each version. One of these versions was used as an individual test, and the other one as a small-group test. Each test consisted of a booklet and an answer sheet.

Design

In order to assess the effects of the intervention programme, we used a Factorial Mixed 2X2 design, with Treatment (experimental and control groups) as the between-subjects factor and Tests (as the within-subjects factor with repeated measures). For the microgenetic study, we carried out several complementary qualitative and quantitative analyses.

PROCEDURES

Test Preparation and Administration

In order to evaluate exploratory talk, reasoning, and problem-solving abilities, children were administered an adapted version of the Raven's Test of Progressive Matrices, before and after intervention, following Wegerif (1996). The original test consists of sixty logical-perceptual problems where subjects select one out of six to eight figures to complete a progressive matrix. Problems are divided into five scales from A to E, which increase in degree of difficulty. From this original version, two parallel, half-sized formats were prepared by assigning each successive problem to either format 1 or 2. Each parallel format was used as either a pre- or post-test. At the same time, during each testing period both versions of the test were administered, one functioning as an individual and the other as a small-group test (in triads). These versions were alternated for the pre- and post-tests. Each triad was composed of one child of high, one of middle, and one of low score, as assessed initially by the individual administration of the test. All triads were of mixed gender. For the microgenetic study, each of the six selected triads was video-recorded while solving the corresponding small-group test, during both pre- and post-tests. The talk children used while solving all the problems was subsequently transcribed verbatim, together with a detailed description of the context following Mercer (e.g., Edwards & Mercer, 1987; Mercer, 2000) (twelve transcriptions in total were analysed, six for the pretest and six for the post-test).

Intervention Programme

We developed a training programme that included a series of educational materials and procedures designed *ex-profeso*. The programme aimed to encourage children to use exploratory talk and was created by adapting culturally, linguistically, and to our school context the original programme called "Thinking Together" designed by Dawes, Mercer, and Wegerif (2000). The materials included games, texts, objects for experiments, activity cards, answer sheets, and software.

Experimental groups were exposed to this training programme, which lasted ten sessions over a period of five months, and was implemented between the pre- and post-tests. The aim was to promote children's use of exploratory talk, so that they could express and share their reasoning while they negotiated their perspectives to solve jointly diverse problems. Training was carried out by the respective group teacher, supported by one researcher. So teachers could implement the training programme, they first underwent training into how to apply it to their respective groups of children; teacher training followed procedures derived from a sociocultural perspective. Teachers subsequently applied the training programme with their respective students in the multipurpose room. During the sessions teachers encouraged their students first to "discover" and then to practice using the ground rules for exploratory talk while working together in small teams to solve a variety of problems. As mentioned in the introduction, the ground rules encouraged children to work collectively so they could present, explore, and negotiate alternatives for solving various problems, making their reasoning visible to others. In particular, the rules used for training the children promoted learning to express and share their ideas, to respect each other's points of view, to argue and justify their perspectives, to constructively criticise and ask others for justifications of their opinions, and to try to reach joint conclusions.

The sessions involved an introduction plenary followed by small-group work and ending with a closing plenary. During small-group work, children applied exploratory talk to different contexts and tasks to induce generalisation of the abilities promoted. Training of the strategies was not embedded within the existing curriculum.

Data Analysis

We developed a method for analysing peer interactions and discourse based on previous proposals developed by Wegerif and Mercer (e.g., 1996). The method takes into account social, discursive, and cognitive processes and their interactions. For that, it combines quantitative and qualitative observations (see Hammersley, 1986) to analyse interaction and discourse at different levels of abstraction and generality, relating the different levels of analysis to each other in a dynamic fashion.

Level I. Analysis of the Interaction

At this level we analyse in detail all the videos of the children interacting while solving the problems, together with the transcripts of all the verbal productions and nonverbal actions and context. These analyses allow us to have a first impression of the quality of the interaction, as well as the orientation of the children towards each other while solving the task. We also put forward some preliminary hypotheses about the types of talk that might be used by the participants to solve different problems.

Level II. Analysis of the Discourse

At this level we look more closely at the orientation children displayed towards each other, as reflected by their talk, when solving each problem. We carried out this analysis at two sublevels. At sublevel IIA, we analysed in detail the type of talk that was most predominantly used by each triad in solving each problem. We considered as a unit of analysis all the verbal exchanges taking place within each problem. For each unit, we characterised the type of talk predominantly used by considering the extent to which the children seemed to be following the ground rules underlying the different types of talk. In this report we present data particularly for exploratory talk. When analysing the data for this type of talk, we saw the need to make a further distinction between what we call "incipient exploratory talk" and "elaborate exploratory talk." The first one suggests exploratory talk is not very consistent nor very prominent in the way children talk, whereas the latter indicates exploratory talk is more consolidated and sophisticated. The Appendix at the end of the chapter presents the specific criteria used to decide whether the orientation predominantly exhibited by the children to solve a problem, on the basis of the underlying ground rules, corresponded to exploratory talk, as well as if this was incipient or elaborate. Using such criteria, we compared the scoring done by two independent judges in all twelve transcripts. We obtained an interobserver reliability measure of 85.5 percent on average (min. = 78.5 percent, max. = 89.3 percent), using the formula: [Agreements/(Agreements + Disagreements)] × 100.

Complementary, at sublevel IIB we looked at various features of the language used, including the speech acts implied by the talk, and particularly the use of arguments. We define an argument as the combination of an assertion plus one or more supports (see Billig, 1987; van Eemeren et al., 2000). All interventions related to the assertion and support(s) and with a unity of meaning and the same intention were considered part of the same argument. An argument finishes when there is a change of perspective. In order to quantify the number of arguments, we counted each argument produced by a child as he or she solved each problem in the test. Then we added up all the arguments produced in the thirty problems contained in the Raven's Test. In this chapter, we report the total number of arguments produced by the selected experimental and control triads during pre- and post-tests.

Level III. Analysis of Problem Solving

Lastly, at this level we looked at performance in group and individual problem solving. For this, we analysed the scores obtained in the Raven's Test in its group and individual versions.

In the next section we illustrate the types of analyses performed at each level and the results obtained in each, by reporting data at levels I, IIA, IIB and III.

RESULTS

Level I. Analysis of the Interaction

In order to illustrate the type of analysis performed at this level, in Figure 16.1 we present the dialogues of three sixth-grade children from the experimental group (one girl, Gala, and two boys, Leonardo and Misael) while they were solving two problems. The first problem (E8) corresponds to the pretest and the second (E9) to the post-test. These two problems are very similar in their degree of difficulty (they are adjacent in the series) and in the type of solution, because they both require that the child selects the elements that are repeated in the intersection of the first and second figure in the horizontal and vertical series of the matrix. That is, the correct figure is the one that contains all the elements that are overlapped when the first and second figures are put together.[1]

Briefly, both Raven items use a crosslike figure, which is embedded in other figures. In Matrix E8 (pretest), the figures are made of a combination of lines and curves, and the correct option is a cross embedded in a square. In Matrix E9 (post-test), the figures are made of straight lines and the correct option is a cross. The essence of the problem in each case is to put together the first two figures in each series and uncover which figure remains after eliminating all the features in both figures that do not overlap. In both matrices the problem relates to the difficulty that the crosslike figure that is the correct option is

---

[1] The original matrices from the Raven's Test cannot be reproduced in Figure 16.1 due to copyright limitations. Please refer to Matrix E8 in the original test to relate to the dialogue corresponding to the pretest – left side, and to Matrix E9 in the same test to relate to the dialogue corresponding to the post-test – right side .

matrix E8
Pre-test

Dialogue produced by the triad while solving problem E8 during pre-test (Response chosen = 2 - incorrect. Correct response = 6).

Leonardo: Which is best?
Gala: Mmmmm.
Leonardo: Here I think it can be this one (points to one option)
Gala: This one (points to another option).
Misael: This one (points to another option).
Misael: (to Leonardo) Ahhh, why?
Leonardo: Oh, no, it's this one (points to another option).
Gala: This one, number two (points at number 2).
Misael: Number 2.
Leonardo: Yes, look (points at figure number 2).
Gala: Yes, come on, yes (writes down number 2).

Key of symbols:

(...)   Inaudible language.

//   Pause of more than two seconds.

]   Simultaneous talk.

matrix E9
Post-test

Dialogue produced by the same triad while solving problem E9 during post-test (Response chosen = 3 - correct).

Misael: Upps.
Leonardo: This one they put it on the other one (puts the pencil on his mouth).
Gala: Here (...) pss, pss. // and here they put a line (points).
Misael: Here they put a line.
Leopold: Aha, and here they removed the line (points).
Misael: Yes (nods).
Leonardo: Here they removed the line and they put it here (points).
Misael: Yes.
Leonardo: But here they removed them, they removed the two in the middle.
Misael: Yes.
Leonardo: (...) they tilted them (points to one option).
Gala: No, let's see, wait, it must be this one because look (removes the hand from the matrix and points to one option).
Misael: Number 8.
Leonardo: Number 7, no?
Gala: Number 7.
Leonardo: No because it's already there.
Gala: No because it's already there.
(Leonardo and Gala point at second figure at bottom of matrix).
Misael: It's already there.
Gala: Then it must be number 5.
Leonardo: No, it's already there.
Misael: It's already there.
Leonardo: It's number 8, but look (...) (points) // because they removed this (points at figure and then option number 8).
Gala: Here it would only be what is left.
Leonardo: But you see, they remove the lines, and there are three left, no?
Gala: Yes, because they remove this, pum, pum, pum, pum, pum, pum (points at parts of the figure) and only the
X remains (points at option number 3).
Leonardo: Number 3 then?.
Misael: Yes, because they remove this (...).
Leonardo: Yes, because they remove the lines.
Misael: Yes (writes down option number 3 on the answer sheet).

Figure 16.1. Dialogues produced by one experimental triad while solving equivalent problems during the pre- and post-tests.

hard to find because it is embedded in other configurations of lines and other shapes.

In the dialogue corresponding to the pretest, the three children simply propose different options (all incorrect) but without giving reasons for their choices. Then, even if Misael challenges Leonardo (with "why?"), the latter responds by changing his opinion but without providing a justification for either choice. Then Gala proposes option 2 and the other two children agree, and they write down number 2, which is incorrect. Here there are no arguments, and the reasoning is not visible in the talk; their talk is mainly cumulative.

In contrast, in the dialogue produced by the same triad in the post-test, the children make more visible their reasoning, as when Gala and Misael say "here they put a line" and Leonardo adds "and here they removed the line." Proposals are expressed and evaluated, as when Gala and Leonardo propose option number 5 and the three children conclude that it cannot be, because it is already in the matrix. Then the three children take turns offering several options and backing them with justifications, as when Gala proposes option number 3 and justifies her position ("Yes, because they remove this... and only the X remains"). The others support this option (which is correct) and provide their own reasoning, as when Leonardo says "Yes, because they remove the lines." Thus, throughout the interaction we can observe an orientation towards exploration of different perspectives and reflexion on the choices. They make their reasoning visible in the talk, with argumentations and co-construction of the solution to the problem. These features characterize elaborate exploratory talk, as defined under "Methods" (also see the Appendix).

Although the contrast and gains seem quite clear in this example, it would be valid to ask: how representative is this case of the talk observed for the whole corpus? The data corresponding to the production of exploratory talk by the six selected experimental and control triads during pre- and post-tests are presented in the next section.

Level II. Analysis of the Discourse

Figure 16.2 shows the percentage of matrices solved using each type of exploratory talk (incipient and elaborate) by each treatment group and in each test ($N = 18$). The figure also includes the chi-square obtained after comparing the test scores of each treatment group and its level of significance. It is important to notice that we considered each triad as one unit (and not each individual child) for carrying out these analyses. It is the triad working as one unit that solved each problem.

We can see that for the experimental groups there is a very substantial increase in their use of exploratory talk, and particularly the elaborate type, between the pre- and post-tests, with highly significant differences ($p < .0001$). In fact, in the post-test, exploratory talk became their most prominent style of interaction (for about 75 percent of all problems). In contrast, the control groups' use of exploratory talk was in general quite low (around 30 percent) and remained so between the pre- and post-tests (nonsignificant differences). Thus, in contrast to the control groups, the experimental groups made very substantial gains in their use of exploratory talk as a result of the training programme.

How did this increase in exploratory talk by the experimental groups relate to some linguistic features of their talk, such as the production of arguments?

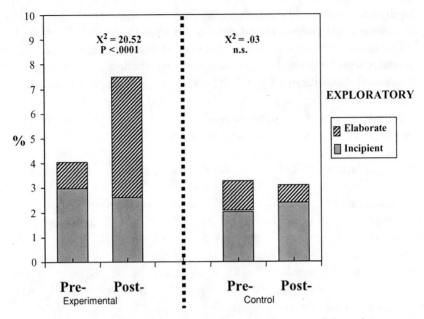

Figure 16.2. Percentage of matrices answered using exploratory talk by each treatment group in each test.

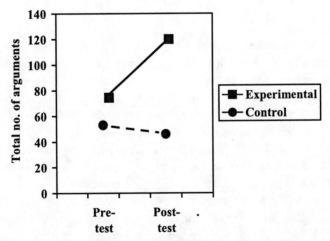

Figure 16.3. Total number of arguments produced by each treatment group in each test.

Figure 16.3 shows the number of arguments produced by the experimental and control groups during the pre- and post-tests.

During pretest both groups performed at a similar, low level, and their scores did not differ significantly ($\chi^2 = 5.57$, d.f. = 1, p > 0.05). In contrast, in the post-test, the experimental group produced significantly more arguments than the control group (almost three times as much: 117 vs. 46) ($\chi^2 = 6.48$, d.f. = 1, p < 0.05). These results indicate that training in exploratory talk produced a very positive effect in the experimental children's linguistic capacity, particularly for argumentation. At the same time, data not reported here showed that not only the quantity of arguments increased but also their quality. In particular, experimental children's arguments after training were more explicit, more coherent (with a greater use of linguistic markers), more clear, more precise, and more concise, and with the use of a wider variety of support statements to back up their opinions (for further details on these data, see Rojas-Drummond & Peón, 2004).

In summary, the data showed that the experimental groups in contrast to the control groups increased very substantially their use of exploratory talk, and particularly the more sophisticated type, after training. This improvement was accompanied by a substantial increase in the quantity (and quality) of production of arguments. Thus, training facilitated children's confronting problems from various perspectives, sustaining different positions, negotiating points of view, and supporting opinions with justifications before arriving at a solution. How did these linguistic gains relate to performance in problem solving?

Level III. Analysis of Problem Solving

In order to assess the effects of the two main factors under study, namely Treatment and Tests, as well as their interactions, on children's capacity for problem solving, two separate analyses of variance (ANOVA) were carried out. The scores obtained in each version of the Raven's Test, small-group and individual, were treated as separate dependent variables. Table 16.1 contains the results of these analyses.

Figures 16.4 and 16.5 illustrate these results visually by showing the mean scores obtained by each treatment group in each test, for the small-group and individual versions of the Raven's Test, respectively.

For the small-group version of the Raven's Test, the ANOVA resulted in significant effects for both of the main factors. However, the also highly significant effect for the interaction between these factors (p <.0005) indicates the need to interpret their effects in combination. This interaction can be clearly appreciated in Figure 16.4: in the pretest both the experimental and control groups performed very similarly. In contrast, in the post-test the experimental groups increased substantially, while the control groups remained at a similar level as that in the pretest.

Table 16.1. Analysis of variance for treatment and tests and dependent variables: Individual and small-group Raven's scores

Factor and test	df	SS	MS	F	Level of significance
Treatment					
Individual	1	4.20	4.20	.21	
S-group	1	240.99	240.99	78.20	***
Tests					
Individual	1	.08	.08	.01	
S-group	1	225.67	225.67	157.29	***
Treatment by Tests					
Individual	1	86.55	86.55	15.73	***
S-group	1	75.08	75.08	52.33	***
Residual					
Individual	80	440.14	5.50		
S-group	92	132	1.43		

*** $p < .0005$

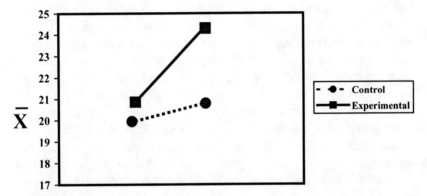

Figure 16.4. Mean scores obtained by each treatment group in the pre- and post-tests. Small-group Raven's Test.

For the individual version, the ANOVA resulted in no significant effects for the main factors but a highly significant effect for the interaction between them ($p < .0005$). This interaction becomes evident in Figure 16.5: while the children in the experimental groups increased very substantially between the pre- and the post-test, the children in the control groups actually decreased between these same tests. Thus, the intervention programme implemented in the experimental group resulted in significant improvements in children's problem-solving capacities at both group and individual levels. No such effects were found for the control group.

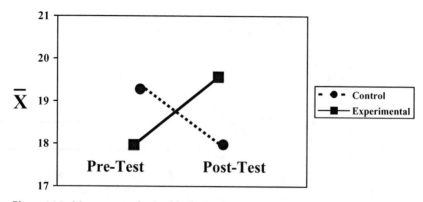

Figure 16.5. Mean scores obtained by each treatment group in the pre- and post-tests. Individual Raven's Test.

DISCUSSION

The results of the present study illustrate the intricate relations holding between language and reasoning in social and educational contexts, supporting a sociocultural perspective to explain the functioning of these processes and their interactions (e.g., Cole, 1996; Coll, 1988, 1990; Mercer, 1995, 2000; Rogoff, 1990; Vygotsky, 1962, 1978; Wertsch, 1985a, 1995b; 1991, 1998). The contexts analysed included small groups of peers solving problems jointly, as well as children solving problems individually. Specifically, our results confirm sociocultural claims made by authors like Mercer and Wegerif (e.g., Mercer, 1995, 2000; Mercer et al., 1999; Wegerif & Mercer, 2000) that language, when used effectively, can function as a powerful tool to facilitate reasoning in social contexts. Among other effects, exploratory talk would seem to have facilitated the creation of an "intermental development zone" by the children when interacting for solving problems jointly (Mercer, 2000). When creating this zone, children's dialogues work as a scaffold to support their joint efforts at reasoning and problem solving, helping each other to reach higher levels of understanding than those they might have achieved by themselves. This perspective has led us to reconceptualise the original concept of scaffolding, which was supposed to facilitate learning mainly between experts and novices (e.g., Rogoff, 1990; Wood, Bruner, & Ross, 1976). Thus, we have extended this concept to account also for peers' interactions and mutual support through effective communication (see Fernández et al., 2001).

In addition, the study illustrates how exploratory talk can serve as an effective tool to enhance children's solving of problems not only collectively but also, and importantly, individually. The latter effect seems particularly difficult to achieve. For example, in the previous study by Rojas-Drummond et al. (2000) reviewed in the introduction, we found group but not individual facilitation of problem solving after training in exploratory talk. Facilitation not only of group but also of individual problem solving, as found in the present study, suggests internalisation and/or appropriation of exploratory talk as an effective tool by the children who underwent training. Thus, they could use this tool adequately not only when interacting with their peers but also when working by themselves, that is, in a self-regulated fashion (Leontiev, 1981; Mercer, 1992; Rojas-Drummond et al., 1998).

The results presented provide answers to the research questions originally posed: (a) the intervention programme implemented had a very positive effect in improving significantly the ability of some Mexican primary school children to use exploratory talk; (b) this improvement had a very positive effect in children's linguistic capacities, and particularly in that for argumentation, enhancing not only quantitatively but also qualitatively the type of arguments children produced; and (c) promotion of exploratory talk resulted, in turn, in improvement of reasoning and group and individual problem-solving in the children. The enhancement of children's capacity for argumentation is a very important outcome of our intervention programme because, as argued in the introduction, learning processes by which we acquire knowledge of the world, by which we overcome our difficulties in comprehension, and by which we renovate and extend our language are all supported in argumentation (Habermas, 1984). Similarly, argumentation is essential for the acquisition and use of scientific knowledge (Candela, 1999).

In conclusion, our findings confirmed previous studies carried out by researchers such as Mercer, Wegerif, and Dawes in British primary schools (e.g., Dawes et al., 2000; Mercer et al., 1999; Wegerif & Dawes, 2004; Wegerif, Mercer, & Dawes, 1999). This confirmation refers to the potential facilitative effects of exploratory talk on problem solving, both at the group and individual levels. Thus, their conclusions do not seem to apply exclusively to British populations; we found similar results in a very different cultural, linguistic, and educational context. This implies that their original findings are fairly robust.

A confirmation of these findings in such a different cultural context is important because the sociocultural claim that language can work as a powerful tool for reasoning both socially and individually is often made but seldom tested empirically. Similarly, results seem to support sociocultural assumptions that acquisition of many psychological functions follows a path from social to individual regulation. In this trajectory, language plays a central role as a mediating tool for activity at both the interpsychological or social plane that facilitates communication, as well as at the intrapsychological or psychological plane, functioning as a tool for self-regulation, which represents a "voice of the mind" (Mercer, 2000; Vygotsky, 1978; Wertsch, 1991).

Thus, results from our study, as well as those of our British colleagues provide confirmation of the preceding claims for two very different cultures and languages, with two very different pedagogical traditions. Exploratory talk would seem to be more akin to the British than to the Mexican pedagogical tradition, and yet we managed to obtain somewhat similar results for both cultures. These results have led the British and Mexican teams of researchers to carry out, among other analyses of our corresponding results, various cross-cultural comparisons (e.g., Wegerif et al., 2005).

As described in previous sections, some of our methods for analysing and promoting exploratory talk, reasoning, and problem solving among primary school children represent linguistic, cultural, and contextual adaptations of those originally developed by Mercer, Wegerif, and Dawes for British populations (e.g., Dawes et al., 2000; Mercer et al., 1999; Wegerif & Mercer, 1996). The adapted analytical methods proved adequate for characterising the types of talk that commonly occur among children when solving problems jointly and could be used by other researchers for similar purposes. Similarly, the methods developed for analysing interaction, discourse, and reasoning at different levels of abstraction and generality, and combining quantitative and qualitative observations, proved very fruitful for providing rich, varied, and complementary data and could be employed for carrying out further studies in these areas. At the same time, the methods employed to promote discursive and cognitive abilities in the students represent useful guidelines into how we can design educational environments to promote the use of better tools for social communication as well as for collective and individual reasoning. Such environments could contribute importantly to improving the quality of the teaching-learning process. Furthermore, they can represent an essential factor to endow children with more effective social, discursive, and cognitive tools to enable them to participate more competently and independently as members of their community inside and outside of the school context.

APPENDIX: CRITERIA FOR CLASSIFYING EXPLORATORY TALK

Exploratory Talk

Exploratory talk is characterised by the social construction of ideas and a group orientation towards the solution of the task. The participants work together, expressing their reasoning to the others for consideration. Participants are able to change their mind if someone else makes an argument. They search together different and new alternatives for the task solution and explain their argument to support their opinions. The communicative intention is to explore different perspectives, to negotiate and eventually to be able to reach consensus. From this frame two types of exploratory talk are distinguished:

Incipient Exploratory Talk

Rudimentary arguments are found related to the task, followed by a point of encounter with a statement by another child. This encounter is an opinion without arguments. Rudimentary arguments are often supported in deixis – for example, "... because look" (pointing out) – in which the opinion can be implicit in the discourse but present in the child's actions. No more than two options are considered. The exploratory orientation is not maintained along the discourse (a systematic); consensus is not necessarily reached.

Elaborate Exploratory Talk

This type exhibits the incipient exploratory talk criteria, as well as at least one of the following:

- A participant gives an opinion, and there is a point of encounter with a statement from another child or with all members, which leads to a reelaboration of the first idea.
- An opinion is presented and followed by a challenge – for example, "... why?" – and by an argument, which is responded to with a counterargument.
- Two or more perspectives are considered, and at least one of them is argued and elaborated – that is, the opinion is supported by making the reasoning visible in the talk.

References

Andrews, R. (1995). *Teaching and learning argument*. New York: Cassell.
Andrews, R., Clarke, S., & Costello, P. (1993). *Improving the quality of argument, 5–16: Final report*. Hull: University of Hull, School of Education, Centre for Studies in Rhetoric.
Barnes, D., Britton J., & Torbe, M. (1990). *Language, the learner and the school*. Portsmouth, NH: Boynton/Cook.

Billig, M. (1987). *Arguing and thinking: A rhetoric approach to social psychology.* Cambridge: Cambridge University Press.

Bronckart, J. P. (1992). El discurso como acción: Por nuevo paradigma psicolingüístico. *Anuario de Psicología* (Universidad de Barcelona), *54*, 3–48.

Brown, A., & Reeve, R. (1987). Bandwidths of competence: The role of supportive contexts in learning and development. In L. Liben (Ed.), *Development and learning: Conflict or congruence?* (pp. 173–223). Hillsdale, NJ: Lawrence Erlbaum.

Bruner, J. (1990). *Acts of meaning.* Cambridge, MA: Harvard University Press.

Candela, A. (1990). Investigación etnográfica en el aula: el razonamiento de lo alumnos en una clase de ciencias naturales en la escuela primaria. *Investigación en la Escuela, 13*, 13–23.

Candela, A. (1995). Consensus construction as a collective task in Mexican science classes. *Anthropology and Education Quarterly, 26* (4), 1–17.

Candela, A. (1997). Demonstrations and problem-solving exercises in school science: Their transformation within the Mexican elementary school classroom. *Science Education, 81*, 497–513.

Candela, A. (1999). *Ciencia en el aula. Los alumnos entre la argumentación y el consenso.* México, D.F: Paidós Mexicana.

Cole, M. (1985). The zone of proximal development: Where culture and cognition create each other. In J. Wertsch (Ed.), *Culture, communication and cognition: Vygotskian perspective* (pp. 146–161). Cambridge: Cambridge University Press.

Cole, M. (1996). *Cultural psychology: A once and future discipline.* Cambridge, MA: Harvard University Press.

Coll, C. (1988). Significado y sentido en el aprendizaje escolar: Reflexiones en torno al concepto de aprendizaje significativo. *Infancia y Aprendizaje, 41*, 131–142.

Coll, C. (1990). *Aprendizaje escolar y construcción del conocimiento.* Barcelona: Paidós.

Coll, C., & Edwards, D. (Eds.). (1996). *Teaching, learning and classroom discourse.* Madrid: Infancia y Aprendizaje.

Coll, C., Palacios, G., & Marchesi, A. (Comp.). (2001). *Desarrollo psicológico y educación: Vol. 2. Psicología de la Educación Escolar.* Madrid: Alianza.

Dawes, L., Mercer, N., & Wegerif, R. (2000). *Thinking together: A programme of activities for developing thinking skills at KS2.* Birmingham: Questions Publishing.

Edwards, D., & Mercer, N. (1987). *Common Knowledge: The development of understanding in the classroom.* London: Methuen/Routledge.

Elbers, E., Maier, R., Hoekstra, T., & Hoogsteder, M. (1992). Internalisation and adult-child interaction. *Learning and Instruction, 2*, 101–118.

Feinman, S. (1992). An integrative look at social referencing. In S. Feinman (Ed.), *Social referencing and the social construction of reality in infancy* (pp. 3–14). New York: Plenum.

Fernández, M., Wegerif, R., Mercer, N., & Rojas-Drummond, S. M. (2001). Reconceptualizing "scaffolding" and the zone of proximal development in the context of symmetrical collaborative learning. *Journal of Classroom Interaction, 36* (2) and *37* (1), 40–54.

Forman, E., & Cazden, C. (1985). Exploring Vygotskian perspectives in education: The cognitive value of peer interaction. In J. Wertsch (Ed.), *Culture, communication and cognition: Vygotskian perspectives* (pp. 323–347). Cambridge: Cambridge University Press.

Freedman, A., & Pringle, I. (1984). Why students can't write arguments. *English in Education*, *18* (2), 73–84.

Gergen, K. J. (1992). *El yo saturado: Dilemas de identidad en el mundo contemporáneo*. Barcelona: Paidós Iberica.

Habermas, J. (1984). *The theory of communicative action: Reason and the rationalization of society*. London: Heinemann.

Hammersley, M. (1986). Revisiting Hamilton and Delamont: A cautionary note on the relationship between "systematic observation" and ethnography. In M. Hammersley (Ed.), *Controversies in classroom research* (pp. 44–48). Milton Keynes: Open University Press.

Hicks, D. (Ed.). (1996). *Discourse, learning and schooling*. Cambridge: Cambridge University Press.

Jadallah, E. (2000). Constructivist learning experiences for social studies and education. *Social Studies*, *91* (5), 221–226.

King, A. (1994). Guiding knowledge construction in the classroom: Effects of teaching children how to question and how to explain. *American Educational Research Journal*, *27* (4), 664–687.

King, A. (1995). Inquiring minds really do want to know: Using questioning to teach critical thinking. *Teaching of psychology*, *22*, 13–17.

Kraf, R. G. (1975). The dead of argument. *College English*, *36* (5), 548–551.

Lave, J. (1991). *La cognición en la práctica*. Barcelona: Paidós.

Lemke, J. (1993). *Talking science: Language, learning and values*. Norwood, NJ: Ablex.

Leontiev, A. (1981). *Problems of the development of mind*. Moscow: Progress.

Light, P., & Butterworth, G. (Eds.). (1992). *Context and cognition: Ways of learning and knowing*. Hertfordshire: Harvester Wheatsheaf.

Maybin, J. (1994). Children's voices: Talk knowledge and identity. In D. Graddol, J. Maybin, & B. Stierer (Eds.), *Researching language and literacy in social context* (pp. 131–150). Milton Keynes: Open University Press.

Mercer, N. (1992). Culture, context and the construction of knowledge in the classroom. In P. Light & G. Butterworth (Eds.), *Context and cognition: Ways of learning and knowing* (pp. 28–46). Hertfordshire: Harvester Wheatsheaf.

Mercer, N. (1995). *The guided construction of knowledge: Talk amongst teachers and learners*. Clevedon: Multilingual Matters.

Mercer, N. (1996). The quality of talk in children's collaborative activity in the classroom. *Learning and Instruction*, *6* (4), 359–375.

Mercer, N. (2000). *Words and minds: How we use language to think together*. London: Routledge.

Mercer, N., & Edwards, D. (1981). Ground-rules for mutual understanding: A social psychological approach to classroom knowledge. In N. Mercer (Ed.), *Language in school and community* (pp. 30–46). London: E. Arnold.

Mercer, N., Wegerif, R., & Dawes, L. (1999). Children's talk and the development of reasoning in the classroom. *British Educational Research Journal*, *25* (1), 95–112.

Newman, D., Griffin, P., & Cole, M. (1989). *The construction zone*. Cambridge: Cambridge University Press.

Rabinow, P., & Sullivan, W. (1979). *Interpretive social science: A second look*. Berkeley: University of California Press.

Rogoff, B. (1990). *Apprenticeship in thinking: Cognitive development in social context.* Oxford: Oxford University Press.

Rojas-Drummond, S., & Alatorre, J. (1994). The development of independent problem solving in pre-school children. In N. Mercer & C. Coll (Eds.), *Explorations in socio-cultural studies: Vol. 3. Teaching, learning and interaction* (pp. 161–175). Madrid: Infancia y Aprendizaje.

Rojas-Drummond, S., & Peón, M. (2004). Exploratory talk, argumentation and reasoning in Mexican primary school children. *Language and Education, 18* (6), 539–557.

Rojas-Drummond, S., Fernández, M., & Vélez, M. (2000). Habla exploratoria, razonamiento conjunto y solución de problemas en niños de primaria. In *La Psicología Social en México* (Vol. 8, pp. 403–410). México, D.F.: Asociación Mexicana de Psicología Social.

Rojas-Drummond, S., Hernández, G., Velez, M., & Villagrán, G. (1998). Cooperative learning and the appropriation of procedural knowledge by primary school children. *Learning and Instruction, 8* (1), 37–62.

Serra, M., Serrat, E., Solé, R., Bel, A., & Aparici, M. (2000). *La Adquisición del Lenguaje.* Barcelona: Aril.

Solomon, G. (Ed.). (1993). *Distributed cognitions: Psychological and educational considerations.* Cambridge: Cambridge University Press.

Spears, R. (1996). Discourse analysis. In A. Manstead & M. Hewstone (Eds.), *The Blackwell Encyclopaedia of Social Psychology* (pp. 120–145). Oxford: Blackwell.

van Eemeren, F. H., Grootendorst, R, Jackson, S., & Jacobs, S. (2000). Argumentación. In T. A. van Dijk (Ed.), *El discurso como estructura y proceso* (pp. 305–333). Barcelona: Gedisa.

Vygotsky, L. S. (1962). *Thought and language.* Cambridge, MA: MIT Press.

Vygotsky, L. S. (1978). *Mind in society: The development of higher psychological processes.* Cambridge, MA: Harvard University Press.

Wegerif, R. (1996). Using computers to help coach exploratory talk across the curriculum. *Computers and Education, 26* (1–3), 51–60.

Wegerif, R., & Dawes, L. (2004). *Thinking and learning with ICT: Raising achievement in primary classrooms.* London: Routledge Falmer.

Wegerif, R., & Mercer, N. (1996). Computers and reasoning through talk in the classroom. *Language and Education, 10* (1), 47–64.

Wegerif, R., & Mercer, N. (2000). Language for thinking: A study of children solving reasoning test problems together. In H. Cowie & G. Aalsvoort (Ed.), *Social interaction and learning and instruction: The meaning of discourse for the construction of knowledge* (pp. 179–192). Amsterdam: Pergamon.

Wegerif, R., Mercer, N., & Dawes, L. (1999). From social interaction to individual reasoning: An empirical investigation of a possible socio-cultural model of cognitive development. *Learning and Instruction, 9,* (6), 493–516.

Wegerif, R., Perez, J., Rojas-Drummond, S., Mercer, N., & Velez, M. (2005). Thinking together in the U.K. and México: Transfer of an educational innovation. *Journal of Classroom Interaction, 40* (1), 40–48.

Wegerif, R., & Scrimshaw, P. (1997). Introduction: Computers, talk and learning. In R. Wegerif, & P. Scrimshaw (Eds.), *Computers and talk in the primary classroom* (pp. 1–18). Clevedon: Multilingual Matters.

Wells, G. (1999). *Dialogic enquiry: Towards a sociocultural practice and theory of education*. Cambridge: Cambridge University Press.

Wertsch, J. (Ed.). (1985a). *Culture, communication and cognition: Vygotskian perspectives*. Cambridge: Cambridge University Press.

Wertsch, J. (1985b). *Vygotsky and the social formation of mind*. Cambridge, MA: Harvard University Press.

Wertsch, J. (1991). *Voices of the mind: A sociocultural approach to mediate action*. Cambridge, MA: Harvard University Press.

Wertsch, J. (1998). *Mind as action*. New York: Oxford University Press.

Wertsch, J., Del Río, P., & Álvarez, A. (Eds.). (1995). *Sociocultural studies of mind*. Cambridge: Cambridge University Press.

Wilkinson, A. (1986). Argument as a primary act of mind. *Educational Review, 38* (2), 127–138.

Wood, D., Bruner, J., & Ross, G. (1976). The role of tutoring in problem-solving. *Journal of Child Psychology and Child Psychiatry, 17,* 89–100.

17

What Kinds of Tools and Resources Are Made Available to Students through Effective Guidance in a Student-Scientist Partnership Program?

Jrène Rahm, Wendy Naughton, and John C. Moore

Partnerships between scientists and students have a long history (John-Steiner, 2000; Pycior, Slack, & Abir-Am, 1996; Tinker, 1997). Typically, through joint activity over prolonged periods of time, old and new ways of thinking are being developed. Given the recognition that "generative ideas emerge from joint thinking, from significant conversations, and from sustained, shared struggles to achieve new insights by partners in thought" (John-Steiner, 2000, p. 3), such models of education also figure prominently in current reform-oriented educational efforts (e.g., Barab & Duffy, 2000; Brown, Collins, & Duguid, 1989; Collins, Brown, & Holum, 1991; Hennessy, 1993; Lave, 1996; Lave & Wenger, 1991; McGinn & Roth, 1999; Richmond & Kurth, 1999). Yet there is a paucity of research on how such ways of knowing and becoming are perceived by students and how they come to influence students' future endeavors.

A second area of concern centers on the low rates of participation of students from different ethnic, racial, cultural, and socioeconomic groups in science and mathematics disciplines, hereafter referred to collectively as underrepresented students. Much has been published on these disparities and the putative reasons behind them (Atwater, 2000; Mortensen, 1995; Oakes, Muir, & Joseph, 2000; Steele, 1997; Tobin, Seiler, & Walls, 1999). Against this backdrop are myriad programs that involve creative collaborations aimed at

The authors wish to thank the students, staff, and parents of COSMOS – the UNC Math and Science Upward Bound Program. Special thanks to E. Bilsky, H. Horton, K. Mallory, K. Melville, C. Peterson, C. Pritekel, and A. Whittemore-Olson for serving as mentors, and to the UNC Departments of Biological Sciences, Chemistry and Biochemistry, and Physics for the use of their facilities. Special thanks also to Michael Opferman for help with data collection and Danielle Nipe for help with data analysis. This work was supported in part by grants from the U.S. Department of Education (P047M 990093–00), the U.S. National Science Foundation (ESI-0119786), and the University of Northern Colorado.

exposing underrepresented students to the cultures of science and mathematics in the hopes of encouraging these students to pursue careers in these disciplines. The performances of these programs in narrowing the disparity are generally summative in nature, providing limited insight into the reasons behind successes or failure (Crane, 1994). Few research studies on the intersection of the creative collaboration and the cultures of underrepresented students are available (for some exceptions, see Calabrese, 2003; Jones, 1997; Rahm et al., 2003; Sosniak, 1995).

While John-Steiner (2000) discusses creative collaborations where new knowledge is co-constructed, we use a similar conceptual approach to understand the value of collaborations between scientists and students for the development of science literacy. Unlike other studies of such partnerships (Barab & Hay, 2001; Richmond & Kurth, 1999; Richtie & Rigano, 1996), we are particularly interested in the students' contributions to and interpretations of such collaborations. Thereby, we aim to better understand the process that makes such partnerships successful in the eyes of the students (Rahm et al., 2003). To do so, we examine collaborations between scientists and students that are part of a six-week residential summer youth program for underrepresented students and that occur during the student's third year of participation.

In this chapter, we explore the kinds of literacies students developed through participation in the student-scientist partnerships. We focus on the nature of the partnerships and discuss the forms that guidance took as science was practiced. In line with the sociocultural-historical theory, it is assumed that for guidance to be effective, it has to occur within the zone of proximal development of the student. Yet effective guidance is also taken to be a highly contextualized, dynamic, and emergent phenomenon. For instance, the form guidance takes can have much to do with the kind of collaboration that comes to define the partnership, the nature of the project, and the students' expectations and beliefs about a project (Rahm et al., 2003). Subsequently, we address the kinds of resources and tools (technical and psychological) that the collaborations made available to the students. We speak of learning outcomes in terms of tools, given the assumption that what is appropriated through joint action will mediate students' future actions (Vygotsky, 1978; Wertsch, 1991).

PROGRAM DESCRIPTION

COSMOS is a Mathematics and Science Upward Bound program funded by the U.S. Department of Education through its TRIO initiatives. As such,

COSMOS is a voluntary longitudinal program involving a six-week residential summer program centering on hands-on research projects that teach students much about the process of science and the use of mathematics and technology as tools in that process. Students join the program as freshmen or sophomores at the age of fifteen and typically stay with it for three consecutive years (summers). The first year, students participate in an integrated math and science curriculum centering on ecosystems and chaos theory. They are given a number of projects, one of which they develop further into a final project that is presented to the whole program. The second year, students do sports physics and spend much time developing an understanding of the mathematics such physics entails. They are also responsible for the development of a project that deals with sports physics (e.g., physics of golfing, physics of a skateboard). In the third year, participants are given the opportunity to participate in a summer research internship. They work with graduate students and scientists and take part in ongoing research projects at the university (see Ebert-May et al., 2004). Monthly school visits, academic assignments, college application guidance, and field trips lend continuity to the program during the school year.

The program accepts students who are in ninth or tenth grade and who are first-generation college bound and/or low-income (annual salary at 150 percent poverty level or less, as defined by the U.S. Department of Education). At least 67 percent of the forty students in the summer of 2000 and the forty-five students in the summer of 2001 (years of this study) fit both categories. The student body is also gender balanced and ethnically diverse (approximately 42 percent European Americans, 40 percent Hispanic, and 18 percent Hmong and Vietnamese). The program, directed by the third author, is managed by seasonal instructional and residence staff and is staffed year-round by two full-time faculty, a part-time administrator, and a curriculum developer and supervisor.

DATA COLLECTION AND ANALYSIS

In this chapter, we rely on data gathered during the second year of a two-year qualitative case study of COSMOS that was initiated in 2000. We focus on the ten third-year students (seven males, three females; ranging in age from seventeen to eighteen years) who were taking part in the student-scientist partnership program. The first two authors of this chapter were involved in following these ten students with a video camera as they did science research. We collected video recordings of their work in laboratories and in the field, which were immediately supplemented with field notes, journals, and logs of the actual video recordings (Hall, 1999). We also interviewed all ten students and their mentors toward the end of the program to assess what the program came to mean to them. In this report, we focus primarily on data gathered through the student and mentor interviews – specifically, the students' and mentors' answers to questions about their perceptions of the mentorship program, their projects, the science they did, and the challenges they faced in accomplishing their projects.

Due to space limitations, we decided to focus on three of the five partnerships studied, namely: biochemistry (two students with two different mentors), ecology (two students with the third author as the mentor), and laser optics (one student with one mentor). Transcripts of interviews of these five students and their mentors were read and reread many times to gain a solid understanding of the form that guidance took in each collaboration and the tools that students could appropriate. Unique or interesting findings that emerged from analysis of these interviews led to further analysis of field notes, journals, and logs to get a broader perspective on how the collaborations developed and the tools and resources they made available. The first two authors of this chapter met several times during the analysis process to discuss preliminary findings, to decide on the best approach for analyzing the data, and to negotiate the final presentation of this analysis, steps typical of interaction analysis (Jordan & Henderson, 1995).

RESULTS

Nature of Projects and Forms of Guidance

The collaborations in biochemistry and ecology can be best described as *scientist-led* partnerships, because students participated in ongoing scientific investigations, whereas the project in physics was rather open-ended and *student-led*. Tinker (1997) also discusses the value of *scientist-guided* collaborations, a form of guidance that became apparent in biochemistry and ecology once the students were familiar with the scientific procedures and required less tight supervision, a form of guidance that was absent in the physics project.

For instance, in ecology, Tia and Hannah studied the effects of herbicide treatments on different sites in the Rocky Mountain National Park, a three-year project initiated by the third author and a colleague at the university. In many respects, Hannah and Tia were initiated into the team like any undergraduate or beginning graduate student in field ecology. They were provided an overview of the project objectives and a copy of the proposal that had been submitted to the park for the funding, and they were instructed to conduct their own review of the literature on the subject. Hannah and Tia played an important role in the beginning stages of the project in that they helped identify and set up three sites (each containing a control and a herbicide treated area), which made possible the collection of data on the vegetation (percent cover) and the extraction of soil samples for the eventual study of the presence of arthropods. In essence, Hannah and Tia were in charge of collecting and analyzing the first round of data – a procedure that was then repeated three times during the remainder of the year and the duration of study by the research team. Hannah and Tia were provided minilessons and vignettes on the field and laboratory techniques that they would have to master to complete the project, and in the process became familiar with running transect lines (setting of measurement tapes in a consistent manner) and the placing of the quadrat along these lines (a rectangle frame also referred to as Daubenmire square, named for its inventor) within which ground cover for a variety of categories could be identified, such as grasses, forbs, sedges, cacti, shrubs, litter, bare ground, and rocks. They also used soil cores to collect a number of soil samples along the transect lines in all the sites. These soil samples were then processed in the lab to extract the arthropods to be identified for further study under the microscope (Moore et al., 2000).

These activities were scientist-led. Data collection and analysis had to be conducted in a systematic manner to count as "real" data, a process that left little room for student transformation. At the same time, being involved in a "real" research project was perceived as valuable, as described by one of the students:

> TIA: It was hard and everything, and I might complain about it, but it was a lot of fun to actually be a part of something that is real . . . something that we are getting funds for to do research on. That is really cool to be able to be part of, you know, the soil lab work.

Tia's reference to the outside financial support for her research project reveals her understanding of a larger science community/hierarchy and also shows that she saw herself as a member of that community. Her final statement also indicates that she perceived herself to be an active contributor to the ecology research group in which she worked. She did not question the fact that the project was primarily scientist-led, but instead perceived it as an avenue to become part of such a community.

The collaborations in biochemistry were also scientist-led, yet for a different reason, as Monica's mentor summarized:

MENTOR: In Frank's lab there was always tight supervision because we were working with narcotics. And, so you'd never leave the kids alone with ecstasy or morphine, or cocaine, which is a lot of the things we use [in the research]. So, for, uh, that mentor it was tight supervision throughout the whole thing, but more and more repetitious and independent work was also involved in terms of their writing, their, um, data collection, after injections were done . . . stuff like that.

Hence, the form of guidance had much to do with the kind of project students were engaged in. Tia, Hannah, Monica, and Edric participated in well-defined projects. Furthermore, Monica and Edric worked with chemicals that demanded tight supervision. They examined the analgesic potency and efficacy of different opioid peptides for pain relief under guidance of two different graduate students and a scientist. They tested the effectiveness of drugs that produce analgesia just like morphine but without its negative side effects. In both projects, mice were injected with opioids and then their pain resistance assessed using a variety of conventional methods. Both students became familiar with the specific procedures for the injections of chemicals, the actual data collection protocols, and data analysis procedures. They also learned much about the chemicals they tested and how the chemicals had to be prepared and administered to the mice. Despite tight supervision in this laboratory, Edric described his collaboration and the mentor's role in very positive terms:

EDRIC: He's played a big role. Uh, he, he's right there with me when I struggled sometimes. I'm the only one in that lab that could do injections the first week I was there. So right away they trusted me like that, you know. So they were just giving me orders and I was carrying them out. And you know, do this, do that, and he's been there, he's been there, you know, helping me with my project, helping with the slides. He helped me watch the mice uh, stretch out . . . so he's been a good help.

For Edric, it was important to have his mentor around. It gave him a sense of belonging and facilitated the development of a trusting relationship, which was crucial for the success of the kind of work that had to be accomplished. Despite much guidance in this laboratory, Monica still perceived the work as challenging:

MONICA: Well um our learning was kind of we started our project right away we had to I think learn a little bit more in depth. Then it was kind of more on your own than in the beginning . . . we didn't have the class where you went and learned about what you were gonna do and then you could do projects about it, you were just kinda thrown into it there like here you go. Here's this and this and this and this and learn about what you're gonna do so.

As Monica's statement illustrates, she did not question the amount of guidance she received. What was challenging for her, however, was the new role it demanded of her as a learner. She had to master the subject matter in greater depth than in school, while she also had to learn through practice. As described by Lave (1996, p. 151) in a somewhat different context, "the apprentices were learning many complex 'lessons' at once." There was no longer a teacher who taught them. Instead, they "were just kinda thrown into it" and worked at the elbows of an expert right away. Given such a new way of learning and doing, the tight supervision was not perceived as negative or challenging but was appreciated and taken as essential.

Interestingly, the project in laser optics was much more open-ended and student-led. An undergraduate student in physics offered to mentor Joe in laser optics and holography, something that was new to both of them. Joe received little guidance from the professor in charge of this laboratory and also did not pursue projects that were ongoing in that lab. Instead, Joe made use of the lab equipment to pursue his own interest in laser optics. His project had two main objectives: to assemble a helium/neon (HeNe) laser, and to generate a hologram, which involved using a laser and properly setting up a laser table. Joe worked independently on the first objective, and with minimal guidance he succeeded in assembling a working laser. Joe and his mentor collaborated more on the second objective: creating a hologram. Because it was the first time that either Joe or his mentor had taken on such a task, it proved to be very challenging. Several attempts were made to create the hologram, which involved modifying the set-up of the laser table (adjusting angles, changing filters, slit lengths, etc.), trying two different types of lasers, and using different types of film. Unfortunately, they failed to create a hologram by the end of the summer. Joe described the co-construction of knowledge that came to define his partnership:

> JOE: Most challenging [about my project]? I would say shooting the holo-
> gram, because both my mentor and I had never done it before. He had
> worked with lasers and objects, but he didn't know how to shoot the
> hologram. So, we both had to read up on it. And, uh, so that was kind
> of challenging, I mean in a way, we were both learning from each other.

Joe's comment that they "were both learning from each other" suggests that he did not perceive lack of expertise as a serious handicap, even though he did refer to it as a challenge. That challenge was further amplified when he consulted his uncle who "shoots holograms." The advice he received contradicted what Joe and his mentor had been trying to do in the lab. Joe also noted that they could not act upon it due to lack of time:

> JOE: I kinda wish I had somebody that was more experienced so they could be like, "Well, you know, this is how I set it up." I was talking with my uncle and he just said a bunch of things that . . . Well, I asked him "How was yours set up?" and he said something that was totally different from what we had. He was all "You might want to try that" and he was like "It took me three weeks to set it up." I was like "Well, we've got two days."

In the end, the hologram never worked, something Joe and his mentor were disappointed about. Despite such an outcome, Joe highly valued his experience and the freedom he was given to pursue something of interest to him. As shown, Joe received tighter supervision at the beginning, as he was introduced to the physics behind laser optics and later to heliography. At the same time, the actual assembly of the laser required little supervision as long as he followed the instructions that came with the kit. Like most other students, he had much freedom in developing his project presentation.

Despite such variations in the kind and amount of guidance, most mentors were surprised by the time commitment such a job entailed, as voiced by Harry who was part of the ecology lab:

> HARRY: I just had no idea that I would be putting in the hours that I would be doing. And, and, it's not that there was a lot of hand-holding that needed to be done. But there was some in some spots. But most of that was not that they didn't know, it's just 'cause they'd never done it before. And once you'd show them how to do it, well then, they were like, "Why are you still here? Let me, let me do this." And then it was hard for me to step away from that and not want to kind of lean over their shoulder and look at what they're doing and stuff. That was hard to not just sit through it with them the whole way, but to let them fumble through it themselves and then come back.

According to Harry, students needed most guidance as they acquired a new skill. Yet, once they mastered it, they were ready to challenge the form guidance took and preferred to "fumble through it themselves." It was difficult for the mentors to step back and let go of their leadership. Yet for the students to come to own their projects, such an approach was essential. As illustrated, collaborations were mutually beneficial in that they helped mentors see the students in new ways while giving them a way to become part of the real world of science. For these reasons, guidance is also best understood as a dynamic process determined in a complex manner by the nature of the project, the nature of the collaboration, the expertise of the students and mentors in the subject area, and the students' and mentors' perceptions of their roles in the project. By looking at three projects, we have made some of these dimensions explicit. We now turn to ways in which such variations came to determine the kinds of tools and resources these partnerships made available to the students.

Tools and Resources That the Students Could Appropriate

Even though we are interested in the science literacies students developed through participation in these projects, these appear secondary to the new ways of learning and being a learner that the collaborations made possible. Not surprisingly, Edric among others, described the program as a physical and emotional challenge – physical given the amount of work that had to be accomplished, and emotional, given the struggles he experienced in "sticking through" with a project in times of difficulties. Naomi experienced the same challenges:

> NAOMI: [The students] understand now the meaning of hard work and dedication and putting it to something that they love. Every single one of them loved their projects. And they took pride in their projects. And it made me very proud to see that they were willing to put in the extra mile to get their project done and at a level that they and I would be proud of, and more importantly, that they would be proud of. Um, they learned dedication. They learned hard work. They learned commitment. They learned time management.

While many other learning outcomes could be noted, we briefly examine in what ways the scientist-led and student-led collaborations resulted in students' dedication to their projects, hard work, and commitment.

Doing was an important variable for both Hannah and Tia. Initially, they struggled with their project in ecology:

> HANNAH: What actually happened to me was that I didn't want to go into anything that dealt with plants. But, once I was in it and once I was doing it, I had fun. . . . I liked it better than I did before I did it.

TIA: Well, I didn't go into the project really too interested. I was kind of nervous about it because I wanted to do something more, like, in terms of the medical field. But what interested me was probably when Amy started showing us the mites and things, and then I started to like it more.

Getting involved was a means to draw both of them into the project and essential for their eventual commitment, hard work, and project dedication. The comments also reveal a common epiphany that scientists undergo during their careers as they cast aside stereotypes and begin to understand that science is about discovery and problem solving, and that the joy comes from this process. It certainly helps to be interested in the topic, but good research questions, regardless of the field, hold and attract interest. Edric also valued the fact that he was actively involved and had the opportunity to do "real" research, yet for a different reason:

EDRIC: Well, [I liked] everything [about the partnership program]. You know, I'm working with a new drug that, that might make it out into the market one day. That would be cool, if it comes out one day, and you know, I worked on that drug... bragging rights. That'd be cool. I like that.

Edric understood the value of his research for the community and felt proud to be involved in something that might eventually make a difference in people's lives. Unlike Hannah and Tia, he was able to perceive the value of his work beyond its immediate context and in remarkably complex terms, both to society and to himself.

The *challenges* and *hard work* the students faced were also crucial for making the collaborations successful in the end. For instance, Edric emphasized the difficulty of sticking through with his project:

EDRIC: Actually, doing the project, like, um, there was something wrong with the drug and it wouldn't work. And we struggled for like a week. So I lost a week there. That's been the most challenging. – Sticking through it. 'Cause I flat out wanted to quit.... And I told her that. But, but we got it to work. – most challenging part is like, actually sticking through the, you know, going with it, seeing what happens. And it was hard, but I did it for some reason.

Edric thought it made him think of science and scientists in new ways, "I have a little bit more respect for the people that like it 'cause it's harder than most people think." Similarly, Hannah described how her experience in

COSMOS has given her a new understanding of what is required of scientists when they do research:

> HANNAH: [Scientists] spend a lot of their time doing research.... I never really knew. Because you look up on the Internet, and they don't really say that much about it. Except just the job requirements and what you have to do and stuff like that. They never really tell you how much time and how much they devote to it.

Hannah realized that even though she had previously used the Internet to find out about careers, she did not really understand how much scientists invest in their research until she became an active participant in this program. Her own experiences doing research enabled her to have such a revelation. In addition, we often observed Hannah questioning scientists and graduate students about what was required of them in order to "do their job." Hannah's understanding of the hard work that accompanies science was contextualized and processed in terms of how it might affect her future career.

Tia, on the other hand, presented a much more immediate and personal discussion of the hard work that accompanies science when she was asked about the most challenging part of the program:

> TIA: Not being able to have as much social time with everyone. We had to get our work finished and research. Like at the camping trip, we couldn't really hang out that much. We just did our work the whole day and that was probably the worst part of the whole thing.

At another point in the interview, Tia said that she sees her role in COSMOS as being "cheap labor." These two statements reveal the fact that Tia struggled with the amount of work that was required of her in the program. The second statement also shows that Tia was aware of the hierarchy that existed within the program and within her research group, but unlike Edric she did not convey an understanding that the experience was of immediate benefit to her or her career plans. If Tia believed that the main outcome of her hard work was the benefit of others, it is not surprising that she had a difficult time getting excited about the large amount of work that was required of her. Tia's understandings and feelings about this hierarchy are not much different from feelings that are occasionally voiced by graduate students or postdoctoral fellows in science. Yet, as discussed by Buxton (2001), they are not often talked about publicly and few students are aware of these social dimensions of scientific work prior to pursuing careers in science. At other points in the interview, Tia acknowledged that she found the hard work rewarding and that she believed the program was designed to show students that hard work will be required of them, but that they can get through it too.

Other kinds of experiences appeared to lead to project dedication and commitment for Joe. Most important for him was the opportunity to work on his own and to manage his time – to gain ownership over his project.

JOE: Well, I think it's learning how to use your time wisely.... 'Cuz you know nobody's gonna be like, well you should be this far with your project, 'cuz it's your own project. They don't know where you should be.

Joe had to learn to manage his time and to take charge of his own learning and pace of work. At the same time, Joe already perceived such learning outcomes as tools for college:

JOE: Oh, it's been really... I think the whole mentor thing for me has really got me thinking about college. Like, in the past years... we were treated as a class still. And college is gonna be, your individual study. It's gonna be the effort that you put into it. The teacher's not gonna try to catch you up so much. You know it's... rather independent, and that's what I think the mentor thing was, you know, 'cuz it was just me working on a project. And I needed to know how far to go, and I needed to, you know, monitor that stuff myself.

Having the opportunity to be in charge of his own learning was empowering to Joe and made his mentor experience meaningful and valuable to him. As his comment makes apparent, the collaboration made it possible for him to become a different kind of learner from what he experienced in school. He was in charge, and he realized that whatever he put into his project would also benefit him in the long run.

Accordingly, the tools and resources the students took with them varied greatly due to the form of their mentor's guidance in the collaborations and the kinds of learning opportunities that emerged. Overall, they experienced what it means to come to own a project while also being a responsible learner and co-participant in the collaborations. They all accomplished something they could be proud of. Thereby, they became confident and came to see learning and success as a possibility for themselves, despite the many odds they face daily as poverty-stricken youth. We take such confidence as one of the most essential tools for their future success.

DISCUSSION

In this chapter we described the forms of guidance in three different kinds of partnerships (in the fields of biochemistry, ecology, and physics) and the tools and resources that were thereby made available to the students, such as dedication, hard work, and commitment – tools we consider essential for their future success in college (the overall aim of the program). In essence, the partnerships promoted new ways of learning and being a learner, a new experience that the students came to value. The partnerships also posed many challenges for the students, some being emotional and others being cognitive. It shows in what ways the cognitive, affective, and social processes of learning always need to be understood together as Vygotsky (1987, p. 282) emphasized:

Thought … is not born of other thoughts. Thought has its origins in the motivating sphere of consciousness, a sphere that includes our inclinations and needs, our interests and impulses, and our affect and emotion. The affective and volitional tendency stands behind thought. Only here do we find the answer to the final "why" in the analysis of thinking.

It is neither solely the science that the students appropriated nor the insights into the processes of science, but an understanding of themselves as learners that made the program meaningful and valuable. Put differently, students learned what it means to work hard, to be dedicated to a project, and committed despite ongoing challenges.

Most important, these experiences led to self-confidence – an essential tool for their future. The students came to see themselves as being able to take charge of their own learning, to manage challenges, and to be successful in the end. For these reasons, we also value the notion of multiple literacies emphasized by Gallego and Hollingsworth (2000; see also Hull & Schultz, 2002). We contend that the collaborations made available to the students both personal and social (or community) literacies – an awareness of ways of knowing and believing about the self and an understanding of ways of talking and being in communities, respectively.

What made the partnerships intriguing to us were also the forms they took as scientists and students came to interact with each other and with science. In essence, each supported the youths' intellectual and social development in a different manner, thereby speaking to the socially and culturally constituted nature of doing and becoming. By emphasizing such a dynamic, we intended to underline the need to think of effective guidance and literacy development in broader terms. In the current discussion of educational reform, it appears too often as if one model of teaching and learning should and can fit all. Furthermore, in the literature on underrepresented students, the focus is often on the external factors that affect access to opportunities. Yet, our analysis shows that most important is how the positions of the mentors and students are recognized, built on, and supported in joint activity. Furthermore, even though underrepresented students are often viewed as problems or as having deficiencies (Heath & McLaughlin, 1993), this study shows how remarkably pedestrian these students are in terms of preparedness and their reaction to meaningful learning opportunities and how much such opportunities come to mean to them. Yet, because the partnership was not structured as a typical course, the institutions (high schools and the university) viewed this as an elective activity. The university awarded credit to the students, but the high schools did not uniformly accept the credits. The university did not compensate the mentors for their time and effort, either. Nevertheless, these experiences are precisely the ones that can guide youth into the sciences and attract students to the university, while they also help mentors (graduate students and faculty) understand the importance of educational outreach efforts, especially efforts aimed at underrepresented groups.

The students you met in this chapter often described themselves as the ones who were not supposed to be successful in math and science. Yet, COSMOS, and in particular the partnership component, has given them the self-confidence needed to challenge such assumptions, a tool much needed for their future success. Joe says it best:

JOE: COSMOS has given me a focus, you know. I am so tired of high school, and yeah, let's skip class, and yeah, I used to, but it gets kind of old. Now I want to learn, do something. I don't want to work eight to five all my life. I want to do something with my life, get an education. You know, we are not expected to go to college and succeed, but COSMOS has given me the confidence that I can.

References

Atwater, M. M. (2000). Equity for black Americans in precollege science. *Science Education, 84*, 154–188.

Barab, S. A., & Duffy, T. M. (2000). From practice fields to communities of practice. In D. H. Jonassen & S. M. Land (Eds.), *Theoretical foundations of learning environments* (pp. 25–55). Hillsdale, NJ: Lawrence Erlbaum.

Barab, S. A., & Hay, K. (2001). Doing science at the elbows of scientists: Issues related to the scientist apprentice camp. *Journal of Research in Science Teaching, 38*, 70–102.

Brown, J. S., Collins, A., & Duguid, P. (1989). Situated cognition and the culture of learning. *Educational Researcher, 18* (1), 32–42.

Buxton, C. A. (2001). Modeling science teaching on science practice? Painting a more accurate picture through an ethnographic lab study. *Journal of Research in Science Teaching, 38* (4), 387–407.

Calabrese Barton A. (2003). *Teaching science for social justice.* New York: Teachers College Press.

Collins, A., Brown, J. S., & Holum, A. (1991). Cognitive apprenticeship: Making thinking visible. *American Educator, 15* (3), 38–46.

Crane, V. (1994). An introduction to informal science learning and research. In V. Crane, H. Nicholson, S. Bitgood, & M. Chen (Eds.), *Informal science learning* (pp. 1–14). Dedham, MA: Research Communications.

Ebert-May, D., Hodder, J., Williams, K., & Luckie, D. (2004). Pathways to scientific teaching. *Frontiers in Ecology and the Environment, 2* (6), 323.

Gallego, M. A., & Hollingsworth, S. (Eds.). (2000). *What counts as literacy: Challenging the school standard.* New York: Teachers College Press.

Hall, R. (1999). Video recording as theory. In A. Kelly & D. Lesh (Eds.), *Handbook of research design in mathematics and science education* (pp. 647–664). Mahwah, NJ: Lawrence Erlbaum.

Heath, S. B., & McLaughlin, M. W. (Eds.). (1993). *Identity and inner-city youth.* New York: Teachers College Press.

Hennessy, S. (1993). Situated cognition and cognitive apprenticeship: Implications for classroom learning. *Studies in Science Education, 22,* 1–41.

Hull, G., & Schultz, K. (2002). *School's out! Bridging out-of-school literacies with classroom practice.* New York: Teachers College Press.

John-Steiner, V. (2000). *Creative collaboration.* New York: Oxford University Press.

Jones, L. S. (1997). Opening doors with informal science: Exposure and access for our underserved students. *Science Education, 81,* 663–677.

Jordan, B., & Henderson, A. (1995). Interaction analysis: Foundations and practice. *Journal of the Learning Sciences, 4* (1), 39–103.

Lave, J. (1996). Teaching, as learning in practice. *Mind, Culture, and Activity: An International Journal, 3* (3), 149–164.

Lave, J., & Wenger, E. (1991). *Situated learning: Legitimate peripheral participation.* Cambridge: Cambridge University Press.

McGinn, M. K., & Roth, W.-M. (1999). Preparing students for competent scientific practice: Implications of recent research in science and technology studies. *Educational Researcher, 28* (3), 14–24.

Moore, J. C., Tripp, B. B., Simpson, R. T., & Coleman, D. C. (2000). Springtails in the classroom: Collembola as model organisms for inquiry-based laboratories. *American Biology Teacher, 62,* 512–519.

Mortenson Research Letter. (1995). *The Mortenson Research Letter on public policy analysis of opportunity for postsecondary education, 41.* Iowa City, Iowa.

Oakes, J., Muir, K., & Joseph, R. (2000). *Course taking and achievement: Inequalities that endure and change.* A keynote presentation at the annual meeting of the National Institute for Science Education, Detroit.

Pycior, H. M., Slack, N. G., & Abir-Am, P. G. (Eds.). (1996). *Creative couples in the sciences.* New Brunswick, NJ: Rutgers University Press.

Rahm, J., Miller, H., Hartley, L., & Moore, J. (2003). The value of an emergent notion of authenticity: Examples from two student/teacher-scientist partnership programs. *Journal of Research in Science Teaching, 40* (8), 737–756.

Richmond, G., & Kurth, L. A. (1999). Moving from outside to inside: High school students' use of apprenticeships as vehicles for entering the culture and practice of science. *Journal of Research in Science Teaching, 36* (6), 677–697.

Richtie, S. M., & Rigano, D. L. (1996). Laboratory apprenticeship through a student research project. *Journal of Research in Science Teaching, 33* (7), 799–815.

Sosniak, L. A. (1995). Inviting adolescents into academic communities: An alternative perspective on systemic reform. *Theory into Practice, 34* (1), 35–42.

Steele, C. (1997). A threat in the air: How stereotypes shape intellectual identity and performance. *American Psychologist, 52,* 613–629.

Tinker, R. S. (1997). Student-scientist partnerships: Shrewd maneuvers. In K. C. Cohen (Ed.), *Internet links for science education: Student-scientist partnerships* (pp. 5–15). New York: Plenum Press.

Tobin, K., Seiler, G., & Walls, E. (1999). Reproduction of social class in the teaching and learning of science in urban high schools. *Research in Science Education, 29,* 171–187.

Vygotsky, L. S. (1978). *Mind in society: The development of higher psychological processes.* Cambridge, MA: Harvard University Press.

Vygotsky, L. S. (1987). *Thinking and speech.* In R. W. Rieber & A. S. Carton (Eds.), *The collected works of L. S. Vygotsky: Vol. 1. Problems of general psychology* (pp. 37–285). New York: Plenum Press.

Wertsch, J. (1991). *Voices of the mind: A sociocultural approach to mediated action.* Cambridge, MA: Harvard University Press.

18

Girls on the Sidelines

"Gendered" Development in Early Childhood Classrooms

Sonja de Groot Kim

In my dissertation on two- and three-year-old children in a child care center (de Groot Kim, 1999), I focused on both verbal and nonverbal communication and was guided by the following broad questions: How do children make themselves understood, and how do children understand the intentions of their peers and their teachers? In this chapter, I focus on the physical activity patterns of some of the two- and three-year-old boys during transition times while they waited in the classroom to go play outside or in the hallway. It appeared that these boys regularly sent their teachers nonverbal, gender-related messages.

I will discuss (1) how socialization of two- and three-year-old boys and girls into their gender roles seemed to be influenced by the sociocultural context of their particular setting, a classroom in a childcare center; (2) how a small group of toddler boys seemed to transform unintentional physical body contact activity into intentional body contact activity, which resulted in gaining earlier access to space and resources and receiving more teacher attention; and (3) how a year later, in response to a different set of sociocultural expectations, some of the three-year-old boys seemed to transform body contact activity into a more socially acceptable, noncontact activity, aided by voice and hand gestures. They similarly gained earlier access to space and resources and received more teacher attention.

I believe that some of the two- and three-year-old boys did not just internalize and reproduce an existing culture but actively participated in co-constructing with their teachers a gendered culture that worked to their advantage. At the same time, the two- and three-year old girls seemed to have accepted an implied cultural message that girls wait.

DISCUSSION OF THE LITERATURE

The views of child development that emphasize the reciprocal nature of children's interactions and the sociocultural context of their development (Corsaro, 1997; de Groot Kim, 2005; Fromberg, 1992; Lubeck, 1996; Vygotsky, 1978) have also given rise to a way of studying children that reflects this complexity. According to Pellegrini (1991, p. 15), "If we are interested in understanding development, or changes within individuals across time, we should study them across time." To date, few studies have examined in a natural context how social communication develops over time in young children between the ages of one and five – especially children in childcare centers where some may spend up to ten hours a day (Blanck & Rosenthal, 1982; Duveen & Lloyd, 1992; Farver, 1992; Garvey, 1990). As Graue and Walsh (1995, p. 140) remark, "For its pervasive presence in children's lives, try to find thick descriptive accounts of children's lives when they leave home and enter the child care situation. There are amazingly few."

We know that from infancy children establish active communication patterns with others that include facial expressions, voice, and movements. I documented how adept these toddlers were in communicating their intentions to, and establishing relationships with, other children and adults. I observed how these young children at first did not always announce their intentions to others verbally. More often, they announced it in different ways, such as exaggeration, the making of noises and faces, and transformations of themselves and of objects to announce to others: *this is play.* When they wanted to play together, they needed to determine what the other child's intentions were and to make their actions intelligible to one another. They did so either verbally, by constructing a line of action ("let's . . . "), or nonverbally, often by jumping directly into a cooperative activity. As Bruner (1987, p. 84) explains, "Very young children had something clearly in mind about what others had in mind, and organized their actions accordingly. I thought of it as the child achieving mastery of one of the precursors of language use: a sense of mutuality in action."

According to Leiman (1999, p. 427), "every act of signification will always involve a three-term relationship between at least two people and 'the object,'" and "an 'object' may be anything, from parts of the body, from gestures, and other actions, to physical things." Children's social worlds are integral to their development, and communication during social interactions helps children to interpret their world (Berk & Winsler, 1995; Vygotsky, 1978). As Cole (1985, p. 159) notes, "There has been a great deal of interest among scholars of many disciplines in the 'real activities of real people.' . . . there also has been an increasingly heavy emphasis on human activity as mutually constituted in interaction."

Throughout their early years children are exposed to patterns of behavior and interactions with others that shape their use of communicative signs and help to determine their manipulation of symbolic transformations (Reis, 1983). They are active participants in this meaning-making process and bring a rich store of knowledge and experience from their own world to their interactions with others (Bruner, 1987, 1996; Dunn, 1993; Nelson, 1986; Rogoff, 1990).

Researchers emphasize the value of social and cultural experiences, including adult-child and peer-peer interaction, for the development of children's understanding, but there seems to be a heavy emphasis on how verbal language and dialogue facilitate children's cognitive growth (Berk, 1994; Nelson, Plesa, & Henseler 1998; Rogoff, 1990; Vygotsky, 1978). Because of this emphasis on verbal language and dialogue, there has been less recognition of the role of nonverbal and other action-related modes of communication in children's construction of understanding of self and others. Leiman (1999, p. 433) concurs: "For Voloshinov, the birthplace of language is the dialogue, the concrete, living speech activity between socially organized persons. . . . It has also seduced Philologists throughout the centuries, as well as linguists and psychologists of our own time, to approach the word from a lexical-semantic point of view."

Some researchers believe that nonverbal messages may serve an important function in interpersonal interaction and in developing children's communicative competence (Boyatis & Satyaprasad, 1994; Feldman, Philippot, & Custrini, 1991; Garvey, 1990; Saarni, 1982). Bruner (1987), and other researchers (Farver, 1992; Garvey, 1984; Göncü, 1993; Wang, Bernas, & Eberhard, 2004) suggest that both nonverbal and verbal communication are meaningful and become increasingly shared or intersubjective.

PHYSICAL CONTACT ACTIVITY GAMES: PUPPY-WRESTLING
IN THE TODDLER ROOM

In the following account, I describe some experiences of the toddlers as they occurred in the context of a regular school day in the toddler classroom. The room was arranged so that it contained all the areas common to many early childhood classrooms. It had separate areas for sociodramatic play, play with manipulatives such as Legos, art activities, book reading, and block play. The morning routine allowed children to play freely with the materials, carry out an art activity project with the teachers, have a snack, and, after that, get ready to go outdoors to the playground. When it was time to go outdoors, one of the teachers took coats from the hook and things out of the bin and dressed one child at a time while the others waited, occupying themselves by looking at the fish in the aquarium. In case of inclement weather, the teachers, Emma or Karen, took a few children at a time to the hallway.

In the toddler room, some physical-activity games involved bodily contact. Three of the boys, Eddy, Ben, and Beau, were enthusiastic participants, while Kurt and Colin, the quieter boys, and the girls did not participate in any of these episodes. These games involved playful aggression and are also called rough and tumble (R&T) play (Garvey, 1990; Pellegrini & Smith, 1998). I used the term "puppy wrestling" for these young toddlers, because it seemed to more accurately reflect the playfulness I perceived in the situation. It seemed that the three boys enjoyed the activity for its physical as well as its social aspect. They laughed, pushed, shoved, and held on to each other. Each time, this activity occurred near the door when the children were ready to leave for the playground or the gym. It resulted in Eddy, Ben, and Beau going out the door first with the teacher, mostly with Eddy in the lead. These three boys seemed to have a mutual understanding that the purpose of the activity was playful, pretend aggression as the following vignette illustrates.

Ben grimaces at Eddy and grabs him by the shoulders. It looks as if they have each other in a good, solid hold. They are shaking each other and laughing. They look like wrestling puppies. Karen finishes dressing several children and says to Emma, "I'll take these out first." Emma responds, "OK, I'll be right out with the others." Karen opens the door and Eddy, Ben and Beau disappear in a flash. Emma, Kurt, Mae and Lea stay in the room.

At the time, I did not view the boys' actions and the teachers' responses as gender-related. However, the analysis of the data collected in the three-year-old classroom revealed distinct patterns of behavior by the children and the teachers. This, in turn, led me to revisit, reexamine, and reinterpret the toddler data.

NON-PHYSICAL-CONTACT ACTIVITY GAMES: LOUD BOYS IN THE THREE-YEAR-OLD ROOM

The activities and schedules in this classroom were similar to the ones I outlined for the two-year-olds except for the dressing and diaper-changing routines, as the three-year-olds were more capable of self-care. The three-year-olds also gathered near the classroom door when they were going outdoors or to the hallway to play. In this classroom, fourteen months later, I found no evidence of the physical contact activity game, puppy wrestling, which was so prevalent in the toddler room. It seemed that this puppy wrestling had been replaced by another kind of physical and verbal behavior by some of the boys. These three-year-old boys, one of whom was a child I had previously observed in the toddler room, were physically and verbally very active. They had established a pattern of behavior near the door that included loud yelling, laughing, slapping one hand high up in the air against another boy's hand (giving each other high-fives), and jumping up and down. These boys, Dean, Eddy, Freddy, and Kurt, were often selected first for out-of-class activities where they received more time, practice, and instruction. Randy, the youngest child, was sometimes near the loud boys, but his voice was so low that he could not be heard over the din of loud boys yelling, jumping, and clapping. Tim and Ted, the boys labeled special needs, usually arrived at 11:00 A.M. and were in the last group to be selected.

Girls were in the second or the last group of children selected for out-of-classroom activities. At times, girls were specifically selected to remain with a teacher and directed to help clean up play areas, even if they had not played there. They would then wait with the teacher for Tim and Ted to arrive and then head outside together for a brief play period. Here is one example.

Bridget Makes It Out First: I watch to see if the girls leave with the first group. It seems, from what I have observed over time, that the girls wind up in the last group which waits with a teacher for Tim and Ted to arrive at 11:00 am. Mandy is patiently waiting near the wall, but Bridget seems determined to be with the first group. As she's heading out the door, I hear Bonny say, "Bridget come back here." But Bridget doesn't hear (or pretends not to hear?) and disappears out the door in the surge of boys.

It was interesting that the three-year-old girls did not participate in boisterous verbal and physical play near the door, just as the toddler girls did not participate in puppy wrestling a year earlier either. If a girl headed for the door, she was called back as the above snapshot of Bridget illustrates. During hallway play, as presented next, the four "loud" boys were selected first.

Kurt and Dean, Playing Hockey: Bridget stands by the door when Sally takes Kurt and Dean out of the room for a hockey game. When Sally brings Kurt and Dean back in and invites two other boys to go out with her, Bridget comes running over again. Sally tells her that she'll definitely be next. Bridget excitedly hops up and down and waits. Sally returns for Bridget and Elly and teaches the girls how to hold the hockey stick. Elly holds the stick up and swings right past the puck. Bridget keeps missing as well. After a few more tries Sally says, "Let's go back inside." She calls Kurt and Dean for another turn. They plant their feet firmly down and give the puck a good swing. The puck goes at least 20 feet.

In the following pastiche, I braided the experiences of three different groups of children and Sally's interactions with each group.

Hallway Play: Who's on First? Dean, Freddy, Eddy and Kurt are excitedly running back and forth. They jockey for position, trying to be near the top of the slide. They experiment with the cars, making them go down different ways. They try the planes and boats. Each time, Sally describes their actions, saying, "Oh, look your car is going downwards, your car is crashing, your car is spinning around." She seems very interested and involved. (group 1, log 26, pp. 342–346)

Sally returns with Elly, Kevin and Mandy. Kevin stands in his walker near the top of the slide where he can push cars down the slide. Sally keeps asking Elly and Mandy to hand Kevin another car. This group seems content to push cars, boats, and planes, down the slide, retrieve them, run around, and slide them down again. Sally makes only verbal requests and gives initial instruction to the three. Then she sits and watches. (group 2, log 26, pp. 342–346)

Sally returns with Bridget, Randy and Tim, the child with speech-related difficulties. Sally tells them what the slide is for, then she sits back. Tim is very energetic, pushing the cars down hard, then retrieving them at the bottom. When they land sideways, he says, "crashing down." Bridget puts two plastic people in the cars. She is the only child who does this. Sally gives no verbal feedback and does not interact with these children. (group 3, log 26, pp. 342–346)

The first group of four boys received most of Sally's energy and involvement, together with more extensive verbal feedback. She seemed to really enjoy these boys. There were lively exchanges between them. Sally's interactions with the second group centered on her requests to Elly and Mandy to give Kevin cars. Sally gave the third group a brief explanation of the activity, then sat back and watched. There was no response to children's actions and comments, even though Randy, a new speaker of English, and Tim, who had speech problems, might have benefited from communicative exchanges with Sally.

DISCUSSION

Researchers consider the R&T play I witnessed in the toddler room to be reflective of boys' creating and maintaining a dominance relationship among their peers and learning to encode and decode social signals between participants. R&T play is also gender-related because girls rarely participate in this type of play. Valsiner and van der Veer (2000, p. 369), in discussing Vygotsky's view of higher mental processes as social, point out that the actions of young children may not have a particular purpose until the adult attributes a certain social or cultural meaning to it. In line with this view, I theorize that the toddler boys may have initially engaged in R&T play for physical activity and/or to establish social dominance among themselves. However, once the teachers interpreted the behavior as a sign of their readiness to go out, and the boys experienced that unanticipated benefit, their behavior may have become intentional, an example of situated learning. "If we act this way, we get to go out first."

In the three-year-old classroom, there was no evidence of R&T play, which is unusual because it is well established that this type of play increases with age (Bjorklund & Brown, 1998; Pellegrini & Smith, 1998). I learned that for the teachers in this class, *being nice* was of great importance and that therefore R&T play may not have been acceptable. In this sociocultural context, however, Eddy, Kurt, Freddy, and Dean's noncontact physical activity play and use of loud voices near the door was acceptable and had the same effect: they were taken out first for outdoor play and for special activities. An important benefit for these boys was that they had a longer period of time to spend outdoors with the first choice of activities and of selecting and using materials, such as balls and tricycles. In hallway play, these boys received more frequent and longer turns and received more verbal feedback and instruction from the teacher. Because there were no girls in these clusters near the door, this gendered selection brought about fewer opportunities for girls.

Historically, there is some consensus (Duveen & Lloyd, 1992) about the different treatment of boys and girls in classrooms, with boys getting more teacher attention, although most of this research was carried out with older children. Berk (1997) writes that teachers create different environments for boys and for girls, referring to the physical environment, including materials. In this study, however, the physical environment was the same for boys and girls. Much more of an issue was unequal access to materials and activities, such as riding tricycles on the playground, or experimenting with gravity on the incline in the hallway. Here, some of the more verbal, physically active boys seemed to have a distinct advantage.

The girls internalized an implied social rule: *girls wait*. Their turn might come later, it might be shorter, or, as I also documented, their turn may not come. The girls complied with this social rule most of the time. One time, Bridget managed to leave with the first group, ignoring the teacher's calls to come back. At this time, another girl, Mandy, was already standing against the wall, quietly waiting for her turn. She seemed to have absorbed the "girls wait" rule. This social rule was never discussed because officially it did not exist. In their comments about social-rule learning, Light (1993) and Smetana (1993) suggest that the acquisition of social-rule knowledge is a necessary task and a positive accomplishment for young children:

Developing an understanding of social rules is to be held "one of the major tasks of childhood," on the grounds that such understanding is necessary if one is to function competently in society. (Light, 1993, p. 195)

... an increasing interest in the effects of day care on children's social development (Clarke-Stewart, 1989; Philips et al., 1987). One study (Siegel & Storey, 1985) has examined the effects of social experience on social rule knowledge. This study demonstrates that social experience in a new setting is necessary to acquire an understanding of the conventional rule of that setting. (Smetana, 1993, p. 128)

Thus, Smetana and Light suggest that children need social experiences to develop an understanding of social rules, in order to function competently in society. On the surface, this seems to be a statement with which few people would disagree. It is important to note that imbedded in social rules are expectancies that people have for the way things are supposed to happen. However, it seems that in the particular cultural contexts of the classrooms I studied, having an understanding of social rules and of how things are supposed to happen was not necessarily a positive accomplishment.

In these classrooms, gaining social experience and adapting to social rules placed the girls at a distinct disadvantage because embedded in the implied social rule about transitions was an expectation that certain boys would go out first and girls would wait their turn. This social rule seemed to constitute a kind of "gentlemen's agreement," which was actively negotiated, silently communicated, and carried out by the teachers and a group of vocal, physically active boys. Its resulting message, "girls wait," was absorbed most of the time by girls. It sent a powerful message to the children, especially the three-year-old girls.

My interpretation of how children seemed to make sense of the verbal and nonverbal messages they sent and received, both to and from other children and adults, saw their meaning-making as deeply rooted in the particular culture of this room and of this center. This concept of development is supported by other researchers (Bruner, 1990; Dunn, 1995; Kessen, 1991; Rogoff, 1990; Wertsch, 1991). Rogoff's ethnographic work situates people squarely in a sociocultural context. In her view, people actively participate in a social setting and appropriate the cultural practices of their environment, with the support of what she calls "socially guided activity settings." Their views reflect the influence of Vygotsky (1978), whose sociocultural theory stresses the role of environment and of people in children's development.

I found that boys received more frequent as well as longer turns and more detailed information about how things work. These results support studies by Wittmer and Honig (1994, p. 119), who contend that, "boys received higher rates of instruction, more verbal interaction, more verbal stimulation to stimulate boys' cognitive development." Serbin et al. (1994) speak about the influence that groups of boys have on adults and other children. Maccoby (1994, p. 96) notes that "there may be a certain recognition among children and adults that boys' groups need to be taken more seriously. They tend to be larger and more of their activities are countercultural."

This viewpoint is interesting in light of my documentation that the physical and vocal behavior of some *loud* boys may have been a reason for teachers to select them first for outside. Maccoby (1994) contends that children learn about gender roles by living in a community where roles and expectations of each gender are subtly and not so subtly communicated. In this study, messages about cultural gender expectations were absorbed by the children, who mostly adapted to them. Bridget, at age three, occasionally communicated her resistance and escaped out the door with the boys.

The young children in this study received important nonverbal, gender-related messages from the adults in the environment. It seemed that especially transition times and subsequent activities became gendered events, during which some of the boys regularly left the room first and thus had earlier access to materials in the hallway, gym, and yard. These boys received more detailed instruction, as well as more frequent and longer turns. The girls became accustomed to waiting for their turns, although they occasionally protested – to no avail. Because these gendered messages tend to derive from deeply held values and implicit beliefs, it may require an outsider to study "what is going on here." Future studies about communication patterns among children, and among children and adults, during classroom interactions, at transition times, and during other group-related events might serve to note and possibly ameliorate gendered patterns of communication.

References

Berk, L. E. (1994). Vygotsky's theory: The importance of make-believe play. *Young Children, 50* (1), 30–39.

Berk, L. E. (1997). *Child development* (4th ed.). Boston: Allyn & Bacon.

Berk, L. E., & Winsler, A. (1995). *Scaffolding children's learning: Vygotsky and early childhood education.* Washington, DC: National Association for the Education of Young Children.

Bjorklund, D. F., & Brown, R. D. (1998). Physical play and cognitive development: Integrating activity, cognition, and education. *Child Development, 69* (3), 604–606.

Blanck, P. D., & Rosenthal, R. (1982). Developing strategies for decoding "leaky" messages: On learning how and when to decode discrepant and consistent social communications. In R. S. Feldman (Ed.), *Development of nonverbal behavior in children* (pp. 203–255). New York: Springer-Verlag.

Boyatis, C. J., & Satyaprasad, C. (1994). Children's facial and gestural decoding and encoding relations between skills and with popularity. *Journal of Nonverbal Behavior, 18* (1), 37–55.

Bruner, J. (1987). The transactional self. In J. Bruner & H. Haste (Eds.), *Making sense: The child's construction of the world* (pp. 81–96). New York: Methuen.

Bruner, J. (1990). *Acts of meaning.* Cambridge, MA: Harvard University Press.

Bruner, J. (1996). *The culture of education.* Cambridge, MA: Harvard University Press.

Clarke-Stewart, K. A. (1989). Infant daycare: Maligned or malignant? *American Psychologist, 44,* 266–273.

Cole, M. (1985). The zone of proximal development: Where culture and cognition create each other. In J. Wertsch (Ed.), *Culture, communication, and cognition: Vygotskian perspectives* (pp. 146–161). Cambridge: Cambridge University Press.

Corsaro, W. A. (1997). *The sociology of childhood.* Thousand Oaks, CA: Pine Forge Press.

de Groot Kim, S. (1999). Making sense of my world: The development of communication in two- and three-year old children in a childcare center. *Dissertation Abstracts International, 60* (6A), 1898. (UMI No. 9935643).

de Groot Kim, S. (2005). Kevin: I gotta get to the market. The development of peer relationships in inclusive early childhood settings. *Early Childhood Education Journal, 33* (3), 163–169.

Dunn, J. (1993). *Young children's close relationships: Beyond attachment.* Newbury Park, CA: Sage.

Dunn, J. (Ed.). (1995). Connections between emotion and understanding in development. *Cognition and Emotion, 9,* 2–3. Hillsdale, NJ: Lawrence Erlbaum.

Duveen, B., & Lloyd, B. (1992). *Gender identities and education: The impact of starting school.* New York: St. Martin's Press.

Farver, J. M. (1992). An analysis of young American and Mexican children's play dialogues: Illustrative study # 3. In C. Howes, *The collaborative construction of pretend* (pp. 55–63). Albany: State University of New York Press.

Feldman, R. S., Philippot, P., & Custrini, R. J. (1991). Social competence and nonverbal behavior. In R. S. Feldman & B. Rime, *Fundamentals of nonverbal behavior* (pp. 329–350). Cambridge: Cambridge University Press.

Fromberg, D. P. (1992). A review of research on play. In C. Seinfeld (Ed.), *The early childhood curriculum: A review of current research* (2nd ed., pp. 42–84). New York: Teachers College Press.

Garvey, C. (1984). *Children's talk.* Cambridge, MA: Harvard University Press.

Garvey, C. (1990). *Play.* Cambridge, MA: Harvard University Press.

Göncü, A. (1993). Development of intersubjectivity in the dyadic play of preschoolers. *Early Childhood Research Quarterly, 8,* 99–116.

Graue, M. E., & Walsh, D. J. (1995). Children in context: Interpreting the here and now of children's lives. In J. A. Hatch (Ed.), *Qualitative research in early childhood settings* (pp. 135–154). Westport, CT: Praeger.

Kessen, B. (1991). Directions: Where do we turn now? *Society for Research in Child Development Newsletter, 2,* 12–14.

Leiman, M. (1999). The concept of sign in the work of Vygotsky, Winnicott, and Bakhtin: Further integration of object relations theory and activity theory. In Y. Engeström, R. Miettinen, & R. L. Punamaki, *Perspectives on activity theory* (pp. 419–434). Cambridge: Cambridge University Press.

Light, P. (1993). Developing psychologies. In M. Bennett (Ed.), *The development of social cognition: The child as psychologist* (pp. 191–200). New York: Guilford Press.

Lubeck, S. (1996). Deconstructing "child development knowledge" and "teacher preparation." *Early Childhood Research Quarterly, 11,* 147–168.

Maccoby, E. (1994). Commentary: Gender segregation in childhood. In C. Leaper (Ed.), Childhood gender segregation: Causes and consequences. *New Directions for Child Development, Number 65,* 87–97. San Francisco: Jossey-Bass.

Nelson, K. (1986). *Event knowledge: Structure and function in development.* Hillsdale, NJ: Lawrence Erlbaum.

Nelson, K., Plesa, D., & Henseler, S. (1998). Children's theory of mind: An experiential orientation. *Human Development, 41,* 7–29.

Pellegrini, A. D. (1991). *Applied child study: A developmental approach.* Hillsdale, NJ: Lawrence Erlbaum.

Pellegrini, A. D., & Smith, P. K. (1998). Physical activity play: The nature and function of a neglected aspect of play. *Child Development, 3,* 577–598.

Philips, D. A., McCartney, K., Scarr, S., & Howes, C. (1987). Selective review of infant daycare research: A cause for concern. *Zero to Three, 7,* 18–21.

Reis, H. T. (Ed.). (1983). *Naturalistic approaches to studying social interaction.* San Francisco: Jossey-Bass.

Rogoff, B. (1990). *Apprenticeship in thinking.* New York: Oxford.

Saarni, C. (1982). Social and affective functions of nonverbal behavior: Developmental concerns. In R. S. Feldman (Ed.), *Development of nonverbal behavior in children* (pp. 123–147). New York: Springer-Verlag.

Serbin, L. A., Moller, L. C., Gulko, J., Powlishta, K. K., & Colburne, K. A. (1994). The emergence of gender segregation in toddler playgroups. In C. Leaper (Ed.), Childhood gender segregation: Causes and consequences. *New Directions for Child Development, Number 65,* 7–17. San Francisco: Jossey-Bass.

Siegal, M., & Storey, R. M. (1985). Daycare and children's conception of moral rules. *Child development, 56,* 1001–1008.

Smetana, J. (1993). Understanding of social rules. In M. Bennett (Ed.), *The development of social cognition: The child as psychologist* (pp. 111–141). New York: Guilford Press.

Valsiner, J., & van der Veer, R. (2000). *Social mind: Construction of the idea.* Cambridge: Cambridge University Press.

Vygotsky, L. S. (1978). *Mind in society: The development of higher psychological processes.* Cambridge, MA: Harvard University Press.

Wang, X., Bernas, R., & Eberhard, P. (2004). Engaging ADHD students in tasks with hand gestures: A pedagogical possibility for teachers. *Educational Studies, 30* (3), 217–229.

Wertsch, J. (1991). *Voices of the mind: A sociocultural approach to mental action.* Cambridge, MA: Harvard University Press.

Wittmer, D. S., & Honig, A. S. (1994). Play, story-song, and eating times in child care: Caregiver responses to toddlers and threes. In H. Goelman & E. V. Jacobs (Eds.), *Children's play in child care settings* (pp. 119–147). Albany: State University of New York Press.

19

Inscripting Predicates

Dealing with Meanings in Play

Bert van Oers

PLAY AND MEANINGS

One of the recurrent issues in the debate about humanity and cultural development is the phenomenon of play. Despite this perpetual attention of philosophers, educators, psychologists, and pedagogues to the element of play in human activities, there is still much controversy about the conceptualisation of the relationship between play and human cultural development. In his famous study of the role of play in human cultures, *Homo Ludens*, the Dutch historian of culture Johan Huizinga investigated many cultures from antiquity until the beginning of the twentieth century and concluded that play is most certainly the basis for all human culture. Institutions such as the law, constitutions, art, crafts, science, sport, and trade are basically rooted in human playful activities (Huizinga, 1938). "Human civilisation," he writes, "emerges and develops in play, as play." In his analysis he stipulates that play has a culture-creating function, and the major determinant in this process is the element of competition, which is intrinsic to all playful activities. In this competition, new or modified meanings are attributed to familiar objects and actions, which subsequently become the basis for new objects and actions.

It is interesting to note that in the beginning of the twentieth century this connection between play and human cultural development was made independently by many academics at different places. For Bakhtin (1964/1994), for example, the element of play was essential for cultural innovations. People can free themselves in play from conventional meanings, and in play they are allowed to explore alternatives and even oppose or ridicule sacrosanct conventions of culture. Bakhtin (1964/1994) designated this basic process in cultural innovations as the carnivalesque element in human culture. Characteristically, Bakhtin relates such playful activities to meaning and the proliferation of meanings in culture. Vygotsky also relates play to meanings, but he focused primarily on a developmental psychological relationship. In a lecture in 1933 (published in Vygotsky, 1978), Vygotsky states that play is a major source of development, especially for children: "a child's greatest achievements are possible in play, achievements that tomorrow will become her basic level of real action and morality." One of the important mechanisms in play that explains its potential is, according to Vygotsky, the inversion of the relationship of action and meaning. In play, meaning is going to dominate over real actions and objects. Meaning, contextualised in an imaginary situation, regulates the real object-oriented and tool-mediated actions of the child, and these actions produce new objects that may be a starting point for new explorations of meanings and the production of new tools. A contemporary example of this can be seen when children play "hospital": they may act as a doctor and scribble something on a piece of paper (i.e., writing a prescription), but when they discover that their actions are not easily understood in the way they are meant, they have to invent new means for clarifying their meanings (e.g., with drawings or pictures). The contradictions between the meanings in play (emerging from the imaginary situation) and the real actions are the main basis for children's development (see Vygotsky, 1978, p. 101).

In my research, I tried to clarify the notion of play and meaning and especially how children deal with meaning in their play activity. In this chapter, I try to demonstrate on the basis of observations of children's play how the construction of new signs in play contributes to the elaboration of meaning.

Before the presentation of my observations, a few preliminary words are needed on the theory of meaning that framed my analysis of children's play.

TOPICS AND PREDICATES

In his article on play, Vygotsky does not elaborate a concise theory of meaning, although it is obvious that the notion of meaning for him is a core element in the explanation of the potentials of play. But we can complement the picture by putting together various elements from different places in Vygotsky's work.

An important piece of a psychological theory of meaning was developed by Vygotsky in his *Thinking and Speech* (1987, chap. 7), in which he tries to give a psychological explanation of the abbreviated character of thinking (or inner speech). Vygotsky notes that this abbreviation is possible when communicating people have a shared attention for some common object. Because of this shared attention, they assume implicitly what the other is referring to in his or her speech. There is no need to repeat this topic of communication every time it might be relevant; rather, it is sufficient to mention those qualities that are *new to the topic under discussion*. These new qualities are called "predicates." The predicate always refers to the topic that is taken to be a shared attentional object, and it enriches that subject matter for that moment while distinguishing it from others. Vygotsky explains that he uses this term in a psychological sense, so it is different from the grammatical predicate. An example of the psychological predicate might be seen in the following: when we hear a noise, then this noise is common in our minds, and we can predicate it as "the door"; then "the door" is something new added to the original noise (the topic in our minds), and this predicate explains the noise in a way and distinguishes it from other noises – for instance, those caused by starting cars, falling trees, or disco music. In this case "the door" is added to the original shared attentional topic and can become a new topic that can be predicated again with new qualities – for example, "the front door" or "it's shut." Then "the front door" is the predicate giving new information about the initial subject, discriminating it from other possible interpretations (noises and doors). Extending Vygotsky's description, we can now say that a topic always contains a potential pool of predicates; in fact, these predicates emerge from the attention to a certain topic, and they are implicitly *meant* by reference to the topic. When a topic is in a person's mind, there is no need to repeat the topic every time. And, likewise, when communicating people have a shared attentional topic, they can confine themselves to talking in predicates.

When we apply this idea to the child's play, we can maintain that the imaginary situation is the topic. In the case of social play (e.g., role play), the imaginary situation is the attentional topic taken as shared. The new actions or propositions of the children are the predicates that contribute to the qualities of the topic. When a child says in a role play, "I was the mother and you were the child," this child predicates the situation with new qualities that define the situation and distinguish it from other situations (e.g., this is not playing hospital, or the new situation may even be distinguished from other situations where the roles of mother and child are reversed). By saying this, the child defines the situation and attributes particular roles and actions to the different players. Even the use of the past tense is a predicative code (in the sense of Bateson, 1973), *meaning* that the situation is not real but pretended.

In play, children use predicates all the time for articulating the imaginary situation and for the elaboration of their play. When a child picks up a block and says, "this is a soap," it predicates the shared attentional object and, by so doing, articulates her meanings (e.g., the meaning of her actions: it is not rubbing another child with a block but is *washing the baby*).

THE PRODUCTION OF INSCRIPTIONS

An essential element in the process of predicating a shared attentional topic is the availability of material codifications that make the meanings and predicates accessible for others. This part of the meaning is usually referred to as the sign. Most theories of meaning take the sign for granted and focus primarily on the negotiation of meanings, the reconstruction of meanings, and the circulation of meanings by the use of signs. Sinha (1988) already pointed out that a more elaborated theory of the material aspect of the sign is needed for a psychological theory of meaning. The innovation of meaning often requires invention of new signs, or at least a reconstruction of old signs in order to articulate the new meanings. Most of the time language is used as the pool of signs, and the combinations of language elements are the inventions of new signs for the reference to new meanings. Often, the success of finding adequate signs determines the efficacy of the communication of new meanings (or predicates).

The importance of the role of signs in the production of knowledge is acknowledged by Latour (1990). He used the notion of inscriptions to refer to the material or materialised tools that people use to represent knowledge and experiences in a number of different places or circumstances. For him, inscriptions are by definition shippable things that can be taken from one place to another and that can be reproduced at will for the express intent of representing the original things and meanings at any time or place. Through inscriptions, meanings can circulate in a community. In addition to this transportability and representativeness, inscriptions have several other advantages: they are fairly stable when transported, their scale can be modified without disturbing the internal proportions, they can easily be (re)combined with other inscriptions, they can easily be inserted in a written or spoken text, and they can be reproduced at a fairly low cost.

Inscriptions emerge in activities and tend to shape that very activity in fundamental ways (see also Meira, 1995). In our observations of young children's play, we frequently observed children making and using such inscriptions to represent other things and meanings. Children (ages five and six), carrying around a construction map for a castle in order to find a place in the classroom to build the castle represented, are very literally – in the sense of Latour – transporting an inscription to reconstruct it at will at another place and another time. These children can read the map and reread it in order to understand how the castle should be built (see van Oers & Wardekker, 1999). Another child (five years old), after having drawn a construction plan of his

own castle, tried to specify the numbers of blocks to be used. He inscribed
the following on his drawing:

But eventually he replaced this digital symbol by another (analogical) one
that he supposed to be more clear:

What we see here is that young children can use transportable inscriptions
in order to reconstruct their meanings at various places. But they can also
inscribe new symbols to their inscriptions in order to focus other people's
attention to specific parts of their drawings and even manipulate their attention to bring specific meanings (predicates) to their minds. The boy who
wrote the analogical number sign on the drawing obviously wanted to make
sure that the observer reconstructs the building with a pile of four blocks on
that specific point.

When we bring the Vygotskian theory of meaning and the Latourian theory
of inscriptions together, we can picture a theory of meaning that conceives of
the development of meaning as a process of producing new predicates (with
conventional means, like language) to a certain topic and that expresses those
predicates more precisely by inventing new appropriate inscriptions. The use
of these new inscriptions in cultural activities often leads to contradictions
with available actions or conventional symbols and subsequently to innovations of meanings (e.g., the invention of new concepts or categories). In the
following section, I describe this process in more detail on the basis of a series
of observations in role-play activities.

CHILDREN'S PLAY AND THE PRODUCTION OF INSCRIPTIONS

The setting that I use here for demonstrating the process of inscription of
predicates has been described several times in other articles, in order to
demonstrate the relevance of semiotic activity in young children's play (van
Oers, 1996), to point out the important role of contextualisation for the
development of children's activities (van Oers, 1998, 2001), and to articulate

the idea of predication in the formation of mathematical symbols (van Oers, 2000). In this chapter, I integrate these different parts in one coherent picture.

Describing the Context

A classroom with five- and six-year-old children in a Dutch school (Amsterdam) has constructed a shoe store in its school as an educative play corner for children. The teacher introduced the idea, but the necessary items for such a store (shoes, boxes, mirror, till, money, counter, brochures, etc.) were collected by both the teachers and the children. Then the children arranged the store together with the teacher. During this process, the children encountered several problems that they had to solve. From a certain point on, the children found the situation more or less ready and started playing in this shoe shop: fitting shoes, buying shoes, looking for shoes. In this play part of the activity, the children also encountered different problems that called for a solution. Sometimes the solution of the play problem was the rearrangement of the store. So we could observe a continuing shift from playing shoe shop to rearranging the situation. For the children these were different meaningful aspects of their activity. The teacher was also part of the activity, switching roles from a customer to adviser or designer. In the situations from which the following observations were taken, about five children were playing in the shoe shop (some dropped in, others dropped out).

A Classification Problem

One of the first tasks that the children had to accomplish during the arrangement of the situation was finding matching pairs of shoes from a heap of shoes and then putting them in the boxes. The children easily did this, but then they noticed that not all the shoe boxes could be displayed on the shelf; also, it was very awkward to find a pair of shoes once they were hidden in the boxes. They had to open all the boxes again and again in order to find "that red sandal" or "the black boots." In their discussions (including the teacher),[1] they decided to put one shoe of each pair on a shelf and leave the other in the box. But then the problem arose of how to retrieve the matching shoe. This was a crucial moment: to solve this problem, the children invented

---

[1] Although the teacher played an important facilitating role in all discussions, suggesting solutions, objecting or revoicing pupils' suggestions, and answering questions, her role is not discussed here. For more details, see van Oers, 1996; 2003, especially part II.

the solution of making labels that could be stuck to the boxes to indicate the kind of shoe that was inside.

The drawings of shoes were literally carried from their working tables to the shoe boxes. So the labels were literally inscriptions in the sense of Latour, and the inscriptions did capitalize on remarkable characteristics of the shoes. After these initial attempts at drawing the shoes, however, the children remained unsatisfied about the difficulty of having to read the drawings in order to find the wanted shoe. During the activity, the children started classifying the shoes for themselves as mama shoes, papa shoes, children shoes, and baby shoes. At the same time, some of the children got the idea of improving their labels by writing letters. They made seemingly meaningless strings of letters in the beginning, like RDTI or RAID. When the teacher discussed the meaning of these letter strings with the children, it turned out that one child wrote MAAR in order to indicate *mama shoe* (the M was for mama, possibly also the A, but that was not discussed). Then the teacher rephrased that invention for the whole group, endorsing the use of letters, for example, M for mama shoes. The children very easily invented P for papa shoes and B for baby shoes.

The initial classification of the shoes was on perceptual qualities (matching pairs), but now the children invented a new meaning of the shoes by classifying them by type. Mama, papa, baby, and children shoes can be seen as predicates of the initial amorphous collection of shoes that articulated the type of shoe and distinguished it from other shoes (a mama shoe is *not* a papa, baby, or child shoe!). The invention of the inscriptions M, P, B, or K (the Dutch word for child is *Kind*) stimulated the use of new predicates for describing the shoes in distinct classes and a reorganisation of the children's classification activities.

Beyond Classification

The inscriptions shape in significant ways the course of the activity from which they emerged. The availability of the inscriptions (the children also could carry them around on labels) led to a new subactivity of classifying the shoes in the four different classes with the help of the labels and then checking to see if the labels indeed matched with the type of shoe inside of the boxes. In this production of appropriate labels, we also observed that the form of the inscription changed in such a way that the letters used were limited to M, P, K, and B, and the other letters that were used in the beginning were left out, as they were not significant for designating the particular types of shoes.

These labels articulated also that the proportion of different types of shoes was very unequal: the children noticed that there were so many mama shoes

Figure 19.1. Diagram of shoe boxes.

and such a small number of papa shoes. Their attention shifted to the number of shoes in the different classes. They had made different piles of the distinguished groups of shoes and wanted to count them. In their counting, however, some of the children touched the boxes and then it happened that the piles of shoes tumbled over. In order to avoid this, the teacher suggested making a precise drawing of the piles of shoes so that they could count not the boxes but their paper drawing. With this drawing, they made a new inscription referring to the situation, focusing attention on the number of the different classes of shoes. Their attention shifted from the individual shoes to the collections of different shoes, and they predicated the collections again by numbers and by the inscriptions M, P, B, and K. For an example of a drawing of the shoe boxes, made by a six-year-old child, see Figure 19.1.

They now use the same inscription (e.g., M) for designating the collection of mama shoes, and they add new predicates to this collection in terms of numbers. They used this inscription in a collaborative counting activity with five- and six-year-old children. The inscription of these predicates (in the form of this diagram) is used as a tool in the children's activity, and again we see how these inscriptions-in-use function as means for elaborating their activities and for developing new, more specific meanings. The basic process here is always the (shared) attention to some topic, the production of new predicates, and materialising these predicates into new inscriptions that can be used for new actions and new tools (like diagrams, symbolic representations, or models).

CONCLUSIONS

In our observations of children's play in a shoe shop corner in a school, we observed that children could construct meaningful symbolic means ("inscriptions") that are helpful for the solutions of the problems that they encounter in their play activity. In the course of the activity, these inscriptions suggest new actions and consequently new developments of the activity (the children went from arranging the shoe shop, to playing in the shoe shop, to classifying, to counting, to combining inscriptions and making diagrams), and in these activities they concurrently reconstructed their initial inscriptions in order to make them useful in the new subactivity. The dialectical relationship between acting and making appropriate inscriptions is an essential element in the evolution of play activity. Our observations show the accessibility of this activity for young children, as well as the close relationship between the needs that emerge in the children's activities, on the one hand, and the articulation of predicates and production of inscriptions, on the other.

References

Bakhtin, M. (1964/1994). Carnival ambivalence: Laughter praise and abuse. In P. Morris (Ed.), *The Bakhtin reader* (pp. 206–226). London: Edward Arnold.
Bateson, G. (1973). *Steps to the ecology of mind.* London: Paladin.
Huizinga, J. (1938). *Homo Ludens.* Groningen: H. D. Tjeenk Willink & Zn.
Latour, B. (1990). Drawing things together. In M. Lynch & S. Woolgar (Eds.), *Representation in scientific practice* (pp. 19–68). Cambridge, MA: MIT Press.
Meira, L. (1995). The microevolution of mathematical representations in children's activity. *Learning and Instruction, 13* (2), 269–313.
van Oers, B. (1996). Are you sure? The promotion of mathematical thinking in the play activities of young children. *European Early Childhood Education Research Journal, 4* (1), 71–89.
van Oers, B. (1998). The fallacy of decontextualisation. *Mind, Culture, and Activity, 5* (2), 135–142.
van Oers, B. (2000). The appropriation of mathematical symbols: A psychosemiotic approach to mathematics learning. In P. Cobb, E. Yackel, & K. McClain (Eds.), *Symbolizing and communicating in mathematics classrooms: Perspectives on discourse, tools, and instructional design* (pp. 133–176). Mahwah, NJ: Lawrence Erlbaum.
van Oers, B. (2001). Contextualisation for abstraction. *Cognitive Science Quarterly, 1,* (3–4), 279–306.
van Oers, B. (2003). *Narratives of childhood.* Amsterdam: VU Press.
van Oers, B., & Wardekker, W. (1999). On becoming an authentic learner: Semiotic activity in the early grades. *Journal of Curriculum Studies, 31* (2), 229–249.
Sinha, C. (1998). *Language and representation: A socio-naturalistic approach to human development.* New York: Harvester Wheatsheaf.

Vygotsky, L. S. (1978). *Mind in society: The development of higher psychological processes.* Cambridge, MA: Harvard University Press.

Vygotsky, L. S. (1987). *Thinking and speech.* In R. W. Rieber & A. S. Carton (Eds.), *The collected works of L. S. Vygotsky: Vol. 1. Problems of general psychology* (pp. 39–285). New York: Plenum.

20

Pretend Play and Preschoolers

Ricardo Ottoni Vaz Japiassu

Although the belief that play is educationally important could already be found in the works of Plato and Aristotle, it was only in the eighteenth and nineteenth centuries that Rousseau and Fröbel, with their pedagogical theories, laid the basis for the construction of educational practices that systematically incorporate playfulness into school education (Brougère, 1998). The discoveries resulting from research in the field of developmental psychology enriched the belief in the educational value of play. This belief corresponds to the liberal progressivist pedagogical concept of Active Education (the New School movement), which, since the early 1900s, has spread throughout the world. Piaget, Vygotsky, Bruner, Usova, and Elkonin are among the most important investigators of the educational dimensions of play, and their research contributed to the elaboration of the idea of an active pedagogy of play (França, 1990). Today, the study of the interrelationships between play and education has awakened the interest of researchers such as Gilles Brougère, Artin Göncü, Suzanne Gaskins, Barbara Rogoff, Jaan Valsiner, James Wertsch, Keith Sawyer, Tia Tulviste, Bert van Oers, Tizuko Kishimoto, Gisela Wajskop, Ingrid Koudela, Maria Cecília R. de Góes, and Zilma Oliveira.

The investigation of the educational dimensions of play in a historical and cultural perspective seeks to associate pretend play with the historical, material, economic, and political development of the relationships between production and the division of labor in human societies. This approach appeals to cross-cultural researchers, whose findings reinforce the hypothesis of the social-historical origins of children's pretend play (Elkonin, 1998). The importance of biological vectors in the orientation of behavior – and their important role in ontogenetic development – should not be ignored:

the emergence of the symbolic function in the child is connected to an innate or instinctive predisposition. The social-historical perspective highlights the subordination of the biological determination to the cultural factors associated with the emergence of the so-called higher mental functions (Toomela, 1996). This new psychological and cultural functioning of the human being is conceived of as the result of the articulation between the use of tools (practical intelligence) and the use of signs (verbal reasoning) (Vygotsky, 1987). The fusion between practical intelligence and verbal reasoning was the result of intersubjective communication underlying the practices of collective labor, which caused an improvement in the material methods of production during phylogenesis (Luria & Vygotsky, 1996). In other words, in the cultural-historical approach, human behavior is intertwined with the historical development of the social and material relations of production that were sculpted in the process of collective labor aimed at the control and transformation of nature – and that secured the survival of the human species.

These studies usually associate the beginning of pretend play with the development of efficient technologies for maximizing agricultural production, the domestication of animals, and the social division of labor. In other words, the growth of the volume of the material production of goods, the sophistication of labor instruments that this requires, and the new and complex forms of social relations and labor division make it difficult to include the child in the production process. As a consequence, teaching the handling of complicated tools and machines necessary for labor was postponed to a later age, which actually contributed to childhood being prolonged: the infantile culture became a requirement of the production process.

According to cultural-historical theory, the development of material production effected two changes in the informal education or enculturation of the child: the necessity of promoting the development of some general and fundamental abilities for the mastery of complicated work tools (development of hand-eye coordination, etc.) and thus the design of playthings; and the creation of a special type of child's play – pretend play, in which children began to have the opportunity to (re-)create some spheres of social life. Therefore, pretend play would have originated in the historical-economic transformations that determined the alteration of the role of the child in the system of social relations and, at the same time, demanded its removal from the production process (Elkonin, 1998, pp. 89–90).

Understanding the cultural-historical origins of pretend play allows the visualization of the importance of this type of play activity in the cultural development and social learning of the child. Therefore, pretend play constitutes an important social area of potential development (Lima, 1995a,

1995b) because it presupposes the experimentation of culturally established and desired roles and conduct. At the same time, it demands complex mental elaborations on the part of the child (Vygotsky, 1996, p. 135).

When children imagine something, they not only confer sense on their physical actions but also (re)discover the cultural meaning of childhood and of "being a child." It is a human activity of social construction and has a sense that requires forms of complicity and cooperation that are part of the existence of childhood itself (Wajskop, 1996, pp. 111–127). The importance of pretend play for the development of the cultural forms of a child's performance has been demonstrated through numerous studies informed by genetic psychology and the pedagogical proposals concerned with guaranteeing the place of childhood in the process of formal education (Kishimoto, 1994, 1996).

From a cultural-historical perspective, pretend play allows children to exercise their understanding of social situations and to practice cultural roles because they make use of temporary representations of these events, roles, characters, and things in this type of play activity. But the roles, characters, things, and situations can be represented dramatically, at first, only with the help of "pivots" (pillars) or material support (Vygotsky, 1996, p. 128). In this way, for example, a pen can become a "comb" or an "intergalactic rocket" in pretend play. This material support to pretend play can already exist in an explicit invitation to infantile playful action, as in playthings produced by artisans, manufacturers, and industries of consumer goods for children (including rag dolls, action figures based on movie and television characters, and miniaturized replicas of furniture, utensils, home appliances, makeup, clothes, cars, etc.).

Pretend play, then, constitutes a complex construction of sociocultural meanings. As a play activity, it becomes an important instrument in the culture of childhood. Pretend play is therefore educational in two ways: it teaches the child to be a child; and it allows the child to appropriate values and social roles from its environment and complex systems of semiotic representation that are widely used by more experienced members of the culture.

The informal education for child's play, through the mass production of children's playthings, has secured the specificity and the extension of childhood in technologically advanced human societies. This practice forces children to recognize themselves as children and to understand roles shared culturally in their social groups (Brougère, 1995). The cultural-historical approach to pretend play comes from the principle that the play activity is necessary for the "preexercise" of future cultural abilities by the child. Therefore, it makes use of the theory of preexercize of Karl Groos, whose ideas have been (re)elaborated to adapt them to the materialist dialectical thought founded by Marx and Engels, a pillar of the social-historical perspective (Elkonin, 1998).

PRETEND PLAY

What is pretend play? What modalities of pretend play can be identified in the child's activity, and what characterizes it? Under what social-historical and cultural circumstances does pretend play appear and develop? What is the importance of pretend play for the cultural development of the child?

First, it is necessary to clarify that I do not intend either to defend absolute truths or to find definitive answers to these questions. My objective is quite the opposite: to outline how infantile pretend play can be studied from a cultural-historical perspective originally developed by Lev Vygotsky (Davidov, 1988). The social-interactionist theories of Henri Wallon, Piagetian cognitivism, Freudian psychoanalysis, and post-Freudian psychoanalysis led to an understanding of the dramatic representation of the child. These different approaches to pretend play present a vital contribution to comprehending this form of typically infantile play activity. In isolation, however, each would not be sufficient to explain the origin and the development of human psychological processes involved in pretend play. Given that pretend play, like any term, may be interpreted in many different ways (Bakhtin, 1993, 1995, 1997), my objective is to understand each one of these theories as they pertain to a specific epistemological "territory," situated in distinct "topological" regions of human knowledge. These "territorial surfaces" may be part of more extensive "frontier zones."

I attempt to work from the fertile soil of the cultural-historical theory of development. I also desire to find some echo or reverberation in the vast "continent" over which the academic knowledge is spread. This knowledge is informed by various points of view and different places from which people can be studied and understood.

A Relative Topic with Different Significations

A difficulty for a researcher interested in examining pretend play is the absence of unified and consensual terminology. Terms such as "child's play" (Freud), "symbolic play" (Piaget), "play" (Vygotsky), "role-playing" (Elkonin), "child drama" (Peter Slade), "dramatization," and "infantile theater" have all been used, without distinction, to refer to representational dramatic actions of a ludic nature by the child.

The profusion of meanings given to the terms based on their conceptualized, cultural use or the internal logic of the webs and theoretical nets that confer specific signification on them (M. B. de Oliveira, 1999) makes it too difficult to determine what they refer to. This difficulty, however, is situated in the environment of another broader discussion that deals with the conceptual boundaries of the word "play." Another tendency in the realm of approaches to play is connected to the studies by the group of researchers at the Laboratoire de Recherche sur le Jeu et le Jouet at the Université Paris-Nord, led by Gilles Brougère and Jacques Henriot. To define play, these researchers focused on the cultural and social-historical context of the use of this word by "contextualizing" (conceptualizing) the word play. Brougère (1998) and collaborators allowed themselves to determine the basic attributes of play: (a) the concept of play is always a part of values and concepts of a specific culture; (b) every play works in accordance with a system of explicit and implicit rules; (c) play can be materialized in objects (e.g., on the chessboard and its pieces).

Relying on this French approach to play, Tizuko Kishimoto, a researcher from the School of Education at the University of São Paulo–FEUSP, proposes that, in the rigorous studies on this phenomenon in Brazil, the expression "child's play" be used to "designate the object as well as the rules governing the child's play (plaything and child's play)." She goes on to say that play "refers to a description of a ludic action involving situations structured by the type of material itself as in chess. . . . The playthings can be used in different ways by the child, but in play activity such as chess (chessboard, pieces), external structured rules are brought in to define the ludic situation" (1994, p. 7).

The term "plaything" has been used without distinction to designate the objects the children use to play with, the determined modes of play practiced by them, and the action of playing itself. Given this profusion of referents, Kishimoto proposes defining plaything exclusively as the "object in support of child's play" understood in its concrete existence (toy). Kishimoto also argues that playthings include artifacts beyond those "created by the adult world, conceived specially for child's play." A child can take any object produced by adults and invest it with ludic meaning: "Spoons, plates and pans have served as a support for play, acquiring ludic meaning, representing, for example, musical instruments, combs, among others" (1994, pp. 7–8).

Tizuko argues that the term child's play should be used only in reference to the "description of a structured conduct, with rules" or the action that the child develops in the act of playing. Brazilian cultural-historical researchers conceive of pretend play as the dramatic representational actions of a ludic nature by the child with playthings that possess certain rules implicit in the imaginary situation.

Pretend play, being an activity that requires the use of imagination, already possesses in itself at least one rule: the child must act in accordance with the cultural meanings of the objects and social relations dramatically represented in her or his ludic "pretending." In other words, the child must act in pretend play in such a way that the meanings applied to the objects, to the partners in the child's play, and to her or his actions should be culturally appropriate and "truthful" (Vygotsky, 1996, p. 125). Pretend play refers to the ludic infantile conduct that makes use of dramatic representation. It does not refer to "exhibition" or "public presentation," or to an aesthetic preoccupation (in the sense that it is something to be appreciated by observers).

According to the cultural-historical theory of human development, pretend play emerges when a child is denied the satisfaction of instantaneous wishes, such as being barred from driving a real automobile, in which case the child would try to satisfy her or his wish in the imaginary plane by "pretending" to drive a car. The infantile pretend play, in the social-historical context, is understood as a temporary activity and flow (spontaneous, improvised, without rehearsal), because the dramatic representations are not initially found to be ready, completely drawn, or finished in the mind of the child. But it is part of the pleasure of (re-)creating reality that the children involved in pretend play possess a high degree of independence for the construction of a dramatic plot, alone or in collaboration with other children. These improvised representational dramatic actions develop as a result of a child's desire to incorporate or take advantage of occasional sensations, perceptions, and associations stimulated by the environment, by the quality of the intersubjective relations in the ludic activity, and by the unpredictable development of a dramatic plot.

The exploitation of these stimuli occurs necessarily in a "flow" or improvised manner. In other words, the child appropriates them without planning and according to the circumstances that give impetus to the development of the imaginary plot. This idiosyncratic incorporation of elements of the visual, olfactory, and tactile configuration of the perceptual field of the subject is related to the personal experience of the child and is done based on syncretic associations, subjective, of an unconscious nature, that invoke facts, behaviors, actions, and objects from the cultural world in which the child finds herself immersed.

But curiously, within pretend play, in parallel with the unconscious exploitation of cultural signs – already internalized or in the process of internalization by the subject – an appropriation of the original cultural meaning of objects, actions, and performances occurs. Cultural-historical theory explains that this can be possible only from a complex (re)elaboration of data and impressions already stored in the affection-related, cognitive, psychomotor memory through recourse to an important "superior" psychic function, the creative imagination: "Imagination is a new psychological process for the child; it represents a specifically human form of conscious activity, not present in the consciousness of very small children and completely absent in animals" (Vygotsky, 1982, p. 122).

To summarize: (1) pretend play is a highly complex psychological activity supported by a superior psychological function; (2) the creative imagination in this ludic activity is set in motion by the impossibility of instantaneous satisfaction of desires for the subject; (3) pretend play articulates, in the subject, affective-emotional, psychomotor, social-communicative, and cognitive dimensions; and (4) creative imagination is a necessary condition to pretend play and, at the same time, is constituted, strengthened, and amplified by it.

Modalities of Pretend Play

Peter Slade, pedagogue and English dramatist, identified two distinct types of dramatic representational actions of a ludic nature in infantile pretend play. According to Slade (1971), pretend play (dramatic infantile play or "child drama," as he calls it) refers to two distinct forms of ludic conduct by the child: personal play and projected play.

Pretend Play with Personification

According to Slade (1971, pp. 3–4), "Personal play [pretend play with personification] is obvious drama; the whole person or self is used. . . . the child journeys about and takes upon himself the responsibility of playing a role . . . the tendency is towards noise and physical exertion." This type of pretend play refers to a child's play in that the child experiments with social roles from its cultural environment (mother, son, doctor, bus driver, etc). The child also tries to act as if he or she were a character (fairy tale hero, or superhero from the movies, television, or videogame) or seeks to represent things (church, automobiles), real living beings and imaginary beings (animals, plants, aliens), elements, and phenomena from nature (fire, thunder).

Pretend play with personification refers to the active and corporeal engagement in assuming roles in dramatic representations (e.g., children in a group playing a "doctor"; child alone playing "school" with her or his dolls and taking on the role of the "teacher"). The pretend play with personification has also been referred to as role-playing (Brougère, 1995; Moreno, 1974; Z. M. R. de Oliveira, 1988), protagonist play (Elkonin, 1998), dramatization, and even, inappropriately, infantile theater.

Projected Pretend Play

According to Slade (1971, pp. 3–4), "projected play [projected pretend play] is drama in which the whole mind is used, but the body is not used so fully. . . . The child stands still, sits, lies prone or squats, and uses chiefly the hands. . . . The objects played with, rather than the person playing, take on life and do the acting, though there may be vigorous use of voice." This type of pretend play is therefore usually called enacting play (Brougère, 1995; Elkonin, 1998).

Projected pretend play refers to the child's play in which the child uses playthings that are "animated" by recourse to manipulations. Such objects can be used to represent roles, characters, places, or things from a dramatic plot that develops on the intramental plane of the child. The imaginary plot conducts and determines the ludic movement of the playthings by the child. The subject in this case converts himself into a type of "theatrical enactor" or "movie director" because he coordinates – at the same time that he also observes – the unfolding of events in the places he imagines.

It is a kind of pretend play that is almost always more lonely and that presents a higher degree of difficulty for interaction between children – although interaction may also occur. The projected pretend play is generally accompanied by vocalizations and verbalizations (oral interior or "egocentric" speech) that tend to progressively disappear as the child grows older. This modality of pretend play refers to the dramatic representational activity of an infantile ludic nature in which the child manipulates objects projecting himself on them from a subjective and intramental plot (e.g., manipulation of toy soldiers in a "battle").

A keen observation of the cultural development of the child's pretend play must allow identification of a trajectory that begins with the pretend play with personification, follows with the projected pretend play, and finally reaches illusion. Illusion refers to the full development of the ludic imagination without any type of aid or material support. It is related to the creation of plots in an exclusively mental plane. It is daydreaming. There is, as yet, no evidence that allows confirmation of an "evolutionary" sequence of modalities of pretend play in ontogenesis, even if the Vygotskian postulate is true, which states that there is a movement "from outside to inside" in the constitution of the human psyche. Projected pretend play as well as illusion must originate from a larger organization of the child's activity.

Projected pretend play and illusion necessarily imply "decontextualization" (deconceptualization) of the child's thought and demand "deattachment" and independence of thought in relation to the physical actions of the subject. They require a separation between perception and motor activity by the child. Projected pretend play can thus exist only as an intermediary stage between pretend play with personification and illusion. Studies on the representational dramatic activity of an infantile ludic nature have identified pretend play with personification as a privileged object of observation. Therefore, it seems necessary to draw attention to researchers who propose to examine projected pretend play. Their studies should serve as indispensable work within the cultural-historical paradigm. Observation of the modalities of pretend play that supposedly follow throughout the cultural development of the child allow an empirical demonstration of the pertinence of Vygotsky's hypothesis about the movement of internalization of social speech and its role in the constitution of the human psyche.

Peter Slade (1971, p. 4) understood projected pretend play (projected play) as a more "primitive" modality of infantile pretend play, that is, as a type of ludic action that precedes pretend play with personification: "projected play is more evident in the earlier stages of a young child, who is not yet ready to use his body fully." But it is not possible to agree with him in the light of cultural-historical theory. The precocious action of children with playthings, on which Slade bases his conclusions to affirm that projected pretend play would supposedly precede pretend play with personification, is, according to Vygotsky, only a mechanical manipulation of these objects, and nothing more. This perspective would view such activity as imitation in which the founding principle of dramatic representation is found in an embryonic stage. The activity is dependent on the needs of sensory-object manipulation, psychomotor proprioceptive coordination, and the visual, hearing, and tactile configuration that delimits circumstantially and momentarily the concrete perceptual field of the subject. These factors are, in effect, also to be found even in those cases where imitation occurs in the absence of a model (deferred imitation):

Things dictate to the child what he must do: a door demands to be opened and closed, a staircase to be climbed, a bell to be rung.... It is remarkable that the child starts with an imaginary situation that initially is so very close to the real one. A reproduction of the real situation takes place.... It is more memory in action than a novel imaginary situation. As play develops, we see a movement toward the conscious realization of its purpose. (Vygotsky, 1978, pp. 96, 103)

In addition to the modalities of pretend play, it is necessary to attend to the existence of a third kind of pretend play that exhibits traits of dramatic representational procedures as in pretend play with personification and in projected pretend play. This mixed modality escaped Peter Slade's analysis. I call this hybrid form pretend play with personification and projection.

Pretend Play with Personification and Projection

Pretend play with personification and projection refers to a special form of ludic activity of the child. When playing "mother and daughter" with a doll, a child will, for example, lend her or his voice to the doll as the "daughter" while also acting in the role of the "mother." The child "acts along" with herself by using her "projection" on the doll and acting out, in parallel, the role of the "daughter." In this type of ludic conduct, the child verbalizes the speech of the "mother" as well as the "daughter" in order to have an imaginary conversation between the two. It is performance of great complexity because the child becomes capable of assuming the perspective of the other – an imaginary person – alternating her dramatic actions with different roles or characters.

DISCUSSION

According to the sequence of infantile pretend play that I have proposed, pretend play with personification and projection must occur in an intermediary transitional stage between pretend play with personification and projected pretend play. To summarize, if there is an ontogenetic sequence of pretend play, it involves: (1) imitation or manipulation of objects, (2) pretend play with personification, (3) pretend play with personification and projection, (4) projected pretend play, and (5) illusion.

The dimensions of pretend play presented here suggest ways to extend research on infantile pretend play. The gaps in current approaches to pretend play need further investigation. Until now, studies of pretend play have focused almost exclusively on pretend play with personification. Further research should take into account the ontogenetic sequence of pretend play proposed in this chapter.

Based on the premises of cultural-historical theory, what alternatives are there to the approach I have presented? I believe that the transition from the manipulation of objects to projected pretend play occurs through pretend play with personification. I next present a developmental sequence model of the dramatic representation in ontogenesis, illustrating it with the ludic actions of a boy with a toy car.

Imitation or Manipulation of Objects

First, the boy manipulates the car acting only as the "motivation nature" of that object. It is what Lewin proposes as the "inherent" power of objects over actions of a small child (Vygotsky, 1978, himself refers to Lewin in *Mind in Society*). The perceptual field of the child determines the manipulation of objects because, at this stage of development, the motivation for the action is linked to the perception of the object. The perception of the object remains integrated in the motor reactions of the subject.

If the boy acts out the sound of the engine by humming, he is imitating the cultural object, the automobile, that he already knows or recognizes miniaturized in the form of a plaything. In this case, it is not about personification or projection but a reproduction of the cultural meaning of the object represented by the plaything (an automotive vehicle). This reproduction can be the fruit of learning how to use, in a ludic manner, that type of object (the toy car) – which would have been the product of "peripheral observations" by the child or from "explicit instructions" received from more experienced members of the culture he finds himself immersed in (Rogoff et al., 1993).[1] It deals with the subject's memory in action: imitation.

Pretend Play with Personification

When the boy starts to act in the role of "driver" – that is, when he starts to make believe he is driving a car using a pan lid as a steering wheel, for example – his perception moves from the visual field to larger voluntary control of his motor activity. He knows that he has in his hands the cultural object of a pan lid but acts in unpredictable action in relation to this object, giving it a new meaning in the context of its dramatic representation. It is as if the cultural object has begun to lose its "determining strength." This change reveals that the child's creative imagination is building and becoming manifest in the ludic action, because, from a cultural-historical perspective, the imagination is a new psychological function of the child (Japiassu, 2001b).

In this case, it is no longer a question of manipulating objects. The use of the pan lid, by itself, does not mean that the child is developing projected pretend play or pretend play with personification and projection, because the projection does not refer to any use of support material in pretend play. There is now authentic pretend play with personification. Further, in pretend play with personification, the "acting" is not limited exclusively to social roles. It also includes characters and things, living beings, elements, and phenomena

---

[1] Barbara Rogoff proposes the concept of guided participation to characterize different processes of learning and explains that it can occur through: (a) peripheral observation – the subject observes "peripherally" the interactions, events, and social behavior of its cultural group without being "actively" engaged in them; (b) explicit instruction – the subject is instructed how to act in a situation that demands its active and corporal engagement.

from nature. For a child to be engaged in pretend play with personification, it is necessary that her imagination has already reached a certain level of development. She must also seek to satisfy her desires in the imaginary plane – and not in the plane of real life. It is one thing for a baby to pretend to cry because no one will give her attention at the moment; it is another for a child to pretend to cry after having received, in the role of "patient" in playing "doctor and patient," a painful injection!

In the imaginary plane, the child must begin to act the different social roles. First, the child focuses only on the most important characteristics of these roles as understood through personal experience (e.g., the child's understanding of what is "mother" or "son," or what it is to "drive an automobile"). Only after this role will the child act a character in a ludic manner (e.g., representing a determined kind of "mother" or a cultural figure such as Batman or a Digimon).

Pretend Play with Personification and Projection

Now, let us say that our boy is still driving his "car," using a lid for a steering wheel, and he starts to have a conversation with an imaginary policeman, represented by a bush. The boy might begin to take turns in the roles of the "driver" and "policeman," dramatizing a supposed conversation between them. There is now pretend play with personification and projection. The child projects himself as the bush to represent the role of the policeman and, at the same time, maintains personified in the role of "driver" with the help or aid of the central factor (the pan lid) that represents the car.

This ludic activity is of great complexity because the dialogue between the "driver" and the imaginary "policeman" is set in the intramental plane of the child – although he uses projection on a material support (the bush) to help him in this task. In this case, the child projects himself into the perspective of the "other" to act with himself. This example illustrates how pretend play with personification and projection demands a higher level of psychological development on the part of the child.

Projected Pretend Play

But now, let's suppose that the boy starts to use the lid to represent an intergalactic spaceship that explores the universe. The child sometimes produces sounds to represent the roar of the spaceship's engines, or verbalizes fragments of orders by the mission commander, or moves the spaceship (the lid) in silence. The "inner speech" of the boy "escapes" and becomes verbalized.

There is now genuine projected pretend play. The dramatic plot develops exclusively in the mind of the child, and the "personification" or "acting" occurs from the projection of the subject on material supports without his "all body" engagement in it. That means the boy does not necessarily need to act or personify corporeally the commander of the spaceship to imagine him present in his dramatic plot. He can now imagine him (as commander) inside the spaceship (the lid).

In this modality of pretend play, the complexity of the ludic activity of the boy is still greater. This complexity occurs because the creative imagination is well developed and is no longer dependent on "corporeal" personification of a social role or character. The roles and characters can be totally represented on the inner plane, although still with the aid of the projection of an intra-mental plot on material support – so that they can confer on his dramatic representations of ludic nature a more "consistent" imaginary existence.

Illusion

Now, let us say that the boy has grown and that he is already a preteenager. He is on vacation, in his parent's car, on the way to his family's farm and, on the road, he begins to imagine the things he will do, the friends he will meet there, and what he should say to someone from the area who he has wanted to date for a long time. All this, in silence, sitting on the backseat of his parent's car, immobilized by the seat belt, without verbalizations or physical actions. The imagination is only in action in the intramental plane. He has illusions, makes plans, he daydreams about the time that he will arrive at the farm. What happens in this case is a psychological condition in which the imagination is fully developed as a consequence of the complete internalization of the "superior" forms of thought.

When I asked various international and Brazilian researchers of pretend play about the existence of an ontogenetic sequence for dramatic representations of a ludic nature of the child, they gave different and conflicting opinions. At least in the small – but significant – portion of the academic world I was able to interview, 60 percent of researchers opposed the possibility of under-standing the development of the dramatic representational actions of ludic nature according to a genetic-developmental perspective; 20 percent con-sidered the sequence proposed by Slade as correct; and 20 percent believed that there is a sequence of infantile pretend play that differs from that pos-tulated by Peter Slade in the manner I have outlined. This result shows a wide variety of points of view on the phenomenon discussed in this text and confirms – once again – the necessity for rigorous research in order to shed light on this complex and intriguing form of infantile ludic conduct.

THE PLACE OF PRETEND PLAY IN PRESCHOOL EDUCATION

It is still necessary to discuss the place of pretend play in preschool education. I have already reviewed how the development of the material conditions of production generated the necessity of the extension of childhood. This delay in the inclusion of children in the productive activity of the community results from the growing complexity of social relationships. The ever-increasing sophistication of the machinery necessary for the production process required the formal education of children prior to their entrance into the workplace. The institution of a single system of basic education that comprises daycare centers and preschools up to the end of high school suggests the importance and necessity of educational influence in the cultural formation of the subject. Compulsory education consolidates discrete social stages of human development: childhood, preadolescence, adolescence, and adulthood. In this manner, scholastic culture represents and constitutes a specific and unique type of reality that distinguishes itself from natural reality as well as from other realities of a social nature. This reality is characterized by the "principle of the ideal activity" (Davidov, 1988, p. 64).

If it is possible to understand childhood as the result of socioeconomic and psychosocial processes promoted by human societies, it does not seem hard to accept the division into periods of ontogenetic development as a cultural product, as cultural-historical activity theory (CHAT) proposes. The division into periods of infantile development is based on the ideas of Vygotsky and deals with the concretization of some of the principal Vygotskian claims, as outlined by Leont'ev, Elkonin, and others. According to CHAT, this "division into periods" of the cultural development of the human being is structured by the substitution of one activity (conceived of by adults as "ideal" for the child) for another. This activity, collectively thought appropriate for a specific period of ontogenesis, is referred to as the "organizing activity" of performance. The organizing activity of the child's acting, assumed for each specific age, moves and unleashes the processes of psychological transformation of the subject. These neoformations or psychological changes that appear for the first time at a certain age then determine the consciousness of the subject, his relations with the social environment, his intramental activity, his external-object activity, and the entire course of his development in the given period. So the neoformations are "organizers" of the developmental process that characterizes the restructuring of the personality on new bases.

If, on the one hand, the neoformations are "organizers" of the behavior at a specific stage in cultural development, then the basis of psychological development, on the other hand, originates from the replacement of one type of organizing activity with another. The organizing activity is conceived of as an area or social situation of development because it reveals the change of an occupied place by the child in the system of social relationships. All the child's relationships with the environment must therefore be intermediated by the "rector activity" of each stage in its cultural development. In the cultural-historical approach, the organizing activity sets in motion the neoformations or main transformations of the forms of mental functioning of the child.

At each characteristic period of human ontogenesis (childhood, pread-olescence, adolescence, and adulthood), there is a corresponding specific organizing activity of social performance. The substitution of one organizing activity by another characterizes the succession of the evolutionary periods. The psychological neoformations constitute and develop in each correspond-ing organizing activity. We can outline the division in periods of the cultural development according to CHAT and its respective organizing activities or "rectors."

1. *Childhood:* The organizing activity during childhood is the direct emo-tional communication with adults, through which interactions with more experienced members of the culture occur, and intersubjective psychic communion is established. Later, the behavior of the child is organized by engagement in object-manipulative actions. The child reproduces the procedures and actions with objects and culturally elaborated things (imitation). The first words are spoken, which begins the construction process of their meanings and sense. Later, pretend play evolves into the organizing activity of the child's behavior. The creative imagination and the semiotic representation processes (cor-poreal representational actions with the use of support materials or central factors that articulate the oral expression, the repertoire of gestures, and the peculiar infantile manner of drawing or writing) are constituted and developed.

2. *Preadolescence.* During preadolescence, the organizing activity is study. Complex modalities of semiotic representation are developed (writing, artistic languages, foreign languages) along with categorical thought, metacognitive capacities (reflection, analysis, and planning), necessi-ties and related reasons for school activities, and participation in group practices with explicit rules (ludic, sportive, religious, etc.).

3. *Adolescence.* The organizing activity of adolescents is useful social realization, including work, study, participation in social organizations
(philanthropic, sportive, political, etc.), sports, and arts. Aspirations
to economic independence and participation in socially relevant work,
interest in sexual practices, growth of scientific curiosity, development
of metacognitive processes, and self-consciousness occur.

4. *Adulthood.* The organizing activity of this period is study and professional training. Interest in professional training and the necessity of
working are developed; moral, ideological, religious, and civic qualities
are formed; and plans for the constitution of a family and biological
reproduction made. The useful social realization of adolescence develops into actual productive realizations: work, sport, religion, political
participation, artistic-aesthetic occupation, commercial ventures, and
the like.

FINAL CONSIDERATIONS

The division of the organizing activities of human performance into periods,
as proposed by CHAT, clarifies the sociohistorical concept of pretend play
as a "rector activity" of the child's way of being in the preschool period of
cultural development. So, the need arises for larger and more careful study
of this intriguing phenomenon of ludic human behavior by those interested
in infantile education. The essence of pretend play is the creation of a new
relationship between a child's imaginary and material fields (Vygotsky, 1978)
such that:

- The action occurs in the imaginary sphere, developing it.
- The voluntary intentions and the consciousness of the subject are strength-
ened.
- The planes of reality and fantasy are created and differentiated.
- The value and sense of cultural relations – and the social roles existing in
them – can be internalized.
- The child advances in the comprehension of the structure and functioning
of semiotic processes of representation, especially of writing.

Vygotsky was absolutely convinced of the cultural-historical and social
character of verbal thought and the importance of organized pedagogical
interventions designed to accelerate formal operations – including directed
activity with dramatic representations of a ludic nature at schools (Japiassu,

1999, 2001a). If the division into periods of cultural development from a sociohistorical perspective considers pretend play as the organizing activity of a child's performance at preschool, promoting the infantile pretend play in this segment of basic education is an adequate way of advancing intellectual activity toward very specific modalities of mental functioning. Pretend play is an important tool – and an indispensable resource – for the cultural development of childhood.

References

Bakhtin, M. (1993). *Questões de literatura e estética*. São Paulo: Hucitec.

Bakhtin, M. (1995). *Marxismo e filosofia da linguagem*. São Paulo: Martins Fontes.

Bakhtin, M. (1997). *Estética da criação verbal*. São Paulo: Martins Fontes.

Brougère, G. (1995). *Brinquedo e cultura*. São Paulo: Cortez.

Brougère, G. (1998). *Jogo e educação*. Porto Alegre: Artes Médicas.

Davidov, V. (1988). *La enseñanza escolar y el desarrollo psiquico*. Moscow: Progresso.

Elkonin, D. B. (1998). *Psicologia do jogo*. São Paulo: Martins Fontes.

França, G. W. (1990). "Tia, me deixa brincar!" O espaço do jogo na Educação pré-escolar. São Paulo: Pontifícia Universidade Católica-PUC. (Dissertação de Mestrado).

Japiassu, R. O. V. (1999). Ensino do teatro nas séries iniciais da educação básica: a formação de conceitos sociais no jogo teatral. São Paulo: ECA-USP. (Dissertação de mestrado).

Japiassu, R. O. V. (2001a). *Metodologia do ensino de teatro*. Campinas: Papirus.

Japiassu, R. O. V. (2001b). Criatividade, criação e apreciação artísticas: a atividade criadora segundo Vygotsky. In M. Vasconcelos (Ed.), *Criatividade – Psicologia, Educação e conhecimento do novo* (pp. 43–58). São Paulo: Moderna.

Kishimoto, T. M. (1994). *O jogo e a educação infantil*. São Paulo: Pioneira.

Kishimoto, T. M. (1996). *Jogo, brinquedo, brincadeira e a educação*. São Paulo: Cortez.

Lima, E. S. (1995a). Culture revisited: Vygotsky's ideas in Brazil. *Anthropology & Education Quarterly, 26* (4), 443–457.

Lima, E. S. (1995b). Vygotsky in the international scene: A brief overview. *Anthropology & Education Quarterly, 26* (4), 490–499.

Luria, A. R., & Vygotsky, L. S. (1996). *Estudos sobre a história do comportamento: o macaco, o primitivo e a criança*. Porto Alegre: Artes Médicas.

Moreno, J. L. (1974). *Psicodrama*. Buenos Aires: Hormé.

Oliveira, M. B. de (1999). Natureza e dinâmica dos conceitos. In M. K. de Oliveira & M. B. de Oliveira (Eds.), *Investigações cognitivas: conceitos, linguagem e cultura* (pp. 35–53). Porto Alegre: Artes Médicas.

Oliveira, Z. M. R. de. (1988). Jogos de papéis: uma perspectiva para análise do desenvolvimento humano. São Paulo: IP-USP (Tese de doutoramento).

Rogoff, B., Mistry, J., Göncü, A., & Mosier, C. (1993). *Guided participation in cultural activity by toddlers and caregivers*. Child Development Publications (Vol. 58, no. 8). Chicago: University of Chicago Press.

Slade, P. (1971). *An introduction to child drama* (8th ed.). London: University of London Press. (Originally published 1958).

Toomela, A. (1996). How culture transforms mind: A process of internalization. *Culture and Psychology, 2* (3), 285–305.

Vygotsky, L. S. (1978). *Mind in society: The development of higher psychological processes.* Cambridge, MA: Harvard University Press.

Vygotsky, L. S. (1982). *El arte e la imaginación en la infancia: ensayo psicológico.* Madrid: Akal.

Vygotsky, L. S. (1987). *História del desarrollo de las funciones psíquicas superiores.* Ciudad de La Habana: Científico Técnica.

Vygotsky, L. S. (1996). *A formação social da mente.* São Paulo: Martins Fontes.

Wajskop, G. A. (1996). Representação do brincar entre professores da educação infantil: Implicações para a prática pedagógica. São Paulo: FEUSP (Tese de doutoramento).

Index